# A GUIDE TO MIDDLE-EARTH

robert foster

MIRAGE

The VOYAGER Series V-105
The ANTHEM Series A-1009

5111 Liberty Heights Ave., Baltimore, Maryland 21207 U. S. A.

**1971**

Portions of this book have appeared in different form as follows: *Niekas* 16 (June 30, 1966) © 1966 by Ed Meskys; *Niekas* 17 (November, 1966), *Niekas* 18 (Spring, 1967), *Niekas* 19 (1968), © 1966, 1967, 1968 by *Niekas* Publications; *Niekas* 20 (Fall, 1968) © 1968 by Ed Meskys, *Niekas* 21 © 1969 by Ed Meskys.

Outside of North America, The Mirage Press's only authorized agent is G. Ken Chapman Ltd., 2, Ross Road, London, S. E. 25, England.

Library of Congress Catalog Card Number 72-94777

Second Printing, November 1971.

A Glossary is not the proper way to explore Middle-earth, for "in that realm [Faerie] a man may, perhaps, count himself fortunate to have wandered, but its very richness and strangeness tie the tongue of a traveller who would report them. And while he is there it is dangerous for him to ask too many questions, lest the gates should be shut and the keys be lost."[1] Just as a snowflake melts when it is handled, so in the study of Faerie the listing of dates and the boundaries of provinces tends to destroy the Realm and obscure that Truth of which facts are merely the more easily discernible handmaidens. The subtle lineaments of that Truth must be discerned for himself by every reader of *The Lord of the Rings* and the other Middle-earth books.

However, a Glossary, so long as it does not seek, and is not permitted, to replace the original universe it describes (and this is as true of the "real" world as of any literary work or glimpse into Faerie), has value in that it can clarify deep-hidden historical obscurities and draw together facts whose relation is easily overlooked, thus aiding the wanderer in that universe in his quest for its particular Truth. This *Glossary* seeks to be no more than an orderly and factually accurate presentation of the material given in *The Lord of the Rings, The Hobbit, The Adventures of Tom Bombadil* and *The Road Goes Ever On,* and also of various scraps of unpublished information that I have gleaned from sources in contact with Professor Tolkien. Knowing that Professor Tolkien holds the key, I have preferred where necessary to remain silent or state my ignorance, rather than speculate with the possibility of error.

These entries in their final form represent four years of slow labor and frequent revision, and although I am sure there are errors, I can hope that by now they are few. It all began with my interest in the cultural and linguistic sources of Middle-earth and in the languages of Middle-earth, which led me to make the lists of characters and places, with brief

[1] J. R. R. Tolkien, *On Fairy Stories*, p. 3.

descriptions and partial page references. These descriptions grew, and eventually various sections of the *Glossary* were published in *Niekas,* a magazine edited by Felice Rolfe and Ed Meskys. I have found that the deeper I delve the more I learn, and so many of the entries that have already appeared in *Niekas* are now revised.

In this *Glossary* I have followed a number of conventions which I believe deserve mention. First, I have used the Ballantine editions of *The Lord of the Rings* and *The Hobbit* as the basic editions of those texts, since they are by far the most widely distributed, although I have also had occasion to refer to the first and revised Houghton-Mifflin editions. On page x there is a rough concordance between the Ballantine and revised Houghton-Mifflin editions of *The Lord of the Rings*. In geographical entries I have not always cited the maps on which the place in question is shown, and in historical entries I have occasionally used dates given in Appendix B without citation; in both cases the references can always be easily found. Also, I have not always provided individual entries for such titles as "the Lord of the Dark Tower" in cases where it is absolutely clear whom the reference is to, and where I have given such entries page references are frequently to the first occurrence only. Entries have been made under the name most commonly used at the end of the Third Age, with a very few exceptions (such as "Khazad-dûm") where one name was more ancient and respectfully bestowed than another. I have not given death dates for those who have gone over Sea, for they live still, although it should be noted that in the Shire it was recorded that Bilbo lived for a hundred and thirty-one years and seven days.

When names are genuine forms in Middle-earth languages, I have indicated this, and have given rough translations wherever I was sure of them. In a few places, I have indicated the meaning of translated Rohirric forms, and have indicated the language of other such forms as "translated ---" when I felt there was a possibility of confusing them with Elvish forms. However, by and large I have not indicated the language of names and terms "Anglicized" into English, Scandinavian or Celtic equivalents; as Professor Tolkien indicates on III 515-18, most Adûnaic, Rohirric, Westron, Mannish and Hobbitish forms have been so translated.

One matter that must be mentioned is the perspective I have used. Although the Red Book of Westmarch, and the books such as *The Lord of the Rings* derived from it, are written from the point of view of Hobbits of the Shire, I have decided that, because of the appended historical materials, which are ultimately derived from Gondor, it would be best to use the point of view of a Dúnadan scholar of Gondor at the end of the Third Age. Thus, all entries not specifically located in time (such as villages) refer to conditions at the time of the War of the Ring, and all value judgments (such as "evil race") are given from the Gondorian perspective. There is one exception to this rule: references to months and days are those of Appendix B, and are thus in the Shire Reckoning. This difference between Hobbit and Dúnadan dates is no more than a day in the spring and summer, since 2 Yule in the Shire Reckoning equalled yestarë in the Stewards' Reckoning. However, following the Dúnedain system I have made FA 1 = TA 3021 (SR 1421), although in the Shire Reckoning FA 1 = SR 1422.

In this *Glossary* I have made use of two sources of unpublished material, for which I am extremely grateful. First, Dick Plotz, the founder of the Tolkien Society of America, has a number of letters from Professor Tolkien, and also visited him at his home in the summer of 1967. Second, Rick Bjorseth obtained some information about Morgoth from Clyde Kilby, which Professor Kilby in turn received from Professor Tolkien.

I would like to thank all the people with whom I have discussed linguistic and historical problems, especially Mark Mandel, who was kind enough to review the manuscript of the geography entries which appeared in *Niekas* and point out a number of errors. Ed Meskys, co-editor of *Niekas* and Thain of the Tolkien Society, has been of great help, especially in encouraging me to persevere by setting deadlines for submitting material and for allowing me to reprint entries published in *Niekasi* 16 through 20. Dick Plotz has aided me at every stage, from suggesting many years ago that I write a *Glossary* to lending me his electric typewriter. I am deeply grateful to the many friends with whom I share Middle-earth for enabling me to perceive its beauty and theirs. Most of all I must thank Professor Tolkien for making it possible and desirable to be a wanderer in Middle-earth, and for always offering the promise of another day's fruitful journey.

*The Fellowship of the Ring*

*The Return of the King*

I — *The Fellowship of the Ring*
II — *The Two Towers*
III — *The Return of the King*
H — *The Hobbit*
R — *The Road Goes Ever On*
TB — *The Adventures of Tom Bombadil*
LotR — *The Lord of the Rings*, or all the above
RB — information from Rick Bjorseth
RP — information from Dick Plotz
HM — first Houghton-Mifflin edition of *LotR*
RHM — revised Houghton-Mifflin edition of *LotR*

Ad. — Adûnaic
B. S. — Black Speech
Hobb. — Hobbitish
Kh. — Khuzdul
Q. — Quenya
Roh. — Rohirric
S. — Sindarin
West. — Westron
gen. — genuine
tr. — translated (Anglicized)

SA — Second Age
TA — Third Age
FA — Fourth Age
SR — Shire Reckoning
WR — the War of the Ring

Also, various standard abbreviations have been used.

# A

**ACCURSED YEARS** the years of Sauron's great and almost undisputed dominion of large portions of Middle-earth, during which many peoples were corrupted or enslaved. The Accursed Years lasted approximately from S.A. 1000, when Sauron settled in Mordor, to 3441, when he was slain by Elendil and Gil-galad. During this period Sauron built the Barad-dûr, forged the Rings of Power and fought the War of the Elves and Sauron.

Also called the Black Years, the Dark Days (by the Elves of Lórien) and the Dark Years. Some of these terms may also refer to the Great Darkness (q.v.). (I 333-4; III 72)

**ADALDRIDA BRANDYBUCK** (fl. TA 29th Cent.) Hobbit of the Shire, wife of Marmadoc Brandybuck. She was born a Bolger. (III 476)

**ADALGRIM TOOK** (TA 2880-2982) Hobbit of the Shire, son of Hildigrim Took. (III 475)

**ADAMANTA TOOK** (fl. TA 29th Cent.) Hobbit of the Shire, wife of Gerontius Took. She was born a Chubb. (III 475)

**ADAN** See: Edain.

**ADELARD TOOK** (TA 2928-FA 3) Hobbit of the Shire, son of Flambard Took. He was a guest at the Farewell Party, and was given an umbrella by Bilbo. (I 64; III 475)

**ADORN** River in western Rohan, flowing westward from its source in the Ered Nimrais until it joined the Isen. (I 16; III 431)

**ADRAHIL** (fl. TA 30th Cent.) Dúnadan of Gondor, Lord of Dol Amroth. Adrahil was the father of Finduilas and perhaps also of Imrahil.

His name was probably of Númenorean origin, and was probably Adûnaic. (III 418).

**ADUIAL** (S.) Undómë (q.v.). (III 485)

**ADÛNAIC** (Ad., from *adûn* 'west') The language of the Edain, so called because it was the everyday tongue of the Dúnedain of Númenor. In the days of the pride of Númenor (SA 2899-3319) Adûnaic was also used at the royal court.

Adûnaic was related to the languages of the Men of the

Vales of Anduin and was the major source of the vocabulary of Westron.

The only examples of Adûnaic in *LotR* are the names of some of the kings of Númenor and perhaps the name of the book, the *Akallabêth*. The names of most of the Edain were originally Adûnaic, but have been translated by Tolkien into Old English or other Germanic equivalents.

Also called Númenorean. (III 391-2, 507)

**ADÛNAKHÔR, AR-** (Ad.: 'lord of the west') (fl. SA 2899) Dúnadan, nineteenth King of Númenor (2899-?) and the first to take his royal name in Adûnaic. He persecuted the Faithful and all who used Eldarin. (III 390, 391-2, 454)

***ADVENTURES OF TOM BOMBADIL, THE*** A Buckland poem about Tom Bombadil, written probably before the WR. (TB 8-9, 11-16)

**AERIE** Supposedly an Elven-realm, in Bilbo's poem *Errantry*. The name is merely an imitation of Elvish, and thus probably bears no meaning in terms of the geography of Middle-earth. (TB 8, 25)

**AFTERLITHE** The seventh month of the Shire Reckoning (q. v.), coming after Yule, and thus corresponding roughly to our July.

Afterlithe was called Mede by the inhabitants of Bree. (III 478, 483)

**AFTERYULE** The first month of the Shire Reckoning (q. v.), coming after Yule, and thus corresponding roughly to our January.

In Bree the name was Frery. (III 478, 483)

**AGLAROND** (S.: 'glittering caves') The caverns of Helm's Deep, used as a refuge and storage-place by the Rohirrim. During the Battle of the Hornburg, Gimli fought in the Aglarond and discovered their great beauty. After the WR, he settled in the caves with some Dwarves of Erebor and became the Lord of the Glittering Caves. The new gates of Minas Tirith were probably forged here, and the Dwarves of Aglarond did many great works for Gondor and Rohan.

Called by the Rohirrim the Caverns of Helm's Deep and in Westron the Glittering Caves; the Glittering Caves of Aglarond was a bi-lingual (and redundant) name (II 193-5; III 451)

**AHA** (Q.: 'rage') The later name for the tengwa 𝕵 (number

11), adopted when this letter came to represent initial breath *h* and medial and terminal *ch*.
See: harma. (III 500)

**AIGLOS** (S.: 'point white as snow') The spear of Gil-galad, a famous weapon used by him in the Battle of Dagorlad. Aiglos was probably destroyed when Gil-galad was slain. (I 319)

**AKALLABÊTH** (West.? Ad.?) A book describing the seduction of Númenor by Sauron and the changing of the world at the end of the Second Age. It may have been a scholarly work composed by Elendil's historians (but then why the non-Elvish title?), or a popular moral and historical tale of early Gondor.
The name may mean 'the Downfall.' (III 390)

**ALCARIN, TAR-** (Q.: 'the glorious') (fl. SA 28th Cent.) Dúnadan, seventeenth King of Númenor. (III 390)

**ALDA** (Q.: 'tree') Name of the tengwa ᔕ (number 28), used in Quenya for *ld* but in Sindarin and Westron frequently representing *lh*. (III 500)

**ALDALÓMË** (Q.: 'tree-shadow') One of the names or epithets given Fangorn Forest by Fangorn the Ent. (II 91)

**ALDAMIR** (Q.: 'tree-jewel') (d. TA 1540) Dúnadan, twenty-third King of Gondor (1490-1540). He died a violent death. (III 395)

**ALDARION, TAR-** (Q.: 'of trees') (d. SA 1075) Dúnadan, sixth King of Númenor. He had tragic relations with his father, Tar-Meneldur, and with his wife, perhaps related to the fact that he left no male heirs. (III 390, 391; RP 9/12/66)

**ALDËA** (Q.: 'tree-day') Quenya form of the Númenorean and Westron names for the fourth day of the enquië, named in honor of the White Tree. The Sindarin form was Orgaladh, and the Hobbitish Trewesdei.
See also: Aldúya. (III 484)

**ALDOR** (tr. Roh.: 'prince, old') (TA 2544-2645) Man, third King of Rohan (2570-2645). Aldor reigned for seventy-five years and completed the conquest of Rohan east of the Isen. In his time Harrowdale and other valleys in the Ered Nimrais were settled.
Aldor was known as "the Old" because of his long life and reign. (III 434)

ALDÚYA   (Q.: 'trees'-day')   Quenya form of the Eldarin name
for the fourth day of the enquië, named for the Two Trees.
The Sindarin form was Orgaladhad. (III 484)

ALFIRIN   (S.: 'mortal tree'?)   A golden flower that grew,
among other places, in the fields of Lebennin. (III 185)

ALPHABET OF DAERON  The Angerthas Moria (q. v.). (III 493)

ALTARIEL   (Q.: 'tree-female')   Galadriel (q. v.). (R 58)

AMAN   (S.? Q.?: 'blessed'?)   The Undying Lands (q. v.), or
that part of them where the Great Armament landed in SA
3319.
Called Aman the Blessed. (III 392)

AMANDIL, TAR-   (Q.: 'lover of Aman') (fl. SA 6th Cent.)
Dúnadan, third King of Númenor. (III 390)

AMANDIL   (d. SA 3319)   Dúnadan, last lord of Andúnië, the
father of Elendil. He perished in the destruction of Númenor.
(III 391)

AMARANTH BRANDYBUCK   (TA 2904-98)   Hobbit of the
Shire, second child of Gorbadoc Brandybuck. (III 476)

AMBARONA   (Q.: 'world---')   One of Fangorn's names or
epithets for Fangorn Forest (q. v.). (II 91)

AMLAITH OF FORNOST   (S.) (d. TA 946)   Dúnadan, first
King of Arthedain (861-946) and eldest son of Eärendur, the
last King of Arnor. (III 394)

AMON AMARTH   (S.: 'mount doom')   The name given Orodruin
(q. v.) by the people of Gondor when it burst into flame before
Sauron's attack on Gondor in SA 3429. (III 393)

AMON DÍN   (S.: 'mount ---')   Hill in Gondor east of Druadan
Forest on which was built the first of the northern beacon-
towers of Gondor.
Called Dín for short. (III 20, 130, 132)

AMON HEN   (S.: 'hill of the eye')   One of the three peaks at
the southern end of Nen Hithoel, located on the western
bank of the Anduin. The Seat of Seeing (q. v.) was built on
the summit of Amon Hen.
Called in Westron the Hill of Sight or, less commonly,
the Hill of the Eye. (I 509-26)

AMON LHAW   (S.: 'hill of the ear')   One of the three peaks
at the southern end of Nen Hithoel, located on the eastern
bank of the Anduin. The Seat of Hearing was built on its
summit.

Called in Westron the Hill of Hearing. (I 509-10, 526)

**AMON SÛL** (S.: 'mount wind') Weathertop (q. v.). See also: the Tower of Amon Sûl. (I 250, 346)

**AMPA** (Q.: 'hook') Name for the tengua **ᗱ** (number 14), used in Quenya for *mp* and often used in other languages for *v.* (III 500)

**AMROTH** (Silvan) (d. c. TA 1981) An Elven-king who built the port of Dol Amroth. He was the lover of Nimrodel. When his white ship was blown out to sea without her he jumped into the water to return to her and was lost.

Although Dol Amroth was in Belfalas, Amroth's high house was in Lórien, on Cerin Amroth. (I 441-2; III 181, 506)

**ANARDIL** (Q.: 'sun-lover') (d. TA 411) Dúnadan, sixth King of Gondor. (324-411). (III 394)

**ANÁRION, TAR-** (Q.: 'sun ---') (c. SA 1200) Dúnadan, eighth King of Númenor. (III 390)

**ANÁRION** (d. SA 3440) Dúnadan, with Isildur the second King of Gondor (3320-3440). With his father Elendil and the remnant of the Faithful he escaped from the wreck of Númenor, and was given as his fief a large part of Gondor, named Anórien after him. Anárion fought in the war of the Last Alliance, and was killed by a stone catapulted from the Barad-dûr. (I 319, 320; III 394, 401)

**ANARYA** (Q.: 'sun-day') Quenya form of the name of the second day of the enquië, named for the sun. The Sindarin name was Oranor, and the Hobbitish name Sunnendei. (III 484)

**ANBORN** (S.) (fl. WR) Dúnadan of Gondor, a Ranger of Ithilien. (II 359, 373-4)

**ANCA** (Q.: 'jaws') Name for the tengwa **ᴄᴅ** (number 15), used in Quenya to represent *nk*. (III 500)

**ANCALAGON** (S.) The greatest of dragons, living probably in the First Age.

He was called Ancalagon the Black. (I 94)

**ANCALIMË, TAR-** (Q.: 'great-light') (fl. SA 1100) Dúnadan, seventh ruler and first Ruling Queen of Númenor (1075-?). She was the only child of the previous king, Tar-Aldarion. (III 390, 391, 410, 453)

**ANCALIMON, TAR-** (Q.: 'great-light') (c. SA 24th Cent.)

Dúnadan, fourteenth King of Númenor. (III 390)

**ANCIENT HOUSES**    The Three Houses of the Elf-friends (q. v.). (II 127)

**ANCIENT TONGUE**    Quenya (q. v.). (I 119)

**ANCIENT WORLD**    The world of the First Age, so called by Aragorn. (I 460)

**ANDAITH**    (S.: 'long-mark')    Tehta showing vowel length, used optionally in the Mode of Beleriand. (III 499)

**ANDO**    (Q.: 'gate')    Name for the tengwa ᑭᗞ (number 5), used for *nd* in Quenya, and frequently representing *d* in other languages. (III 500)

**ANDUIN**    (S.: 'great-river')    The greatest river of northwestern Middle-earth, flowing from its sources in the far north for about 1500 miles to its delta in the Bay of Belfalas. Anduin and its many tributaries drained the area between Mirkwood and the Misty Mountains (known as the Vales of Anduin), and also Anórien, Ithilien and much of Rohan and Lebennin. Its principal tributaries were the Gladden, Celebrant, Limlight, Entwash, Morgulduin, Erui, Sirith and Poros.
Called in Westron the Great River.
See also: the Carrock, Sarn Gebir, Rauros, Nindalf, Nen Hithoel, Ethir Anduin, Cair Andros. (I 21, 483, 488ff.)

**ANDÚNIË**    (Q.: 'west')    Fief in western Númenor, home of the Faithful. The Lords of Andúnië were descended from Valandil, the first Lord, who was the son of Silmariën. (III 391)

**ANDÚRIL**    (Q?: 'west-flame')    The sword of Aragorn II, forged from the shards of Narsil (q. v.) by elven-smiths in Rivendell in TA 3018. On its blade was a design of seven stars (for Elendil) between the crescent moon (for Isildur) and the rayed sun (for Anárion), as well as many runes. Because of its heritage and its bearer, and because of its great brightness, Andúril quickly became a famous weapon.
Called in Westron the Flame of the West. Also known as the Sword that was Broken, the Sword re-forged, etc. (I 233, 362; II 147, 176; III 150)

**ANDWISE ROPER**    (b. TA 2923)    Hobbit of the Shire, first son of Roper Gamgee. Like his father, he was a roper in Tighfield.
Called Andy for short. (II 276; III 477)

**ANFALAS** (S: 'long-coast')   Fief of Gondor, a coastal area between the Lefnui and the Morthond.
Called in Westron Langstrand. (I 16; III 50)

**ANGA** (Q.: 'iron')   Name for the tengwa **ᴄᴄſ** (number 7), usually used in Quenya to represent **ŋg**. (III 500)

**ANGAMAITË** (Q.: 'iron---')  (fl. TA 1634)   Dúnadan, great-grandson of Castamir and a leader of the Corsairs of Umbar. He and his brother Sangahyando led a raid on Pelargir in 1634 in which King Minardil of Gondor was slain. (III 407)

**ANGBAND** (S.: 'iron---')   Country in which Morgoth dwelled in the First Age, in the far north of Middle-earth. Angband may have been located where the Northern Waste was at the time of the WR. (I 260)

**ANGBOR** (S.: 'iron---')  (fl. WR)   Man of Gondor, probably a Dúnadan, lord of Lamedon at the time of WR. Angbor led the defense of Linhir against the Corsairs, and commanded the army that marched to Minas Tirith after that battle. (III 185, 187, 193)

**ANGELICA BAGGINS** (b. TA 2981)   Hobbit of the Shire, daughter of Ponto Baggins and a guest at the Farewell Party. Because of her vanity, she was given a convex mirror by Bilbo. (I 64; III 474)

**ANGERTHAS DAERON** (S.: 'long rune-rows of Daeron')   A mode of the cirth, said to have been developed in the First Age by Daeron along the lines of the Tengwar. The Angerthas achieved great popularity (and a cursive script) in Beleriand and Eregion, and later were adopted by the Dwarves of Khazad-dûm.

The additions attributed to Daeron may actually have been made by the Noldor of Eregion, but Daeron's contribution lay at least in organizing the cirth into a consistent phonemic system.

Also called the Alphabet of Daeron and Daeron's runes. (III 493, 501-4)

**ANGERTHAS MORIA** (S.: 'long rune-rows of Khazad-dûm') Dwarfish adaptation of the mode of the Angerthas Daeron in use with Eregion, used by Durin's Folk both in Khazad-dûm and in Erebor. The Dwarvish changes, which were unsystematic, were basically a result of the need to represent Khuzdul sounds not occurring in Elvish, and of the desire to represent weak vowels. The Dwarves of Erebor further adapted this system; their changes showed a tendency to return to the original Elvish mode. (III 495, 501-4)

ANGLE    The land between the Mitheithel and the Bruinen. Between TA 1150 and 1350 many Stoors lived here, but left because of the threat of war and the terror of Angmar. At the time of the WR the Angle seems to have been largely deserted, except for the trolls of the Trollshaws. (III 396, 457)

ANGLE    Egladil (q. v.). (I 450)

ANGMAR    (S.: 'iron-home)    Witch-kingdom on both sides of the northern Misty Mountains, north of the Ettenmoors, ruled by the Lord of the Nazgûl, who was then known as the Witch-king of Angmar. Its capital was Carn Dûm. Angmar was peopled with Orcs, Hill-men, and other such creatures.
    Angmar arose about TA 1300 and, for the next 700 years, attempted to destroy the Dúnedain of the North. Cardolan and Rhudaur fell quickly, the former effectively destroyed by 1409 and the latter infiltrated even earlier, but Arthedain, aided by the Elves of Rivendell and Lindon, held out until 1974, although nearly defeated in 1409. In 1975, the Witch-king was defeated in the Battle of Fornost by armies from Lindon (led by Círdan and Eärnur and strengthened by the latter's army from Gondor) and Rivendell (led by Glorfindel); he was driven from the North and his servants west of the Misty Mountains slain or scattered. Those few who survived east of the Mountains were destroyed soon after by the Éothéod (q. v.). (I 270; III 397-400, 411-12, 429, 457-58)

ANGRENOST    (S.: 'iron-fortress')    Isengard (q. v.). (II 95)

ANNA    (Q.: 'gift')    Name for the tengwa ᴄᴛ (number 23). (III 500)

ANN-THENNATH    (S.)    A mode of song among the Elves. The original version of the song of Beren and Lúthien was composed in this form.
    Spelled "ann-thannath" in the RHM Index; this spelling may be the correct one. (I 260; RHM III 437)

ANNÚMINAS    (S.: 'sunset-tower')    City built by Elendil on the shore of Nenuial, the first capital of Arnor. Annúminas was deserted sometime between TA 250 and 861 because of the decline of Arnor, and the court removed to Fornost. Annúminas was rebuilt at the beginning of the Fourth Age by Elessar, and became the northern capital of the Reunited Kingdom.
    The chief palantír (q.v.) of the North was kept at Annúminas

until its loss. (I 320; II 259; III 402)

ANÓRIEN (S.: 'sun-land') That part of Gondor north of the Ered Nimrais, west of Anduin and east and south of Rohan, originally the fief of Anárion. Anórien contained the Druadan Forest, and also much fertile farmland. Its capital and chief city was Minas Tirith.

Called in Rohirric Sunlending. *Anórien* was derived from the older Sindarin form *Anóriend*. (III 14, 19, 127)

ANSON ROPER (b. TA 2961) Hobbit of the Shire, son of Andwise Roper. He probably lived in Tighfield, and was probably a roper. (III 477)

ANTANI (Q.) The Edain (q. v.). (III 506)

ANTO (Q.: 'mouth') Name for the tengwa ᛄ (number 13), used in Quenya to represent *nt* and frequently in other languages for *dh*. (III 500)

APPLEDORE Surname used by Men of Bree. (I 212; III 335)

AR- (Ad.: 'royal, king') Prefix attached to the royal names of those rulers of Númenor who took their names in Adûnaic. The Kings and Queens are entered in this *Glossary* under the root of their royal names.

Cf.: Tar-. (III 390)

ARADOR (S.: 'royal---') (d. TA 2930) Dúnadan, fourteenth Chieftain of the Dúnedain of the North (2912-30). He was slain by hill-trolls in the Coldfells. (III 394, 420)

ARAGLAS (S.: 'royal-leaf') (d. TA 2455) Dúnadan, sixth Chieftain of the Dúnedain of the North (2327-2455). (III 394)

ARAGORN I (S.: 'royal-tree') (d. TA 2327) Dúnadan, fifth Chieftain of the Dúnedain of the North (2319-27), killed by wolves. (III 394, 401)

ARAGORN II (TA 2931-FA 120) Dúnadan, sixteenth and last Chieftain of the Dúnedain of the North (2933-3019), restorer of the Dúnedain kingdoms in Middle-earth and, as Elessar, first King of the Reunited Kingdom (3019-FA 120). As the heir of Ísildur, he was raised secretly in Rivendell to protect him from Sauron, and was known as Estel until he was twenty, when Elrond revealed to him his lineage.

Aragorn then went off into the Wild, and for nearly seventy years fought against Sauron in many ways and learned the customs of various peoples, until he was the hardiest and the wisest man of his time. During this period Aragorn served in disguise Thengel of Rohan and Ecthelion of

Gondor. In Gondor he was known as Thorongil because of the star of the Rangers that he wore; his greatest feat there was a raid on Umbar in 2980 in which he destroyed a large part of the fleet of the Corsairs. In 2956 he met Gandalf, and the two became close friends. In 3017, after thirteen years of intermittent searching at Gandalf's request, Aragorn captured Gollum. The next year, he met Frodo and his companions at Bree and helped them to get to Rivendell. Aragorn was one of the Nine Companions, and led the Fellowship after Gandalf fell in Khazad-dum.

During the War of the Ring, Aragorn was one of the leaders of the defense at the Battle of the Hornburg; during his time in Rohan he and Éomer became fast friends. Then, accompanied by Legolas, Gimli and a company of Rangers, Aragorn took the Paths of the Dead, acting on information gleaned from the palantír of Orthanc, which he had claimed from Gandalf as its rightful possessor. As the heir of Isildur, Aragorn caused the Dead to obey him, and with their aid defeated the Corsairs at Pelargir and captured their fleet. He then brought a large body of men from southern Gondor to Minas Tirith to turn the tide of the Battle of the Pelennor Fields. Later, he was captain of the Army of the West (q. v.).

After the WR, Aragorn became King of the Reunited Kingdom and Lord of the Western Lands as Elessar Telcontar, and married Arwen. During his 120-year reign he extended the borders of the Kingdom and re-established long-absent peace and prosperity.

In addition to the wisdom he gained through his long period of fighting Sauron, Aragorn had Elven-wisdom and the foresight of the Dúnedain. It was said of him with justice that in him the nobility of the Númenoreans of old was restored.

Aragorn met Arwen when he was twenty, just before he departed from Imladris. He loved her from that moment, and they plighted their troth in 2980. Elrond, however, would not consent to marry his daughter to any Man who was less than the King of both Arnor and Gondor, and so the two were not married until after the WR. Aragorn and Arwen had one son, Eldarion, and a number of daughters.

From the time of its forging in 3018, Aragorn bore the sword Andúril.

Aragorn was called Elessar and Elfstone by Galadriel

and the people of Gondor during the WR because of the emerald brooch he wore; he took this name, which was foretold for him, as his royal name. He was called Strider in Bree before the WR, and he took the Quenya equivalent of this name, Telcontar, as the name of his family. Also called Isildur's Heir, the Renewer, Longshanks and Wingfoot; the last name was given him by Éomer after the journey of the Three Hunters. (I 91, 231, 233, 313, 324, 332-33, 365, 387, 486; II 254-55; III 150-52, 169-80, 284, 302, 394, 417-18, 420-28, 438, 461, 462)

ARAGOST (S.: 'royal-fortress') (d. TA 2588) Dúnadan, eighth Chieftain of the Dúnedain of the North (2523-88). (III 394)

ARAHAD I (S.: 'royal---') (d. TA 2523) Dúnadan, seventh Chieftain of the Dúnedain of the North (2455-2523). (III 394, 401)

ARAHAD II (d. TA 2719) Dúnadan, tenth Chieftain of the Dúnedain of the North (2654-2719). (III 394)

ARAHAEL (S.: 'royal---') (d. TA 2177) Dúnadan, second Chieftain of the Dúnedain of the North (2106-77). (III 394)

ARAN- (S.: 'royal-man') The royal prefix used by the Kings of Arthedain after Malvegil and by the Chieftains of the Dúnedain of the North to indicate their claim to all of Arnor. Unlike the Númenorean prefixes Ar- and Tar-, the element Aran- was an integral part of the name, and was given at birth.
Sometimes shortened to Ara- or Ar-. (III 394, 410)

ARANARTH (S.: 'royal-realm') (d. TA 2106) Dúnadan, first Chieftain of the Dúnedain of the North (1974-2106). He was the eldest son of Arvedui, the last King of Arthedain. (III 394, 398)

ARANTAR (Q.) (d. TA 435) Dúnadan, fifth King of Arnor (339-435). (III 394)

ARANUIR (S.: 'royal---') (d. TA 2247) Dúnadan, third Chieftain of the Dúnedain of the North (2177-2247). (III 394)

ARAPHANT (S.: 'royal---') (d. TA 1964) Dúnadan, fourteenth King of Arthedain (1891-1964). During his reign contact with Gondor was renewed. (III 394, 409, 411)

ARAPHOR (S.: 'royal---') (d. TA 1589) Dúnadan, ninth King of Arthedain (1409-1589). While still a youth, with aid from Círdan he drove the forces of Angmar away from Fornost and the North Downs in 1409. During Araphor's long reign

Arthedain seems to have been at peace, since Angmar was temporarily subdued by the Elves of Lindon and Rivendell. (III 394, 397)

**ARASSUIL**   (S.: 'royal---') (d. TA 2784)   Dúnadan, eleventh Chieftain of the Dúnedain of the North (2719-84). In his time Eriador was troubled by Orcs. (III 394, 401-2)

**ARATHORN I**   (S.: royal---') (d. TA 2848)   Dúnadan, twelfth Chieftain of the Dúnedain of the North (2784-2848). He died a violent death. (III 394)

**ARATHORN II**   (TA 2873-2933)   Dúnadan, fifteenth Chieftain of the Dúnedain of the North (2930-33). He was slain by Orcs while fighting with Elladan and Elrohir.
   Arathorn married Gilraen in 2929; their only child was Aragorn II. (III 394, 420)

**ARAVAL**   (S.: 'royal') (d. TA 1891)   Dúnadan, thirteenth King of Arthedain (1813-91). (III 394)

**ARAVIR**   (S.: 'royal') (d. TA 2319)   Dúnadan, fourth Chieftain of the Dúnedain of the North (2247-2319). (III 394)

**ARAVORN**   (S.: 'royal---') (d. TA 2654)   Dúnadan, ninth Chieftain of the Dúnedain of the North (2588-2654). (III 394)

**ARAW**   (S.)   A Vala, the huntsman of the Valar and the only one of his people to come frequently to Middle-earth (in the First Age). He was prominent in the Battle of the Valar. Araw was said to have introduced the mearas (q. v.) to Middle-earth. The Kine of Araw were named after him.
   The Quenya form of his name was Oromë, and he was Called Béma by Men, probably in (translated) Adûnaic. He was known as Oromë the Great. (III 29, 138, 395, 431)

**ARCHET**   Village of the Bree-land on the northern edge of the Chetwood. (I 205, 245)

**ARCIRYAS**   (Q.: '---ship') (TA 19th Cent.)   Dúnadan, younger brother of Narmacil II of Gondor. He was an ancestor of Eärnil II. (III 410)

**ARDA**   (Q.: 'region')   Name for the tengwa $\gamma$ (number 26), usually used to represent *rd* in Quenya and *rh* in Sindarin and Westron. (III 500)

**ARDA**   The land where the Valar came at the beginning of time, and which was prepared by them for the Erusen. Arda was probably equivalent to Valinor or the entire Undying Lands.
   Called in Westron the Realm. (R 66)

ÁRE   (Q.: 'sunlight')   Early name for the tengwa Ȝ (number 31), originally áze and later esse (qq. v.). (III 500)

ÁRE NUQUERNA   (Q.: 'áre reversed')   One of the names for the tengwa Ȝ (number 32).
   See: áre, esse nuquerna. (III 500)

ARGELEB I   (S.: 'royal-silver')   (d. TA 1356)   Dúnadan, seventh King of Arthedain (1349-56). On his accession, since no heirs of Isildur remained in either Rhudaur or Cardolan, Arthedain claimed lordship over all of Arnor. Rhudaur, which was controlled by Angmar, contested this claim. In the war that followed, Argeleb fortified the Weather Hills but was slain in battle. (III 394, 397)

ARGELEB II   (d. TA 1670)   Dúnadan, tenth King of Arthedain (1589-1670). In 1600 he gave permission to Marcho and Blanco to settle the Shire. (I 23; III 394, 398)

ARGONATH   (S.: 'stones of the kings')   The carved rocks at the upper end of the chasm at the northern entrance to Nen Hithoel, on Anduin. They were two immense and awesome statues of Isildur and Anárion, one on either side of the river. The Argonath was built by Rómendacil II about TA 1340 to mark the northern boundary of Gondor.
   Also called the Pillars of the Kings, the Gates of the Kings and the Gates of Gondor; the first was probably the actual Westron name, although all three were commonly used. (I 508-9; III 405)

ARGONUI   (S.: 'royal-stony')   (d. TA 2912)   Dúnadan, thirteenth Chieftain of the Dúnedain of the North (2848-2912). (III 394)

ARKENSTONE   A great white jewel found deep beneath Erebor by Thráin I. The Arkenstone was the greatest treasure of the Kings of Erebor, but was left in Erebor when Smaug drove the Dwarves out in TA 2770. In 2941, while a member of Thorin and Company, Bilbo found it when he explored Smaug's hoard. The Arkenstone was used by him to attempt a reconciliation between Thorin and the Elves and Men besieging him, and was later buried with Thorin.
   Also called the Heart of the Mountain. (III 439, 440; H 220, 225-6, 257, 275)

ARMY OF THE WEST   The small army of Men of Gondor and Rohan, led by Aragorn, Gandalf, Imrahil and Éomer, which during the WR marched on the Morannon to divert Sauron's attention from his search for Frodo. The Army was on the brink of annihilation by Sauron's forces when the Ring was destroyed and Sauron's power broken. The Army then won a great victory over the Haradrim and Easterlings allied with Sauron, as well as over the now-leaderless orcs and trolls.

Pippin, Legolas, Gimli, Beregond, Elladan and Elrohir also marched with the Army.

Also called the Host of the West. (III 193-208, 278-80)

**ARNACH**   See: Lossarnach. (III 152, 508)

**ARNOR**   (S.: 'royal-land')   The senior Dúnedain Kingdom of Middle-earth, founded in SA 3320 by Elendil, who ruled directly as its first king. At its greatest Arnor included all the lands between the Gwathlo-Bruinen and the Lune. Arnor's first capital was Annúminas, but before 861 the capital was moved to Fornost, the chief city of the country. Unlike Gondor, Arnor did not prosper, and the dwindling of the Dúnedain began with the disastrous Battle of the Gladden Fields (q.v.) in TA 2. However, throughout all its troubles, the rulers of Arnor, the heirs of the Line of Isildur, were preserved.

When Eärendur, the tenth King, died in TA 861, Arnor was split among his three sons, the eldest becoming King of Arthedain (q. v.). The Dúnedain in the other two kingdoms, Cardolan and Rhudaur (qq. v.) quickly dwindled, and in 1349 Arthedain claimed lordship over all of Arnor. After this time, what was properly speaking Arthedain was sometimes called Arnor.

Angmar and Rhudaur used this claim as a pretext to attack Arthedain, and in 1974 the kingdom fell. The heirs of Isildur became the Chieftains of the few Dúnedain of the North, until after the WR, when Arnor was re-established by Elessar.

Also called the North-kingdom. (I 181; III 394, 396-454, 456)

**AROD**   (tr. Roh.: 'quick, swift') (fl. WR)   A swift and fiery horse of Rohan, lent to Legolas and Gimli by Éomer. Arod bore them during the WR through Rohan and the Paths of the Dead, and probably also bore Legolas in the Battle of the Pelennor Fields. (II 51; III 70)

**ARTAMIR**   (Q.: '---jewel') (d. TA 1944)   Dúnadan of Gondor, son of King Ondoher. He was killed in battle with the Wain-riders. (III 409)

**ARTHEDAIN**   (S.: 'realm of the Edain')   Dúnadan kingdom, one of the divisions of Arnor, founded in TA 861. Its capital was Fornost. Arthedain included the land between the Lune and the Brandywine, and also the land north of the Great East Road as far east as Weathertop. Arthedain had in its possession the two palantíri of the North kept by Men in the Third Age.

The Kings of Arthedain were descended from Amlaith, the eldest son of Eärendur, the last King of Arnor, and so in them the Line of Isildur was maintained.

In 1349, Argeleb I claimed lordship over all of Arnor due to the extinction of the royal families of Cardolan and Rhudaur; but Rhudaur, aided by Angmar, contested the claim and attacked Arthedain. Sometimes aided by Cardolan, Lindon and Rivendell, Arthedain repulsed major attacks in 1356 and 1409, as well as various minor attacks, with waning strength. In 1974, Fornost was captured by Angmar; King Arvedui fled to the Ered Luin and then to Forochel, but was drowned the next spring. However, Angmar was defeated by the Elves of Lindon and Rivendell and the remnant of the army of Arthedain, aided by a large force from Gondor commanded by Eärnur. Arthedain was not re-established; Fornost was deserted and the Dúnedain of the North became a scattered people.

Although for most of its history Arthedain was estranged from Gondor, during the reign of King Araphant (1891-1964) contact between the two realms was renewed. Arvedui married Princess Fíriel, the daughter of Ondoher of Gondor, and although his claim to the throne was rejected in 1944, the realms remained friendly. Without Gondor's aid in 1975 Angmar could not have been defeated.

Also called the North-kingdom. (III 394, 396-400, 410-11)

**ARVEDUI** (S.: 'king-last') (d. TA 1974 or 1975) Dúnadan, fifteenth and last King of Arthedain (1964-74). At his birth, Malbeth the Seer foretold that he was to be the last king, which is why Arvedui was given his name. In 1944, on the death of Ondoher of Gondor and his sons, Arvedui claimed the crown of Gondor because of his descent from Isildur, who was King of Gondor with Anárion, and because he was the husband of Fíriel, Ondoher's only surviving child, who was heiress to the throne by the laws of Númenor. Although Arvedui's claim was rejected, King Eärnil of Gondor promised to give him aid in need. Late in 1973, Arvedui asked for aid against Angmar, but before the fleet sent by Eärnil arrived, the Witch-king overran Arthedain. Arvedui sent his sons to Lindon, but he remained on the North Downs until the last. He then hid in the dwarf-mines in the northern Ered

Luin until forced by hunger to seek refuge with the Lossoth. In March of 1974 (or, possibly, 1975) Cirdan sent a ship to Forochel to rescue Arvedui. He and his men boarded the ship, but it was trapped in the ice and Arvedui was drowned. (III 394, 398-400, 409-11, 458)

**ARVEGIL** (S.: 'royal---') (d. TA 1743) Dúnadan, eleventh King of Arthedain (1670-1743). (III 394)

**ARVELEG I** (S.: 'royal---') (d. TA 1409) Dúnadan, eighth King of Arthedain (1356-1409). After his father's death, he drove the forces of Angmar and Rhudaur back from the Tower Hills, with the aid from Lindon and Rivendell, and for fifty years Arveleg, together with Cardolan, maintained a frontier along the Weather Hills, Great East Road and lower Hoarwell. In 1409, Arveleg was killed while unsuccessfully defending the Tower Hills against a massive assault by Angmar and Rhudaur. (III 394, 397)

**ARVELEG II** (d. TA 1813) Dúnadan, twelfth King of Arthedain (1743-1813). (III 394)

**ARVERNIEN** (S.: 'royal---land') A dwelling-place of Eärendil, probably in Beleriand. (I 308)

**ARWEN** (S.) (TA 241-FA 121) Elven lady, daughter of Elrond and Celebrían. For nearly three thousand years she lived in contentment in Imladris and Lórien, until in 2951 she met Aragorn in Rivendell. In 2980 they plighted their troth on Cerin Amroth, and after the WR they were wed, and Arwen became Queen of Gondor. She bore her husband one son and a number of daughters. However, by marrying Aragorn she chose not to accompany her father over Sea at the end of the Third Age, and thus became mortal. After Aragorn died in FA 120, Arwen went to Lórien, where she died the next winter. Her grave was made on Cerin Amorth.

Arwen was noted for her beauty, which was said to resemble that of Lúthien. Because of this beauty, which was never again to appear among the Elves in Middle-earth, she was called Undómiel, or its Westron equivalent, Evenstar, and she was known as the Evenstar of her people. (I 299-300; III 310, 312, 421-28, 456)

**ASËA ARANION** (Q.? Va?: 'leaf of the kings') Athelas (q. v.). (III 172)

**ASFALOTH** (S.: '---blossoms')(fl. WR) Glorfindel's swift white horse, which bore Frodo to Rivendell from the Ford of Bruinen. (I 279, 281-82, 284-86)

**ASH MOUNTAINS, ASHEN MOUNTAINS** The Ered Lithui (q. v.). (I 17; III 245)

**ASPHODEL BURROWS** (TA 2913-3012) Hobbit of the Shire, daughter of Gorbadoc Brandybuck and wife of Rufus Burrows. She was a guest at the Farewell Party. (III 476)

**ASTAR** (Q.: 'month') The month of the various Dúnedain and Westron calendars. The Astar usually contained 30 days, although two months in the Kings' Reckoning had 31 days. (III 481)

**ASTRON** Fourth month of the Shire Reckoning (q. v.), corresponding roughly to our April.
Called Chithing in Bree. (III 478)

**ATANAMIR, TAR-** (Q.: 'adan-jewel') (fl. SA 23rd Cent.) Dúnadan, thirteenth King of Númenor (2251-?). He was the first King to speak openly against the Ban of the Valar and to claim that the descendents of Elros had a right to immortality. This resulted in the division of Númenor into pro- and anti-Eldarin factions.
He was called Tar-Atanamir the Great. (III 390, 391, 454)

**ATANAMIR ALCARIN** A typographical error for Atanatar Alcarin. See: Atanatar II. (III 457)

**ATANATAR I** (Q.: 'king of the Edain') (d. TA 748) Dúnadan, tenth King of Gondor (667-748). (III 394)

**ATANATAR II** (d. TA 1226) Dúnadan, sixteenth King of Gondor (1149-1226). In his time Gondor reached the height of its power and splendor. Atanatar, however, loved luxury, and did nothing to maintain the power of Gondor. The watch on Mordor was neglected, but the royal crown was replaced with a jewelled crown of precious metals.
Atanatar was known as Alcarin, the Glorious, because of the luxury and power of his realm. Called Atanamir Alcarin in error on III 457. (III 395, 401, 402, 404, 457)

**ATENDËA** (Q.: 'double-middle') The leap-year of the Númenorean calendar system and of those derived from it, so called because the year was lengthened by doubling Loëndë, the middle day of the year. (HM III 386)

**ATHELAS** (S.: 'kingsfoil') A healing plant brought to Middle-earth by the Númenoreans, which grew only in places where they had lived or camped. Athelas had a heartening fragrance, and in the hands of the heirs of Elendil had great powers for curing wounds and counteracting poisons and evil influences. Aragorn used athelas by crushing and boiling its leaves in water and then either washing his patient's wounds in the tincture or by having the patient breathe the steam.

Called kingsfoil in Westron and asëa aranion in either Quenya or Valinorean. (I 266, 436-37; III 170-77)

AULË (Q.) A Vala, closely connected with the Dwarves and their origin; he gave them their name and seems to have had an influence on their emotional characteristics.

Aulë was called Aulë the Smith; he was probably the smith of the Valar. (III 518, 519)

AUTHORITIES The Valar (q. v.). (I 33; RP 9/12/65)

AZANULBIZAR (Kh.) The valley outside the Great Gates of Khazad-dûm, lying between two arms of the Misty Mountains. Azanulbizar contained the Kheled-zâram and the source of the Silverlode. In TA 2799 the Battle of Azanulbizar, the final and greatest battle of the War of the Dwarves and Orcs, was fought here.

Called Nanduhirion in Sindarin and the Dimrill Dale in Westron. (I 370, 432-34; III 442)

ÁZE (Q.: 'sunlight') Earliest name for the tengwa Ɛ (number 31), used when the letter had the value z in Quenya. When the z-sound became merged with weak r, the name became áre or esse (qq. v.). (III 500)

ÁZE NUQUERNA (Q.: 'áze reversed') Earliest name for the tengwa Ȝ (number 32). Its use parallelled that of áze (q. v.). (III 500)

AZOG (d. TA 2799) Orc, king of the Orcs of Khazad-dûm. His murder and defilement of Thrór in 2790 touched off the War of the Dwarves and Orcs. In the Battle of Azanulbizar, the final battle of the war, Azog led the Orkish forces. He killed Náin, but was in turn slain by Dáin II. (III 441-42, 443)

# ʙ

**BACK-DOOR** The stone door in the eastern side of the Misty Mountains through which Bilbo escaped from the Orcs who had captured him in TA 2941. The back-door was located west of the Carrock.

Perhaps also called the Goblin-gate. (H 12, 94-95, 100)

**BADGER-BROCK** The head of the Badger-folk in the Old Forest, in the poem *Adventures of Tom Bombadil*. He—and they—were quite possibly fictional. (TB 12-13)

**BADGER FOLK** A family of badgers living in the Old Forest, in the poem *Adventures of Tom Bombadil*. (TB 13)

**BAG END** A dwelling in Hobbiton, built about TA 2880 by Bungo Baggins at the end of Bagshot Row. Bungo, Bilbo and Frodo Baggins lived there, and after Frodo went over Sea it seems that Sam Gamgee and his heirs lived there. From September, 3018 until her imprisonment and his death, Lobelia and Lotho Sackville-Baggins lived in Bag End, and Saruman made it his headquarters in the Shire.

Bag End was a typical, if somewhat more luxurious than the ordinary, hobbit-hole. Its street address was probably Number 1, Bagshot Row.

Also spelled Bag-End. (I 43; III 356, 367-71, 376; H 15-20)

**BAGGINS** A well-to-do family of Hobbits of the Shire, with members living all over the Shire. The Bagginses were connected with most of the aristocratic families of the Shire, as well as the Chubb-Bagginses and Sackville-Bagginses.

The Bagginses were in general an unexceptionable (by Hobbit standards) family, their more eccentric members having a considerable portion of Took blood. (I 30; III 474)

**BAGSHOT ROW** Street in Hobbiton leading from the Water up to Hobbiton Hill. Before the WR, the Gamgees lived at Number 3 Bagshot Row, Daddy Twofoot lived next door and the Bagginses lived in Bag End. The Old Grange was also on Bagshot Row. During the WR, Bagshot Row was torn up by Saruman and made into a gravel and sand quarry. After the War, Bagshot Row was rebuilt and named New Row. (I 44, 45; III 359, 366, 373-74)

**BAIN** (d. TA 3007) Man, second king of Dale (2977-3007). He was the son of Bard I and the father of Brand. (I 301; III 462, 463)

**BALBO BAGGINS** (b. TA 2767) Hobbit of the Shire. He married Berylla Boffin; they had five children. (III 474)

**BALCHOTH** (S.: '---people') Tribe of Easterlings controlled by Sauron, who in the twenty-fifth century of the Third Age lived in Rhovanion east of Mirkwood. They frequently raided the Vales of Anduin south of the Gladden, and greatly distressed its inhabitants. As their power grew, the Balchoth began attacking Gondor's outposts on the Anduin. In 2510 they crossed Anduin and invaded Calenardhon. In the Battle of the Field of Celebrant, the Balchoth, although aided by Orcs of the Misty Mountains, were annihilated by Cirion of Gondor and the Éothéod. After this battle the Balchoth pass from history. (III 415)

**BALDOR** (d. TA 2569) Man of Rohan, eldest son of King Brego. At the feast held to celebrate the completion of Meduseld he vowed to tread the Paths of the Dead. During the WR, his body was found there by the Grey Company.

On III 459 the year of Baldor's death is given as 2570; unless he did not immediately fulfill his vow, or survived for a long time inside the Mountains, this must be an error. (III 71, 84, 315, 434)

**BALIN** (TA 2763-2994) Dwarf of the House of Durin, King of Khazad-dûm (2989-94). Balin was a follower of Thráin, and later of Thorin, from the time of the War of the Dwarves and Orcs. Balin accompanied Thráin on the journey in 2841 that cost him his life, and a century later he was one of the members of Thorin and Company. After the death of Smaug he settled in Erebor, but in 2989 he went to Khazad-dûm with many Dwarves of Erebor and set up a dwarf-colony there. Five years later he was slain by an Orc in Azanulbizar.

Balin and Bilbo became quite friendly in 2941; he seems to have been kindlier than many Dwarves. (I 316, 416, 418-19, III 445, 446, 450; H 21, 26, 286)

**BALROGS** (S.) Evil beings, servants of Morgoth in the First Age. Most of them perished when the Host of Valinor overthrew Morgoth, but at least one escaped. This Balrog, referred to in the Third Age as "the Balrog," hid at the root of the mithril-vein in Khazad-dûm until TA 1980, when he was accidentally released from his prison by the Dwarves. After he killed two Kings of Durin's Folk in two years, the Dwarves fled. About 2480 Sauron peopled Khazad-dûm with orcs and trolls; the Balrog ruled over these by his terror. The Balrog was slain by Gandalf in TA 3019 after a ten-day battle.

Balrogs possessed great power and terror, and wielded both shadow and flame. In the Third Age the Balrog of Moria was second only to Sauron in evil power; his strength was almost equal to that of Gandalf. Balrogs were possibly lesser Valar who had joined Morgoth in his rebellion.

The Balrog of Khazad-dûm was also known as Durin's Bane (because of his murder of Durin VI) and the Terror. (I 423-25, 428-30, 461; II 134-35; 439)

**BAMFURLONG** A place in the Marish, near the Maggot farm. (TB 21)

**BANAKIL** (gen. West.: 'halfling') See: Hobbits. (III 519)

**BANAZÎR** (gen. Hobb.: 'half-wise') See: Samwise Gamgee. (III 517)

**BANDOBRAS TOOK** (TA 2704-2806) Hobbit of the Shire, the second son of Thain Isengrim II. In 2747, he led the force of Tooks that defeated an Orc-band in the Battle of Greenfields. His descendents included the North-tooks of Long Cleeve.

Bandobras was the third tallest hobbit in history; he was four feet five inches tall and able to ride a horse. He was nicknamed Bullroarer. (I 20, 25; III 402, 474; H 30)

**BANKS** Hobbit surname in Bree and in the Shire. (I 212, III 475)

**BAN OF THE VALAR** The one restriction placed on the Númenoreans by the Valar at the beginning of the Second Age, which was that the Dúnedain could never set foot on the Undying Lands or sail west out of sight of Númenor. When the Ban was broken by Ar-Pharazôn in SA 3319, the Valar laid down their guardianship of the world and Númenor was destroyed by Eru. (III 390, 392)

**BARAD-DÛR** (S.: 'tower-dark') The fortress of Sauron, built by him with the power of the One Ring between SA 1000 and 1600. At the end of the Second Age it was besieged and captured (3434-41), but its foundations could not be destroyed while the Ring survived. Sauron began to rebuild the Barad-dûr in TA 2951, but it was destroyed in 3019 when the Ring was unmade.

The Barad-dûr was located at the southern end of a great spur of the Ered Lithui, and was the greatest fortress in Middle-earth in the Second and Third Ages.

Called in Orkish Lugbúrz and in Westron the Dark Tower. (I 519; II 422; III 245, 276, 453, 455, 462)

**BARAHIR** (S.: 'tower-lord') (First Age) Adan of the First House of the Edain, the father of Beren. He was slain in the wars against Morgoth.

Barahir was given a ring by Finrod which later became an heirloom of the House of Isildur. (I 260; III 388, 400)

**BARAHIR** (d. TA 2412) Dúnadan, eighth Ruling Steward of Gondor (2395-2412). (III 395)

**BARAHIR** (Fourth Age 2nd Cent.) Dúnadan, Prince of Ithilien and grandson of Faramir. Barahir wrote *The Tale of Aragorn and Arwen.* He may have been Steward of Gondor. (I 38)

**BARANDUIN** (S.: 'goldenbrown-river') River flowing south and southwest from its source, Nenuial, into the Sea, so called because of its color. It was crossed by the Great East Road in the Shire by the Bridge of Stonebows.

The original (and genuine) Hobbitish name for the river was Branda-nîn, meaning "border-water," which was later corrupted to Bralda-hîm, "heady ale," its normal name at the time of the WR. The translated Hobbitish name was the Brandywine. (I 16; III 515, 520)

**BARANOR** (S.: 'tower-sun') (fl. c. TA 2990) Man of Gondor, father of Beregond. He came from Lossarnach. (III 36, 49)

**BARAZ** Barazinbar (q. v.). (I 370)

**BARAZINBAR** (Kh.: 'redhorn'?) One of the Mountains of Moria, the furthest west and north. Barazinbar had sheer, dull-red sides, and was topped with a silver crown of snow. The world's only mithril-vein was located beneath Barazinbar, and here the Balrog was imprisoned.

Called Barazinbar the Cruel by the Dwarves because of its bad weather. Called in Sindarin Caradhras and in Westron Redhorn.

See: Redhorn Gate, Redhorn Pass. (I 370, 374-84, 432; III 439)

**BARD I** (d. TA 2977) Man, a descendent of Girion of Dale and a noted archer. He was born and raised in Esgaroth, and in 2941 he organized the defense of the town against Smaug, and killed the dragon. After this, Bard became the leading figure in Esgaroth, and led the army of Men that fought in the Battle of the Five Armies. Bard used his share of Smaug's hoard to rebuild Dale, and he also gave a considerable amount to the Master of Esgaroth for the rebuilding of the town. He became the first King of the re-founded Dale, and his heirs ruled after him.

Although Bard was somewhat grim of spirit and face, he was wise and an able leader.

Called Bard the Bowman and Bard the Dragon-shooter. (H

234-42, 250, 275-76, 286)

**BARD II** (fl. Fourth Age 1st Cent.) Man, fourth King of Dale (TA 3019-FA ?). With Thorin III, Bard led the army of Men and Dwarves that broke the siege of Erebor during the WR. (III 469)

**BARDINGS** The Men of Dale (q. v.). (I 301)

**BARLIMAN BUTTERBUR** (fl. WR) Man of Bree, keeper of the Prancing Pony at the time of the WR and a friend of Gandalf's. Physically, Barliman was short, fat, bald and red-faced. Mentally, he was by no means quick-witted and had a bad memory, but was good-hearted and perceptive in the long run. (I 209-10 ff., 291)

**BARROW-DOWNS** Downs east of the Old Forest. On the Barrow-downs were the Great Barrows, from which the Downs took their name. Because of the barrows the Downs were revered by the Dúnedain.

During the wars with Angmar, in TA 1409 the Dúnedain of Cardolan took refuge here. About 1636 the barrows were inhabited by evil Barrow-wights from Angmar, and the Barrow-downs became a place of great dread.

The Sindarin name was Tyrn Gorthad. (I 188-202; III 398)

**BARROWFIELD** The field outside Edoras where the Kings of Rohan were buried. At the end of the Third Age there were two groups of barrows, nine on the west side for the Kings of the First Line and eight on the east for the Kings of the Second Line. Simbelmynë grew on the west side of the mounds. (II 142; III 314)

**BARROW-WIGHTS** Evil spirits from Angmar who infested the Great Barrows after TA 1636. The wights tried to entrap people in the barrows and then sacrifice them. (I 193-98, 347; III 398; TB 13-15)

**BATTLE OF AZANULBIZAR** The final battle of the War of the Dwarves and Orcs, fought in the winter of TA 2799. At first the battle went against the Dwarves, but with the aid of the Dwarves of the Iron Hills, who arrived late, the Orcs were defeated and Azog was killed. Many Dwarves were killed, including a number of members of the royal family of Durin's Folk. The Orcs of the Misty Mountains suffered even greater losses, and were so weakened by the battle that they did not recover their strength for over a century.

Also called the Battle of Nanduhirion and the Battle of Dimrill Dale, by Elves and Men respectively. (III 442-44)

**BATTLE OF BYWATER**  The last battle of the WR, fought on November 3, TA 3019. In the battle about a hundred of the Chief's Men were defeated by a band of Hobbits led by Merry and Pippin. Seventy ruffians and nineteen hobbits were killed. (III 364-65)

**BATTLE OF DAGORLAD**  Battle fought in SA 3434 between the forces of the Last Alliance and the armies of Sauron. According to Gollum, the battle lasted for months, but in the end the Last Alliance had the victory, for Gil-galad and Elendil were invincible. Many of the graves of the slain were later engulfed by the Dead Marshes.

  The Battle of Dagorlad may actually have been a siege of the Morannon, with a number of sorties made by the defending orcs. (I 319; II 294, 297)

**BATTLE OF DALE**  Battle of the WR, fought March 15-17, TA 3019, in which the Men of Dale, aided by the Dwarves of Erebor, were defeated by Easterling allies of Sauron. Both King Brand and King Dáin II were slain, and the remnants of their armies were besieged in Erebor. (III 467)

**BATTLE OF FIVE ARMIES**  See: the Battle of the Five Armies. (H 266)

**BATTLE OF FORNOST**  Battle fought in TA 1974 or 1975 in which Círdan and Eärnur of Gondor, aided by the remnants of the people of Arnor and a force from Rivendell led by Glorfindel, utterly defeated the Witch-king, annihilated his army and broke the power of Angmar.

  It is said that the Shire sent a company of bowmen to the battle. (I 24; III 411-12)

**BATTLE OF GREENFIELDS**  Battle fought in TA 2747 in the Northfarthing between a band of Tooks, led by Bandobras, and a band of marauding orcs, led by Golfimbul. The hobbits had the victory.

  Also called the Battle of the Green Fields. (III 365; H 30)

**BATTLE OF NANDUHIRION**  The battle of Azanulbizar (q. v.), as called by the Elves. (III 442-43)

**BATTLE OF THE CAMP**  Battle fought in North Ithilien in TA 1944 between Gondor and the Wainriders, in which Eärnil, leading the Southern Army of Gondor and the remnants of the Northern Army, defeated the unprepared Wainriders as they were celebrating their conquest of Gondor in their camp. Earnil drove the panic-stricken Wainriders out of Ithilien; some fled eastward over Dagorlad, but many perished in the Dead Marshes. This battle, coupled with Earnil's earlier

victory over the Wainriders and Haradrim in South Ithilien,
ended the Wainrider threat to Gondor. (III 409, 458)

**BATTLE OF THE CROSSINGS OF ERUI**   Battle fought in
TA 1447 during the Kin-strife (q. v.), in which Eldacar defeated Castamir's army and slew the usurper. The remnants
of the rebel army fled to Pelargir, where they were besieged
by Eldacar. (III 406)

**BATTLE OF THE CROSSINGS OF ISEN**   Battle fought in TA
2758 in which the Rohirrim, led by Helm, were defeated by
Wulf and his army of Dunlendings. The Rohirrim were thrown
back to Edoras, the Hornburg and their other refuges. (III 432)

**BATTLE OF THE CROSSINGS OF POROS**   Battle fought in
Ithilien in TA 1885 in which Steward Túrin, with aid from Folcwine of Rohan, defeated the Haradrim. In the battle the twin
sons of Folcwine, Fastred and Folcred, were slain. (III 416)

**BATTLE OF THE FIELD OF CELEBRANT**   Battle fought in
TA 2510 in northern Gondor. The Northern Army, led by
Steward Cirion, had advanced against the Balchoth, who had
overrun Calenardhon, but the latter were reinforced by a
horde of Orcs of the Misty Mountains. The Northern Army
was surrounded, but as the invaders were preparing to massacre it, the Éothéod, led by Eorl, swept down from the
north in answer to a previous request for aid and routed the
enemy. For this victory, which ended the Balchoth threat
to Gondor, the Éothéod were given Calenardhon. (II 148;
III 415, 429)

**BATTLE OF THE FIVE ARMIES**   Battle fought on and around
Erebor in TA 2941 between the Men of Esgaroth and Dale,
the Elves of Northern Mirkwood and the Dwarves of Erebor
and the Iron Hills on one side and a huge army of Orcs of
the Misty Mountains and Wargs on the other. Thanks to timely
aid by Beorn and the Eagles of the Misty Mountains, the
forces of good had the victory, but Thorin II was slain. The
Men were led by Bard, the Elves by Thranduil and the
Dwarves by Thorin II and Dáin Ironfoot; the Orcs were led
by Bolg. Other noteworthies in attendance were Gandalf and
Bilbo. Also called the Battle of Five Armies. (III 461; H
266-70, 273-74)

**BATTLE OF THE FORDS OF ISEN**   See: the Battles of the
Fords of Isen.

**BATTLE OF THE GLADDEN FIELDS**   Massacre occurring in
TA 2, in which Isildur and his people, marching to Arnor

after the defeat of Sauron, were ambushed by Orcs of the Misty Mountains. Isildur and his three eldest sons were slain and the Ring was lost in the marshes of the Gladden Fields. Only three men escaped from the massacre, but the shards of Narsil were saved. Arnor never really recovered from this loss of a considerable part of its manhood. (I 83, 320; III 456)

**BATTLE OF THE GREEN FIELDS** The battle of Greenfields (q. v.). (H 30)

**BATTLE OF THE HORNBURG** Battle of the WR, fought March 3-4, TA 3019, between Saruman's army of Dunlendings and Orcs and the Rohirrim, led by Théoden and Éomer. The Rohirrim, including Aragorn, Legolas and Gimli, were besieged in Helm's Deep or the Hornburg by the invaders, who tried unsuccessfully during the night of the 3rd to breach the defenses; although the gate of the Hornburg was broken no enemy was able to enter inside. At dawn on the 4th, the Riders of Rohan, with Théoden, Éomer and Aragorn at their head, sallied forth from the Hornburg, and the foot-soldiers in the Hornburg and Helm's Deep also attacked. The invaders were pushed back to the Deeping Coomb, where they were trapped between Théoden's army, Erkenbrand's army (and Gandalf), and the Huorns. The Dunlendings surrendered, while the Orcs passed into the Huorn-forest and were slain. (II 171-87; III 466)

**BATTLE OF THE PEAK** The final two-day battle between Gandalf and the Balrog, fought on the summit of Zirak-zigil on January 23-25, TA 3019. The battle ended with the casting-down and death of the Balrog and the passing of Gandalf. In the battle Durin's Tower and the Endless Stair were destroyed. (II 134-35)

**BATTLE OF THE PELENNOR FIELDS** The greatest battle of the WR and of the Third Age, fought on March 15, TA 3019 between the armies of Sauron, composed of 30,000 Haradrim and a great number of Easterlings, Variags and Orcs, led by Lord of the Nazgûl, and the forces of Minas Tirith, aided by 3000 to 4000 men from the southern fiefs, the forces of Osgiliath and Ithilien and 6000 Riders of Rohan. Before dawn the Lord of the Nazgûl broke the Great Gates of Minas Tirith (see: the Siege of Gondor), but was prevented from entering the city by the unexpected arrival of the Rohirrim, who, led by Théoden, vanquished a Haradrim army early in the morning. Then, however, the Lord of the Nazgûl scattered the Rohirrim and slew Théoden, but was in turn killed by Éowyn and Merry.

Éomer then led the Rohirrim in a furious attack against the Haradrim, but by mid-morning, despite aid from the cavalry of Gondor, led by Imrahil, the southward advance of the Rohirrim had been slowed, for the Oliphaunts of the Haradrim could not be conquered, and the enemy had many more troops than the Rohirrim. Meanwhile, Gothmog, the new enemy commander, had thrown his reserve forces into the battle, and the foot-soldiers of Gondor were being driven back to Minas Tirith. About noon the Rohirrim were surrounded about a mile north of the Harlond, but at this point Aragorn, with a great fleet from southern Gondor, where he had defeated the Corsairs, landed at the Harlond. Then the forces of Gondor swept the Pelennor Fields, and by sunset all the invaders had been killed or driven beyond the Rammas Echor. (III 137-52)

**BATTLE PIT** A sand-pit near Bywater where the Chief's Men slain in the Battle of Bywater were buried. (III 365)

**BATTLE PLAIN** Dagorlad (q. v.). (II 265)

**BATTLES OF THE FORDS OF ISEN** Two battles fought during the WR between the Riders of Rohan and Saruman's forces, composed of Dunlendings and Orcs. In the First Battle, fought February 25, TA 3019, Saruman's forces defeated an army led by Prince Théodred. Théodred was killed, but the enemy did not cross the Isen. In the Second Battle, fought on the following March 2, Erkenbrand was defeated by the invaders, who this time crossed the river. The casualties in the Second Battle, however, were lighter than originally thought, since the Rohirrim were scattered early in the battle, before they could be destroyed. (II 167-68, 199; III 437, 465, 466)

**BAY OF BEL, BAY OF BELFALAS** The great bay between Gondor and Umbar. (I 493; TB 8, 36)

**BEATER** Name given to Glamdring (q. v.) by the Orcs. (H 73)

**BEECHBONE** (d. TA 3019) Ent, burned to death in the Ent's attack on Isengard during the WR. (II 221)

**BELBA BOLGER** (TA 2856-2956) Hobbit of the Shire, eldest daughter of Mungo Baggins and wife of Rudigar Bolger. (III 474)

**BELECTHOR I** (S.: '---eagle'?) (d. TA 2655) Dúnadan, fifteenth Ruling Steward of Gondor (2628-55). (III 395)

**BELECTHOR II** (d. TA 2872) Dúnadan, twenty-first Ruling Steward of Gondor (2811-72). At his death the White Tree died and no sapling could be found to replace it. (III 395, 416)

**BELEG** (S.) (d. TA 1029) Dúnadan, second King of Arthedain (946-1029). (III 394)

**BELEGORN** (S.: '---tree') (d. TA 2204) Dúnadan, fourth Ruling Steward of Gondor (2148-2204). (III 395)

**BELEGOST** (S.: '---fortress') A Dwarvish city of the First Age, located in the Ered Luin. Belegost was ruined at the breaking of Thangorodrim, and many of its people went to Khazad-dûm at the beginning of the Second Age. (III 439)

**BELERIAND** (S.: '---land') In the First Age, the land west of the Ered Luin, where the Sindar and, later, the Exiles and the Edain, lived. At the end of the First Age, probably because of the breaking of Thangorodrim, most of Beleriand was broken and drowned, leaving only Lindon. Beleriand contained the Elven-realms of Doriath, Gondolin and Nargothrond, and perhaps also Morgoth's realm, Angband.

Called also the Land of the Elves in the West. (I 319; II 421; 422; III 438)

**BELFALAS** (S.: '---coast') Fair coastal area of Gondor, located between the Morthond and the Gilraen. Its main city was Dol Amroth.

Belfalas was the fief of the Princes of Dol Amroth. (I 16-17; III 14, 23)

**BELL GAMGEE** (TA 30th Cent.) Hobbit of the Shire, wife of Hamfast Gamgee. She bore him six children, including Samwise. Bell was born a Goodchild. (III 477)

**BELLADONNA BAGGINS** (TA 2852-2934) Hobbit of the Shire, ninth child of Gerontius Took. She married Bungo Baggins about 2880; Bilbo was their only child. (III 474, 475)

**BELMARIE** A country, in Bilbo's poem *Errantry*. The name is an imitation of Elvish, and Belmarie was probably fictitious. (TB 8, 25)

**BÉMA** Araw (q. v.). (III 431)

**BEORN** (fl. TA 30th Cent.) Man, chieftain of the Beornings, a berserker. Beorn violently hated Orcs and was in general distrustful of all strangers, but he was a good guy. After Gandalf overcame his initial suspicions in TA 2941, Beorn fed and protected Thorin and Company, and was later instrumental in winning the Battle of the Five Armies. In that battle he killed Bolg, the leader of the Orkish forces.

See: Beornings. (H 117; 118, 120-36, 274, 278)

**BEORNINGS** Men of the Vales of Anduin, living on both sides of the river near the Carrock. The Beornings were descended from the Edain or their close kin, and thus spoke a language related to Adûnaic and Rohirric. At the time of the WR the Beornings were not very friendly to any outsiders, but in return for tolls kept the High Pass and the Ford of Carrock safe for merchants; they greatly hated Orcs. After the WR the Beornings and the Woodmen were given the central portion of Eryn Lasgalen.

The only Beorning encountered in *LotR* is Beorn, who as a skin-changer was probably not representative of his people.

The Beornings were famed for their baking, especially of honey-cakes. They did not eat meat, and were very friendly with animals. They may originally have come from the Misty Mountains, whence they were driven by the Orcs. (I 301, 478; III 429, 468, 508)

**BEREGOND** (S.: '—stone'?) (d. TA 2811) Dúnadan, twentieth Ruling Steward of Gondor (2763-2811) and one of the greatest captains in the history of Gondor. (III 395, 416)

**BEREGOND** (fl. WR) Man of Gondor, perhaps a Dúnadan, soldier in the Third Company of the Citadel. During the Siege of Gondor, he left his post and killed men in the Hallows to prevent Denethor II from burning Faramir, to whom Beregond was devoted. After the WR, he was banished from Minas Tirith for this offense, but was made the first Captain of the Guard of Faramir. (III 36, 153-62, 195, 207, 305)

**BEREN** (tr. Ad.) (First Age) Adan of the First House of the Edain, hero and elf-friend. His father, Barahir, was slain by the forces of Morgoth, and Beren fled through the Mountains of Terror, where he slew a great spider, until he reached Doriath. There he met Lúthien, and together they performed many great deeds, including escaping from the dungeons of Sauron, recovering Barahir's ring and wresting a Silmaril from the Iron Crown of Morgoth. Some time in the course of these adventures Finrod gave his life to save Beren, and Beren lost a hand. Eventually, however, Beren was slain by the Wolf from Angband.

Beren and Lúthien had at least one child, Dior.

Called also Beren One-hand and Beren Húrin. (I 258-61; III 281, 388, 400, 453, 507; RHM III 406)

**BEREN** (d. TA 2763) Dúnadan, nineteenth Ruling Steward of Gondor (2743-63). During his reign, in 2757, Gondor was attacked by three great fleets from Umbar, and the attackers were repulsed with difficulty. Beren gave Isengard to

Saruman to dwell in, thinking that the wizard would protect
Rohan, which had been weakened by the Long Winter and
Wulf's invasion. (III 395, 415-16)

**BERGIL** (S.: '---star') (b. TA 3008 or 3009) Man of Gondor,
son of Beregond. He remained in Minas Tirith during the
Siege of Gondor. (III 47 ff.)

**BERILAC BRANDYBUCK** (b. TA 2980) Hobbit of the Shire, son
of Merimac Brandybuck and a guest at the Farewell Party.
(III 476)

**BERT** (d. TA 2941) A troll of the Trollshaws, one of the
three encountered by Thorin and Company and turned to
stone as a result of Gandalf's trick. (H 46-52)

**BERÚTHIEL** (S.: ? *bereth* 'queen' + *iel* 'female') Elven-
queen whose cats were proverbial for their ability to find
their way home. (I 405)

**BERYLLA BAGGINS** (f. TA 2800) Hobbit of the Shire, wife
of Balbo Baggins. She was born a Boffin. (III 474)

**BIFUR** (fl. TA 2941-3018) Dwarf, a member of Thorin and
Company. After 2941 he lived in Erebor. (I 302; III 450;
H 23, 26)

**BIG FOLK, BIG PEOPLE** Men (q. v.). (I 19, 112)

**BILBO BAGGINS** (TA 2890-    ) Hobbit of the Shire, adventurer, Elf-friend, Ring-bearer, author and scholar. Bilbo's
involvement in the affairs of Middle-earth began in 2941,
when Gandalf coerced him into being the burglar for Thorin
and Company. In the course of this adventure he went to
Rivendell and other far-away places, stole the One Ring and
played an important part in the death of Smaug and the success of the expedition. He returned home to Bag End with
his modest share of the dragon's hoard and the Ring, and
lived a comfortable life in the Shire for sixty years. In 2980,
on the death of Drogo and Primula Baggins, Bilbo adopted
their son Frodo and made him his heir. In 3001, Bilbo gave a
huge birthday party, the Farewell Feast, and then disappeared
leaving his goods, including the Ring, to Frodo. Bilbo then
went to Imladris and, except for a trip to Dale and Erebor in
3001 or 3002, stayed there for twenty years, writing poetry
and studying Elven-lore. In 3021 Bilbo went over Sea with
the Last Riding of the Keepers of the Rings.

Bilbo wrote the account of his expedition to Erebor with
Thorin and Company which appears in the Red Book of Westmarch and, edited by Professor Tolkien, forms *The Hobbit.*

He also wrote numerous poems, including *Errantry* and a long poem about Eärendil (I 308-11). Bilbo's chief scholarly contribution was his *Translations from the Elvish;* his primary interest was with the First Age.

Bilbo lived for most of his life in Bag End, Hobbiton. He was, unlike most hobbits, a bachelor. Bilbo was the longest-lived hobbit in history, being 131 years and 8 days old when he went over Sea; his longevity was partly due to the influence of the Ring, which otherwise affected him to a surprisingly small degree. Bilbo's Fallohide blood showed in his uncommon love of Elves and adventure and his skill with languages, but apart from this he was very much a normal hobbit.

Bilbo's sword was the famous Elven-knife Sting; he wore a mithril-coat given him by Thorin II. (I 31-32, 303-5; III 381-84, 387, 474, 475; H 9, 15-17, 277; TB 7, 8)

**BILBO GAMGEE** (b. FA 15) Hobbit of the Shire, tenth child of Samwise Gamgee. (III 477)

**BILL** (fl. WR) Pony, bought in Bree by Frodo in TA 3018 from Bill Ferny, after whom he was named. When bought, Bill was half-starved, but under the care of Sam Gamgee he became healthy and happy. Bill bore Frodo part of the way to Rivendell, and was later used by the Company of the Ring as a pack animal. He was set free outside the West-gate of Khazad-dûm, and eventually found his way back to Bree. There he was recovered after the WR by Sam, who dearly loved him. (I 242, 273, 366, 396, 402; III 338, 380)

**BILL BUTCHER** Hobbit of the Shire, the butcher of Michel Delving in the poem *Perry-the-Winkle.* Bill Butcher was perhaps a historical character, but his surname may be more of an epithet than a true family name. (TB 42)

**BILL FERNY** (fl. WR) Man of Bree, an agent of Saruman. After making trouble in Bree in TA 3019 he went to the Shire and was put in charge of the gate at the Brandywine Bridge. He was expelled from the Shire by Frodo on October 30, 3019.

Called the Chief's Big Man by the Hobbits at the Bridge. (I 224-25, 242, 244; III 335, 343)

**BINDBALE WOOD** Forest in the Northfarthing. (I 40)

**BINGO BAGGINS** (TA 2864-2960) Hobbit of the Shire, husband of Chica Grubb. Their son Falco was the first Chubb-Baggins. (III 474)

**BITER** Name given to Orcrist (q. v.) by the Orcs. (H 72)

**BLACK BREATH** Name given to the fell influence of the Nazgûl, which resulted in despair, unconsciousness and bad dreams, and after prolonged exposure in death. Athelas was an effective remedy.

Also called the Black Shadow, by the doctors of Minas Tirith; Black Breath was the name used by Aragorn. (I 235-36; III 171)

**BLACK CAPTAIN** The Lord of the Nazgûl (q.v.), as commander of the army that attacked Minas Tirith during the WR. (III 110)

**BLACK GATE** The Morannon (q. v.). (I 319)

**BLACK HAND** The hand of Sauron on which he wore the Ring, so called by Gollum. It was black because of Sauron's inability to assume a fair form after the destruction of his body in the wreck of Númenor, and in the Third Age had but four fingers, because Isildur had cut one off to get the Ring. Also used attributively for Sauron. (II 311, 315)

**BLACK LAND** Mordor (q. v.). (I 203)

**BLACK NÚMENOREANS** Those Númenoreans loyal to the King (and thus opposed to the Eldar and Valar) who had settled in Middle-earth, especially those of Umbar. In the course of the Second Age they were corrupted by Sauron and came to hate all good peoples, especially the Faithful; they loved power and domination. After the fall of Sauron in SA 3441, the Black Númenoreans mixed their blood with the Haradrim, but inherited undiminished their hatred for the Dúnedain of Gondor, the descendants of the Faithful. In the Third Age, operating from Umbar, they frequently attacked the coasts of Gondor, but their power was broken in 933 when King Eärnil I of Gondor took Umbar. They were permanently scattered when Hyarmendacil broke their siege of Umbar in 1050.

The Black Númenoreans were originally known as the King's Men. (III 202, 403)

**BLACK PIT** Khazad-dûm (q. v.). (I 370)

**BLACK PITS** Something somewhere in Mordor, where Sauron punished his errant servants. The Black Pits were perhaps the dungeons of the Barad-dûr. (III 222)

**BLACK RIDER** The Lord of the Nazgûl (q. v.), when riding a horse. (III 125)

**BLACK RIDERS** The Nazgûl (q.v.), when riding horses. (I 118)

**BLACKROOT** The Morthond (q. v.). (III 73)

**BLACKROOT VALE** The valley of the upper Morthond, in

southern Gondor. Erech was in the Blackroot Vale.
Also called Morthond Vale. (III 49, 73)

**BLACK SHADOW** The Lord of the Nazgûl, so called by the
Men of Gondor at the beginning of the WR when his presence
was felt during the attack on Osgiliath. Possibly this refers
to all the Nazgûl, or to the Black Breath. (I 322, 336)

**BLACK SHADOW** The Black Breath (q. v.), as called by the
doctors of Minas Tirith. (III 165-66)

**BLACK SPEECH** The language devised by Sauron in the Second Age for use by him and his servants. The Black Speech
died out at the end of the Second Age, but was re-introduced
by Sauron in the Third, when it was used in its pure form only
by him, the Nazgûl and other of his close servants, and the
Olog-hai. Orcs of Mordor spoke a debased form of the Black
Speech, and some of the words of their dialects, such as
*ghâsh,* meaning "fire," spread throughout all Orcdom.
    The Black Speech was probably based to some extent on
Quenya or Valinorean, and was perhaps an inversion of one
of these languages. It was a very harsh language. The only
example given of the pure Black Speech is the Ring-inscription; a number of the Orcs of Mordor have names in their
debased form of the Black Speech. (I 333-4; III 498, 511, 512)

**BLACK WINGS** The flying Nazgûl (q. v.). (II 321)

**BLACK YEARS** The Accursed Years (q. v.). (I 333-34)

**BLADORTHIN** (S.: '---grey') A king, probably an Elf, who
ordered spears from the Dwarves of Erebor but died before
they were delivered. He died sometime between TA 1999
and 2770. (H 220)

**BLANCO** (fl. TA 1601) A Fallohide Hobbit of Bree, who
with his brother Marcho settled the Shire in 1601. (I 23)

**BLESSED REALM** The Undying Lands (q. v.). (III 388; R 62)

**BLOOTING** The name used in Bree for the eleventh month
of the year.
    See: Blotmath, Shire Reckoning. (III 483)

**BLOTMATH** The eleventh month of the Shire Reckoning,
corresponding to our November. The name was pronounced
"Blodmath" or "Blommath" at the time of the WR.
    Called Blooting in Bree. (III 478, 483)

**BLUE MOUNTAINS** The Ered Luin (q. v.). (I 16, 72)

**BOAR OF EVERHOLT** (d. TA 2864) Famous boar of the
Firienwood, slain by King Folca of Rohan, who died of the

wounds given him by the boar. (III 435)

**BOB** (fl. WR) Man or Hobbit of Bree, one of the servants at the Prancing Pony. Bob seems to have been in charge of the stables. (I 210, 241-42; III 333)

**BOBO PROUDFOOT** (fl. TA 2900) Hobbit of the Shire, husband of Linda Baggins and father of Odo Proudfoot. (III 474)

**BOFFIN** A Hobbit family, with members living all over the Shire at the time of the WR. The Boffins, judging by their many marriages with the Tooks and Bagginses, were probably an upper-class and well-to-do family. Since there is no record of any Boffin-Brandybuck marriage, there may have been few Boffins living in the eastern part of the Shire.

Boffin is an Anglicization of the genuine Hobbit surname Bophîn, of unknown meaning and forgotten origin. (I 30; III 474, 475, 516)

**BOFUR** (fl. TA 2941-3018) Dwarf, a member of Thorin and Company. Although descended from Dwarves of Khazad-dûm, he was not of Durin's line.

After 2941, Bofur lived in Erebor. (I 302; III 450; H 23, 26, 208)

**BOLG** (d. TA 2941) Large Orc of the Misty Mountains, perhaps an uruk, the son of Azog. Bolg led the Orcs and Wargs at the Battle of the Five Armies, in which he was slain by Beorn.

He was known as Bolg of the North. (III 448; H 265, 274)

**BOLGER** An old and aristocratic family of Hobbits of Fallohide origin living in the Shire. The Bolgers frequently gave high-sounding names to their children. (I 52; III 474, 475, 476, 516)

*BOMBADIL GOES BOATING* A Buckland poem about Tom Bombadil, probably written after the WR. (TB 8-9, 17-23)

**BOMBADIL, TOM** See: Tom Bombadil.

**BOMBUR** (fl. TA 2941-3018) Dwarf, a member of Thorin and Company. Bombur was descended from Dwarves of Khazaddûm, though he was not of Durin's line. After 2941 he lived in Erebor.

Always fat, in later life Bombur was so heavy that he could not move by himself, and it required six dwarves to lift him. (I 302; III 450; H 23, 26, 144-50, 208)

**BONFIRE GLADE** Glade in the Old Forest where the Hobbits of Buckland sometime before the WR burnt many trees during the attack of the Forest on Buckland. No trees grew there afterward, but there was a profusion of grass, weeds, nettles and other similar plants. (I 157, 158-59)

**BOOK OF MAZARBUL** (Kh.: 'records') The chronicle kept by Balin's expedition to Khazad-dûm from TA 2989 to 2994. The Book was found in the Chamber of Mazarbul by the Fellowship of the Ring; Gimli took it and may well have preserved it throughout the WR. (I 417-19)

**BOOK OF THE KINGS** One of the chronicles of Gondor that has survived to the present day, and has been used by Professor Tolkien in writing *LotR*. (HM I, 7)

**BOOKS OF LORE** Compendia of Elvish wisdom, in Rivendell. Extracts of these Books of Lore were translated by Bilbo Baggins toward the end of the Third Age and, supplemented by oral sources, formed his *Translations from the Elvish*. (III 380)

**BOPHÎN** (gen. Hobb.) See: Boffin. (III 516)

**BORGIL** (S.: '---star') Betelgeuse, as called by the Elves. (I 120, 159)

**BORIN** (TA 2450-2711) Dwarf of Durin's line, second son of Náin II. Borin lived in the Grey Mountains until 2590, when he went to Erebor with Thrór. (III 440, 450)

**BOROMIR** (S. *boro* + Q. *mir* 'jewel') (d. TA 2489) Dúnadan, eleventh Ruling Steward of Gondor (2477-89). In 2745, Boromir defeated the uruks and drove them out of Ithilien, but received a Morgul-wound which shortened his life.

Boromir was one of the greatest Captains of Gondor, noble and strong of body and will. (III 395, 414-15, 507)

**BOROMIR** (TA 2978-3019) Dúnadan of Gondor, eldest son of Denethor II, named after the preceding. After leading the defense of Osgiliath against Sauron's armies in June, 3018, Boromir went to Imladris to find the answer to a dream he and his brother had had. Arriving there after a long and arduous journey, he took part in the Council of Elrond and became one of the Companions of the Ring. On Amon Hen, the spell of the Ring, which had tempted him at least since Lórien, proved too great for him and he tried to kill Frodo. He immediately repented, but his madness drove Frodo to decide to carry on the Quest alone. This was a good thing, since later that day Amon Hen was raided by Orcs. Boromir died defending Merry and Pippin. Aragorn, Legolas and Gimli gave him a proper funeral and set his body afloat down Anduin.

Although a strong and handsome man and one of the greatest captains of Gondor, Boromir cared little for anything save arms and battle, and was overly proud. As Denethor's heir, he bore those titles and positions usually possessed by the heir of the Steward. (I 315, 321-23, 365, 484, 514-17; II 17-18, 22-24, 337; III 414, 419)

**BOUNDERS**  The Shire border-guard, a branch of the Watch. The Bounders turned back undesirable persons and animals at the borders of the Shire. Their number varied as the need for them changed. (I 31, 73-74)

**BOWMAN COTTON**  (b. TA 2986)  Hobbit of the Shire, fourth child and third son of Tolman Cotton.
    Bowman was usually called Nick. (III 354, 477)

**BRACEGIRDLE**  A family of Hobbits of the Shire, probably well-to-do. At least some of the Bracegirdles lived in Hard-bottle. (I 52; III 372, 474, 476)

**BRALDAGAMBA**  (gen. Hobb.: 'ale-buck')  See: Brandybuck. (III 520)

**BRALDA-HÎM**  (gen. Hobb.: 'heady-ale')  See: Baranduin. (III 520)

**BRAND**  (d. TA 3019)  Man, third King of Dale (3007-3019), a strong ruler. Brand was slain in the Battle of Dale. (I 301; III 463, 468)

**BRANDAGAMBA**  (gen. Hobb.: 'borderland-buck')  See: Brandy-buck. (III 520)

**BRANDA-NÎN**  (gen. Hobb.: 'border-water')  The Baranduin (q. v.). (III 520)

**BRANDYBUCK**  One of the most important Hobbit families of the Shire, containing a strong Fallohide strain. The family traced its descent from Gorhendad Oldbuck, who about TA 2340 moved to Buckland from the Marish and changed the family name to Brandybuck. Ever after, the head of the family was the Master of Buckland, and, with his relatives, lived in Brandy Hall.
    The actual name of the family was Brandagamba, which meant "march-buck" in Hobbitish. Braldagamba, meaning "ale-buck," was not used, but Professor Tolkien has trans-lated the name of the family as *Brandybuck* in order to pre-serve the original similarity between the name of the family and the name of the river, the Brandywine. (I 27; III 476, 516, 520)

**BRANDY HALL**  The chief dwelling of the Brandybucks, a large smial beneath Buck Hill in Buckland. The excavation of Brandy Hall was begun by Gorhendad Oldbuck about TA 2340. (I 40, 45; III 476)

**BRANDYWINE** The Baranduin (q. v.). (I 24)

**BRANDYWINE BRIDGE** The most common name for the Bridge of Stonebows (q. v.) at the time of the WR. (III 341)

**BREE** Town of Men and Hobbits, the principal settlement of the Bree-land. Bree was founded in the Second Age, sometime before the foundation of Arnor in 3320, but its Hobbits did not settle there until about TA 1300. In the days of the glory of Arnor Bree was an important town, since it was situated at the crossing of the Great East Road by the North Road, but by the time of the WR it had dwindled in importance considerably. However, the Prancing Pony, Bree's ancient and famous inn, was still an important source of news. In the Fourth Age Bree doubtless flourished once more.

Bree was built against Bree Hill. The side not facing the Hill was surrounded by a hedge and a dike. There were two gates in this wall for the entrance and exit of the Great East Road. At the time of the WR Bree contained about a hundred stone houses in which Men lived, and a smaller number of Hobbit dwellings. (I 23, 29, 205-7; III 457, 462, 483, 509)

**BREE HILL** The big hill in the Bree-land, north of Bree. Also spelled Bree-hill. (I 205, 206; III 332)

**BREE-LAND** The wooded area at the intersection of the Great East and North Roads, inhabited by Men and Hobbits. The Bree-land contained four villages, Bree, Archet, Staddle and Combe, and a number of scattered dwellings.

The Bree-land was founded in the Second Age by Men from Dunland, and somehow managed to survive through all the wars of Middle-earth. The Bree-land was part of Arnor and later Arthedain; after the fall of the North-kingdom it was protected by the Rangers of the North. Its economy dwindled when the North-kingdom failed and trade declined, but the Bree-land doubtless revived in the Fourth Age. In any case, its farms provided for a comfortable existence for all its inhabitants. (I 205)

**BREE RECKONING** The calendar system of Bree, similar to the Shire Reckoning (q.v.) except that the first, fourth, sixth, seventh and ninth through twelfth months were called Frery, Chithing, Lithe, Mede, Harvestmath, Wintring, Blooting and Yulemath. Also, the Lithes were called the Summerdays. The year 1 of the Bree-reckoning corresponded to TA 1300, the year of the settlement in Bree of Hobbits. (III 482, 483)

**BREGALAD** (S.: 'swift-tree') (fl. WR) Ent of Fangorn Forest, physically resembling and caring for rowan trees. Bregalad

hosted Merry and Pippin during the Entmoot of TA 3019 because, as a result of Saruman's slaughter of his rowan trees, he had already made up his mind about what course of action should be taken. In general, he thought and acted much more quickly than most Ents, which is how he got his name.
Called in Westron Quickbeam. (II 109-11)

**BREGO** (TA 2512-70) Man, second King of Rohan (2545-70). He drove the last remnants of the Orcs and Balchoth out of the Wold, and built the hall of Meduseld. Brego died of grief over the loss of his son Baldor. (III 84, 85, 434)

**BREREDON** Village in Buckland, near Haysend. (TB 9)

**BRIDGEFIELDS** Area in the Eastfarthing near the Bridge of Stonebows. (I 40)

**BRIDGE INN** Inn in the Shire, located on the Great East Road near the west end of the Brandywine Bridge. (III 344)

**BRIDGE OF MITHEITHEL** Three-arched stone bridge crossing the Mitheithel, on the Great East Road.
The Bridge was called the Last Bridge because it was the easternmost bridge on the Road. (I 269; III 464)

**BRIDGE OF STONEBOWS** Bridge across Baranduin, on the Great East Road, built by Arnor.
Also called the Great Bridge and the Brandywine Bridge; the latter was the most common name, at least among hobbits, at the time of the WR. (I 23; III 341, 402)

**BROCKENBORINGS** Village in the Eastfarthing near the hills of Scary. During the WR Fredegar Bolger made Brockenborings the headquarters for his band of rebels.
Also called the Brockenbores. (I 40; III 372)

**BROCKHOUSE** Surname used by Hobbits in Bree and the Shire. (I 52, 212)

**BROWN** A family of working-class Hobbits of the Shire. (III 477)

**BROWN LANDS** Area between Mirkwood and the Emyn Muil, desolate and treeless. Of old the Entwives made their gardens here, but they were driven away and the land ruined during the war between Sauron and the Last Alliance at the end of the Second Age.
Also called the Noman-lands. (I 17, 492; II 100)

**BROWNLOCK** A family of Hobbits of the Shire, perhaps rather well-to-do. (III 474)

**BRUINEN** (S.: 'loud-water') River in Eriador, which joined the Mitheithel at Tharbad to form the Gwathlo. The Bruinen was crossed by the Great East Road at the Ford of Bruinen. The river was under the control of Elrond, who could cause it to flood whenever an enemy tried to cross it.

Also called the River of Rivendell and, in Westron, Loudwater. (I 268-69, 283-86)

BRYTTA (TA 2752-2842) Man, eleventh King of Rohan (2798-2842). During his reign Rohan was troubled by Orcs driven from the Misty Mountains by the War of the Dwarves and Orcs.

Brytta was called Léofa (tr. Roh.: 'beloved') by his people because of his generosity. (III 435)

BUCCA OF THE MARISH (fl. TA 1979) Hobbit, first Thain of the Shire (1979-?). Bucca was probably the founder of the Oldbuck family. (III 458)

BUCK HILL Hill near Bucklebury in which was delved Brandy Hall. (I 143)

BUCKLAND Area of the Shire, located between Baranduin and the Old Forest, the folkland of the Brandybucks. Buckland was settled by Gorhendad Oldbuck in TA 2340. It was originally outside the Shire, but was officially added to it by the gift of King Elessar in FA 42, and was then known as the East March.

Buckland was ruled by the Master of Buckland, although the rule was of course largely nominal.

Also called "the Buckland." (I 30, 141-42; III 459; TB 8-9)

BUCKLAND GATE Gate in the High Hay, the entrance to Buckland from the Great East Road. (III 341, 342)

BUCKLEBURY Chief village of Buckland, in central Buckland about a mile east of the Brandywine. (I 101, 142)

BUCKLEBURY FERRY Ferry across the Brandywine between Bucklebury and the Marish. The Ferry was self-operated, and the boat was kept on the east side of the river. (I 40, 138, 141, 142)

BUDGE FORD Ford across the Water north of Whitfurrows in the Eastfarthing. (I 40)

BUDGEFORD Village or town in Bridgefields, the Eastfarthing. (I 153)

BULLROARER Bandobras Took (q. v.). (H 30)

BUMPKIN (fl. WR) One of the ponies provided by Merry for Frodo's journey from Buckland to Rivendell in TA 3018. Bumpkin was driven off in Bree, but was later recovered; he spent the rest of his life working for Barliman Butterbur.

Bumpkin was named by Tom Bombadil. (I 198, 199, 242)

**BUNCE**   A Hobbit family, living in the Shire. At least some
Bunces seem to have lived in Michel Delving.

Mrs. Bunce, a character in Sam Gamgee's poem *Perry-the-
Winkle,* may have been a historical personage. (III 474; TB
41-42)

**BUNDUSHATHÛR**   (Kh.: 'cloudyhead'?)   One of the three
Mountains of Moria.

Called in Westron Cloudyhead, and by Elves Fanuidhol the
Grey. Called Shathûr for short by the Dwarves. (I 370)

**BUNGO BAGGINS**  (TA 2846-2926) Hobbit of the Shire, father
of Bilbo. Bungo married Belladonna Took about 2880, and
built Bag End to be the family residence. (III 474; H 16-17)

**BURROWS**   Hobbit family of the Shire, perhaps well-to-do.
Spelled "Burrowes" on H 284. (I 52; III 474; H 284)

**BUTCHER**   See: Bill Butcher. (TB 42)

**BUTTERBUR**   A family of Men of Bree, owners of the Prancing
Pony. (I 29)

**BYWATER**   Village in the Westfarthing, located on the Great
East Road about three miles west of the Three Farthing
Stone. In TA 3019 the Battle of Bywater was fought here.
The chief inn of Bywater was the Green Dragon.

See: Pool Side, Pool of Bywater. (I 40, 48, 72; III 349 ff.)

**BYWATER POOL**   The Pool of Bywater (q. v.). (I 40)

**BYWATER ROAD**   Road leading from the Great East Road
through Bywater and then northwest along the Water for about
thirty miles. (I 40; III 364, 366)

# C

**CAIR ANDROS** (S.: 'ship long-foam') Island in Anduin about fifty miles north of Minas Tirith. Cair Andros was fortified by Gondor about TA 2900 to protect Anórien from attack from the east; the island was captured by an army from the Morannon during the WR, but was soon freed.

Cair Andros was shaped like a ship, and had a high prow facing upstream against which Anduin broke with much foam. (III 103, 199, 416, 466)

**CALACIRIAN** (Q.: 'region of Calacirya') That part of Eldamar near and in the entrance to the Calacirya. Here the light from the Two Trees before their poisoning was strongest and the land the most beautiful.

The full form of the name was Calaciriande, with the spelling anglicized from *kalakiryande*. (I 310; R 62)

**CALACIRYA** (Q.: 'light-cleft') The great ravine in the Pelóri, through which the light of the Two Trees flowed eastward into Eldamar, before their poisoning. The Calacirya was the main, and perhaps the only, pass through the Pelóri. (I 489; R 62)

**CALEMBEL** (S.) Town in Lamedon, Gondor, near the Ciril. (III 15, 75)

**CALENARDHON** (S.) Area of Gondor between the Anduin and Isen, possibly extending west of the Isen. Largely depopulated by the Great Plague of TA 1636, Calenardhon was overrun by the Balchoth in 2510, and its remaining inhabitants slain or driven away. In that year, Calenardhon was given to the Éothéod by Steward Cirion in return for their services in the Battle of the Field of Celebrant.

For the history of Calenardhon after 2510, see: Rohan. (III 406, 415, 430, 459)

**CALENDAR OF IMLADRIS** A perhaps-typical calendar system of the Elves in Middle-earth, used by the Elves of Rivendell. The yén was divided into 144 loa of six seasons and various extra days. The loa began with yestarë, the first day, which was approximately equivalent to March 29 in the Gregorian calendar. The first three seasons were tuilë, lairë and yávië, which contained 54, 72 and 54 days respectively. Then followed three enderi, and then the seasons of quellë (or lasse-lanta), hrívë and coirë, which also contained 54, 72 and 54 days respectively. The loa closed with mettarë, the last day.

Every twelfth loa, except the last of every third yén, the enderi were doubled to correct the inaccuracies of this system.

The Calendar of Imladris also contained an astronomical year, the coranar, and a six-day ritual week, the enquië (qq.v.). Also called the Reckoning of Rivendell. (I 480, 486)

**CALENHAD** (S.)   The sixth of the northern beacon-tower hills of Gondor. (III 20)

**CALIMEHTAR** (Q.: ? 'light---')  (fl. TA 14th Cent.)   Dúnadan of Gondor, younger brother of Rómendacil II and grandfather of Castamir. (III 406)

**CALIMEHTAR** (d. TA 1936)  Dúnadan, thirtieth King of Gondor (1856-1936). In 1899, Calimehtar won a great victory over the Wainriders, who were weakened by a rebellion among their slaves in Rhovanion. (III 395, 409)

**CALIMMACIL** (Q.) (fl. TA 19th-20th Cent.)   Dúnadan of the royal house of Gondor, nephew of King Narmacil II and grandfather of Eärnil II. (III 410)

**CALMA** (Q.: 'lamp')   Name for the tengwa $\mathcal{C}$ (number 3). (III 498, 500).

**CALMACIL, TAR-**   (Q.: 'lamp-bright spark')  (d. SA 2899) Dúnadan, eighteenth King of Númenor (?-2899). (III 390)

**CALMACIL** (d. TA 1304)  Dúnadan, eighteenth King of Gondor (1294-1304). During his reign Gondor was governed by his son, Minalcar. (III 395, 404)

**CALMATÉMA** (Q.: 'calma-series')   Name given to the velar stops and spirants *(k, g, kh, gh)* by Elvish grammarians. The calmatéma was usually represented by téma III or IV of the Tengwar. The values for the fifth and sixth grades of the calmatéma were optional, but were usually velars. (III 496-7, 500)

**CAMELLIA BAGGINS** (fl. TA 2900)  Hobbit of the Shire. She was born a Sackville, but married Longo Baggins. She bore him one son, Otho Sackville-Baggins. (III 474)

**CAPE OF FOROCHEL**   Cape in Forochel coming down from the north and partially enclosing the Bay of Forochel.

Part of the Cape is visible on the HM maps. (III 399)

**CAPTAIN OF DESPAIR**  The Lord of the Nazgûl (q.v.). (III 112)

**CAPTAIN OF SHIPS**   The title of the head of the fleets of Gondor. (III 406)

**CAPTAIN OF THE HAVEN**  Title of the ruler or of some high person of Umbar, in TA 2980. (III 417)

**CAPTAIN OF THE HOSTS**  Chief military leader of the armies of Gondor. (III 403)

**CAPTAIN OF THE SOUTHERN ARMY**  Title of the head of the Southern Army of Gondor. The only Captain named in *LotR* is Eärnil, who held the post prior to his election to the throne in TA 1945. (III 409)

**CAPTAIN OF THE WHITE TOWER**  Title of the head of the Guards of the Citadel, a position traditionally held in the time of the Ruling Stewards by the heir of the Steward, and probably in the time of the Kings by the heir to the throne. (III 419)

**CAPTAINS OF THE WEST**  The leaders of the Army of the West. The Captains were King Éomer of Rohan, Aragorn, Prince Imrahil of Dol Amroth, Gandalf and perhaps Elladan and Elrohir. Aragorn was the chief Captain.

The Captains were also called the Lords of the West, although this term may have referred only to Aragorn, Éomer and Imrahil. (III 193, 198ff.)

**CARACH ANGREN**  Isenmouthe (q. v.). (III 241)

**CARADHRAS**  (S.: 'red-horn')  Elvish name for Barazinbar (q. v.). (I 370; III 487)

**CARAS GALADON**  (S.: 'city of the trees')  Chief city of Lórien, site of the court of Celeborn and Galadriel. Caras Galadon consisted of many large telain in a walled grove of very large mellyrn. The city was deserted with the passing of Galadriel and the removal of Celeborn to East Lórien, at the end of the Third Age.

The name of the city was probably of Silvan origin, adopted to Sindarin. Called in Westron the City of the Trees. (I 455-56, 457-80; III 468, 506)

**CARC**  (fl. TA 2770)  Raven of Erebor, friendly with the Dwarves of the Mountain. (H 244)

**CARCHOST**  (S.: 'red-tooth')  One of the Towers of the Teeth (q. v.). (III 215)

**CARDOLAN**  (S.: 'red-hill-land'?)  Kingdom, one of the divisions of Arnor, founded in TA 861. Cardolan included all the land between the Baranduin, the Great East Road and the Gwathlo-Mitheithel. The Dúnedain of Cardolan defended their land against Angmar until 1409, when the country was overrun and the surviving Dúnedain were forced to take refuge in the Old Forest or the Barrow-downs. In this war the last prince of Cardolan was killed, but when Angmar was for a time defeated by the Elves the people of Cardolan returned to their homes. In 1636, the Great Plague killed the last of the Dúnedain of Cardolan, and large portions of the country, especially Minhiriath in the south, were depopulated. After this time Cardolan does not seem to have existed as a nation, although there were doubtless still scattered settlements there at the time of the WR. (III 396, 397, 398)

CARL  (b. TA 2863)  Working-class Hobbit of the Shire, the second son of Cottar. (III 477)

CARL COTTON  (b. TA 2989)  Hobbit of the Shire, youngest son of Tolman Cotton. He was usually called Nibs. (III 354, 477)

CARN DÛM  (S.)  Fortress and chief city of Angmar, located at the northern end of the Misty Mountains. (I 198, 201; III 412)

CARNEN  (S.: 'red-water')  River flowing from its source in the Iron Hills into the River Running. The Carnen was about 250 miles long. The name of the river formed by the confluence of the Carnen and the River Running is not given. Called in Westron the Redwater. (III 440)

CARNIMÍRIË  (Q.: 'red-jewel')  Rowan tree of Fangorn Forest, cut down by Orcs of Isengard near the end of the Third Age. (II 110)

CARROCK   A great rock in the Anduin about thirty miles north of the Old Ford. Beorn carved steps and a high seat in the Carrock, and often came there. (H 116-7)

CASTAMIR  (Q.: '--jewel') (d. TA 1447)  Dúnadan, twenty-second King of Gondor (1437-47). The grandson of a younger brother of Rómendacil II, at the time of the Kin-strife he was Captain of Ships. He aided in the overthrow of King Eldacar and, as the most popular of the rebels (he commanded the loyalty of the entire fleet and of the peoples of the coasts), he was made King. However, Castamir proved to be a cruel and arrogant ruler. He put Eldacar's captured son Ornendil to death, and lavished all his affection on the fleet, ignoring the land and the army. In the tenth year of his reign, therefore, when Eldacar returned, the people of inland Gondor rebelled against Castamir. He attempted to flee, but was defeated and slain by Eldacar in the Battle of the Crossings of Erui.

He was known as Castamir the Usurper. (III 395, 406)

*CAT*  A traditional Shire-poem, reworked by Sam Gamgee. (TB 7, 51)

**CATBARION**  An error for Oatbarton (q. v.). (I 40)

**CAUSEWAY**  Road in the Shire, going through Stock and Rushy. (I 138-39; TB 9, 20)

**CAUSEWAY**  Walled road in Gondor, leading from Osgiliath to Minas Tirith. (III 23, 97)

**CAUSEWAY FORTS**  Fortifications in the Rammas Echor guarding the Causeway at the time of the WR. The Causeway Forts were guarded by Faramir against the army of the Lord of the Nazgûl during the WR, but were easily captured.
   Also called the Guard-towers. (III 23, 97, 110, 467)

**CAVERNS OF HELM'S DEEP**  The Aglarond (q.v.). (II 193-95)

**CELANDINE BRANDYBUCK**  (b. TA 2994)  Hobbit of the Shire, youngest child and only daughter of Seredic Brandybuck. She was a guest at the Farewell Party. (III 476)

**CELDUIN**  (S.: 'running-river')  The River Running (q. v.). (III 405)

**CELEBDIL**  (S.: 'silvertine')  Elvish name for Zirak-zigil (q. v.). Also Celebdil the White. (I 370)

**CELEBORN**  (S.: 'silver-tree') (First Age- )  Sindarin lord, kinsman of Thingol and husband of Galadriel. After somehow surviving the wars against Morgoth, Celeborn dwelt in Lindon for a while at the beginning of the Second Age. After that, he and Galadriel went to Eregion, and later settled in Lórien, where Celeborn was for long Lord of the Galadrim. During the WR Celeborn led the army of Lórien that took Dol Guldur. In the Fourth Age, he was for a while King of East Lórien, but without Galadriel he grew weary of Middle-earth and went to Rivendell. Sometime after that he went over Sea.
   Although Celeborn was an Elven-lord of great fame and was called Celeborn the Wise, in *LotR* he does not seem especially bright. (I 39, 459-62; III 452, 468; R 60)

**CELEBRANT**  (S.: 'silver---')  Fair river flowing from springs in Nanduhirion through Lórien and into Anduin. Its tributaries included Nimrodel and other mountain streams.
   Also called Silverlode in Westron and Kibil-nâla in Khuzdul. (I 370, 434 ff., 449)

**CELEBRIAN**  (S.: 'silver---') (First Age- )  Eldarin lady, daughter and seemingly only child of Celeborn and Galadriel. In TA 100 she wed Elrond; she bore him three children,

Elladan, Elrohir and Arwen. In 2509, while travelling from Imladris to Lórien, her party was ambushed by Orcs in the Misty Mountains. She was soon rescued by her sons, but received a poisoned wound which caused her to go over Sea the next year. (I 300, 486; III 401, 456, 459)

**CELEBRIMBOR** (S.: 'silver-people---') (d. SA 1697) Noldorin Elf of the House of Fëanor, lord of Eregion. A great craftsman, he was one of the makers of the Great Rings, and the sole forger of the Three Rings. Celebrimbor perceived Sauron's treachery in the making of the Rings, and hid the Three Rings and prepared for war. He was slain when Eregion was overrun during the War of the Elves and Sauron. (I 318, 332, 398; III 453-54)

**CELEBRINDOR** (S.: 'silver---') (d. TA 1272) Dúnadan, fifth King of Arthedain (1191-1272). (III 394)

**CELEPHARN** (S.: 'silver---') (d. TA 1191) Dúnadan, fourth King of Arthedain (1110-91). (III 394)

**CELOS** (S.: 'silver-snow') River in southern Gondor, flowing from its sources in the Ered Nimrais into the Sirith. The Celos was about 60 miles long.
Also spelled Kelos. (III 14, 185)

**CEMENDUR** (Q.) (d. TA 238) Dúnadan, fourth King of Gondor (158-238). (III 394)

**CEORL** (fl. WR) Man, a Rider of Rohan. He fought under Erkenbrand in the Second Battle of the Fords of Isen. (II 167-68)

**CERIN AMROTH** (S.) Hill in Lothlórien where Amroth had his house. By the time of the WR, the house was no longer there, and the hill was covered with grass, elanor and niphredil. Aragorn and Arwen plighted their troth on Cerin Amroth, and here Arwen came to die. (I 454; III 425, 428)

**CERMIË** (Q.) Seventh month of the Kings' and Stewards' Reckonings and the fourth of the New Reckoning, corresponding roughly to our July.
The Sindarin form of the name, used only by the Dúnedain, was Cerveth. (III 483)

**CERTAR** (Q.: 'runes') The Cirth (q. v.). (III 493)

**CERTHAS DAERON** (S.: 'rune-rows of Daeron') The original form of the cirth (q. v.), although I do not know why it was named after Daeron. (III 500)

**CERVETH** (S.) Cermië (q. v.). (III 483)

**CHAMBER OF MAZARBUL** (Kh.: 'records') The Chamber of Records of Khazad-dûm, the center of Balin's Dwarf-colony. Balin's throne and tomb were here, and here the last members of his colony were slain. During the Quest the Fellowship of the Ring recovered the records of the Dwarf-colony, but were attacked by Orcs. They retreated through the east door of the Chamber, but when Gandalf attempted to guard the door against the Balrog it and the roof of the Chamber collapsed.

The Chamber was on the Seventh Level, and was the Twenty-first Hall of the North-end. (I 415-25)

**CHAMBERS OF FIRE** The Sammath Naur (q. v.). (III 269)

**CHETWOOD** The forest of the Bree-land. (I 23, 205, 245-46)

**CHICA BAGGINS** (fl. TA 2900) Hobbit of the Shire, wife of Bingo Baggins and mother of Falco Chubb-Baggins. She was born a Chubb. (III 474)

**CHIEF, THE** Name by which Lotho Sackville-Baggins was known during his control of the Shire, short for Chief Shirriff. (III 343, 360)

**CHIEF'S MEN** Those Men who during the WR served Lotho Sackville-Baggins and, when he came to the Shire, Saruman. They were offensive, coarse, ugly and greedy.

The Chief's Men seem to have been a motly assortment of ruffians, at least some of whom were agents of Saruman's before the WR. They tended to be squint-eyed, sallow-faced and otherwise esthetically displeasing; they may have been selected from among the more mannish of Saruman's Orcs. (See: Half-orcs)

Also called Sharkey's Men. (III 347-73 passim.)

**CHIEFTAINS OF THE DÚNEDAIN OF THE NORTH** The rulers of the Dúnedain of the North after the fall of Arthedain, the heirs of Arvedui, last king of Arthedain. The line of the Chieftains never failed, and most of them lived out their full lifespan despite the fact that they were almost continually involved in the struggle to protect Eriador from Orcs and other evil creatures. In addition, the waning of the lifespan of the Chieftains was slower than that of the Dúnedain of Gondor. The sixteenth and last Chieftain was Aragorn II, who became King of the Reunited Kingdom after the WR.

The Chieftains were raised in Imladris, and the heirlooms of their house, the Line of Isildur, were also kept there. (III 394, 400-02)

**CHITHING** Name given Astron (q. v.) in Bree. (III 483)

**CHUBB** A family of Hobbits of the Shire, probably rather well-to-do. (I 52; III 474, 475)

**CHUBB-BAGGINS** A family of Hobbits in the Shire, tracing its descent from Falco, the son of Bingo Baggins and Chica Chubb. (III 474)

**CÍRDAN** (S.: 'ship-wright') (b. First Age) Elda, master of the Grey Havens and builder of the ships that sailed over Sea from that harbor. Círdan had great wisdom and was one of the greatest of the Eldar of Middle-earth in the Second and Third Ages. He was given Narya, one of the Three Rings, by Celebrimbor at its making, but gave it to Gandalf when the latter came to Middle-earth about TA 1050. Círdan fought against Sauron with the army of the Last Alliance, and in the Third Age frequently aided the Dúnedain of the North. After the passing of Gil-galad at the end of the Second Age, Círdan seems to have been the highest Elf of Lindon, and may have ruled that land as well as the Grey Havens. It is said that Círdan remained in Middle-earth until the sailing of the last white ship sometime in the Fourth Age. (I 315, 320; III 383-84, 396, 397, 411, 456)

**CIRIL** (S.) River in Lamedon, Gondor, flowing into the Ringló. Also spelled *Kiril.* (III 14, 75, 184)

**CIRION** (S.: 'ship---') (d. TA 2567) Dúnadan, twelfth Ruling Steward of Gondor (2849-2567). During his reign Gondor was greatly troubled by its enemies, chiefly the Corsairs of Umbar and the Balchoth, and although Cirion was an able ruler, Gondor did not have the strength to repel its foes. However, with the unexpected aid of the Rohirrim, Cirion won the Battle of the Field of Celebrant in 2510, which effectively ended the Balchoth threat. Cirion then granted Calenardhon to the Rohirrim in return for the Oath of Eorl. This alliance greatly aided both kingdoms, and without it Gondor probably would have been overwhelmed in the WR, or even earlier. (III 395, 415)

**CIRITH GORGOR** (S.: 'pass haunted') Great pass into Mordor at the meeting of the Ered Lithui and the Ephel Dúath. The great gate of the Morannon was built across the pass, which connected Dagorlad and Udûn. Cirith Gorgor was further guarded by the Towers of the Teeth. Called in Westron the Haunted Pass. (II 308; III 258)

**CIRITH UNGOL** (S.: 'pass of the spider') Pass over the

Ephel Dúath just north of Minas Morgul, guarded by the Tower of Cirith Ungol. This pass was used in TA 2000 by the Nazgûl when they issued forth from Mordor to besiege Minas Ithil, and also by Frodo during the Quest to get into Mordor. Although well-guarded, it was an easier route to travel undetected than was the main pass behind Minas Ithil.

Cirith Ungol was actually only the road and cleft east of Shelob's Lair, but in common usage referred to the entire path from Imlad Morgul to the Morgai.

Also spelled *Kirith Ungol*. *The Pass of Cirith Ungol* was a bi-lingual redundancy in common usage. (II 380-81, 382, 403 ff.; III 15, 212 ff.)

**CIRTH** (S.: 'runes') Alphabet devised by the Sindar in Beleriand for inscriptions, and later adapted in modes of varying elegance by the Noldor of Eregion and various groups of Men, Dwarves and Orcs. The cirth originally represented only the sounds of Sindarin (see: Certhas Daeron), but the Angerthas Daeron (q.v.) represented a Quenya adaptation and the Angerthas Moria (q.v.) a Dwarvish mode. The original system, although based on the Tengwar, was unsystematic, as were all of its descendents except the Angerthas Daeron.

Called in Quenya certar and in Westron runes. (III 493, 495, 500-04)

**CIRYAHER** (Q.: 'ship-lord') See: Hyarmendacil I. (III 395)

**CIRYANDIL** (Q.: 'ship-lover') (d. TA 1015) Dúnadan, fourteenth King of Gondor (936-1015) and the third Ship-king. Ciryandil continued his father's policy of building ships, but was killed in Haradwaith while fighting the Haradrim. (III 395, 403)

**CIRYATAN, TAR-** (Q.: 'ship-Adan') (d. SA 2251) Dúnadan, twelfth King of Númenor. During his reign the colonization, subjection and taxation of the coasts of Middle-earth by the Númenoreans began. (III 390)

**CITADEL** The seventh level of Minas Tirith, containing the Place of the Fountain and the White Tower. (III 25, 26 ff.)

**CITADEL OF THE STARS** Osgiliath (q.v.). (I 321)

**CITY, THE** Minas Tirith (q.v.). (I 330)

**CITY OF THE CORSAIRS** The city of Umbar (q.v.). (I 17)

**CITY OF THE TREES** Caras Galadon (q.v.). (I 458)

**CLEFT** The narrow path, surrounded on either side with sheer cliffs, at the top of Cirith Ungol. (II 435, 436)

**CLOSED DOOR** Fen Hollen (q. v.). (III 123)

**CLOUDYHEAD** Westron name for Bundushathûr (q.v.). (I 370)

**COIRË** (Q.: 'stirring') The last division of the Eldarin loa (q. v.), corresponding to our February and March.
Called in Sindarin echuir. (III 480)

**COLD-DRAKE** A kind of dragon, found in the Ered Mithrin. In TA 2589 a cold-drake slew King Dáin I and drove Durin's Folk out of the Ered Mithrin. (III 440)

**COLDFELLS** Wild region north of Rivendell, perhaps the Ettenmoors. (III 420)

**COMBE** Village in a valley in the eastern Bree-land. (I 205, 245)

**COMMON SPEECH** Westron (q. v.), so called because it was the *lingua franca* of Middle-earth beginning in the late Second Age. (I 23; III 508)

**COMPANIONS OF THE RING** The members of the Company of the Ring (q. v.). (III 306)

**COMPANY OF THE RING** The company of Free Peoples which accompanied Frodo Baggins on the first stage of the Quest of Mount Doom. The Company was composed of Frodo, Sam Gamgee, Peregrin Took and Merry Brandybuck, representing Hobbits, Aragorn II and Boromir, representing Men, Legolas, representing Elves, Gimli, representing Dwarves, and Gandalf. The Company did not plan to accompany Frodo all the way to Mordor; Boromir was going to Minas Tirith and the plans of some of the other Companions were uncertain. As the Company was deliberating its course of action on Amon Hen, it was broken by Boromir's attempt to seize the Ring and an attack of Orcs. Boromir was slain and Merry and Pippin captured by the Orcs. Aragorn, Legolas and Gimli followed the Orcs, while Frodo and Sam continued the Quest. Gandalf, the leader of the Company, had earlier been lost, in Khazad-dûm.
Also called the Companions of the Ring, which referred specifically to the members of the Company, the Fellowship of the Ring, the Nine Walkers (as opposed to the Nine Riders, the Nazgûl), and the Nine Companions. (I 360; III 320)

**CORONAR** (Q.: 'sun-round') A period, corresponding to one astronomical year, observed by the Eldar in Middle-earth. (III 480)

**CORMALLEN** See: Field of Cormallen.

**CORMARË** (Q.: 'ring-day') Feast-day of the New Reckoning, falling on Frodo's birthday, Yavannië 30. In leap years Cormarë was doubled. (III 486)

**CORSAIRS OF UMBAR** Name given to any of the groups of pirates and raiders based at Umbar, among the greatest enemies of Gondor. The first Corsairs were the Black Númenoreans and their allies, whose attacks on Gondor began before TA 933. After the Kin-strife, Umbar was seized by the defeated followers of Castamir, who soon became Corsairs and raided Gondor's coasts until 1810, when King Telumehtar Umbardacil took Umbar and killed the last descendents of Castamir. Umbar was soon lost to Men of the Harad, who again quickly became Corsairs. From this time, Umbar was merely one of the kingdoms of the Harad, although because of their sea-power the Corsairs were always an immediate threat to Gondor. The Corsairs were probably destroyed by King Elessar at the beginning of the Fourth Age.

The Corsairs at the time of the WR sailed in ships with black sails. (III 148-49, 186-87, 403, 405-06, 407, 408, 415, 417)

**COTMAN** (b. TA 2860) Working-class Hobbit of the Shire, who gave his name to the Cotton family, his descendents.

Cotman's real name, in Hobbitish, was Hlothram, which meant "cottager." (III 477, 520)

**COTTAR** (b. TA 2820) Working-class Hobbit of the Shire, father of Cotman and Carl. (III 477)

**COTTON** Working-class family in the Shire, at least some of whose members were farmers. At the time of the WR, Tolman Cotton was one of the most prominent Hobbits in Bywater, and as a result of his role in the Battle of Bywater and the close connection of his family with the Gamgees, the family at this time became quite influential and rather well-to-do.

The real name of the family, in genuine Hobbitish, was Hlothran, which was derived from Hlothram (Cotman), the first member of the family, or from the village of Hlothran (q. v.). (III 365, 477, 520)

**COUNCIL** The White Council (q. v.). (I 328)

**COUNCIL OF ELROND** Council held at Rivendell on November 25, TA 3019 to discuss the Rings of Power, especially the One Ring, and to answer questions of various groups of Free Peoples. Those in attendance included Elrond, who presided, Gandalf, Glorfindel, Erestor and other counsellors of Elrond's household, Frodo, Bilbo, Sam, who was not invited, Glóin and Gimli, come to seek counsel for the Dwarves of Erebor, Galdor, representing Círdan, Legolas, representing Thranduil, and Boromir, who had come to Rivendell seeking the answer to a dream he and Faramir had had.

The Council learned of the state of the West and Sauron's preparations for war, the treachery of Saruman, the escape of Gollum and the history of the Rings and Sauron's attempts to recover the One. The outcome of the Council was the decision to destroy the Ring in the Sammath Naur, and Frodo's undertaking of this Quest. (I 314-55)

**COUNCIL OF GONDOR**  Council of the highest officials of Gondor, both civil and military, serving the Kings and Ruling Stewards in an advisory capacity. In the days of the Kings the Steward was the head of the Council. (III 108, 409)

**COUNCIL OF THE NORTH-KINGDOM**  Advisory body to the Kings of Arnor and Arthedain. In FA 14 the Thain and Mayor of the Shire and the Master of Buckland were made Counsellors. (III 471)

**COUNCIL OF THE WISE**  The White Council (q. v.). (I 83)

**COURT OF THE FOUNTAIN**  Plaza in the Citadel of Minas Tirith containing a fountain in the middle of which stood the White Tree, or the Withered Tree.

Also called the Place of the Fountain. (III 25, 26, 27)

**CRACK OF DOOM**  The great volcanic rent in the floor of the Sammath Naur of Orodruin. In the depths of the Crack of Doom burned the Fire of Doom, the flame in which the One Ring was forged and the only flame in which it could be unmade.

Also called the Cracks of Doom. (I 94; III 274-76)

**CRAM**  Travelling food prepared by the Men of Esgaroth, a hard and tasteless but very nutritious biscuit or small cake. (I 478; H 232, 247)

**CREBAIN**  (S.)  Black crows of Fangorn and Dunland. At the time of the WR they were controlled by Saruman and were used by him as spies.

The crebain may not actually have come from Fangorn; at the time Aragorn made this claim he had never been to the Forest.

The singular form of the word is *craban*. (I 372-73; II 48, 237)

**CRICKHOLLOW**  Place in Buckland, north of Bucklebury. The

Brandybucks had a house here, in which Frodo stayed after leaving Hobbiton in TA 3018. (I 40, 101, 143-44)

**CROSSINGS OF ERUI**  Ford across the Erui in Lebannin, site of a major battle during the Kin-strife. (III 406)

**CROSSINGS OF ISEN**  The Fords of Isen (q. v.). (III 432)

**CROSSINGS OF POROS**  Ford across the Poros on the Harad Road, site of a great victory over the Haradrim by Gondor in TA 2885. (III 15, 416)

**CROSS-ROADS OF THE FALLEN KING**  The crossing of the Morannon-Harad and Morgul-Osgiliath roads, in central Ithilien. In the early Third Age the Men of Gondor grew tall trees about the Cross-roads and set up a statue of a crowned king. The statue was later despoiled by the servants of Sauron, but was restored during the WR by the Army of the West. (II 395; III 196-97)

**CURUNÍR**  (S.: 'man of skill')  Saruman (q. v.). (III 455)

**ꝺ**

**DAERON** (S.) (First Age) Elf, the minstrel and loremaster of King Thingol. The systematization of the cirth, the Angerthas Daeron, was attributed to him. (III 493)

**DAERON'S RUNES** The Angerthas Daeron or any of its adaptations. In this case, the Angerthas Moria is meant. (I 416)

**DAGORLAD** (S.: 'battle-plain') The great, treeless, open plain between the Dead Marshes and Cirith Gorgor. Dagorlad was the site of the great battle between Sauron and the Last Alliance in SA 3434, and in the Third Age was the gateway into Gondor for many groups of Easterling invaders and the site of many battles with them, especially in 1899 and 1944.
Called the Battle Plain in Westron. (I 319; II 294; III 409, 455, 458)

**DÁIN I** (TA 2440-2589) Dwarf, King of Durin's Folk (2585-89). He was slain in his palace in the Ered Mithrin by a cold-drake. (III 440, 450)

**DÁIN II IRONFOOT** (TA 2767-3019) Dwarf, King of Durin's Folk (2941-3019). A great warrior, Dáin first won fame by killing Azog in the Battle of Azanulbizar in 2799. In 2805, Dáin became lord of the Dwarves of the Iron Hills. In 2941 he led an army to the aid of Thorin II, who was besieged in Erebor, and later was one of the commanders on the good side of the Battle of the Five Armies. Thorin died in that battle, and Dáin, as his rightful heir, became King of Durin's Folk and King under the Mountain. He ruled wisely and justly and brought wealth to Erebor, until the WR, when he was killed in the Battle of Dale while defending the body of his friend King Brand. (III 443-44, 448-49, 450, 468; H 246, 275)

**DAISY BOFFIN** (b. TA 2950) Hobbit of the Shire, daughter of Dudo Baggins and wife of Griffo Boffin. She was a guest at the Farewell Party. (III 474)

**DAISY GAMGEE** (b. TA 2972) Hobbit of the Shire, third child and eldest daughter of Hamfast Gamgee. (III 477)

**DAISY GAMGEE** (b. FA 13) Hobbit of the Shire, eighth child and fourth daughter of Sam Gamgee. (III 477)

**DALE** City-kingdom of Men, located on the southern slopes of Erebor. The Men of Dale traced their descent to the Edain, and Dale may have been quite ancient when it was destroyed in TA 2770 by Smaug. The Men of Dale were then scattered, and many went to Esgaroth. After the death of Smaug in 2941, Dale was rebuilt by Bard, a descendent of the old Kings of Dale, who became its first King. With the simultaneous re-founding of the Kingdom under the Mountain, the ancient friendship between the two realms was re-established and Dale again became wealthy and famous. During the WR Dale was attacked by Easterlings allied with Sauron, but its inhabitants took refuge in Erebor after an initial defeat; the combined force of Men and Dwarves broke the seige after the downfall of Sauron. In the Fourth Age Dale retained its independence, but was allied with and protected by the Reunited Kingdom.

At the time of the WR, Dale extended far to the east and south of the city, and probably included all the land between the Carnen and the River Running. (I 51, 301, 302-03; III 440, 460, 461, 468-69; H 34-36, 195, 234)

**DAMROD** (S.) (fl. WR) Dúnadan of Gondor, a Ranger of Ithilien. (II 338)

**DARK DAYS** The Accursed Years, as called by the Elves of Lórien. (I 445)

**DARK DOOR** The north entrance to the Paths of the Dead, at the foot of the Dwimorberg.
Also called The Door, the Forbidden Door and the Gate of the Dead. (III 69-70, 85, 459)

**DARKNESS, THE** The Great Darkness (q. v.). (II 89)

**DARKNESS, THE** An emanation sent by Sauron which covered Gondor and Rohan in the days preceding the Siege of Minas Tirith. The Darkness had a depressing effect. It lifted at the arrival of the Rohirrim at the beginning of the Battle of the Pelennor Fields. (III 52, 95, 98)

**DARK PLAGUE** Name given to the Great Plague (q. v.) of TA 1636-37 in the Shire. (I 24)

**DARK POWER OF THE NORTH** Morgoth (q. v.). (III 507)

**DARK TOWER** The Barad-dûr (q. v.). (I 320)

**DARK YEARS** Either the Accursed Years or the years of of Morgoth's domination of Middle-earth.
Cf.: the Accursed Years, the Dark Days, the Great Darkness. (II 40, 422; III 23)

**DAWNLESS DAY** The first day of the Darkness, March 10, TA 3019. (III 95, 466)

**DAY, THE**   Possibly the time (or untime) during which the Valar prepared the West for the Eldar and Middle-earth was being made. In any case, the Day occurred before the chronicled years of the First Age. (I 321)

**DAYS OF DEARTH**   The Long Winter (q.v.) of TA 2758-59 and the ensuing famine, so called in the annals of the Shire. (I 24)

**DAYS OF THE RINGS**   The period during which the Rings of Power were influential in the affairs of Middle-earth, extending from SA 1590 to TA 3019. (III 383)

**DEAD MARSHES**   Marshes east of the Emyn Muil. The marshes expanded eastward throughout the Third Age, and at some point engulfed the graves of the Men and Elves slain in the Battle of Dagorlad. The graves became the Mere of Dead Faces (q.v.). In TA 1944 many of the Wainriders defeated in the Battle of the Camp were driven into the Dead Marshes, where they perished. (I 332; II 294-98; III 409, 458)

**DEAD MEN OF DUNHARROW**   Men of the White Mountains, related to the Dunlendings. When Gondor was founded, they swore allegiance to Isildur, but as they had been corrupted by Sauron during the Accursed Years they broke their oath when called to battle by the Last Alliance. For this betrayal, they were condemned to remain in and near the White Mountains, as spirits, until called to fulfill their oath by the heir of Isildur.

For the entire Third Age the Dead Men haunted the area above Dunharrow, especially the Paths of the Dead. In 3019, during the WR, they were called by Aragorn to fulfill their oath, and repaid their debt by routing the Corsairs of Umbar at Pelargir. They then vanished from Middle-earth.

The Dead Men were also known as the Dead, the Sleepless Dead, the Grey Host, the Shadow Host, the Shadow-men, the Shadows, the Shadows of Men, the Men of the Mountains and the Oathbreakers. (III 64-65, 71-75, 186, 509)

**DEADMEN'S DIKE**   Name given to Fornost (q.v.) after its ruin and desertion in TA 1974. (I 321; III 337)

**DEAD ONES**   The corpses in the Mere of Dead Faces (q.v.). (II 296-98)

**DÉAGOL**   (d. TA 2463)   Stoor of the Gladden Fields. While fishing with his cousin Sméagol, he found the One Ring, and was murdered by Sméagol, who coveted it.

The name Déagol is a translation into Old English of the Northern Mannish name Nahald, meaning "secret." (I 84-85;

III 459, 509, 518)

**DEATH DOWN** Mass grave outside Helm's Dike in which the Huorns buried the Orcs killed in the Battle of the Hornburg. The Death Down was a large mound of stones built over a deep pit. (II 201; III 58)

**DEEP-ELVES** Probably one of the Three Kindreds of the Eldar (q. v.), perhaps corresponding to the Noldor. (H 164)

**DEEPHALLOW** Village in the southern part of the East-farthing, near where the Shirebourn flowed into the Brandy-wine. (I 40; TB 9)

**DEEPING COOMB** Valley in Rohan near Helm's Deep. The side of the Coomb near the Hornrock was fortified, and was known as Helm's Dike. The Deeping Stream flowed through the Deeping Coomb, not surprisingly. (II 170)

**DEEPING STREAM** Stream in Rohan coming from Helm's Deep. It passed around the Hornrock, over Helm's Dike and through the Deeping Coomb into Westfold Vale. (II 169-70)

**DEEPING WALL** The wall across Helm's Gate, guarding the entrance to Helm's Deep. The Deeping Wall was twenty feet high and broad enough for four men to walk abreast on its top; it was unscalable. The only flaw in the Wall was that there was a rather sizable culvert in its base through which the Deeping Stream flowed. During the Battle of the Hornburg soldiers of Saruman twice entered Helm's deep through this culvert. (II 169, 173 ff.)

**DEFICIT** The millenial errors in the Kings' and Stewards' Reckonings and, by extension, the adjustments made to correct them. The original Deficit corrected the small error caused by the inaccuracy of the leap year system. In the Third Age adjustments had to be made because of the dis-location of the end of the century, since TA 1000 was equivalent to SA 4441. These adjustments eventually led to the Stewards' Reckoning. (III 481)

**DENETHOR I** (S.: '---eagle') (d. TA 2477) Dúnadan, tenth Ruling Steward of Gondor. Toward the end of his rule Ithilien was overrun by uruks from Mordor, but they were defeated by Denethor's son, Boromir. (III 395, 415)

**DENETHOR II** (TA c. 2935-3019) Dúnadan, twenty-sixth and last Ruling Steward of Gondor (2984-3019). Denethor was a noble man, valiant, proud and wise, yet in his younger days he was overshadowed by Thorongil. It was later be-lieved that he realized that Thorongil was actually Aragorn

II, and feared that Aragorn and Gandalf were plotting to supplant him; Denethor, like his predecessors, was opposed to giving the crown of Gondor to the heir of Isildur.

In 2976, Denethor married Finduilas of Dol Amroth. She bore him two children, Boromir and Faramir, but died in 2988. After her death Denethor became grim and withdrawn. Desiring knowledge of Sauron's plans, for he knew that the great attack against Gondor would come in his time, Denethor began to look into the palantír of Minas Tirith. Although he gained knowledge with which he was able to prepare Gondor as well as possible for the onslaught, Denethor was aged prematurely and became fixed in pride and despair. When his elder and favorite son, Boromir, died in 3019, and Faramir was stricken with the Black Breath, Denethor lost his reason and tried to cremate Faramir. Although prevented in this by Beregond and Gandalf, Denethor succeeded in burning himself. It is likely that a third cause for Denethor's fatal depression was a vision in the palantír of the fleet of the Corsairs sailing up Anduin; since Sauron was able partially to control the image Denethor saw, the Steward was unable to know that the ships were in reality commanded by Aragorn.

Despite his dislike of Gandalf, which hindered the wizard and deprived Gondor of an excellent counsellor, Denethor was an able ruler, worthy of honor despite his ignoble end. (I 330-31; III 27, 28-29ff., 115, 121-23, 153-62, 395-96, 417-19)

**DÉOR** (TA 2644-2718) Man, seventh King of Rohan (2699-2718). During his reign Rohan was troubled by the Dunlendings. (III 435)

**DÉORWINE** (d. TA 3019) Man of Rohan, chief of the knights of Théoden's household. He was killed in the Battle of the Pelennor Fields. (III 146, 152)

**DERNDINGLE** Great bowl in Fangorn, site of Entmoots. (II 103, 104-09)

**DERNHELM** Name used by Éowyn (q. v.) when she disguised herself as a Rider of Rohan in order to ride with the Rohirrim to the Battle of the Pelennor Fields. (III 93)

**DERRILYN** Supposedly a river, in Bilbo Baggins' poem *Errantry*. The name is an imitation of Elvish, and Derrilyn was probably fictitious.

However, see: Shadow-land. (TB 8, 24)

**DERUFIN** (S.) (d. TA 3019) Man of Gondor, son of Duinhir

of Morthond. He and his brother Duilin were archers, and were slain in the Battle of the Pelennor Fields while attacking the Oliphants of the Haradrim. (III 49, 152)

**DERVORIN** (S.) (fl. WR) Man of Gondor, son of the lord of Ringló Vale. He led his father's troops to the defense of Minas Tirith during the WR, and fought in the Battle of the Pelennor Fields. (III 49)

**DESOLATION OF SMAUG** From TA 2770 to 2941, Erebor and the surrounding area, devastated by Smaug's rather extravagant breathing habits and general unsociability.

Also called the Desolation of the Dragon and, probably, the Waste. (I 303; H 13, 195)

**DESOLATION OF THE MORANNON** The foul and reeking area between the Morannon and Dagorlad, despoiled by the servants of Sauron. The Desolation was scarred with many pits and slag-mounds. (II 302-03; III 467)

**DIAMOND TOOK** (fl. FA 7) Hobbit of the Shire, wife of Peregrin Took. Diamond came from Long Cleeve, and was probably a North-took. (III 471, 475)

**DIMHOLT** Small forest of black trees in Rohan, near the Dark Door. (III 69, 81)

**DIMRILL DALE** Westron name for Azanulbizar (q. v.). (I 370)

**DIMRILL GATE** The Great Gates (q. v.). (I 430)

**DIMRILL STAIR** Path leading from Azanulbizar to the Redhorn Pass. The Dimrill Stair was built along the bank of a swift and many-falled stream. (I 359, 370, 432)

**DINGLE** The valley of the Withywindle in the Old Forest, the center of the evil in the Forest. Many willow trees, including Old Man Willow, grew in the Dingle. (I 163-70; TB 8-9, 11)

**DINODAS BRANDYBUCK** (b. TA 2914 to 2919, d. after 3001) Hobbit of the Shire, youngest son of Gorbadoc Brandybuck. He was a guest at the Farewell Party. (III 476)

**DIOR** (S.? tr. Ad.?) (First Age) Son of Beren and Lúthien and father of Elwing. Dior was Thingol's heir, and so may have been King of Doriath.

Dior's race is not mentioned. (I 261)

**DIOR** (d. TA 2435) Dúnadan, ninth Ruling Steward of Gondor (2412-35). (III 395)

**DIRHAEL** (S.) (fl. TA 2930) Dúnadan of the North, a descendent of Aranarth. Dirhael was the husband of Ivorwen and the father of Gilraen. (III 420)

**DÍS** (b. TA 2760)   Dwarf of Durin's Line, third child and only daughter of Thráin II. Dís was the mother of Fíli and Kíli. (III 440, 449, 450)

**DODERIC BRANDYBUCK** (b. TA 2989)   Hobbit of the Shire, eldest son of Seredic Brandybuck. He was a guest at the Farewell Party. (III 476)

**DODINAS BRANDYBUCK** (b. TA 2908 to 2913, d. before 3001)   Hobbit of the Shire, fourth son of Gorbadoc Brandybuck. (III 476)

**DOL AMROTH** (S.: 'hill of Amroth')   Castle and port, the chief city of Belfalas, Gondor. Until about TA 1981, the white ships of the Elves of Lórien sailed from Dol Amroth, and the Dúnedain of that city were said to have elven blood in their veins.

See also: Morthond, Sea-ward Tower. (III 23, 50, 181, 301; TB 8, 37-38)

**DOL BARAN** (S.: 'golden-brown hill')   The southernmost foothill of the Misty Mountains, rounded and covered with heather. (II 248)

**DOL GULDUR** (S.: 'hill of black magic')   Fortress in southwestern Mirkwood. Dol Guldur was probably built by Sauron about TA 1050; it was first mentioned about 1100, when the Wise discovered that an unknown evil power had settled there. For the next thousand years, the power grew stronger and corrupted the forest. In 2063 Gandalf went to Dol Guldur to learn the identity of its master, but the evil power fled. The power returned with increased power in 2460, but in 2850 Gandalf again entered the fortress and discovered that its master was Sauron. Sauron continued to rule his many servants from Dol Guldur until 2941, when he was driven out by the White Council. Sauron retreated to Mordor, but ten years later sent three of the Nazgûl to occupy Dol Guldur. During the WR, armies from Dol Guldur attacked Lórien and the Woodland Realm, but they were defeated. After the fall of Sauron, Celeborn took Dol Guldur and Galadriel threw down its walls and cleansed its pits. (I 328, 336; III 415, 448, 456-59, 460, 461, 462, 467, 468, 469)

**DOME OF STARS** Building in Osgiliath where the palantír of the city was kept. The Dome of Stars was ruined during the Kin-strife.

Also called the Tower of the Stone of Osgiliath. (II 259; III 406)

**DONNAMIRA BOFFIN** (TA 2856-2948) Hobbit of the Shire, tenth child of Gerontius Took. She married Hugo Boffin. (III 475)

**DOOM OF MEN** The later name for the ban set on Men by Eru in the beginning, which was that all Men must age and die. The Doom of Men was originally conceived of as a great blessing, and was therefore called the Gift of Men, but later Men, especially the Númenoreans, considered mortality a curse. (III 390, 425, 427-28)

**DORA BAGGINS** (TA 2902-3006) Hobbit of the Shire, eldest child of Fosco Baggins. She was a guest at the Farewell Party, and was given a waste-paper basket. Dora was noted for her lengthy letters and good advice. (I 64; III 474)

**DOR-EN-ERNIL** (S.: 'land-middle-prince'?) Area of Gondor west of the Gilrain. (III 14)

**DORI** (fl. TA 2941-3018) Dwarf of the House of Durin, a member of Thorin and Company. Dori settled in Erebor after the expedition. (I 302; III 450; H 22, 26, 44)

**DORIATH** (S.) An Elven-kingdom of the First Age, located in the forest of Neldoreth in Beleriand. Doriath is referred to as a hidden kingdom; it was probably surrounded by mountains and was almost inaccessible.

The most famous King of Doriath was Thingol.

Doriath is once referred to as Elvenhome (I 258). (I 258-60, 319; III 506)

**DORTHONION** (S.) Highland area in Beleriand. Many pine trees grew here.

Also called Orod-na-thôn. (II 90)

**DORWINION** (S.) Somewhere in Middle-earth. The wines drunk by the Elves of the Woodland Realm were made here. (H 172, 175)

**DOWNLANDS** The area of the Barrow-downs. (I 223)

**DRAGONS** Evil creatures, found in and perhaps native to the Ered Mithrin. Physically, dragons were dragons--large, scale-covered, long-lived, usually fire-breathing flying creatures. Dragons were greedy, crafty and conceited; they were easily influenced by Sauron.

Dragons were present in the First Age, but were not mentioned after that time until about TA 2570, when they began to reappear in the Ered Mithrin and harass the Dwarves and the Éothéod. The greatest of these dragons was Smaug, who in 2770 took Erebor.

There appear to have been two kinds of dragons, regular dragons and cold-drakes (q.v.).

Also called the Great Worms. (III 440, 459; H 35, 207, 212, 214; TB 54)

**DROGO BAGGINS** (TA 2908-80) Hobbit of the Shire, second child and eldest son of Fosco Baggins. Drogo married Primula Brandybuck; their only child was Frodo Baggins. Drogo and his wife died in a boating accident on the Brandywine.

Until his irregular death, Drogo was considered a proper and unexceptionable Hobbit, and was very fond of good food. (I 45-46; III 474, 476)

**DRUADAN FOREST** (S.: '---man') Forest in Anórien, thirty miles northwest of Minas Tirith, the home of the Woses (q.v.). After the WR, in return for the aid they gave the Rohirrim, King Elessar gave the forest to the Woses and forbade anyone to enter it without their permission.

Also called the Grey Wood. (III 15, 127, 313)

**DUDO BAGGINS** (TA 2911-3009) Hobbit of the Shire, youngest child of Fosco Baggins. He was a guest at the Farewell Party. (III 474)

**DUILIN** (S.: 'river-song'?) (d. TA 3019) Man of Gondor, son of Duinhir, the lord of Morthond. Duilin, with his brother Derufin, was trampled to death by Oliphaunts during the Battle of the Pelennor Fields. (III 49, 152)

**DUINHIR** (S.: 'river-lord') (fl. WR) Man of Gondor, lord of Morthond at the time of the WR. He fought in the Battle of the Pelennor Fields, in which he lost both his sons. (III 49)

**DUMBLEDORS** A probably-imaginary race of insects in Bilbo's poem *Errantry*. (TB 27)

**DÚNADAN** See: Dúnedain.

**DÚNADAN, THE** Aragorn (q.v.). (I 304)

**DÚNEDAIN** (S.: 'edain of the west') Men, those of the Edain (q.v.) who at the beginning of the Second Age sailed to Númenor (q.v.), and their descendents. After the fall of Númenor in SA 3319, the Dúnedain survived only in the Faithful (q.v.) and the Black Númenoreans of Umbar (qq.v.). Two kingdoms were founded by the Faithful, Gondor and Arnor (qq.v.), and after the death of Elendil in SA 3441 the Dúnedain were split into two groups, those of the North and those of Gondor.

The Dúnedain of the North were attacked from TA 1300

onward by Angmar, and slowly they lost territory and their numbers dwindled. The Dúnedain of Rhudaur were few by 1409, and the last Dúnedain of Cardolan perished in the Great Plague of 1636. After the fall of Arthedain in 1974, the Dúnedain of the North became few, and survived only with the aid of Elrond. However, adversity preserved their hardiness, and many or all of the male Dúnedain became Rangers, who protected the innocent Men and Hobbits of Eriador and were implacable foes of Sauron and his servants. The Dúnedain of the North were ruled by the Line of Isildur, which never failed.

In Gondor, the Dúnedain flourished for many years despite threats from Harad and Rhûn, but many of the Dúnedain became decadent and over-proud. The Line of Anárion, the family of the Kings of Gondor, failed five times because of the childlessness or early death of the king. Also, the Dúnedain of Gondor, like their forebears in Númenor, became concerned with their shortened lifespan (which waned more rapidly than that of their northern kinsmen), and even had a disastrous civil war, the Kin-strife, about this. The purity of the Dúnadan blood was lessened by intermarriage with lesser Men, especially the Northmen, and, more importantly, by sloth and love of luxury. However, some of the Dúnedain families, notably the House of Húrin and the house of the Princes of Dol Amroth, retained their nobility; the blood of the latter family was enriched by Elvish blood. By the time of the WR, although Gondor was still strong and some of her Dúnedain were still noble and wise, the Dúnedain of Gondor had waned considerably.

The Dúnedain were superior to other Men in nobility of spirit and body, although they were of course capable of evil if corrupted. They were tall, with dark hair and grey eyes. The lifespan of the royal family, originally three times that of lesser Men, was by the time of the WR still about 150 or more years; lesser Dúnedain lived somewhat shorter lives. The age of adulthood seems to have been about 25 or 30, although most of the Kings did not succeed their fathers until they were much older. The Dúnedain, especially those of high rank, possessed great wisdom and discernment, and occasional foresight. The Faithful and their descendents loved the Elves and were liked by them; there was great hatred between them and Sauron.

The Dúnedain spoke Westron, which they enriched with many Elvish words. Many of the Dúnedain knew Sindarin, and some also knew Quenya. The Dúnedain of Númenor, and probably also those of Umbar, spoke Adûaic.

The Dúnedain were also known as the Men of Westernesse and the Númenoreans. They were also called the Kings of Men (the Westron equivalent of "Edain"), the Men of the Sea (since the Númenoreans were great mariners) and, in the lore of Gondor, the High Men of the West. The singular of *Dúnedain* is *Dúnadan*. (I 29, 326, 330; II 335-38, 362-63; III 394-419, 507-08)

**DÚNHARG**  See: Dunharrow. (III 492)

**DUNHARROW**  Fortress and refuge above Harrowdale, built in the Accursed Years by an unknown race. Dunharrow was used by Gondor and later by Rohan; it was one of the chief refuges of the latter country.

Dunharrow was easily defended, since it was reached by a switch-back path that went up a steep cliff; each level was overlooked by the ones above.

Dunharrow is a modernized form of the translated Rohirric "Dúnharg." "Dunharrow" referred to the area generally, while "the Hold of Dunharrow" referred specifically to the refuge. (II 163; III 14, 65, 76 ff.)

**DÚNHERE**  (d. TA 3019)  Man of Rohan, lord of Harrowdale. He was killed in the Battle of the Pelennor Fields. (III 79, 83, 152)

**DUNLAND**  Area west of the Misty Mountains and south of the Glanduin, at the time of the WR neither prosperous, civilized nor organized into a state, being a land of backward herdsmen and hillmen.

Dunland was inhabited before the founding of Gondor by the Dunlendings. (q. v.). About TA 1150 some Stoors came to Dunland, but migrated to the Shire in 1630. From approximately TA 2770 to 2800 Dwarves who had escaped from the sack of Erebor, led by Thrór, lived in Dunland. At the time of the WR, Dunland, though a fair, fertile land, was sparsely inhabited. (I 16; II 168, 180; III 322, 325, 441, 457, 505)

**DUNLENDINGS**  Men, last remnant of the people that once inhabited the valleys of the Ered Nimrais. Some of these folk were assimilated by Gondor; one group became the Dead Men of Dunharrow. In the Second Age, however, some of these people had moved north; some settled in Dunland, while others moved into Eriador. The Men of Bree were the northernmost surviving branch at the time of the WR.

In Dunland the Dunlendings preserved their ancient

language and primitive culture. In the Third Age they hated the Rohirrim, who had driven them out of the northern valleys of the Ered Nimrais and the plains of western Rohan, and so they frequently attacked that country. The two greatest Dunlending attacks on Rohan were in 2758, when they were led by Wulf, and during the WR, when the Dunlendings were aroused by Saruman.

The Dunlendings were tall and somewhat swarthy; they had dark hair. They were primitive, uncultured and superstitious. (II 180; III 432, 434, 435, 505, 509)

**DURIN I** (First Age) Dwarf, eldest of the Seven Fathers of the Dwarves and the ancestor of Durin's Folk, the most important family of the Dwarves in the Third Age. Durin named Azanulbizar and its prominent features, and began the building of Khazad-dûm.

Durin lived to a very great age, and for that reason was called "the Deathless." It was believed by the Dwarves that he would one day rise again. (I 411-12; III 438-39)

**DURIN II** (c. SA 750) Dwarf, King of Durin's Folk and of Khazad-dûm. He was probably King at the time of the building of the West-gate, although the Durin referred to could be Durin III. (I 398)

**DURIN III** (fl. SA 16th Cent.) Dwarf, King of Durin's Folk and of Khazad-dûm at the time of the forging of the Rings of Power. He was given the chief of the Seven Rings by Celebrimbor. (III 445)

**DURIN VI** (TA 1731-1980) Dwarf, King of Durin's Folk and of Khazad-dûm. In his time the Balrog was released, and Durin was slain by it. (III 439, 450)

**DURIN VII** (Fourth Age or later) Dwarf, last King of Durin's Folk. (III 450)

**DURIN'S AXE** The weapon of Durin I, a great heirloom of the Dwarves of Durin's Folk. Durin's Axe seems to have remained in Khazad-dûm when it was deserted in TA 1981; Balin's expedition found it in 2989. When Balin's colony was destroyed in 2994, the Axe was lost once again. (I 418)

**DURIN'S BANE** The Balrog (q. v.) who dwelt in Khazad-dûm, so called by the Dwarves because of his murder of Durin VI in TA 1980. (I 413)

**DURIN'S BRIDGE** A single fifty-foot arch of stone spanning the great abyss in the Second Hall of Khazad-dûm, built as a last defense against invaders from the east. During

the Quest of Mount Doom Gandalf defended the Bridge
against the Balrog, and broke it.

Also called the Bridge of Khazad-dûm and the Bridge.
(I 419, 427-30; II 134)

**DURIN'S CROWN** Constellation of seven stars, first seen
by Durin I reflected around his head in Kheled-zâram. Ever
after, the reflection of Durin's Crown could be seen in
the lake, even in the daytime. (I 433-34)

**DURIN'S DAY** The time of Durin I, early in the Fourth Age.
(I 412, 454)

**DURIN'S DAY** The first day of the Dwarvish year, so called only if the moon and the sun shone in the sky at the
same time. The Dwarves' New Year was the first day of the
last new crescent moon of autumn. (H 62-63)

**DURIN'S FOLK** The eldest and greatest of the seven folk
of the Dwarves, descended from Durin I. All the Dwarves
in *LotR,* except for some unnamed Dwarves at the Battle
of Azanulbizar, were of Durin's Folk. The ancestral hall of
Durin's Folk was Khazad-dûm, where they flourished until
TA 1980, growing rich from the treasure they mined there,
especially mithril. Although Durin's Folk weathered all
assaults from without, they were driven from Khazad-dûm
by the rising of the Balrog in TA 1980. Durin's Folk then
became a fragmented and wandering people, settling at
various places in the Ered Mithrin, and in Erebor, until
they were driven out by dragons. By TA 2800 only their
paltry mines in the Ered Luin and the Iron Hills remained
to them. In 2790, Thrór attempted to visit Khazad-dûm, but
was slain by the Orcs who dwelled there. His son Thráin
in revenge began the War of the Dwarves and Orcs (2793-
99), in which Durin's Folk played the major role.

In 2941 Thorin II recovered Erebor, and Durin's Folk
once more had a home and could become wealthy. Although
Balin's colonization of Khazad-dûm in 2989 failed, with the
death of the Balrog and the passing of Sauron in the WR
Khazad-dûm may have been recovered by Durin's Folk in
the Fourth Age.

Durin's Folk were ruled by the Kings of Durin's Folk
(q. v.), who were the heirs of Durin. Because the Kings
possessed the last and greatest of the Seven Rings, they
and their people were the especial targets of Sauron's
malice throughout the Third Age.

Durin's Folk were also known as the Longbeards; many

of them had long, frequently plaited and forked beards; which perhaps Dwarves of the other houses did not have. (III 439-50)

**DURIN'S STONE**  Pillar in Azanulbizar marking the spot where Durin I first looked into Kheled-zâram and saw Durin's Crown. Balin was slain here in TA 2994. (I 418, 433)

**DURIN'S TOWER**  Chamber at the top of the Endless Stair of Khazad-dûm, carved in the rock of the pinnacle of Zirakzigil. Durin's Tower was ruined in the Battle of the Peak in TA 3019. (II 135)

**DURTHANG**  (S.: 'dark-fang')  Castle built early in the Third Age by Gondor on the ridge on the western side of the Udûn, used to guard that entrance to Mordor. Durthang, together with other similar fortifications, was deserted about TA 1640, and was later turned into an orc-hold. (III 15, 251)

**DWALIN**  (TA 2772-FA 92)  Dwarf of Durin's Folk, second son of Fundin. Dwalin was one of the companions of Thráin during his wanderings from 2841 to 2845, and later was a member of Thorin and Company. After the recovery of Erebor Dwalin settled there. (III 446, 450; H 20, 26)

**DWALING**  Village in the northern Eastfarthing. (I 40)

**DWARF RINGS**  See: the Seven Rings.

**DWARROWDELF**  Khazad-dûm (q. v.). (III 519)

**DWARVES**  One of the speaking races of Middle-earth, and one of the Free Folk. The Dwarves claimed descent from Seven Fathers who lived in the First Age, and consequently were divided into seven Folk, each with its own King and ancestral halls. The eldest Father was Durin, and his Folk (see: Durin's Folk) were the most famous and seemingly the most numerous in the Third Age.

Through the ages, the numbers of the Dwarves waned; there were three reasons for this. The Dwarves suffered heavily in wars with Elves (in the First Age) and Men who coveted their treasure or offended the touchy pride of the Dwarves. Also, they were attacked by Sauron and his servants, and by dragons, and in the Third Age became a wandering people. Finally, because of individual pride Dwarves frequently did not marry.

Dwarves were short, about four and a half to five feet

tall, but broad, strong and extremely hardy. They lived about 250 years, and married about the age of 100. They were proud and easily angered, and never forgot wrongs done them. They were greedy for gold and riches, and once gold-lust awoke in a Dwarf it was extremely hard to quiet. Except for this, however, Dwarves were fair, but not overly generous, to those of other races. Dwarves were great miners and craftsmen, and worked great wonders with stone, metals and jewels. In battle they used axes.

The Dwarves had their own language, Khuzdul (q. v.), but it was a secret language, and in public Dwarves used the tongue of their neighbors, in the Third Age usually Westron or other tongues of Men. The names of the Dwarves in *LotR* are of northern Mannish form, and are thus Anglicized equivalents of names in the languages of Dale or Esgaroth. The Dwarves wrote with modified versions of the cirth; Durin's Folk used the Angerthas Moria.

The Dwarves called themselves the Khazad (q. v.); the Elves in the First Age called them the Naugrim, and in the Third Age the Nogothrim. (III 396, 430, 438-51, 455, 493-95, 501-04, 512-13, 514, 518-19; H 16, 165, 204, 227, 263)

**DWARVISH**    See: Khuzdul. (III 488)

**DWIMMERLAIK**    (tr. Roh: 'work of necromancy, spectre') Name given to the Lord of the Nazgûl by Éowyn during the Battle of the Pelennor Fields. (III 140-42; RHM III 421)

**DWIMORBERG**    (tr. Roh.: 'haunted-mountain')    Mountain in the Ered Nimrais behind Dunharrow, in which was the Dark Door.

Called in Westron the Haunted Mountain. (III 69 ff., 81)

**DWIMORDENE**    (tr. Roh.: 'haunted-valley')    Name given Lórien (q. v.) by the Rohirrim. (II 150)

**EAGLES OF THE MISTY MOUNTAINS** The greatest and noblest of all birds of Middle-earth, descending from Thorondor, who lived in the Encircling Mountains in the First Age. Toward the end of the Third Age, their lord, Gwaihir (q. v.), was a friend of Gandalf's, and this, coupled with their natural dislike of Orcs, caused the Eagles to play a key part in the Battle of the Five Armies (2941), and later to perform other services for Gandalf and Radagast before and during the WR.

The Eagles were large enough to carry Men. They lived at least to the age of 100.

Also called the Eagles of the North and the great eagles. The Sindarin for "eagle" is *thoron*. (I 342-43; III 278; H 108, 110-16, 273)

**EÄRENDIL** (Q.: 'sea-lover') (First Age) Adan, son of Tuor and Idril, husband of Elwing and father of Elros and Elrond. When the Edain and Elves were finally defeated by the forces of Morgoth, Eärendil, being a great mariner, tried to sail to Valinor to request aid from the Valar. Although he may have made earlier attempts to reach Valinor in vain, this voyage was successful, for Eärendil bore on the prow of his ship the Silmaril given him by Elwing. Eärendil pleaded his case before Elbereth and Manwe, and his request was granted. However, Eärendil was not permitted to return to Middle-earth, and he and his ship, bearing the Silmaril, were set in the sky to give hope and comfort to those in Middle-earth oppressed by Morgoth or his servants.

As a star, Eärendil seems to have corresponded to Venus, and was referred to as the Flammifer of Westernesse, as well as the Morning Star and the Evening Star. He was the star most beloved of the Elves, and his light had great power. (See: the Phial of Galadriel)

As a person, he was known as Eärendil the Mariner. (I 308-12; III 389)

**EÄRENDIL** (d. TA 324) Dúnadan, fifth King of Gondor (238-324). (III 394)

**EÄRENDUR** (Q.: 'sea---') (d. TA 861) Dúnadan, tenth King of Arnor (777-861). At his death Arnor was divided among his sons. (III 394)

EÄRENYA (Q.: 'sea-day') Sixth day of the Númenorean and subsequent enquier.
Called in Sindarin (used only by the Dúnedain) Oraeron, and Meresdei by the Hobbits. (III 484)

EÄRNIL I (Q.: 'sea---') (d. TA 936) Dúnadan, thirteenth King of Gondor (913-36) and the second Ship-king. Eärnil repaired Pelargir, built a great navy and took Umbar from the Black Númenoreans. He died when his fleet was caught in a great storm off Umbar. (III 395, 403)

EÄRNIL II (d. TA 2043) Dúnadan, thirty-second King of Gondor (1945-2043). A great soldier, Eärnil was Captain of the Southern Army, which in 1944 defeated the Haradrim and the Wainriders in two decisive battles that saved Gondor from being overrun. Since King Ondoher and both his sons had been killed by the Wainriders, after a year of dissension the crown was given to Eärnil, who as a descendent of Umbardacil was a member of the royal family.
    Eärnil was a wise ruler; he strengthened Gondor and in 1974 dispatched a fleet commanded by his son Eärnur (q. v.) to the aid of Arthedain. (III 395, 409-11)

EÄRNUR (Q.: 'sea---') (d. TA 2050) Dúnadan, thirty-third King of Gondor (2043-50). In 1974, Eärnur, then Captain of Gondor, was sent to Arthedain by his father Eärnil to aid the Dúnedain of the North against Angmar. His army comprised the major part of the Host of the West which defeated Angmar in the Battle of Fornost in 1975. Eärnur, however, was shamed when his horse would not endure the presence of the Lord of the Nazgûl, but bolted. In 2043, when the Lord of the Nazgûl was in Minas Morgul and Eärnur was King of Gondor, the former challenged the king to personal combat, taunting that Eärnur had fled from him in 1975. Eärnur was restrained by Mardil the Steward, but in 2050 he was challenged again and rode off to Minas Morgul, whence he never returned.
    Eärnur was a great captain, but was proud and cared little for anything but arms. He took no wife, and thus produced no heir. At his death the Line of Anárion ended. (III 303, 395, 411-13)

EAST-ELVES The Silvan Elves (q. v.). (III 505)

EASTEMNET That part of Rohan east of the Entwash. (I 17, II 35)

**EASTERLINGS** The Men of Rhûn. Beginning in TA 490, waves of Easterlings of various tribes and races periodically attacked Gondor, usually over Dagorlad. Some of these invasions were clearly military, and were no doubt inspired by Sauron, but others, such as the invasion of the Balchoth in 2510, seem to have involved the migration of entire peoples, perhaps because of pressure from a warlike nation further eastward.

The Easterlings were in general primitive, and were motivated chiefly by hate for Gondor and greed for her riches. In the Fourth Age, the Easterlings living nearest Gondor were subdued by Elessar.

The Easterlings who fought in the Battle of the Pelennor Fields were tall and bearded, and bore great axes, but they seem to have been atypical.

See: Balchoth, Wainriders. (I 322; III 115, 148, 403, 404-05, 438, 468-69)

**EASTFARTHING** One of the Four Farthings of the Shire, whose inhabitants had a strong Stoorish strain. (I 40)

**EASTFOLD** Area of Rohan bounded by the Mering Stream, the Entwash, the Snowbourn and the Ered Nimrais. (III 14)

**EAST LÓRIEN** An Elven-realm founded by Celeborn at the beginning of the Fourth Age and peopled with Silvan Elves from Lórien. East Lórien comprised all of Eryn Lasgalen south of the Narrows. (III 468)

**EAST MARCH, THE** Buckland (q. v.). (I 30)

**EAST WALL** The great cliff at the western edge of the Emyn Muil (q. v.), which marked the eastern boundary of Rohan at that point. (II 29-30)

**EAST-WEST ROAD** The Great East Road (q. v.). (I 72, 189)

**ECHUIR** (S.) The Sindarin form of coirë (q. v.). (III 480)

**ECTHELION I** (S.) (d. TA 2698) Dúnadan, seventeenth Ruling Steward of Gondor (2685-98). (III 395)

**ECTHELION II** (d. TA 2984) Dúnadan, twenty-fifth Ruling Steward of Gondor (2953-84). During his rule Aragorn, disguised as Thorongil, served Gondor, and in 2980 destroyed a large part of the fleet of Umbar. (III 395, 417)

**EDAIN** (S.: 'fathers of men') Three kindred of Men in the First Age. Their original home was near what is now Lake Baikal, but early in the First Age the Edain migrated to Beleriand, where they aided the Eldar in the War of the

Great Jewels. Although the Edain produced great heroes, they were defeated by the power of Morgoth. However, Eärendil, an Adan, obtained aid from the Valar, and Morgoth was defeated. The Edain were then granted the island of Elenna, near Eressëa, to dwell in, secure from the troubles of Middle-earth. Those of the Edain who sailed there founded the realm of Númenor in SA 32, and became known as the Dúnedain (q.v.); their kindred who remained in Middle-earth, such as the ancestors of the Rohirrim, mingled with those peoples closely related to them, and pass from history until the Third Age.

Of the Three Houses of the Edain, the Third House, the House of Hador (q. v.), was the most renowned in the wars against Morgoth, and also the only house whose members had blond hair. The Edain were no doubt much like the Dúnedain physically and emotionally, although their life-span was probably shorter.

The language of the Edain was that tongue later called Adûnaic; many of the Edain also knew Sindarin.

The singular of *Edain* was *Adan;* the Quenya form of the word was *Antani* (singular *atan*). The Edain were also known as the Elf-friends and the Three Houses of the Elf-friends.

See also: First House of the Edain. (III 388, 390-93, 404, 506-07, 508; RP summer 1967, oral)

**EDGE OF THE WILD**  The boundary between the settled lands of Eriador and the dangerous lands of the Wild, roughly speaking a line drawn north and south through a point slightly west of the Ford of Bruinen. (H 12, 65)

**EDORAS**  (tr. Roh.: 'the courts')  Capital of Rohan, located on the Snowbourn at the foot of the Ered Nimrais. Edoras was built by Eorl and Brego, and contained the great feast-hall of Meduseld. (I 343; II 141, 144 ff.; III 430, 432, 433)

**EGALMOTH**  (S.) (d. TA 2743)  Dúnadan, eighteenth Ruling Steward of Gondor (2698-2743). (III 395)

**EGLADIL**  (S.)  The heart of Lórien, the area between Anduin and Celebrant near their confluence.

Called in Westron the Angle. (I 450)

**EGLANTINE TOOK**  (fl. TA 3000)  Hobbit, wife of Paladin Took and mother of Peregrin Took. She was born a Banks, and was a guest at the Farewell Party. (III 475)

**EILENACH**  (S.)  The second of the northern beacon-tower hills of Gondor, located in Druadan Forest. (III 20, 127)

**ELANOR** (S.: 'star-sun') Yellow winter flower of Lórien, shaped like a star. (I 454)

**ELANOR GAMGEE** (b. FA 1) Hobbit of the Shire, eldest child of Sam Gamgee. In her youth she was a maid of honor to Queen Arwen. In FA 31 Elanor married Fastred of Greenholm, and in 35 they moved to the Tower Hills, where they lived at Undertowers. In 62 Elanor was given the Red Book of Westmarch by her father, and the Book was kept by her descendents, the Fairbairns of the Tower.

Elanor was called "the Fair" because of her beauty; she had blonde hair. (III 378-79, 402, 470, 471-72, 477)

**ELBERETH GILTHONIEL** (S.: 'star-queen star-kindler') A Vala, the mightiest queen of the Valar and the spouse of Manwe, with whom she lived in a great palace on top of Taniquetil. A figure of worship and praise for the Elves, Elbereth was believed to have created the stars. After the revolt of Fëanor, it was Elbereth who cast Valinor in shadow at the summons of Manwe. Elbereth and Manwe were the Valar who received Eärendil in Valinor, and it was Elbereth who set his Silmaril in the sky as a star. In later ages she acted through this star in answering the prayers of Men and Elves; during the WR she aided Sam in his struggle against Shelob.

Elbereth is her Sindarin title; in Quenya she is called Varda ("the exalted") or Tintallë ("star-kindler"). Another Sindarin title she bears is Fanuilos ("snow-white"). (I 117, 310, 312, 489; II 430; III 234; R 60, 61, 64-66; RHM III 421)

**ELDACAR** (Q.: 'high-elf---') (d. TA 339) Dúnadan, fourth King of Arnor (249-339). (III 394)

**ELDACAR** (d. TA 1490) Dúnadan, twenty-first King of Gondor (1432-37, 1447-90). Because his mother was not a Dúnadan, and because he had been born in Rhovanion and called in his youth Vinitharya, Eldacar was believed to be less than a true Dúnadan of Gondor, and so the royal family rebelled against him. This rebellion, the Kin-strife, lasted for five years, for Eldacar was a noble man and a valiant soldier, and was not easily defeated. Eventually, however, he was besieged in Osgiliath, but escaped and fled to Rhovanion. Ten years later, in 1447, Eldacar returned to Gondor with an army of Northmen, and gained much support from the people of northern Gondor. He slew his cruel successor, Castamir the Usurper, in the Battle of the Crossings of Erui, and recovered his throne.

Despite his mixed blood, Eldacar did not age more swiftly than other Dúnedain, and he proved a good ruler. (III 395,

405-07)

**ELDAMAR**  (Q.: 'elvenhome')  The home of the Eldar in the
West. Eldamar comprised the island of Eressëa and that
part of Valinor east of the Pelóri. The chief city of Eldamar
seems to have been the haven of Tirion (q. v.).

Called Faerie in *The Hobbit*. The Westron name was Elvenhome. (I 309, 482; III 289, 506; H 164; TB 63; R 62)

**ELDAR**  (Q.: *'elda* + plural')  Three kindreds of Elves. Early
in the First Age they received a summons from the Valar to
migrate to Valinor, and so undertook the Great Journey.
Arriving at the coast of the Sea, the Eldar became divided
into two groups; most of the Eldar sailed over Sea to Valinor, but some, who became known as the Sindar (q. v.),
lingered in Beleriand. The Eldar of Valinor lived in Eldamar
for many years in great happiness. However, when Morgoth
stole the Silmarils, Fëanor, one of the noblest of the Noldor
(q. v.), one of the Three Kindreds, led his people back to
Middle-earth to recover the jewels. For doing this against
the will of the Valar, the Noldor were forbidden to return
to Valinor, and became known as the Exiles.

In Middle-earth, the Noldor, aided by the Sindar and later
by the Edain, waged a futile war against the forces of
Morgoth from the Elven-realms of Gondolin, Nargothrond and
Doriath. The first two realms fell to Morgoth and many of
the Eldar were slain, but when they were utterly defeated
Eärendil, an Adan, obtained aid from the Valar and Morgoth
was overthrown. The Exiles, with the exception of Galadriel,
the only one of the leaders of the Noldorin rebellion to
survive the War of the Great Jewels, were forgiven and were
permitted to return to Valinor. Thus, at the end of the First
Age many Eldar, including a large number of the Sindar,
returned to the Undying Lands.

In the Second Age, many of the Eldar of Middle-earth lived
in Lindon, where they were ruled by Gil-galad, last heir of
the Eldarin kings in Middle-earth, while others, led by
Celebrimbor, founded Eregion. Still others of the Eldar, such
as Thranduil, Galadriel and Celeborn, went further east and
founded Elven-realms peopled mostly by Silvan Elves. However, the Eldar were troubled by Sauron, and their numbers
dwindled and they did little new. At the end of the Third
Age many of the Eldar, including the now-forgiven Galadriel,
Elrond and Gildor, passed over Sea. Throughout the Second
and Third Ages the Eldar of East and West remained close

to the Dúnedain, visiting them in Númenor when they were welcome, and aiding them at need in Middle-earth. In the Fourth Age, without the Three Rings, the power of the Eldar was diminished, and those few of their kindred remaining in Middle-earth dwindled.

The Eldar were tall, grey-eyed and fair, with a nobility exceeding that of other Elves. They otherwise resembled other Elves, except that the House of Finrod, one of the noblest Noldorin families, was golden-haired. The Eldar were wise and strong, with power against both the Seen and the Unseen. They had great skill in all things, but especially with words. Within all Eldar burned a desire for Valinor; never quieted in the minds of the Exiles, it slept in the Sindar, but once awakened could not be ignored. The Eldar worshipped the Valar, especially Elbereth.

The Eldar originally spoke Quenya, and perhaps also some variant dialects of it, but by the end of the First Age the Eldar of Middle-earth spoke a changed form of Quenya, called Sindarin. They wrote with the Tengwar or the Cirth, both of which scripts they devised.

The identity of the Three Kindreds is uncertain. On H 164 they are listed as the Light-elves, the Deep-elves and the Sea-elves. The only kindred mentioned elsewhere is the Noldor, who would have to correspond to the Deep-elves.

Also called the High Elves (in Westron), the West-elves, the Three Kindreds, the People of the Great Journey and the People of the Stars. (I 294, 472; III 388, 389, 390, 392, 393, 455, 505-06, 514, 519; H 164; R 60, 62, 65-66)

**ELDARIN** General name for the languages spoken by the Eldar. The two of which examples are given in *LotR* are Quenya and Sindarin (qq. v.). (III 506)

**ELDARION** (Q.: 'of the Eldar') (b. FA 1st Cent.) Dúnadan, second King of the Reunited Kingdom (FA 120-?). He was the only son of Elessar and Arwen. (III 427)

**ELDER DAYS** The First Age (q. v.). In the Fourth Age all earlier ages were sometimes called the Elder Days, but this was incorrect. (I 21; III 452)

**ELDER KINDRED** The Elves (q. v.). (III 308)

**ELDER KING** Manwe (q. v.). (I 310; III 392)

**ELDER RACE** The Elves (q.v.), or perhaps the Eldar. (III 101)

**ELENDIL, TAR-** (Q.: 'star-lover' or 'elf-friend') (fl. SA 600)

Dúnadan, fourth King of Númenor. During his reign Númenorean ships first returned to Middle-earth. (III 390, 391; RHM III 398)

**ELENDIL** (d. SA 3441) Dúnadan of Númenor, first King of Arnor and Gondor (3320-3441). Elendil was one of the Faithful, and, as the son of the last Lord of Andúnië, the noblest of his kind to survive the fall of Númenor. With his sons Isildur and Anárion, Elendil escaped to Middle-earth with nine ships, the Palantíri and a seed of the White Tree. In Middle-earth he established the kingdoms of Arnor and Gondor, ruling over the former directly as High King and committing the governing of the latter to his sons. Elendil was one of the leaders of the Last Alliance which overthrew Sauron, and with Gil-galad its greatest warrior. He was slain, along with Gil-galad, by Sauron on the slopes of Orodruin, but they in turn overthrew their enemy.

Elendil's sword was the famous Narsil.

He was known as Elendil the Tall. (I 83, 319, 320; III 303, 391, 392-93, 394)

**ELENDILMIR** (Q.: 'Elendil-jewel') The Star of Elendil (q. v.). (III 401)

**ELENDUR** (Q.) (d. TA 777) Dúnadan, ninth King of Arnor (652-777). (III 394)

**ELENNA** (S. or Q.: 'star---') Island, the furthest west of mortal lands, lying in the Sea within sight of Eressëa. Númenor was founded on Elenna in SA 32 after the island was given to the Edain by the Valar. In SA 3319, when Ar-Pharazôn landed on Aman the Blessed, Elenna was destroyed and sunk beneath the Sea.

Called in Westron the Land of the Star, since the Edain reached it using Eärendil as a guide. (III 390)

**ELENYA** (Q.: 'star's-day') The first day of the enquië in all Elven, Dúnedain and related calendars.

Called in Sindarin Orgilion, and Sterrendei by the Hobbits. (III 484)

**ELESSAR** (Q.: 'elf-stone') The name under which Aragorn (q. v.) took the throne of the Reunited Kingdom. It was foretold for him by Galadriel, and was given him by the people of Gondor during the WR because of the great emerald brooch, a gift from Arwen, which he wore. (I 486; III 302-10)

**ELF-FRIENDS** The Three Houses of the Elf-friends, the Edain (q. v.).

"Elf-friend" was also a title or epithet bestowed by Elves upon those of other races who aided them or liked them. Bilbo and Frodo, for example, were elf-friends. (I 119; III 507; H 277)

**ELFHELM** (fl. WR) Rider of Rohan, marshal of the éored with which Éowyn and Merry rode to the Battle of the Pelennor Fields. Later in the WR, Elfhelm commanded the Rohirrim that defended Anórien while the Host of the West rode to the Morannon. (III 127, 135, 193)

**ELFHILD** (d. TA 2978) Woman of Rohan, wife of King Théoden. Elfhild died while giving birth to her only child, Théodred. (III 437)

**ELFSTAN FAIRBAIRN** (b. FA 34) Hobbit of the Shire, eldest son and heir of Fastred and Elanor, and first of the Fairbairns of the Tower. He was probably Warden of Westmarch.

Elfstan's name means "elfstone" in translated Hobbitish; he was probably named after King Elessar. (III 471)

**ELFWINE** (early F. A.) Man, nineteenth King of Rohan (63-?). He was known as Elfwine the Fair. (III 438)

**ELLADAN** (S.: 'elf-man') (TA 139-FA ?) Elda, son of Elrond and Celebrían and identical twin brother of Elrohir. With his brother he rescued Celebrían from an Orc-hold in TA 2509, and ever after the brothers rode against the Orcs with the Rangers to avenge their mother's torment. During the WR Elladan and Elrohir rode south with Halbarad, and accompanied Aragorn from Rohan to the Morannon. Because of their Elven-wisdom and the counsel they had received from their father before setting forth, Elladan and Elrohir were present at the councils of the Lords of the West, and may themselves have been numbered among the Lords.

Elladan and Elrohir remained in Imladris well into the Fourth Age, and since they did not accompany Elrond over Sea they seem to have chosen to become mortal. (I 39, 300; III 60, 389, 456)

**ELROHIR** (S.: 'elf-horse-master') (TA 139-FA ?) Elda, son of Elrond and Celebrían and identical twin brother of Elladan (q. v.). (I 39, 300; III 60, 456)

**ELROND** (S.: 'star---') (First Age- ) One of the Peredhil, the son of Elwing and Eärendil, renowned for his wisdom and knowledge of lore. He was present at the Battle of the Valar. At the end of the First Age Elrond chose to become of Elven-kind, and was made by the Valar an Eldarin lord of great power and a master of wisdom. He dwelt in Lindon with Gil-galad until SA 1695, when he was sent by the latter to Eregion to aid in the defense of that realm against Sauron. When Eregion was overrun in 1697, Elrond fled with the surviving Noldor and founded Imladris, which became, especially after the fall of Gil-galad, one of the greatest Elven refuges in Middle-earth. During the war of the Last Alliance Elrond was Gil-galad's herald, and stood by him when he fell.

In TA 100 Elrond married Celebrían, the daughter of Galadriel and Celeborn; their children were Elladan, Elrohir and Arwen. Throughout the Third Age Elrond gave aid and counsel to the Dúnedain of the North, first military aid for the protection of Arnor and Arthedain and later shelter for the Dúnedain, especially the women and children of the royal line. At the end of the Third Age Elrond departed over Sea with the Last Riding of the Keepers of the Rings.

Elrond bore the greatest of the Three Rings, Vilya, which he was given by Gil-galad. (I 258, 292, 296, 299, 319; III 381-84, 389, 454, 456; H 60-61)

**ELROS** (S.: 'star-foam'?) (FA?-SA 442) One of the Peredhil, son of Eärendil and Elwing and brother of Elrond. At the end of the First Age he chose mortality, and, taking the royal name Tar-Minyatur, became the first King of Númenor (32-442), with a life-span many times that of lesser Men. His heirs were the Kings of Númenor, Arnor and Gondor. (III 389-90, 453)

**ELVENHOME** Eldamar (q. v.). (I 309; III 289; TB 63)

**ELVENHOME** Doriath (q. v.), or perhaps Beleriand, in the song of Beren and Lúthien. (I 258)

**ELVENHOME** Probably an Elven-realm somewhere in Beleriand. (TB 8, 53)

**ELVENKING, THE** Thranduil (q. v.). (H 168)

**ELVEN RINGS** The Three Rings (q. v.).

**ELVEN SMITHS** The Noldor of Eregion, ruled by Celebrimbor. In SA 750 Eregion was settled by Noldor from Lindon because of its proximity to the mithril-mine in Khazad-dûm. The Elven-smiths were friendlier with Durin's Folk than any other Elves and Dwarves ever were, and together the two peoples performed great works.

However, about 1200 Sauron seduced the smiths, and instructed them in many skills. About 1500 they began forging the Rings of Power under his direction. When the Rings were completed in 1590, Sauron betrayed the smiths and forged the One Ring. Celebrimbor discovered the treachery, but in 1697 Sauron's armies overran Eregion, killing Celebrimbor and most of the Noldor.

Elrond led the few surviving Elven-smiths to Rivendell. It is likely that these smiths forged Andúril for Aragorn in TA 3018. (I 318; III 453, 453-54)

**ELVES** The eldest and noblest of the speaking races of Middle-earth. Early in the First Age the Elves became divided into two groups: the Three Kindreds of the Eldar (q. v.), nobler than the rest, who received the call of the Valar to go to Valinor, and the Silvan Elves (q.v.). These two groups were sometimes called the West-elves and the East-elves, respectively. The Elves flourished in the First Age, but by the Third their power was waning. Many of the Elves of Middle-earth in the Third Age lived in Elven-realms and refuges such as Lindon, Imladris, the Woodland Realm and Lórien, where Eldarin lords ruled over Silvan Elves; many Elves were members of Wandering Companies. In the Fourth Age, with almost all the Eldar having gone to Valinor, the Silvan Elves dwindled and became a secret people.

Elves were about six feet tall and somewhat slender; they were graceful but strong, and were resistant to the extremes of nature. Their senses, especially of hearing and sight, were much keener than those of Men. Elves did not die naturally, but could be killed. Elves, or at least the Eldar, seem to have aged physically only until they reached the appearance they most desired. Elves did not sleep, but rested their minds by thinking of past ages or looking at beautiful things. They, or at least the Eldar, could talk directly from mind to mind without words. Elves, especially the Eldar, were very wise and had power to shape or realize the thoughts of others; they also had an insatiable curiosity about all things, and even at one point taught the trees of Fangorn Forest to speak so that they could find out what they were thinking. The Elves loved all beautiful things, but especially growing things such as trees, music and above all the stars.

Elves and Men were on good terms until the Fourth Age, when Men ceased to understand them. There was some intermarriage between the Eldar and the Edain and Dúnedain,

and perhaps between Silvan Elves and Men as well. Because
of great strife of some kind in the First Age, Elves and
Dwarves were not very friendly. Elves hated all things evil
and ugly, and so were usually at enmity with Sauron, but at
various times Elves were seduced by people evil but fair.

The Elves had the Three Rings of Power, which were
given to the three greatest of the Eldar.

The Elves called themselves Quendi, which in Quenya
meant "the Speakers." They were also called the Elder
Kindred, the Elder Race, the Elder People, the Fair Folk
and the Firstborn. (I 17, 123-24, 472, 503; II 37, 84, 90; III
181-82, 289, 325-26, 421, 519; H 57-60, 150-53, 164-65; TB 53)

**ELVET-ISLE**  Island in the lower Withywindle; in Hobbit-
lore the home of the Old Swan. (TB 19, 23)

**ELVISH**  See: Eldarin, Silvan.

**ELWING**  (S.: 'star---') (First Age) Eldarin princess, daughter
of Dior and wife of Eärendil, to whom she gave her Silmaril.
Elwing bore Eärendil two children, Elrond and Elros.

Elwing was known as Elwing the White. (I 261, 309)

**EMBLEMS**  Identifying insigniæ used on banners, shields,
and sometimes also used attributively.

The emblems described in *LotR* are:

Anárion--the (setting) sun. (I 362)

Dol Amroth--a white swan-ship on a blue field, or a swan
and a white ship. (III 180)

Dúnedain of the North--a many-pointed silver star. (II 60)

Durin and his heirs--an anvil and hammer surmounted by a
crown set with seven eight-rayed stars. (I 397, 399; RHM III
439-40)

Eldar--Galathilion, bearing a crescent moon. (I 397)

Elendil and his heirs in Gondor--The White Tree, surmounted
by a silver crown and surrounded by Seven Stars (q. v.). In the
North, the emblem was just the Seven Stars. (III 26, 150)

Eregion--holly. (I 395)

Gondor--the White Tree. (III 150)

House of Fëanor--an eight-rayed silver star. (I 397; RHM
III 439)

Isildur--a (rising) moon. (I 362)

Minas Morgul--a moon (for Minas Ithil) disfigured by a
death's-head. (III 219)

North-kingdom--the Star of Elendil (q. v.). (RHM III 439)

Rohan--a white horse on a green field. (III 138, 438)

Saruman--a white hand on a black field, sometimes with an s-rune. (II 20)

Sauron--The Red Eye or the Lidless Eye. (II 21; III 117)

Stewards of Gondor—a white field with no device. (III 414)

**EMYN ARNEN** (S.: 'hills of the royal water'?) Hills in South Ithilien, across Anduin from Minas Tirith. After the WR Emyn Arnen was the dwelling-place of the Princes of Ithilien. (I 23, 305)

**EMYN BERIAD** (S.: 'tower-hills') The Tower Hills (q. v.). (III 471)

**EMYN MUIL** (S.: 'hills---') Rough hill-country on either side of Anduin above Rauros, mostly composed of sharp ridges and deep valleys running north and south. (I 492, 498; II 27 ff., 265 ff.)

**ENCHANTED RIVER** River in Mirkwood, flowing from its source in the Mountains of Mirkwood north until it joined the Forest River. Anyone who drank of its waters or bathed in it fell into a deep sleep and dreamed of Elven-feasts in Mirkwood. (H 13, 133, 142-45, 149)

**ENCIRCLING MOUNTAINS** Mountains in the First Age, home of Thorondor, the first of the great eagles. The Encircling Mountains may have been in Beleriand. (III 278)

**ENDERI** (Q.: 'middle-days') Days added to the calendar in the middle of the year to make the year of the proper length without ruining the equal lengths of the months.

In the Calendar of Imladris there were three enderi between the yávië and quellë, and six in leap years. In the Kings' and Stewards' Reckoning, the two enderi replaced loëndë in leap years, while in the New Reckoning there were three enderi between Yavannië and Narquelië, the second of which was called Loëndë. The Lithe was in the Shire Reckoning equivalent to the enderi. (III 480)

**ENDLESS STAIR** Spiral stair in Khazad-dûm going from the lowest dungeon to Durin's Tower. The Endless Stair was built early in the First Age and was ruined in TA 3019, during the Battle of the Peak. (II 134)

**ENDORE** (Q.: 'middle-land') Middle-earth (q. v.). (III 490)

**ENEDWAITH** (S.: 'giant-waste'?) Land south of the Gwathlo perhaps including Dunland. Once part of Gondor, Enedwaith was devastated by great floods in TA 2912, and whatever people still lived there at that time left or died. (I 16; III 461)

**ENNOR**  (S.: 'middle-land)  Middle-earth (q. v.). (III 490)

**ENQUIË**  (Q.: 'week')  The six-day ritual week of the Eldar, and the seven-day weeks of the Númenoreans, the Dúnedain and the Westron area. The Quenya names for the days of the Eldarin enquië were Elenya, Anarya, Isilya, Aldúya, Menelya and Valanya or Tárion. The Dúnedain names were the same except that Aldëa was the fourth day, Valanya was the seventh day, and Eärenya was the sixth.

The enquië was adopted throughout Middle-earth by Men and Hobbits. For Hobbits, and probably also for others, Highdei (Valanya) was the chief day. (III 479, 484)

**ENT-DRAUGHTS**  The drinks given to Merry and Pippin by Fangorn, which seem to have comprised, with water, the sole nourishment of the Ents. Two kinds of Ent-draughts are described, one primarily refreshing, and the other primarily nourishing. The Ent-draughts made the Hobbits uncommonly large. (II 93, 103)

**ENTISH**  The language of the Ents, a "slow, sonorous, agglomerated, repetitive" language with very fine distinctions of tone and length. No one not an Ent had ever managed to learn Entish, as the language was exceedingly difficult and unlike all others. (III 510)

**ENTMOOT**  A formal council of Ents, traditionally held in the Derndingle in Fangorn Forest. The Entmoot held in TA 3019 which decided to attack Isengard lasted only three days, which seems to have been rather short. (II 103, 105-09)

**ENTS**  Tree-herders, perhaps the oldest speaking race in Middle-earth. Created sometime early in the morning of the world, the nature of the Ents was closely connected with that of the trees they protected and guarded. Sometime in the First Age the Ents came in contact with the Eldar, who taught them Quenya and Sindarin. Later in the First Age the male and female Ents became estranged; the Entwives crossed Anduin and tended their favorite plants--small trees, grasses, fruit trees, flowers and vegetables--in what was later called the Brown Lands, while the male Ents tended their larger trees in the forest that stretched from the Old Forest to Fangorn, and was called the Great Wood. The Entwives were greatly honored by Men, to whom they taught the skills of agriculture, but sometime before the end of the Second Age their gardens were destroyed and they vanished.

The Ents in the Third Age remained in the  Forest of

Fangorn, growing old without hope of having children. Some of the Ents grew "treeish" and ceased moving or speaking, but some, like Fangorn, remained active and alert. About TA 2950 Saruman began harassing the Ents and cutting down their trees; in 3019, as a result of the appearance of Merry and Pippin, Fangorn realized that something had to be done. He aroused the remaining active Ents, and they attacked and destroyed Isengard. In the Fourth Age the Ents probably remained in Fangorn Forest and dwindled.

An Ent looked like a fourteen-foot-tall cross between a tree and a Man; a full description of an Ent is given on II 83, although Fangorn's beard may have been exceptional. Ents resembled different trees, and individual Ents cared for and honored the kind of tree they looked like, and to a certain extent possessed the personality one might expect of that tree. Ents did not die naturally; their skin was extremely tough, but they could be burned. Ents thought slowly and were slow to act, but once aroused they possessed the strength of the age-long action of trees compressed in a few seconds; they could crack rocks and move large quantities of earth easily and quickly. Ents were nourished by Ent-draughts.

The Ents spoke Entish. They also knew many other languages, but preferred Quenya, which they spoke after the same fashion as they did Entish.

The name "Ent" was given them by the Rohirrim, and means "giant" in Old English. They were called Onodrim or Enyd in Sindarin by the Elves; the singular was *Onod*. (I 73; II 83, 84, 88-89, 99-100, 105-16, 131, 196-97, 216-22; III 320-21, 510)

**ENTWADE** Fords on the Entwash northeast of Edoras. (II 45; III 14)

**ENTWASH** River coming out of Fangorn and flowing through Rohan to Anduin, which it joined in a large marshy delta, the Mouths of Entwash. (I 17; II 38; III 14)

**ENTWASH VALE** The valley of the lower Entwash, including the Mouths of Entwash. Entwash Vale was a green, fenny area. (II 30)

**ENTWOOD** Fangorn Forest, so called in Rohan. (II 197)

**ENYD** (S.) The Ents (q. v.). (III 510)

**ÉOMER** (TA 2991-FA 63) Man, eighteenth King of Rohan (TA 3019-FA 63), son of Théodwyn and Éomund and nephew of King Théoden. Before the WR, Éomer was the Third Marshal of Riddermark, and was in charge of the East-mark. He was a valiant warrior and a discerning man, friendly to Gandalf and hating Gríma. Although he fell into Théoden's disfavor as a result of Gríma's plots, his loyalty was proven and during the WR he fought nobly at the Hornburg, the Pelennor Fields and the Morannon, and became friendly with Aragorn. Théoden, at his death during the Battle of the Pelennor Fields, named Éomer as his heir. After the WR Éomer became King of Rohan, and renewed the Oath of Eorl with King Elessar. During his long reign he ruled Rohan well, and often fought beside Elessar in foreign lands.

In 3020 Éomer married Lothíriel of Dol Amroth; she bore him at least one child, Elfwine the Fair. (II 42-51; III 135, 144-52, 437-38)

**ÉOMUND** (d. TA 3002) Man of Rohan, husband of Théodwyn and father of Éomer and Éowyn. Éomund was the chief marshal of the Mark, and was in charge of the east marches. He was noted for his hot and unwary pursuit of raiding Orcs, and during one of these pursuits was ambushed and slain. Éomund came from Eastfold. (II 42; III 437)

**ÉORED** A fighting-force of Rohan, composed of the men of a lord's household. Éomer's, which was perhaps typical, had 104 men. All the éoreds were probably cavalry units. (II 39, 45, 48; III 127)

**EORL** (TA 2485-2545) Man, Lord of Éothéod (2501-10) and first King of Rohan (2510-45). In 2510, answering a summons for aid from Cirion of Gondor, Eorl and his Riders defeated an army of Balchoth and Orcs in the Battle of the Field of Celebrant. As a reward, the Riders were given Calenardhon, and Eorl swore the Oath of Eorl. He was slain in a battle in the Wold with Easterlings.

Eorl was a great warrior and horse-master. His horse, Felaróf, was the first of the mearas (qq. v.). Eorl was known as "the Young" because he succeeded his father Léod in his youth, and kept his yellow hair throughout his life. (II 143, 148; III 415, 428-31, 434)

**EORLINGAS** The Rohirrim (q. v.), so called because they considered themselves the descendents of Eorl. (II 155; III 430)

**ÉOTHAIN** (fl. WR) Man of Rohan, a member of Éomer's éored. (II 45)

**ÉOTHÉOD**   Land near the sources of Anduin, named after
the Éothéod (q. v.), who founded it in TA 1977 after the
fall of Angmar, which had previously controlled the area.
In 2510 Eorl Lord of Éothéod led an army to Gondor to
fight in the Battle of the Field of Celebrant, and he and
his people then settled in Rohan. (III 428-29, 458)

**ÉOTHÉOD, THE**   Men of the Vales of Anduin, related to the
Third House of the Edain. They originally lived between
the Carrock and the Gladden, but in TA 1977, being crowded
and hearing of the fall of Angmar, moved to an area near
the sources of Anduin. They drove out the Orcs living there
and named the land Éothéod.

In 2510, under their lord Eorl, the Éothéod rode to Gondor
to aid Cirion against the Balchoth. After winning the Battle
of the Field of Celebrant, the Riders of Éothéod were granted Calenardhon to live in. From this time on they called
themselves the Eorlingas and were called the Rohirrim
(q. v.) by the men of Gondor.

*Éothéod* is translated Rohirric, in Old English it meant
"horse-folk." (III 428-29, 458)

**ÉOWYN**   (TA 2995-FA ?)   Woman of Rohan, daughter of Éomund and Théodwyn and sister of Éomer. During the WR
she met and fell in love with Aragorn; when he rode the
Paths of the Dead she despaired greatly, thinking him lost.
Being of a martial spirit, in her desperation she disguised
herself as a man and, calling herself Dernhelm, rode to
Gondor with Elfhelm's éored. In the Battle of the Pelennor
Fields, with the aid of Merry she won great renown by slay-
ing the Lord of the Nazgûl and his steed. The evil coming
from contact with the Nazgûl-lord, amplified by the years of
waiting on Théoden in his dotage and her hopeless love for
Aragorn, caused in her a severe case of the Black Breath.

Aragorn released her from the illness with athelas, and
while recovering she realized her true heart. Giving up her
desire to be a free, independent shield-maiden, she married
Faramir and became Lady of Ithilien.

Éowyn was very beautiful; she was tall, slim and graceful, with golden hair. (II 152; III 91, 93, 141-45, 174-77,
291-300, 315-16, 437)

**EPHEL DÚATH**   (S.: 'outer-fences dark-collective plural')
The mountains forming the west and south borders of Mordor,
a great chain perhaps 800 miles long. In the north the Ephel
Duath met the Ered Lithui at Isenmouthe and Cirith Gorgor.

Called in Westron the Mountains of Shadow or the Shadowy Mountains. (I 17; II 308, 402-47 passim.; III 236)

**ERADAN** (S.) (d. TA 2116) Dúnadan, second Ruling Steward of Gondor (2080-2116). (III 395)

**EREBOR** (S.: 'single-mountain') Mountain east of Mirkwood and West of the Iron Hills. Erebor was first settled by Thráin I, who came there with a large part of Durin's Folk after fleeing from Moria, and founded the Kingdom under the Mountain in TA 1999. The Kingdom was for a while (from about 2190 to 2590) lessened in numbers and glory while the Kings of Durin's Folk dwelled in the Ered Mithrin, but dragons caused Thrór to return to Erebor in 2590. The fame and richness of Erebor grew for nearly two hundred years, until in 2770 Smaug plundered the Dwarf-kingdom. Smaug dwelled in Erebor with his hoard until 2941, when he was disturbed by Thorin and Company and slain by Bard. Dáin II re-established the Kingdom under the Mountain, and its halls became once more fair and its people wealthy. During the WR Erebor was besieged by an army of Easterlings, but after the downfall of Sauron the Dwarves and the Men of Dale routed the besiegers. In the Fourth Age Erebor was independent, but was allied with and protected by the Reunited Kingdom.

Called in Westron the Lonely Mountain and the Mountain.

See: Great Hall of Thráin, the Lower Halls, the Front Gate, Ravenhill. (I 302-03; III 439, 459-61, 468-69; H 196-271 passim.)

**ERECH** Hill in Lamedon upon which stood the Stone of Erech (q. v.). Here the King of the Mountains swore allegiance to Isildur, and throughout the Third Age Erech was haunted by the Dead Men of Dunharrow.

*Erech* is of pre-Númenorean origin, and thus comes from some Mannish tongue of the Second Age. Also called the Hill of Erech. (III 14, 64-65, 73-74, 508)

**ERED LITHUI** (S.: 'ashy mountains') The mountain chain forming the northern border of Mordor, stretching east about 400 miles from the Morannon.

Called in Westron the Ash Mountains or the Ashen Mountains. (I 17; II 308)

**ERED LUIN** (S.: 'blue mountains') Mountains running north and south from the Gulf of Lune, forming the border between Beleriand (later Lindon) and Eriador. Dwarves dwelled in the Ered Luin from the First Age into the Fourth, and between TA 2810 and 2941 the Kings of Durin's Folk lived here. In TA 1974 deserted dwarf-mines in the northern Ered Luin were for a time the hiding-place of Arvedui. The ruined Dwarvish cities of Belegost and Nogrod were in the Ered Luin.

Called in Westron the Blue Mountains and the Mountains of Lune. (I 16, 72; II 90; III 396, 398, 439, 445)

**ERED MITHRIN** (S.: 'grey mountains') Mountains north of Mirkwood, home of the dragons. About TA 2200, most of Durin's Folk gathered in the Ered Mithrin, but they were forced to leave by 2589 due to the rise of dragons and cold-drakes. (I 17; III 430, 440, 459)

**ERED NIMRAIS** (S.: 'white mountains') Mountain chain of Gondor, running westward from Minas Tirith almost to the Sea. Originally home of a race of Men related to the Dunlendings (q. v.), in the Third Age the Ered Nimrais was chiefly the site of retreats of the Rohirrim and Men of Gondor such as Dunharrow and Helm's Deep. The Paths of the Dead went through the Ered Nimrais.

Important peaks of the Ered Nimrais included Mindolluin, Dwimorberg, Starkhorn, the Thrihyrne and the peaks of the northern beacon-towers of Gondor.

Called in Westron the White Mountains. (I 338; II 167, 371; III 416)

**EREGION** (S.) Land between the Glanduin and the Bruinen, settled about SA 750 by Celebrimbor and other Noldorin Elven-smiths (q. v.). Eregion was laid waste in 1697 during the War of the Elves and Sauron.

Called in Westron Hollin. Both the Westron and Sindarin names may mean "land of holly," since holly was the emblem of the Elven-smiths. (I 76, 318, 369 ff.; III 396, 453, 453-54)

**ERELAS** (S.: 'single-leaf'?) The fourth of the northern beacon-tower hills of Gondor. (III 20)

**ERESSËA** (Q.: 'lonely-isle') The island close to the shore of Valinor in the Undying Lands, part of Eldamar.

Also called the Lost Isle, reflecting the meaning of the name *Eressëa* and the remoteness of the island from Middle-earth. (I 321; III 289, 390, 452; R 62)

**ERESTOR** (S.) (fl. WR) Elf of Rivendell, Elrond's chief counsellor. (I 315)

**ERIADOR** (S.: 'land of the kings'?) Land between the Misty
Mountains and the Ered Luin, bounded on the south by
Gwathlo and Glanduin and on the north by the Forodwaith.
Once a prosperous and well-populated area, Eriador was
decimated by the wars with Angmar and the Great Plague,
until by the end of the Third Age only a few people lived
in Rivendell, the Bree-land, the Shire and a few other
scattered habitations.

See also: Minhiriath, Eregion, Rivendell, Arnor, Rhudaur,
Arthedain, Cardolan, the Shire, the Bree-land. (I 16; III
396, 454, 457)

**ERKENBRAND** (fl. WR) Man of Rohan, master of Westfold
and the Hornburg, a noted warrior. Erkenbrand commanded
the forces of Rohan at the Second Battle of the Fords of
Isen, and regrouped his forces after the battle and returned
to Helm's Deep in time to complete the rout of Saruman's
forces at the Battle of the Hornburg. (II 168, 170, 172,
186, 191)

**ERLING** (b. TA 2854) Hobbit of the Shire, of the working
class. Erling was the third child of Holman the greenhanded. (III 477)

*ERRANTRY* A cyclical narrative poem contained in the Red
Book of Westmarch, probably written by Bilbo Baggins soon
after 2941. Although most of the names in the poem are
borrowed from Elvish verse, the poem is not serious and
the names are not real.

*Errantry* does, however, contain some possible references
to the history of the Dúnedain of Numenor, and it is not
inconceivable that on his trip to Erebor with Thorin and
Company Bilbo heard scraps of tales of the Second Age and
used them, somewhat fancifully, in the poem. (TB 7-8, 24-27)

**ERU** (S.: 'the one') God, more or less. Eru is that power
superior to the Valar and for whom they labored in the creation of the world. He created the peoples of Middle-earth,
and His was the over-all plan for the world. It is not clear
which races acknowledged or worshipped Him; He was
associated most definitely with Elves and Men.

Also called the One. (III 392; R 66; RP 9/12/65)

**ERUI** (S.) River of Gondor, flowing from Lossarnach into
Anduin.

See: Crossings of Erui. (III 15, 185)

**ERUSĒN** (S.? Q.?: 'children of God') Men and Elves, seemingly the chosen races, best loved by Eru and the Valar. It was for the Erusēn that Arda was prepared. However, since mortals were not permitted to sail to the West, the Erusēn seem to have been more specifically Elves than Men. (R 66)

**ERYN LASGALEN** (S.: 'wood of green leaves') Name given Mirkwood after its cleansing in TA 3019. The southern part, ruled at the beginning of the Fourth Age, was called East Lórien, while the part north of the Mountains was the Woodland Realm. The land in between was inhabited by the Beornings and the Woodmen. (III 468)

**ESGALDUIN** (S.: '---green-river') Enchanted river of Doriath, beside which Beren first saw Lúthien. (I 260)

**ESGAROTH** City of Men, located on the Long Lake. Its location was good for commerce, and Esgaroth supplied food and drink to Erebor and the Woodland Realm from the south and east, while the products of Erebor and Dale were funneled through Esgaroth. Esgaroth was destroyed by Smaug in TA 2941, but was rebuilt using gold from his hoard.

Esgaroth was governed by a Master, chosen by the people, or perhaps by the important local merchants.

Esgaroth was built of wood on stilts driven into the bottom of the Long Lake. (I 55; H 172, 185-93, 234-38, 239, 286)

**ESMERALDA BRANDYBUCK** (b. TA 2936) Hobbit of the shire, wife of Saradoc Brandybuck and mother of Merry. Esmerelda was the fifth and youngest child of Adalgrim Took. She was a guest at the Farewell Party. (I 56; III 475, 476)

**ESSE** (Q.: 'name') Alternate name for the tengwa ƺ (number 31, used when this sign represented ss after the original z (as in áze) had changed to r. (III 500)

**ESTEL** (S.: 'hope') The name by which Aragorn II (q. v.) was known in his youth, to keep Sauron from learning that he was the heir of Isildur. (III 420)

**ETHIR ANDUIN** (S.) The delta of Anduin, in southern Gondor. Called in Westron the Mouths of Anduin. (I 518)

**ETHRING** (S.) Fords or town on the Ringló, on the road from Erech to Pelargir. (III 15)

**ETHUIL** (S.) The Sindarin form of tuilë' (q. v.). (III 480)

**ETTENDALES, ETTENMOORS**  Troll-fells north of Rivendell. The source of the Mitheithel was in the Ettenmoors.
The Ettenmoors and the Coldfells may have been the
same place. (I 268, 271; III 458)

**EVENDIM**  Name given to undómë (q. v.) in the Shire. (III 485)

**EVARARD TOOK**  (b. TA 2980)  Hobbit of the Shire, youngest child of Adelard Took. He was a guest at the Farewell
Party. (I 54; III 475)

**EVEREVEN**  Valinor, after it was drowned in shadow by
Elbereth as a result of the rebellion of Morgoth and the
revolt of the Noldor.
       Also called Ever-eve. (I 310, 482)

**EVERHOLT**  A place in the Firien Wood. (III 435)

**EVERMIND**  Simbelmynë (q. v.). (II 142)

**EVERNIGHT**  See: the Shadows. (I 309)

**EXILES**  Those of the Noldor (q. v.) who returned to Middle-
earth with Fëanor to recover the Silmarils from Morgoth.
Most of the Exiles were slain in the War of the Great
Jewels, and the survivors, except Galadriel, were permitted
to return to Valinor at the end of the First Age. (III 506)

**EXILES**  Elendil and the Faithful who survived the fall of
Númenor and escaped to Middle-earth. (III 393)

**EYE**  The Eye of Sauron, the form of his appearance to the
outside world at the time of the WR and his emblem. The
Eye was rimmed with fire, but glazed like a cat's; its
pupil was a slit. As an emblem, the Eye was usually all
red.
       Also used attributively for Sauron.
       Also called the Evil Eye, the Great Eye, the Lidless
Eye, the Red Eye and the Eye of Barad-dûr. (I 471, 519;
II 21, 61, 131, 248, 267; III 117, 202)

# F

**FAERIE**  Eldamar (q. v.). (H 164)

**FAERIE**  An Elven-realm, in Bilbo's poem *Errantry*. Any relationship to real places of any Age is probably accidental. (TB 25)

**FAIRBAIRN OF THE TOWER**  A Hobbit family, descended from Elfstan Fairbairn, son of Fastred of Greenholm and Elanor Gamgee. The Fairbairns were Wardens of Westmarch; they also kept, added to and made copies of the Red Book of Westmarch. The Fairbairns lived at Undertowers. (I 37; III 471, 477)

**FAITHFUL**  Those few Númenoreans who remained friendly with the Eldar and continued to honor the Valar despite the estrangement of Tar-Atanamir (SA 2251) and later kings from the West. In SA 2350 the Faithful founded Pelargir, which became their chief haven in Middle-earth. Beginning in 2899, the Faithful were persecuted by the Kings of Númenor, but nonetheless persisted in their beliefs and in the use of the Eldarin languages. A remnant of the Faithful, led by Elendil, survived the fall of Númenor in 3319 and in 3320 founded the Dúnedain realms of Arnor and Gondor in Middle-earth.

Most of the Faithful were found in Andúnië, and they were led by the Lords of Andúnië. (III 391-93)

**FALASTUR**  (Q.: 'coast-lord') (d. TA 913)  Dúnadan, twelfth King of Gondor (830-913) and the first Ship-king. His birthname was Tarannon; he took the crown as Falastur to commemorate his victories as Captain of the Hosts. Falastur began the policy, kept until after 1200, of building great fleets and extending Gondor's power along the coasts of the Bay of Belfalas, and even further to the south.

Falastur was the first childless king, and was succeeded by his nephew Eärnil. (III 394, 403)

**FALCO CHUBB-BAGGINS**  (TA 2903-2999)  Hobbit of the Shire, son of Bingo Baggins and Chica Chubb. Falco was the first Chubb-Baggins. (III 474)

*FALL OF GIL-GALAD, THE*  Elven-song, translated into Westron by Bilbo. The song dealt with the death of Gil-Galad during the Siege of the Barad-dûr. (I 250, 251)

**FALLOHIDES**   The least numerous of the three strains of Hobbits. About TA 1150 the Fallohides left their ancestral home on the upper Anduin, crossed the Misty Mountains north of Rivendell and entered Eriador, where they mingled with other Hobbits. Because of their adventurous spirit, Fallohides were frequently found as leaders of tribes of other kinds of Hobbits. Marcho and Blanco, the founders of the Shire, were Fallohides, as were the Tooks, Brandybucks and Bolgers. Bilbo and Frodo Baggins also had Fallohide blood.

The Fallohides were taller and slimmer than other Hobbits, and had fairer skin and hair. They liked trees and forests, and had more skill in the arts than in handicrafts. They were friendlier with Elves than were other Hobbits. (I 22; III 457, 516)

**FANG**   (fl. WR)   One of Farmer Maggot's wolf-like dogs. (I 133, 134)

**FANGORN**   (S.: 'beard-tree') (First Age-   ) Ent, the guardian of Fangorn Forest. At the time of the WR Fangorn was the oldest surviving Ent, and thus the oldest living being in Middle-earth. Fangorn was responsible for arousing the Ents against Saruman during the WR, and probably also sent the Huorns to the Hornburg.

Fangorn was bearded, and seems to have resembled an evergreen tree.

Called in Westron Treebeard; he was called Eldest by Celeborn. (II 83 ff., 131; III 317-21, 510)

**FANGORN FOREST**   Wood of great age east of the southern end of the Misty Mountains, watered by the Entwash and Limlight. Fangorn was the eastern remnant of the great forest that once covered all of Eriador and extended into Beleriand. The Ents lived in Fangorn Forest.

During the last century of the Third Age Orcs of Isengard did great damage to Fangorn, but this stopped with the destruction of Isengard by the Ents during the WR.

Fangorn was a wild, visibly old forest. There were places in it where the shadow of the Great Darkness had never been lifted.

Fangorn was named after Fangorn the Ent, the oldest Ent living there at the time of the WR and the guardian of the Forest. Called the Entwood by the Rohirrim; also called Fangorn and the Forest of Fangorn. Ambarona, Tauremorna, Aldalómë and Tauremornalómë were epithets applied to the Forest by Fangorn the Ent. (I 17, 484; II 55, 80 ff., esp. 89,

90-91)

**FANTASIE**   A probably-imaginary land in Bilbo's poem *Errantry*. (TB 25)

**FANUIDHOL**   (S.: 'cloudy-head')   Elvish name for Bundusha-thûr (q. v.).
Also called Fanuidhol the Grey. (I 370)

**FANUILOS**   (S.: *'fana*-ever-white')   Elbereth (q. v.). (I 312; R 66)

**FARAMIR**   (Q.?: '---jewel') (d. TA 1944)   Dúnadan of Gondor, son of King Ondoher. He was slain in battle with the Wainriders. (III 409)

**FARAMIR**   (TA 2983-FA 82)   Dúnadan of Gondor, second son of Denethor II. Faramir was a gentle, discerning man, a lover of lore and music and a reader of men's minds. Unlike his brother Boromir, he did not care for battle for its own sake, but was nonetheless a brave warrior, much loved by his soldiers. Because of his gentle nature and his love of Gandalf, he displeased his father.
Before the WR, Faramir was Captain of the Rangers of Ithilien. During the WR Faramir led the retreat from Osgiliath to Minas Tirith before the Siege of Gondor. He fell under the Black Breath, and was nearly cremated by Denethor in his madness. After being rescued by Beregond and Gandalf, he was healed by Aragorn. While recovering, he met and fell in love with Éowyn, whom he married after the WR. With the return of the King to Gondor, Faramir was made Steward of Gondor, Prince of Ithilien and Lord of Emyn Arnen. (II 336 ff.; III 101, 114-15, 153-62, 171-73, 292-303, 315, 396, 419, 462)

**FARAMIR TOOK**   (FA 10-?)   Hobbit of the Shire, son of Peregrin Took and thirty-third Thain of the Shire, from FA 64 to his death. Faramir married Goldilocks Gamgee in 43. (III 471, 475)

**FARAWAY**   Hills in Eriador near the western border of the Shire, home of the Lonely Troll in the Shire-poem of the same name. Faraway may have been fictitious. (TB 41, 43)

**FAR DOWNS**   Down marking the western boundary of the Shire until its expansion in FA 32. The Far Downs were originally called the Fox Downs. (I 16, 24; III 383, 471)

**FAREWELL PARTY**   Birthday party held in the Party Field on September 22, TA 3001 to celebrate the eleventy-first birthday of Bilbo and the coming of age of Frodo. The Party was quite spectacular, with 144 guests, huge amounts of food, fireworks by Gandalf and presents made as far away as Erebor. Toward the end of the Party, Bilbo put on the One Ring and disappeared from the Shire. (I 50-56; III 473)

**FAR HARAD**  The southern part of Harad. The Men of Far Harad were allied with Sauron in the WR, and some of them fought in the Battle of the Pelennor Fields. (III 148)

**FARIN**  (TA 2560-2803)  Dwarf of Durin's line, son of Borin and father of Fundin and Gróin. (III 450)

**FARMER COTTON**  Tolman Cotton (q. v.). (III 365)

**FARMER MAGGOT**  See: Maggot. (I 132)

**FAR WEST**  The Undying Lands (q. v.). (III 452)

**FASTOLPH BOLGER**  (TA 29th Cent.)  Hobbit of the Shire. He married Pansy Baggins. (III 474)

**FASTITOCALON**  A giant, perhaps mythical beast, the last of the Turtle-fish, in the Hobbitish poem of the same name. Fastitocalon was mistaken for an island by sailors, who were drowned when he submerged. (TB 48-49)

*FASTITOCALON*  A Hobbit-poem found in a margin of the Red Book of Westmarch. The poem may be a nonsense-rhyme. (TB 48-49)

**FASTRED**  (TA 2858-85)  Man of Rohan, son of King Folcwine and twin brother of Folcred. He and his brother led an army to aid Rohan against the Haradrim. The enemy was defeated in the Battle of the Crossings of Poros, but both Fastred and his brother were slain. (III 436)

**FASTRED**  (d. TA 3019)  Man of Rohan, slain in the Battle of the Pelennor Fields. (III 152)

**FASTRED OF GREENHOLM**  (FA 1st Cent.)  Hobbit of the Shire. In FA 31 he married Elanor Gamgee, and later moved with her to Undertowers. Fastred was probably the first Warden of Westmarch. (III 471, 477)

**FATHERS OF MEN**  The Edain (q. v.). (III 506)

**FATTY LUMPKIN**  (fl. WR)  Tom Bombadil's pony. (I 199)

**FËANOR**  (S.: '---sun') (First Age)  Noldorin Elf of noble lineage, the greatest Elven craftsman of all time. Fëanor invented silima, and he alone could make it. From silima he fashioned the Silmarils. When Morgoth stole them, against the will of the Valar Fëanor led a great part of the Noldor back to Middle-earth to recover the jewels, since he was also the proudest of the Eldar. He was slain in the War of the Great Jewels.

Fëanor was also credited with inventing the Tengwar in the form in which they were used in Middle-earth, and perhaps with fashioning the palantíri. (II 258, 260; III 388, 493)

**FELAGUND**  See: Finrod. (III 400)

**FELARÓF**  (b. before TA 2500, d. 2545)  Horse, the mount of King Eorl and the first of the mearas. Originally a wild horse in Éothéod, Felaróf slew Léod, Eorl's father and a great horse-tamer, when Léod tried to mount him. As a wergild for this, Felaróf submitted himself to Eorl.

Felaróf was called Mansbane because he had slain Léod, and "father of horses" because he was the ancestor of the mearas. (II 143; III 430-31, 434)

**FELL WINTER**  The winter of TA 2911 as called in the annals of the Shire. Many rivers in Eriador, including the Baranduin, froze over, and much of the land, including the Shire, was invaded by White Wolves. (I 239, 377; III 461)

**FELLOWSHIP OF THE RING**  The Company of the Ring (q. v.). (III 320)

**FENGEL**  (TA 2870-2953)  Man, fifteenth King of Rohan (2903-53). Fengel was quarrelsome, greedy and gluttonous, and was very unpopular. (III 436)

**FEN HOLLEN**  (S.: 'the closed door')  Door in the western side of the sixth level of Minas Tirith, through which one went to reach the Hallows. Fen Hollen was so called because it was kept closed and guarded by a porter at all times, and was opened only for funerals.

Called in Westron the Closed Door. Also called the Steward's Door. (III 121, 123, 160)

**FENMARCH**  Area in Rohan, west of the Mering Stream and including all the land between the Mouths of Entwash and the Firien Wood. (III 14, 93-94)

**FERDIBRAND TOOK**  (b. TA 2983)  Hobbit of the Shire, son of Ferdinand Took. He was a guest at the Farewell Party. (III 475)

**FERDINAND TOOK**  (b. TA 2940)  Hobbit of the Shire, son of Sigismond Took. He was a guest at the Farewell Party. (III 475)

**FERNY** Family of Men of Bree. (I 212)

**FERUMBRAS TOOK** (TA 2701-2801) Hobbit of the Shire, son of Isumbras Took. As Ferumbras II he was the twenty-fourth Thain of the Shire (2759-2801). (III 475)

**FERUMBRAS TOOK** (TA 2916-3015) Hobbit of the Shire, son of Fortinbras Took. As Ferumbras III he was the thirtieth Thain of the Shire (2980-3015). Ferumbras was unmarried. He was a guest at the Farewell Party. (III 475)

**FIELD OF CELEBRANT** Meadow-lands between the Limlight and Silverlode, site in TA 2510 of the Battle of the Field of Celebrant. (I 17)

**FIELD OF CORMALLEN** (S.: 'ring-gold') Place in northern Ithilien near Henneth Annûn. The celebration of the downfall of Sauron in the WR was held here. (III 284-90)

**FIELDS OF PELENNOR** See: the Pelennor. (III 426)

**FIERY MOUNTAIN** Orodruin (q. v.). (I 94)

**FÍLI** (TA 2859-2941) Dwarf of Durin's Line, son of Dís and nephew of Thorin II. He was a member of Thorin and Company, and was slain, with his brother Kíli, defending Thorin's body in the Battle of Five Armies. (III 450; H 22, 26, 275)

**FILIBERT BOLGER** (fl. TA 3000) Hobbit of the Shire. He married Poppy Baggins, and was a guest at the Farewell Party. (III 474)

**FIMBRETHIL** (S.: 'thin-birch') An Entwife, loved by Fangorn. Called in Westron Wandlimb. (II 99, 100; III 510; RHM III 423)

**FINARPHIR** (S.? Q.?) (First Age) Noldorin Elf, founder of the royal house of which Galadriel and Finrod were members. (III 506)

**FINDEGIL** (S.: 'hair---star') (fl. FA 172) Man of Gondor, a King's Writer. Findegil made a copy of the Red Book of Westmarch for the Thain of the Shire. (I 38)

**FINDUILAS** (S.: 'hair---leaf') (TA 2950-2988) Dúnadan of Gondor, daughter of Adrahil of Dol Amroth, wife of Denethor II and mother of Boromir and Faramir. A beautiful and gentle woman, Finduilas after her marriage missed the Sea and the freedom of the south, and dreaded the Shadow of Mordor; she faded and died twelve years after marrying Denethor in 2976. (III 296, 418, 461, 462)

**FINGLAS** (S.: 'hair-leaf') (First Age-    ) Ent, one of the

three eldest Ents still living at the time of the WR. By the
end of the Third Age Finglas had grown quite sleepy and
"tree-ish," and moved very little. He was covered with
leaf-like hair.

Called in Westron Leaflock. (II 97-98)

**FINROD FELAGUND** (S.: 'hair-power---'?) (First Age)  Eldarin prince of the House of Finarphir, King of Nargothrond
and brother of Galadriel. Finrod gave his life to save Beren,
and for that was called "Friend-of-Men."

Finrod was golden-haired.

*Felagund* may be translated Adûnaic. (III 453, 506, 519)

**FIREFOOT** (fl. WR)  A horse of Rohan, mount of Éomer during
the WR. (II 164)

**FIRE OF DOOM**  The flames of the heart of Orodruin, found
in the depths of the Crack of Doom. (III 272)

**FÍRIEL** (Q.: 'mortal-woman') (fl. TA 1940)  Dúnadan of Gondor, daughter of King Ondoher. In 1940 she married Arvedui
of Arthedain. (III 409; TB 8)

**FÍRIEL** (fl. FA 100)  Hobbit of the Shire, daughter of Elanor
and Fastred. (TB 8)

**FÍRIEL**  Woman of Gondor, chief character in a Hobbit poem
originally derived from Gondor. Fíriel was very beautiful,
and for this reason Elves departing over Sea offered to take
her with them. Fíriel, however, was unable to do so because
of her mortality. (TB 61-64)

**FIRIENFELD** (tr. Roh.: 'mountain-field')  The meadow of
Dunharrow. (III 80-81)

**FIRIEN WOOD, FIRIENWOOD**  Oak-wood at the foot of the
Ered Nimrais, on the border between Rohan and Gondor. The
boar of Everholt dwelled in the Firienwood until it was slain
by Folca in TA 2864. The last of Gondor's beacon-tower hills,
Halifirien, was in the Firien Wood. (III 14, 92, 94, 435)

**FIRITH** (S.)  Sindarin name for quellë (q.v.). (III 480)

**FIRST AGE**  The first of the recorded ages of Middle-earth.
The First Age began near the beginning, possibly with the
Great Journey, and ended with the overthrow of Morgoth. In
the First Age racial friendships and enmities were established, and the events of this period formed the framework for
later ages. The Edain and the Elves became allied, and the
Dwarves and the Elves hostile. Morgoth rebelled and came

to Middle-earth, and Fëanor's attack on him in the War of the Great Jewels resulted in the destruction of Beleriand and of Morgoth, the foundation of Númenor, and the hatred of Morgoth's surviving servants for the Edain. In the First Age such evil creatures as Orcs and Trolls were first bred, but also the Peredhil were born, whose descendents were illustrious among Men and Elves ever after.

Also called the Elder Days. (III 452, 519)

**FIRST BATTLE OF THE FORDS OF ISEN** See: Battles of the Fords of Isen. (III 465)

**FIRST-BORN** The Elves (q. v.), or perhaps the Eldar. (I 294)

**FIRST DEEP** Level of Khazad-dûm just below the Great Gates. (I 426)

**FIRST EASTFARTHING TROOP** See: the Watch. (III 347)

**FIRST HOUSE OF THE EDAIN** One of the three houses of the Edain. Beren and Barahir were of the First House. (III 388)

**FIRST LINE** The first nine Kings of Rohan. The First Line began with Eorl, and the Kings of the First Line were descended from father to son. The last king of the First Line was Helm, who was succeeded by his nephew, his sons having fallen in the war against Wulf. (III 434-35)

**FIRST SHIRRIFF** An office and title of the Mayor of Michel Delving in his capacity of head of the Watch. (I 31)

**FISHER BLUE** A kingfisher of the Withywindle, in the Shire-poem *Bombadil Goes Boating*. (TB 18, 23)

**FLADRIF** (S.: 'skin-bark') (First Age-    ) Ent, one of the three eldest surviving Ents at the time of the WR. Fladrif lived west of Isengard, and when Saruman became evil he was wounded by Orcs and many of his trees killed. After this, Fladrif retreated to the higher slopes of Fangorn and refused to come down from there.

Fladrif probably resembled a birch tree.

Called in Westron Skinbark. (II 97-98)

**FLAMBARD TOOK** (TA 2887-2989) Hobbit of the Shire, son of Isembard Took. (III 475)

**FLAME OF ANOR** Whatever it was that Gandalf wielded. Possibly "Anor" is used in its secondary sense of "setting sun, west," and the Flame of Anor was some force or power of the Undying Lands.

Possibly equivalent to the Secret Fire. (I 429)

**FLAME OF UDÛN** The fire of the Balrog. See: Udûn. (I 429)

**FLAMMIFER OF WESTERNESSE** Eärendil (q. v.), as a star, so called because it guided the Edain to Númenor. (I 311)

**FLET** Talan (q. v.). (I 444)

**FLOATING LOG, THE** A good inn in Frogmorton, closed during the WR by Sharkey's Men. (III 345-46)

**FLÓI** (d. TA 2989) Dwarf. Flói went to Khazad-dûm with Balin in 2989 and was slain by an orc-arrow in a battle outside the Great Gates. It seems that Flói before he was slain killed an important enemy fighter, perhaps a troll or an uruk. He was buried near the Mirromere. (I 418)

**FOLCA** (TA 2804-64) Man, thirteenth King of Rohan (2851-64), a great hunter. Folca killed the last of the Orcs remaining in Rohan from the invasion of 2799, and also slew the boar of Everholt. He died of the tusk-wounds given him by the boar. (III 435)

**FOLCO BOFFIN** (fl. WR) Hobbit of the Shire, a good friend of Frodo Baggins. Folco was most probably a guest at the Farewell Party. (I 71, 102)

**FOLCRED** (TA 2858-85) Man of Rohan, son of King Folcwine and twin brother of Fastred (q. v.). (III 436)

**FOLCWINE** (TA 2830-2903) Man, fourteenth King of Rohan (2864-2903). Folcwine recovered the area between the Adorn and Isen from the Dunlendings, and in 2885 sent an army commanded by his twin sons Fastred and Folcred to the aid of Gondor in the Battle of the Crossings of Poros. (III 435-36)

**FOLDE** Area of Rohan, located in western Eastfold. (III 14, 92, 93)

**FORBIDDEN DOOR** The Dark Door (q. v.). (III 459)

**FORD OF BRUINEN** Ford across the Bruinen, on the Great East Road. On their way to Rivendell in TA 3018, Frodo and his companions were attacked here by the Nazgûl, but the Black Riders were defeated by Aragorn and Glorfindel and a flood created by Elrond.

Also called the Ford of Rivendell. (I 16, 269; H 12, 55)

**FORD OF CARROCK** Ford across Anduin, kept open at the time of the WR by the Beornings.

In *H*, the Ford of Carrock only connects the Carrock and the east bank of the Anduin; perhaps the reference on I 301 should be to the Old Ford. (I 301; H 116-18, 131)

**FORD OF RIVENDELL**  The Ford of Bruinen (q.v.). (I 283)

**FORDS OF ISEN**  Fords across the Isen in western Rohan, the chief entrance into Rohan from the west. In TA 2758 the Fords were the site of a battle between King Helm and Wulf, and during the WR two battles were fought here between the Rohirrim and Saruman's forces.

Also called the Crossings of Isen. (II 168, 198-99; III 432)

**FORELITHE**  The sixth month of the Shire Reckoning (q.v.), coming before the Lithe, and thus roughly corresponding to our June.

Called Lithe in Bree. (III 478, 483)

**FOREST GATE**  Western entrance to an elf-path crossing northern Mirkwood. Thorin and Company were shown this gate by Beorn in TA 2941, and entered Mirkwood through it. (H 13, 140)

**FOREST RIVER**  River flowing from the Ered Mithrin through northern Mirkwood and into the Long Lake. (H 13, 172, 180)

**FOREYULE**  The last month of the Shire Reckoning (q.v.), roughly corresponding to our December.

Called Yulemath in Bree and the Eastfarthing. (III 478, 483)

**FORGOIL**  (Dunlending: 'strawhead')  Name given the Rohirrim by the Dunlendings. (II 180; III 509)

**FORLINDON**  (S.: 'north Lindon')  That portion of Lindon north of the Gulf of Lune. In the Second Age Gil-galad lived in Forlindon. (I 16; III 452)

**FORLOND**  (S.: 'north-haven')  Harbor on the northern side of the Gulf of Lune. (I 16; III 411)

**FORLONG**  (d. TA 3019)  Man of Gondor, Lord of Lossarnach. Although old, he fought valiantly in the Battle of the Pelennor Fields, but was slain by Easterlings after he was separated from his men.

He was called Forlong the Fat because he was. *Forlong* is of pre-Númenorean (early-Second-Age) Mannish origin. (III 49, 148, 152, 508)

**FORMEN**  (Q.: 'north')  Name for the tengwa ⟨ (number 10). This tengwa was commonly used to indicate the compass-point "north," even in languages in which the word for "north" did not begin with this sign. (III 500)

**FORN**  Name given Tom Bombadil (q.v.) by the Dwarves. (I 347)

**FORNOST ERAIN**  (S.: 'north fortress of the kings')  City on the North Downs, second capital of Arnor and its chief city. Fornost was also the capital and chief city of Arthedain, but was captured by Angmar in TA 1974. Although freed the next year in the Battle of Fornost, Fornost was deserted, since the North-kingdom ended.

A palantír (q. v.) was kept at Fornost until 1974.

Called Norbury, or Norbury of the Kings, in Westron. After its abandonment, Fornost was known as Deadman's Dike. (I 16, 320-21; III 337, 398, 411)

**FOROCHEL** (S.: 'north---') Cold barren area in northern Middle-earth, about 300 miles north of the Shire. The Lossoth were its sole inhabitants in the Third Age, although in the First it was of some importance, since its great cold was imposed on the area by Morgoth.

See: Cape of Forochel. (I 16; III 398-400)

**FORODWAITH** (S.: 'north---') Area north of Carn Dûm, perhaps equivalent to the Northern Waste or Norland (qq. v.). (III 399)

**FORSAKEN INN, THE** Inn one day's journey east of Bree, the easternmost inn on the Great East Road. (I 253)

**FORTINBRAS TOOK** (TA 2745-2848) Hobbit of the Shire, son of Ferumbras Took and, as Fortinbras I, twenty-fifth Thain of the Shire (2801-48). (III 475)

**FORTINBRAS TOOK** (TA 2878-2980) Hobbit of the Shire, son of Isumbras II and, as Fortinbras II, twenty-ninth Thain of the Shire (2939-80). (III 475)

**FOSCO BAGGINS** (TA 2864-2960) Hobbit of the Shire, paternal grandfather of Frodo Baggins. He married Ruby Bolger. (III 474)

**FOUR FARTHINGS** The Shire (q. v.). (I 306)

**FOURTH AGE** The age of the Dominion of Men. The Fourth Age began with the passing of the Three Rings and various heroes of the Third Age after the defeat of Sauron (September, TA 3021), but the first day of the Fourth Age was March 25, TA 3021.

In the Fourth Age most of the Elves, especially the Eldar, passed over Sea, and those of the non-Mannish races that remained in Middle-earth dwindled and hid, for their time was past and Men no longer understood them.

Also called the New Age and the Younger Days. (III 308, 387, 470, 486)

**FOX DOWNS** Earlier name for the Far Downs (q. v.). (I 24)

**FRAM** (fl. TA 21st Cent.) Man, Lord of Éothéod, son of Frumgar. Fram slew the dragon Scatha and won his hoard. He later quarreled with the Dwarves, who claimed the treasure, and may have been slain by them. (III 430)

**FRÁR** (d. TA 2994) Dwarf. Frár went to Khazad-dûm with Balin, and was slain in the defense of Durin's Bridge and the Second Hall. (I 419)

**FRÉA** (TA 2570-2659) Man, fourth King of Rohan (2645-59). (III 434)

**FRÉALÁF** (TA 2726-98) Man, tenth King of Rohan (2759-98) and the first of the Second Line, son of Hild, King Helm's sister. During the Dunlending invasion of 2758, Fréaláf took refuge in Dunharrow with many of the Rohirrim, and early the next spring he took Meduseld and Edoras in a surprise attack in which Wulf was slain. In the course of 2759, Fréaláf, with aid from Gondor, drove the Dunlendings out of all of Rohan. Since King Helm and his sons had died in the invasion, Fréaláf was made king.

During Fréaláf's reign Saruman came to Isengard, and the wizard aided the Rohirrim, who had been greatly weakened by the war with Wulf and the Long Winter. (III 433, 435)

**FRÉAWINE** (TA 2594-2680) Man, fifth King of Rohan (2659-80). (III 435)

**FRECA** (d. TA 2754) Man of mixed Rohanish and Dunlending blood, father of Wulf. Freca was very rich and powerful, and had much land near the Adorn. King Helm distrusted him, and after Freca insulted the king for refusing an offer to marry his daughter to Wulf, Helm slew Freca. (III 431-32)

**FREDEGAR BOLGER** (fl. WR) Hobbit of the Shire, son of Odovacar Bolger and a guest at the Farewell Party, a good friend of Frodo Baggins. He came from Budgeford. In 3018 Fredegar helped cover Frodo's departure from Crickhollow, and was nearly slain by the Nazgûl. During Lotho's and Saruman's control of the Shire, Fredegar led a band of rebels in the Brockenbores, but was captured and imprisoned in the Lockholes.

Fredegar was called Fatty before he was imprisoned and half-starved. He was a typical Hobbit in that, despite his friendship with Frodo, he had no desire to leave the Shire with him in 3018 to seek adventure, but became a guerilla when it was necessary. (I 71, 153, 238-39; III 372, 475)

**FREE FAIR** Fair held once every seven years on the Lithe.

The Fair was held on the White Downs and was attended by Hobbits. The Mayor of the Shire was elected at the Free Fair. (I 31; III 377)

**FREE FOLK**   See: the Free Peoples. (I 368)

**FREE LORDS OF THE FREE**   A general term used by Boromir to refer to the mighty lords of the Free Peoples such as the Steward of Gondor and Elrond. (I 350)

**FREE PEOPLES**   The "good" races of Middle-earth: Men (especially the Dúnedain), Elves, Dwarves and Hobbits. The term was used specifically to refer to those races which were in opposition to Sauron.

The Free Folk were those individuals who comprised the Free Peoples.

Also called the Free. (I 361, 368)

**FRERIN**   (TA 2751-2799)   Dwarf of Durin's line, second son of Thráin II and younger brother of Thorin II. Frerin escaped with his family from Erebor when Smaug attacked the Dwarf-kingdom in 2770, and wandered with Durin's Folk until he was slain in the Battle of Azanulbizar. (III 440, 443, 450)

**FRERY**   In Bree and the Eastfarthing, the name given Afteryule (q. v.). (III 483)

**FRODO BAGGINS**   (TA 2968-   )   Hobbit of the Shire, Ring-bearer, Elf-friend and hero, the only son of Drogo Baggins and Primula Brandybuck. In 2980, on the death of his parents, he was adopted by his cousin Bilbo, and went to live with him in Bag End. In 3001, when Bilbo left the Shire, Frodo inherited all his goods, including Bag End and the One Ring.

In 3018, on Gandalf's advice, Frodo, under the name of Mr. Underhill, went to Rivendell to escape the Nazgûl. Along the way, he met Aragorn and was nearly slain by the Lord of the Nazgûl. In Rivendell, he volunteered to undertake the Quest of Mount Doom. After great adventures and heroic deeds with the Fellowship of the Ring, Frodo reached the Sammath Naur, but at the last moment claimed the Ring for himself. However, Gollum bit off Frodo's ring-finger and then fell into the Sammath Naur, thus fulfilling the Quest.

After the WR, Frodo was for a while (November 3019-Mid-year's Day, 3020) Mayor of Michel Delving. However, he was discontented in mind and wounded in body (from his stabbing by the Nazgûl-lord and his poisoning by Shelob), and so passed over Sea with the Last Riding of the Keepers of the Rings, leaving his goods to his beloved servant and friend, Sam Gamgee.

Frodo wrote the account of the War of the Ring and the Quest of Mount Doom contained in the Red Book of Westmarch.

Even before the WR, Frodo was more thoughtful and moody than Hobbits were wont to be, and eagerly sought out news of far lands. Although this was in part because of Frodo's responsibility as Ring-bearer, he was also uncommonly perceptive of the hearts of those he met. The Ring influenced Frodo surprisingly little; although it caused him to age very slowly, and although he was greatly troubled by the burden and eventually succumbed to it, his resistance was very great. Frodo knew Sindarin and a little Quenya, and was said to show uncommon skill in pronouncing foreign languages; he was quite literate. He seems to have had few friends of his own age, although he was close to Bilbo and a number of Hobbits younger than himself. He was unmarried.

Called the Ring-bearer and Frodo of the Nine Fingers. (I 32, 43-44, 45, 154; III 271-77, 303-04, 312, 331, 373, 380-84, 474, 475, 476, 490; TB 9)

**FRODO GARDNER** (b. FA 3) Hobbit of the Shire, second child and eldest son of Samwise Gamgee. Frodo was founder of the family of Gardner of the Hill. He probably lived in Bag End. (III 382, 477)

*FRODOS DREME* See: *The Sea-Bell.* (TB 9)

**FROGMORTON** Village in the Eastfarthing on the Great East Road. The Floating Log, a good inn, was located in Frogmorton, and during Lotho's control of the Shire the village was the headquarters of the First Eastfarthing Troop of the Watch. (I 40; III 345-46)

**FRONT GATE** The main gate of Erebor, out of which flowed the River Running. The Front Gate was the only gate to Erebor not blocked up by Smaug, and he used it as his entrance.

Also called the Gate of Erebor and the Gate. (III 449, 468; H 33, 196, 230, 246-48)

**FRONT PORCH** Name given by a group of Orcs of the Misty Mountains to the cave forming the main entrance to their tunnels. The Front Porch opened onto the High Pass, and was built sometime in the years immediately preceding TA 2941. (H 66-67, 71)

**FRÓR** (TA 2552-89) Dwarf of Durin's Folk, second son of

Dáin I. He was slain with his father in the Ered Mithrin by a dragon. (III 440, 450)

**FRUMGAR** (fl. TA 1977) Man, Chieftain of the Éothéod. In TA 1977 he led the Éothéod north from their previous home between the Gladden and the Carrock to the land called Éothéod.

Misspelled "Frungor" on III 458. (III 430, 458; RHM III 368)

**FUNDIN** (TA 2662-2799) Dwarf of Durin's line, son of Farin and father of Balin and Dwalin. He was slain in the Battle of Azanulbizar. (III 443, 450)

# G

**GALABAS** (gen. Hob.)   See: Gamwich. (III 520)

**GALADRIEL**   (S.: 'lady of light' or 'tree-lady')   (First Age-   )
Noldorin Princess of the House of Finarphir, the noblest Elf
in Middle-earth in the Third Age. Galadriel was one of the
princes and queens who led the rebelling Noldor to Middle-
earth to battle Morgoth, and she was the only one to survive
the War of the Great Jewels. At the end of the First Age a
ban was set on her return to Valinor.

In the Second Age Galadriel, with her husband Celeborn
and her daughter Celebrían, dwelled for a time in Lindon and
Eregion, and then founded and became Queen of Lórien, which
she sustained (and perhaps made) with the aid of her own
power and that of Nenya, one of the Three Rings, which was
given to her at its making. Throughout the Second and Third
Ages Lórien remained safe from Sauron, for Galadriel's
power was such that she knew his mind, but hers was closed
to him, and she could protect Lórien from assault by any
power less than Sauron himself.

During the WR, Galadriel gave shelter and great gifts to
the Companions of the Ring, and refused the One Ring when
it was offered to her by Frodo. Because of this, and because
of her endless opposition to Sauron, at the end of the Third
Age the Valar permitted her to return to Valinor. Galadriel
fulfilled her age-old desire in TA 3021, when she went over
Sea with the Last Riding of the Keepers of the Rings.

Galadriel was very tall and beautiful, and she had the
golden hair of her family.

The Quenya form of her name was Altariel. She was known
as the Lady of Lórien, the Lady of the Wood, the Lady of the
Galadrim, the Sorceress of the Golden Wood (by Gríma), the
Mistress of Magic (by Faramir), the White Lady and Queen
Galadriel. (I 456, 459 ff., esp. 462, 472, 503; II 150; III
381-84, 451, 453, 506; R 60)

**GALADRIM** (S.: 'tree-people')   The Elves (mostly Silvan) of
Lórien, ruled by Celeborn and Galadriel. The Galadrim flourished from the founding of Lórien in the Second Age until TA
1980, when with the freeing of the Balrog in Khazad-dûm
many of the Galadrim fled south to Dol Amroth. Many of the

Galadrim at this time sailed over Sea. Although forced to become more military, the Galadrim lived happily in Lórien until the end of the Third Age, when with the departure over Sea of Galadriel Lórien was deserted. Most of the Galadrim went with Celeborn to East Lórien.

The Galadrim lived in telain (see: talan) built in the trees of Lórien. They spoke a dialect of Sindarin.

Called in Westron the Tree-people. (I 442; III 458, 468, 506)

**GALATHILION** (S.: 'tree-moon') The White Tree of the Eldar, a sapling of Telperion. Galathilion grew in Eressëa, and was the emblem of the Eldar. Unlike Telperion, Galathilion did not shine. Nimloth was descended from it.

Called the White Tree, the Tree of Silver, and the Tree of the High Elves. (I 321, 397; III 308; RHM III 440)

**GALBASI** (gen. Hob.) See: Gamgee. (III 520)

**GALDOR** (S.) (fl. WR) Elf of the Grey Havens, messenger of Círdan and his representative at the Council of Elrond in TA 3018. (I 315, 327-28)

**GALENAS** (S.: 'pipe-weed') See: pipe-weed. (I 29; RHM III 438)

**GALION** (S.) (fl. TA 2941) Elf of the Woodland Realm, butler of Thranduil. (H 173-76)

**GÁLMÓD** (fl. TA 30th Cent.) Man of Rohan, the father of Gríma. (II 151)

**GALPSI** (gen. Hob.) See: Gamgee. (III 520)

**GAMGEE** A Hobbit family of the Shire, originally of the working class. The Gamgees took their name from the village of Gamwich, where they came from; at the time of the WR one branch of the family lived at Number 3, Bagshot Row, Hobbiton. The most illustrious member of the family was Samwise, who as the heir of Frodo and the son-in-law of Tolman Cotton was both well-to-do and influential; he was elected Mayor of the Shire seven times. Samwise's children included the founders of the families of the Fairbairns of the Tower and the Gardners of the Hill.

The name Gamgee evolved through such forms as Gammidge and Gammidgy, from the original Gamwich. The genuine Hobbitish forms were Galpsi, from Galbasi, from Galabas. (I 44; III 477, 520)

**GAMLING** (fl. WR) Man of Rohan, leader of the men that guarded Helm's dike before the Battle of the Hornburg. Gamling was probably Erkenbrand's lieutenant.

He was known as Gamling the Old, because at the time of the WR he was. (II 172, 178-79, 180)

**GAMMIDGE** See: Gamgee. (III 477)

**GAMMIDGY** See: Gamgee. (III 520)

**GAMWICH** A village in the Shire, home of Hamfast of Gamwich, the founder of the Gamgee family.

Gamwich is the translated Hobbitish form of the genuine Hobbitish *Galabas,* which was a common Shire village-name meaning "game-village." (III 477, 520)

**GAMWICH** Hobbit surname, used by a working-class family in the Shire c. TA 2800. The name was derived from the village of Gamwich.

The genuine Hobbitish form was Galbasi.

See: Gamgee. (III 477, 520)

**GANDALF** One of the Istari, as Gandalf the Grey the second most powerful of the Order. Gandalf can be said to have been the person most responsible for the victory of the West and the downfall of Sauron in the Third Age; he labored ceaselessly and ever-faithfully for two thousand years towards that goal, and by his foresight built up many powers to oppose Sauron in the final struggle.

On his arrival in Middle-earth about TA 1000, Círdan gave him Narya, one of the Three Rings. Gandalf had many adventures and trials during the Third Age, only the chief of which can be mentioned here. In 2063, at the request of the White Council, he went to Dol Guldur as a spy, but was unable to determine the identity of its lord. In 2850 he again entered Dol Guldur, discovered that its lord was Sauron, received the key to Erebor from Thráin and managed to escape. Later, in 2941, Gandalf interested Thorin in the recovery of Erebor, his goal being the establishment of a strong realm in the north to oppose an attack by Easterlings allied with Sauron. Gandalf's further action of persuading Thorin to hire Bilbo Baggins as burglar for the expedition, perhaps because he wished to use the latent strength of the Shire-folk at a later date, had even more important consequences, since Bilbo obtained the One Ring. Gandalf suspected that Bilbo's treasure was indeed the One, and from 2941 to 3001, with the aid of the Rangers put a close watch over Bilbo and the Shire. In 3001 Gandalf persuaded Bilbo to give the Ring to Frodo (an unparalleled action which confirmed Gandalf's high opinion of Hobbits), and in 3018 set into motion the Quest of Mount Doom. Gandalf was an important influence at the Council of Elrond, since he alone knew the full history of the Ring and of Saruman's treachery, and later was one of the Companions of the Ring. Although he was slain defending the Company from the Balrog in Khazad-dûm, he was sent back to Middle-earth as Gandalf the White to complete his task. During the WR he released King Théoden from Gríma's spells, cast Saruman out of the order of Istari and was invaluable to the counsels of Gondor and Rohan. During the Battle of the Pelennor Fields Gandalf contested the gates of Minas Tirith with the Lord of the Nazgûl for a few crucial minutes between their breaking and the arrival of the Rohirrim.

After the successful completion of the WR, his task being completed, Gandalf went over Sea with the Last Riding of the Keepers of the Rings.

Gandalf looked like a grey-cloaked, grey-haired (after his resurrection, his hair and cloak were white) bent old man, and passed easily for a meddlesome old conjuror; at times, however, he revealed his true majesty and power. Prior to his fight with the Balrog, it seems that he was mortal, and was vulnerable both to weapons and "magical" force, but as Gandalf the White no weapon could touch on him, and his power over the Unseen was greatly increased.

Gandalf travelled mostly in the West, and had no permanent home. Of all the Istari, he was the closest to the Eldar, and the only Wizard who truly cared about things of seemingly small value like Hobbits and trees. He was a great master of lore and (perhaps due to Narya) of fire. Gandalf was a friend and teacher to Aragorn seemingly above all other Men, and the two helped each other greatly. After 2941, in addition to his staff Gandalf bore the great sword Glamdring. In 3018, after escaping from Isengard, he tamed Shadowfax, the greatest of the mearas of Rohan, and rode him for the rest of the WR.

"Gandalf" was the name given him by the Men of the North. He was called Mithrandir by the Elves; the Westron forms Grey Wanderer and Grey Pilgrim were also used. He was called Tharkûn by the Dwarves, Incánus by the Haradrim, Gandalf Greyhame by the Rohirrim, and at various times Stormcrow (by Théoden), Láthspell (by Gríma) and the Grey Fool (by Denethor II, who disliked him because of his friendship with Thorongil, the rival of his youth). He was also known as the Enemy of Sauron and (during the WR) the White Rider. His real name, given him in Valinor in his youth, was Olórin. (I 57-63, 299, 336-47, 366, 380, 387; II 46, 86, 134-35, 149, 353; III 100, 125-26, 303-04, 308, 383, 418, 447-48, 455-56, 459, 460; H 17-20, 26, 29, 100, 184)

**GAP OF ROHAN**   Area in Rohan between the White and Misty Mountains. (I 338)

**GARDNER OF THE HILL**   Famous and influential family of Hobbits of the Shire, whose first member was Frodo, eldest son of Samwise Gamgee. The Gardners, who took their name from Sam's trade, most probably lived in Bag End. (III 473, 477)

**GÁRULF**   (d. TA 3019)   Man of Rohan, a Rider of Éomer's éored. He was killed in the battle between the éored and Uglúk's Orcs. (II 51)

**GATE OF EREBOR**   The Front Gate (q. v.). (III 449)

**GATE OF KINGS**   The Argonath (q. v.). (II 24)

**GATE OF THE DEAD**   The Dark Door (q. v.). (III 69-70)

**GERONTIUS TOOK**   (TA 2790-2920)   Hobbit of the Shire, son of Fortinbras Took and twenty-sixth Thain of the Shire (2848-2920). He married Adamanta Chubb; they had twelve children.
    Gerontius reached the second greatest age of any Hobbit in history, being surpassed only by Bilbo. He was known as the Old Took. (II 80-81; III 475; H 17)

**GHÂN-BURI-GHÂN**   (fl. WR)   Man, chieftain of the Woses. During the WR Ghân-buri-Ghân guided the Rohirrim through Druadan Forest, thus enabling them to avoid the superior force of Orcs and Easterlings guarding the Great West Road.
    Also called Ghân. (III 129-33, 313)

**GIANTS**   See: stone-giants. (H 99-100, 118)

**GIFT OF MEN**   The Doom of Men (q. v.). (III 390)

**GILDOR INGLORION**   (S.: 'star--- ---') (fl. WR)   Elda of the House of Finrod. At the time of the WR he lived at Rivendell. He sailed over Sea with the Last Riding of the Keepers of the Rings. (I 118-24; III 381; R 65-66)

**GIL-GALAD**   (S.: 'star-light') (FA-SA 3441)   Noldorin Elf, last heir of the Noldorin kings of Middle-earth. In the Second Age he was King of Lindon. When Sauron arose after the fall of Númenor and attacked Gondor, Gil-galad formed the Last Alliance of Men and Elves with Elendil, and with Elendil led the army that in 3434 defeated Sauron in the Battle of Dagorlad and besieged the Barad-dûr. In 3441 Gil-galad and Elendil overthrew Sauron, but were themselves slain; Gil-galad was burned to death by Sauron's heat.
    Gil-galad's weapon was the famous spear Aiglos. He was the first bearer of Vilya, the greatest of the Three Rings.

(I 83, 250, 257, 319-20, 332; III 389, 452, 453-55; R 65)

**GILLY BAGGINS** (d. after TA 3001) Hobbit of the Shire, wife of Posco Baggins and a guest at the Farewell Party. She was born a Brownlock. (III 474)

**GILRAEN** (S.: 'star---') (TA 2907-3007) Dúnadan of the North, daughter of Dírhael. In 2929 she married Arathorn II, and in 2931 their only child, Aragorn, was born. Gilraen lived in Rivendell from the death of her husband in 2933 until 2954, when she returned to her home somewhere in Eriador.

She was called Gilraen the Fair. (III 420, 422, 426, 461, 463)

**GILRAIN** (S.: 'star---') River in Lebennin, Gondor, flowing from its source in the Ered Nimrais southward until it entered the Bay of Belfalas just west of the Ethir Anduin. Its principal tributary was the Serni. (III 14, 185)

**GIMILZÔR, AR-** (Ad.) (fl. SA 3100) Dúnadan, twenty-second King of Númenor. (III 390)

**GIMLI** (TA 2879-   ) Dwarf of Durin's line, son of Glóin. He probably spent his youth in the Ered Luin, and moved to Erebor with his father in 2941. In 3018 Gimli accompanied Glóin to Imladris. There he was chosen to represent the Dwarves in the Company of the Ring, and guided the Companions through Khazad-dûm. He was the first Dwarf to enter Lórien since Durin's Day, and in that land became devoted to Galadriel and a close friend of Legolas. After the breaking of the Fellowship, Gimli travelled with Legolas and Aragorn to Rohan, where he fought valiantly in the Aglarond during the Battle of the Hornburg. He then travelled the Paths of the Dead and came to Minas Tirith with Aragorn, fighting in the Battle of the Pelennor Fields and the battle outside the Morannon.

After the WR, Gimli brought a group of Dwarves from Erebor to Rohan, and became Lord of the Glittering Caves. He remained friendly with Legolas and the other members of the Fellowship of the Ring, and forged new gates of mithril and steel for Minas Tirith. In FA 120, after the passing of Elessar, Gimli sailed over Sea with Legolas. This action was unprecedented; it was no doubt prompted by Gimli's love for Legolas.

Gimli was called Elf-friend. He was known as Lock-bearer because of the lock of her hair given him by Galadriel. (I 315, 361, 365-66, 453-54, 461-62, 464-65, 481, 486-87; II

193-95; III 317, 387, 449-51)

**GIRDLEY ISLAND**   Island in the Brandywine just above the Bridge of Stonebows, perhaps a part of the Shire. (I 40)

**GIRION**   (S.?) (d. TA 2770)   Man, last King of Dale of the old line. He was killed by Smaug, but his wife and children escaped to continue the royal line. (H 215, 220, 237, 239)

**GIRITHRON**   (S.)   Name for Ringarë (q. v.), used only by the Dúnedain. (III 483)

**GLADDEN**   River flowing east from its source in the central Misty Mountains. It emptied into the Anduin in a marsh. An important pass over the Misty Mountains was located at the source of the Gladden. (I 17, 359)

**GLADDEN FIELDS**   Marshy fields at the meeting of the Gladden and Anduin. In TA 2 the Battle of the Gladden Fields was fought here, and the One Ring remained hidden here from that time until TA 2463, when it was found by Déagol. A band of Stoors lived in or near the Gladden Fields from about TA 1410 until after 2460, and this may have been the original home of the Stoors. (I 17, 83, 320; III 456)

**GLAMDRING**   (S.: 'foe-hammer')   The sword of Gandalf. Glamdring was originally made by the Elves of Gondolin for the wars against Morgoth, and was worn by the King of Gondolin. After the fall of Gondolin, Glamdring eventually found its way into a troll-hoard, where it was found by Gandalf in TA 2941. Gandalf used Glamdring from then until the end of the WR. It is not said if he took the sword over Sea with him.

As with all such weapons, Glamdring shone with a blue light in the presence of Orcs. It was the mate of Orcrist (q.v.). Called by the Orcs Beater. (I 366, 429; III 336; H 53, 61, 73)

**GLANDUIN**   (S.)   River flowing west from its source in the Misty Mountains and joining the Mitheithel above Tharbad.

Called Swanfleet in Westron because of the many swans that lived on the lower reaches of the river. (III 325, 396)

**GLÉOWINE**   (fl. WR)   Man of Rohan, Théoden's minstrel. After the WR he made a song about Théoden and his death, and composed no song after that. (III 314)

**GLITTERING CAVES**   The Aglarond (q. v.). (II 195)

**GLÓIN**   (TA 2136-2385)   Dwarf, King of Durin's Folk (2283-2385) in the Ered Mithrin. (III 450)

**GLÓIN**   (TA 2783-FA 15)   Dwarf of Durin's line, son of Gróin and father of Gimli. He was a companion of Thráin and Thorin in their wanderings after the Battle of Azanulbizar, and was a member of Thorin and Company, as a result of which expedition he became rich and important in Erebor. In 3018, with Gimli, Glóin went to Rivendell to obtain advice from Elrond on behalf of the Dwarves of Erebor, and took part in the Council of Elrond. (I 300, 316-17; III 445, 450; H 22, 26)

**GLORFINDEL** (S.: 'dream-hair---'?) Eldarin lord of great power, probably of the House of Finrod. At the time of the WR Glorfindel seems to have been the second most important Elf, after Elrond, in Rivendell. Glorfindel led the Elvish force that helped rout Angmar in the Battle of Fornost in TA 1975. In 3018 he met and protected Frodo and his companions on their way to Rivendell, and fought the Nazgûl at the Ford of Bruinen.

Glorfindel's horse was the great white steed Asfaloth. (I 279-81, 294, 299; III 412)

**GOATLEAF** Family of Men of Bree. (I 212)

**GOBLIN-GATE** An entrance to the Orc-tunnels of the Misty Mountains, probably the back-door (q. v.). (H 12)

**GOBLIN-WARS** The War of the Great Jewels (q. v.). (H 61, 72)

**GOD** Eru (q. v.). (R 66)

**GOLASGIL** (S.: 'leaf-star') (fl. WR) Man of Gondor, probably a Dúnadan, lord of Anfalas. (III 50)

**GOLDBERRY** (fl. WR) Woman, wife of Tom Bombadil. She was the daughter of the River-woman of the Withywindle.

Goldberry was fair and golden-haired, gracious and calm, with a beauty like to that of Elves yet more easily encompassed by Hobbitish hearts. (I 168, 169, 172 ff., 187-88; TB 11-12, 15-16)

**GOLDEN HONEYCOMB** Trophy or prize of war won by the messenger of *Errantry*, probably fictitious. (TB 27)

**GOLDEN PERCH** Inn in Stock, reputed at the time of the WR to have the best beer in the Eastfarthing. (I 128)

**GOLDEN TREE** Laurelin (q. v.). (I 482)

**GOLDEN WOOD** Lórien (q. v.). (I 439)

**GOLDILOCKS TOOK** (b. FA 10) Hobbit of the Shire, daughter of Sam Gamgee and wife of Faramir Took. She was most probably golden-haired. (III 382, 477)

**GOLDWINE** (TA 2619-99) Man, sixth King of Rohan (2680-99).

(III 435)

**GOLDWORTHY**    Family of Hobbits of the Shire, perhaps well-to-do. (III 476)

**GOLFIMBUL**    (d. TA 2747)   Orc, King of the Orcs of Mount Gram and leader of the Orc-band that was defeated in the Battle of Greenfields. In that battle, Golfimbul was slain by Bandobras Took, who knocked his head off with a club.
      The name "Golfimbul" is either facetious and fictitious or else translated Westron, since Professor Tolkien derives the source of the game and name of "golf" from Golfimbul. Also, since the Orc-band was probably not very large, Golfimbul, if a historical personage, was probably somewhat less than a king. (H 30)

**GOLLUM**    (TA c. 2430-3019)   Hobbit of the Stoor strain, born in the Stoor settlement near the Gladden Fields. About 2463 his cousin Déagol found the One Ring while fishing, and Gollum murdered him for it. Soon he became odious to his family and was driven out of the Stoor community. Gollum hid in the Misty Mountains, falling more and more under the control of the Ring until 2941, when he lost it. Bilbo Baggins found the Ring and took it with him to the Shire. Gollum, suspecting that Bilbo had the Ring, came out of the Misty Mountains to search for Bilbo, his need for the Ring overcoming his hatred and fear of the sun, the moon and other living things.
      A few years before the WR, Gollum was captured by Sauron, who thus discovered about Bilbo. Sauron released Gollum in 3017 and he was captured by Aragorn, who turned him over to Gandalf. The wizard learned that part of the story of the Ring which he had not previously known, and then gave Gollum over to the Elves of the Woodland Realm. In June, 3018, Gollum escaped during an Orc-raid, and immediately went off in search of the Ring. He caught up with Frodo and the Company of the Ring outside the West-gate of Khazad-dûm, and followed the Company through Moria. Gollum was captured by Frodo and Sam in the Emyn Muil; and, partly out of fear of the Ring-bearer and partly to ensure that Sauron did not recover the Ring, Gollum led the Hobbits faithfully to Cirith Ungol, the only unguarded route into Mordor. However, there he betrayed Frodo and Sam to Shelob, hoping to recover the Ring when Shelob discarded their clothing. His plan failed, and so he followed the Hobbits to Orodruin. There his last ambush of Frodo failed, but when the latter claimed the Ring as his own Gollum attacked him once more. In the struggle which

followed, Gollum bit off Frodo's ring-finger and thus got the Ring, but in his joy fell into the Crack of Doom, destroying both himself and the Ring.

Gollum originally looked like a normal Hobbit, but his long years in darkness and dampness under the influence of the Ring drastically affected his appearance. The descriptions of him given in *LotR* vary somewhat, but he seems by the time of Bilbo and Frodo to have been extremely thin and wiry, with black skin, flat feet, long thin hands and pale large eyes. Although his sight was poor, his hearing was acute, and he could move silently and climb like an insect. Because of his long domination by the Ring, Gollum pathologically feared all things Elven; Elven ropes burned his flesh and lembas tasted like dust. He hated all creatures and was, due to the influence of the Ring on his naturally somewhat nasty character, generally despicable.

Gollum's real name was Trahald, a northern Mannish name meaning "burrowing, worming in"; the Anglicized Mannish equivalent was Sméagol. He was called Gollum because of the disgusting noise he made in his throat; the name was originally given to him by his family after he found the Ring. He called himself "my preciouss," perhaps confusing himself and the Ring. Sam devised two names, Slinker and Stinker, for the two aspects of Gollum's nature while he was serving Frodo. The former referred to his fawning behavior toward Frodo as Ringbearer and his sworn master, which was in part a sincere desire to be a good person and escape the control of the Ring, while the latter referred to Gollum's spiteful, treacherous, hating behavior toward all else, which sometimes carried over to Frodo. (I 32-34, 85-91, 329-36 ff., 497; II 278-80 ff.; III 279-86 ff., 459, 462, 463; H 79-93)

**GONDOLIN** (S.) Hidden city and kingdom of elves in Beleriand in the First Age, ruled by Turgon. Eärendil was born here, and Glamdring and Orcrist were forged here. Gondolin was attacked by Morgoth near the end of the First Age and was destroyed. (I 319, 412; III 389; H 61, 72)

**GONDOR** (S.: 'stone-land') One of the Dúnedain kingdoms in Middle-earth, founded by Elendil in SA 3320 and committed by him to the joint rule of his sons Isildur and Anárion. At the height of its power (c. TA 1100), Gondor extended north to Celebrant, east to the Sea of Rhûn, south to the River Harnen inland and Umbar on the coast, and west to Gwathlo. In addition, various realms to the east and south were tributary states. The chief cities of Gondor were Osgiliath, Minas Anor, Minas Ithil, Dol Amroth and Pelargir.

From its founding, Gondor was always under attack by Sauron or his allies in Rhûn, Harad or Umbar. Ithilien was invaded a number of times, beginning in SA 3429, until in TA 2002 Minas Ithil was taken by the Nazgûl and held until the end of the WR. In the Third Age, Gondor suffered three great evils, the Kin-strife of 1432-48, the Great Plague of 1636 and the invasions of the Wainriders between 1851 and 1954. These difficulties, combined with the degeneration of the Dúnedain, sapped Gondor's strength, decreased her population and dulled her vigilance.

After the death of Elendil in SA 3441, Gondor was ruled by the Line of Anárion (q. v.) until it failed in TA 2050. From that time until the restoration of the kingdom by Elessar in 3019, Gondor was governed by the Ruling Stewards.

Gondor was a feudal kingdom. Originally the two greatest fiefs, the royal fiefs of Ithilien (Isildur) and Anórien (Anárion and his heirs), were of equal rank, but after the removal of Isildur to Arnor and the moving of the capital from Osgiliath to Minas Anor, Anórien became more important than Ithilien.

Also called the South-kingdom, in opposition to Arnor. Called Stonelending and Stoningland by the Rohirrim.

See: Calenardhon, Lebennin, Belfalas, Enedwaith, etc. (I 319, 321; II 363; III 394-96, 402-19, 454-62 passim.)

**GOODBODY** Family of Hobbits of the Shire, perhaps of the upper class. (I 52; III 474)

**GOODCHILD** Family of Hobbits of the Shire, perhaps of the working class. (III 477)

**GOOLD** Family of Hobbits of the Shire, perhaps of the upper class. (III 476)

**GORBADOC BRANDYBUCK** (TA 2860-2963) Hobbit of the Shire, Master of Buckland (2910-63). He married Mirabella Took; they had seven children, including Frodo's mother Primula.

Gorbadoc was noted for his generous table and matching waistline; he was called "Broadbelt." (I 45; III 475, 476)

**GORBAG** (d. TA 3019) Uruk of Minas Morgul, captain of a company of Orcs. He was killed in the fight between his company and Shagrat's over Frodo's mithril coat. (II 437; III 223-24)

**GORBULAS BRANDYBUCK** (b. TA 2908, d. before 3001) Hobbit of the Shire, son of Orgulas Brandybuck. (III 476)

**GORGOROTH** (S.: 'haunted---') The great plateau of north-western Mordor, a desolate area scarred with countless Orc-dug pits. Points of interest in Gorgoroth included Orodruin and the Barad-dûr. (I 519; II 308; III 245-67)

**GORGÛN** Orcs (q. v.), as called by Ghân-buri-Ghân. (III 133)

**GORHENDAD OLDBUCK** (fl. TA 2340) Hobbit of the Shire. He originally lived in the Marish, but in 2340 he crossed the Brandywine, settled Buckland and built Brandy Hall. He changed the family name to Brandybuck; his heirs were the Masters of Buckland. (I 141; III 476, 520)

**GORMADOC BRANDYBUCK** (TA 2734-2836) Hobbit of the Shire, Master of Buckland (?-2836). He married Malva Head-strong; they had many children.

Gormadoc was called "Deepdelver"; perhaps he enlarged Brandy Hall. (III 476)

**GOTHMOG** (fl. WR) The lieutenant of Minas Morgul and commander of Sauron's army during the Battle of the Pelennor Fields after the fall of the Lord of the Nazgûl.

Gothmog may have been a Nazgûl. (III 148)

**GRAM** (TA 2668-2741) Man, eighth King of Rohan (2718-41). (III 435)

**GREAT ARMAMENT** The fleet built by Ar-Pharazôn between SA 3310 and 3319 for the assault on Valinor. (III 454)

**GREAT BARROWS** The graves on the Barrow-downs (q. v.), in which were buried chieftains of the Edain, and also Dúnedain of Cardolan. The Barrows were taken over by Barrow-wights in the middle of the Third Age. (I 181)

**GREAT BATTLE** The battle between the Host of Valinor and Morgoth at the end of the First Age, which resulted in the casting-out of Morgoth and the ruin of Beleriand.

Also called the battle of the Valar. (III 138, 452)

**GREAT BRIDGE** The Bridge of Stonebows. (III 402)

**GREAT DANGER** Term used by Frodo to describe the period of the WR, when the Shire (and the rest of Middle-earth) was nearly enslaved by Sauron. (III 382)

**GREAT DARKNESS** Term referring to the domination and evil influence of Morgoth. Although most of the references to the Great Darkness are clearly placed in the First Age, some of the references can also apply to Sauron.

Also called the Darkness.

Cf.: the Accursed Years, the Dark Days, the Dark Years.

(II 89, 90, 96, 99, 113)

**GREAT EAGLES** The Eagles of the Misty Mountains (q. v.). (I 343)

**GREAT EAST ROAD** The road running from the Grey Havens to Rivendell, passing through the Shire and the Bree-land. Also called the Great Road, the East-West Road, the East Road, the Road and the Old Road. (I 16, 72, 189, 202 ff.)

**GREAT ENEMY** Morgoth (q. v.). (I 260)

**GREAT GATE OF MINAS TIRITH** The gate in the first level of Minas Tirith, the chief entrance to the city. The Gate was broken by the Lord of the Nazgûl during the Siege of Gondor, but after the WR was rebuilt of mithril and steel by the Dwarves of Aglarond.
Also called the Gate of the City and the Gate. (III 24, 25, 125, 301, 451)

**GREAT GATES** The eastern gate of Khazad-dûm, facing the Dimrill Dale. The Gates were broken when Balin's Dwarf-colony was attacked in TA 2994, and had not been repaired by the time of the WR.
Also called the Dimrill Gate and the Gate. (I 430; III 441, 443-44)

**GREAT GOBLIN** (d. TA 2941) Orc, perhaps leader of all the Orcs of the Misty Mountains, or at least of those near the High Pass. The Great Goblin was slain by Gandalf after he had captured Thorin and Company. (H 70-72)

**GREAT HALL OF THRÁIN** The main hall of Erebor.
Also called the Great Hall. (III 440)

**GREAT HORN** Heirloom of the House of the Stewards of Gondor from the time of Vorondil (c. TA 2000) until the WR. The Horn was made from the horn of one of the Kine of Araw, and was borne by the heir of the Steward. It was believed that if the Horn were blown anywhere within the ancient boundaries of Gondor, help would come. In TA 3019, Boromir blew it when attacked by Orcs near Rauros. Although Denethor and Faramir heard the call hundreds of miles away, no help arrived and Boromir was slain and the horn cloven in two. The Horn was set on Boromir's funeral barge, but the shards were recovered by Denethor. (I 315; II 17, 18, 22, 347, 364; III 29)

**GREAT HOUSE** The dwelling of the Master of Esgaroth. (H 189-91, 236)

**GREAT JEWELS** The Silmarilli (q. v.). (I 362)

**GREAT JOURNEY** The migration of the Eldar from Middle-earth to Eldamar at the beginning of the First Age. All of the Eldar, except for the Sindar, completed the Journey. (III 506, 519; R 66)

**GREAT ORCS** The Uruk-hai (q. v.). (II 48)

**GREAT PLACE OF THE TOOKS** Room in the Great Smials. Gerontius Took spent the last part of his life here, and the room was left untouched after his death. (II 80)

**GREAT PLAGUE** The plague that swept across Middle-earth from the southeast in TA 1636-37. Harad, and perhaps also Rhûn, suffered greatly. Gondor, which was struck next, was devastated. King Telemnar and all his children, and also the White Tree, died. Osgiliath was especially hard hit, and those of its inhabitants who survived by fleeing to the country did not return. The guard on Mordor was discontinued as a result of the Plague.

In Eriador, especially in the north, the Plague was somewhat less severe, but most of the inhabitants of Cardolan, including all the Dúnedain, perished.

Called in the Shire the Dark Plague. (I 24; III 398, 407-08)

**GREAT RING** The One Ring (q. v.). (I 331)

**GREAT RINGS** The Rings of Power (q. v.). (I 333)

**GREAT RIVER** Anduin (q. v.). (I 17)

**GREAT ROAD** The Great East Road (q. v.). (III 396)

**GREAT SEA** See: the Sea. (I 452)

**GREAT SHELF** The dwelling place of the King of the Eagles, located in the Misty Mountains near the Old Forest Road. (H 112-13)

**GREAT SIGNAL** The signal from the Barad-dûr or Orodruin during the WR that sent the army of Minas Morgul against Gondor on March 10, TA 3019. This signal may also have served to unleash Sauron's other armies. (II 399, 441)

**GREAT SMIALS** Chief dwelling of the Tooks, a vast series of tunnels at Tuckborough. The excavation of the Great Smials was begun by Isengrim II in TA 2683.

Also called the Smials. (I 27; II 80; III 357, 459)

**GREAT SPIDERS** Large and evil creatures, originally found in the Mountains of Terror in the First Age. When Beleriand was destroyed the spiders were slain, but at least one, Shelob, survived. She fled to the Ephel Dúath, and her incestuous offspring spread through the mountains of Mordor. In the Third Age, great spiders of Mordor moved to Mirkwood when Sauron established himself there, and for the rest of the Age plagued the Woodmen and the Elves of the Woodland Realm. The spiders of Mirkwood were probably destroyed early in the Fourth Age, and Shelob may have died of wounds given her by Sam Gamgee, but the lesser spiders of Mordor probably survived well into the Fourth Age.

Shelob stood at least five feet tall, for Sam was able to stand underneath her belly, and all the great spiders of Beleriand were probably this size. The spiders of Mirkwood and Mordor were smaller than this, but were still quite large. (II 422-23; H 153-62)

**GREAT WEST ROAD**   The West Road (q. v.). (III 14)

**GREAT WORMS**   The Dragons (q. v.). (H 10)

**GREEN DRAGON**   Inn in Bywater, located on the Hobbiton side of the village, frequented by Hobbits from both villages. (I 72; III 350)

**GREENFIELDS**   Village or area in the Shire, probably in the Northfarthing. In TA 2747 the Battle of Greenfields was fought here.
Also spelled Green Fields. (III 365)

**GREENHAND**   Family of working-class Hobbits of the Shire, descended from Halfred, the eldest son of Holman the green-handed. The Greenhands lived in Hobbiton, and were gardners; the name was no doubt derived from the epithet applied to Holman because of his skill in his trade. (III 477)

**GREEN HILL COUNTRY**   Wooded area in the East- and South-farthings. (I 40, 107 ff.)

**GREEN HILLS**   Hills in the South- and Westfarthings, the center of Tookland. (I 40; III 357)

**GREEN HILLS**   The Pinnath Gelin (q. v.). (III 50)

**GREENHOLM**   Town in the Shire, located on the Far Downs. Greenholm was the home of Fastred of Greenholm. (III 471)

**GREENWAY**   Name given to the North Road (q. v.) in the latter part of the Third Age, when it was not frequently used. (I 29, 210)

**GREENWOOD THE GREAT**   The vast forest east of Anduin. About TA 1050 the shadow of Dol Guldur fell on the forest, and it became known as Mirkwood (q. v.). After its cleansing at the end of the Third Age, it was renamed Eryn Lasgalen (q. v.). (III 404, 408, 456)

**GREY COMPANY** Those who rode the Paths of the Dead with Aragorn during the WR. The Grey Company was composed of Legolas, Gimli, Elladan, Elrohir and a company of Rangers of the North. (III 73)

**GREYFLOOD** Gwathlo (q. v.). (I 268)

**GREY HAVENS** Town and harbor of Círdan, located at the head of the Gulf of Lune. The Grey Havens were founded in SA 1, and it is said that Círdan dwelled there until the last white ship sailed over Sea, which took place sometime in the Fourth Age.

Called in Sindarin Mithlond. Also called the Havens. (I 72, 74, 315; III 383, 453, 456)

**GREY MOUNTAINS** The Ered Mithrin (q. v.). (III 440)

**GREY WOOD, GREYWOOD** Thickets east of Amon Dîn, in Anórien. The Grey Wood may have been part of Druadan Forest. (III 15, 132, 313)

**GRIFFO BOFFIN** (fl. TA 3000) Hobbit of the Shire, husband of Daisy Baggins. He was a guest at the Farewell Party. (III 474)

**GRÍMA** (d. TA 3019) Man of Rohan, chief counsellor to King Théoden. Gríma was an agent of Saruman, and gave his master information about Rohan at the same time as he enfeebled Théoden with his lying counsel; his reward was to have been Éowyn. After Gandalf renewed Théoden, Gríma fled to Isengard, where he kept Saruman company during his imprisonment by Fangorn. Gríma accompanied Saruman to the Shire, where, after great mistreatment by his master, he killed him in front of Frodo and was himself slain by Hobbits.

Gríma was called Wormtongue in Rohan because of his evil counsel; Saruman shortened this to Worm. (II 148-51, 158-60; III 323-24, 369-70)

**GRIMBEORN** (fl. WR) Man, son of Beorn and chieftain of the Beornings. He was perhaps a shape-shifter like his father. During his rule, the High Pass and the Ford of Carrock were kept open, and no Orc or wolf dared enter the land of the Beornings.

He was known as Grimbeorn the Old. (I 301)

**GRIMBOLD** (d. TA 3019) Man and Marshal of Rohan, from Grimslade. He was distinguished in the Battles of the Fords of Isen, and later commanded the third éored in the Battle

of the Pelennor Fields. He was slain in the latter battle.
(III 135, 152; RHM III 424)

**GRIMSLADE**   Place in Rohan, home of Grimbold. (III 152)

**GRINDWALL**   Village in the southern part of Buckland, outside the High Hay. (TB 9, 19)

**GRIP**   (fl. WR)   One of Farmer Maggot's wolf-like dogs. (I 133,
134)

**GRIP**   Bill Butcher's dog, in the poem *Perry-the-Winkle*. Grip
may have been modelled on a historical personage. (TB 42)

**GRISHNÁKH**   (d. TA 3019)   Orc of the Barad-dûr, captain of
the Mordor-orcs in the band that slew Boromir and captured
Merry and Pippin. Somehow, Grishnákh knew of the Ring;
and, desiring it for himself and presuming that Merry or Pippin had it, he stole the two Hobbits away from their guard
of Isengard Orcs while the Orc-camp was surrounded by the
Rohirrim. Although slain by the Rohirrim, he carried Merry
and Pippin far enough to enable them to escape the slaughter.
(II 60-75 passim.; III 511)

**GRÓIN**   (TA 2671-2923)   Dwarf of Durin's line, second son of
Farin and father of Óin and Glóin. (III 450)

**GROND**   The Hammer of the Underworld. (III 124)

**GROND**   The great, hundred-foot-long battering ram prepared in
Mordor to break the Great Gate of Minas Tirith during the
WR. Grond's head was made of black steel and was formed
in the shape of a wolf's-head.
   Grond was named after the Hammer of the Underworld. (III
124-25)

**GRÓR**   (TA 2563-2805)   Dwarf of Durin's line, youngest son
of Dáin I and father of Náin. He founded the Dwarvish realm
in the Iron Hills. (III 440, 450)

**GRUBB**   A family of Hobbits of the Shire, perhaps of the upper
class. (I 52; III 474)

**GUARD OF FARAMIR**   The White Company (q. v.). (III 305)

**GUARDS OF THE CITADEL**   An elite military unit of Gondor
which guarded the Citadel of Minas Tirith and the White Tree,
and participated in official functions. There were at least
three companies of the Guards, each of which had its own
storehouse. Beregond and Pippin belonged to the Third Company.
   The Guards wore Númenorean sea-helms (see: the Silver
Crown) made of mithril and black surcoats bearing the livery
of Elendil. The Guards were the only ones in Gondor to bear

this livery in the time of the Stewards.

The traditional Captain-general of the Guards was the heir of the Steward, and in the time of the Kings the Captain was probably the heir to the throne. (III 26, 37-39, 45, 96-97, 123, 162)

**GULF OF LUNE**  Great gulf in Lindon, fed by the River Lhûn. The Gulf of Lune was perhaps an estuary created in the breaking of Beleriand. Its harbors were the Harlond, the Forlond and the Grey Havens. (I 16; III 396)

**GUNDABAD**  Mountain in the northern Misty Mountains, at the time of the War of the Dwarves and Orcs the site of the northernmost Orc-hold in the Mountains captured by the Dwarves. (I 17; III 442)

**GUNDABALD BOLGER**  (fl. TA 29th Cent.)  Hobbit of the Shire. He married Salvia Brandybuck. (III 476)

**GUTHLÁF**  (tr. Roh.: 'survivor of the battle')  Man of Rohan, banner-bearer of Théoden in the Battle of the Pelennor Fields. He was slain in the battle. (III 137, 145)

**GÚTHWINË**  (tr. Roh.: 'battle-friend')  The sword of Éomer. (II 176)

**GWAERON**  (S.: 'wind---')  Sindarin form of Súlimë, used only by the Dúnedain. (III 483)

**GWAIHIR**  (S.: 'wind-lord') (fl. TA 2941-3019)  Chief of the Eagles of the Misty Mountains. Gwaihir befriended Gandalf when the wizard healed him of a poisoned wound. In 2941 he and his eagles rescued Gandalf and Thorin and Company from Orcs. Gwaihir later brought his Eagles to the Battle of the Five Armies, in which they played a crucial role. In the time of the WR he aided Gandalf three times, first freeing him from Isengard, then rescuing him from the peak of Zirak-zigil after his fight with the Balrog, and finally rescuing Frodo and Sam from the slopes of Orodruin. Gwaihir and his people also served Gandalf and Radagast as messengers and spies.

Sometime after 2941 Gwaihir became the King of All Birds. (I 343; II 126, 135; III 278, 280-82; H 107-08, 112-13, 116, 270, 273)

**GWATHLO**  (S.: 'greyflood')  Large river forming the boundary between Minhiriath and Enedwaith, formed by the meeting of the Mitheithel and Glanduin at Tharbad.

Called in Westron the Greyflood. (I 268)

**GWIRITH**  (S.)  Sindarin form of Víressë, used only by the Dúnedain. (III 483)

# ᚻ

**HADOR** (tr. Ad.: 'bright') (First Age)   Adan, elf-friend and hero, founder of the Third House of the Edain. He was perhaps also the ancestor of the Rohirrim.

He was called Hador the Goldenhaired, because he was. (I 355; II 364; III 389)

**HADOR** (d. TA 2395)   Dúnadan, seventh Ruling Steward of Gondor (2278-2395). In 2360 he made the last millenial adjustment in the Stewards' Reckoning. (III 395, 481)

**HALBARAD** (S.: 'tall-tower') (d. TA 3019)   Dúnadan, Ranger of the North. Halbarad led the company of Rangers that met Aragorn in Rohan during the WR, and accompanied him through the Paths of the Dead. He was Aragorn's standard-bearer during the Battle of the Pelennor Fields, and was slain in that battle. (III 55, 152)

**HALDIR** (S.: 'tall-watch') (fl. WR)   Elf of Lórien, one of the three brothers who intercepted the Company of the Ring and escorted them to Caras Galadon.

Haldir had travelled outside Lórien, and knew Westron. (I 445-60, 464)

**HALETH** (d. TA 2758)   Man of Rohan, eldest son of King Helm. He was slain while defending the doors of Meduseld against Wulf. (III 432)

**HALFAST OF OVERHILL** (b. TA 2972)   Hobbit of the Shire, son of Halfred of Overhill. He lived in Overhill and worked there for a Mr. Boffin. Halfast enjoyed hunting in the Northfarthing, and once saw an Ent there. (I 73; III 477)

**HALFLINGS**   The name given to Hobbits (q.v.) by Men. (III 510)

**HALF-ORCS**   Servants of Saruman, used by him as spies and soldiers. They were seemingly the product of a cross between Men and Orcs. Although they were as tall as Men, they were sallow-faced and squint-eyed. The Chief's Men were half-orcs.

The half-orcs (the term is not used in *LotR*) were definitely not Uruk-hai. (II 96, 218; III 350, 364)

**HALFRED GAMGEE** (b. TA 2969)   Hobbit of the Shire, second son of Hamfast Gamgee. He moved to the Northfarthing. (III 477)

**HALFRED GREENHAND** (b. TA 2851) Hobbit of the Shire, eldest son of Holman the greenhanded and the first greenhand. He lived in Hobbiton, and was a gardêner. (III 477)

**HALFRED OF OVERHILL** (b. TA 2932) Hobbit of the Shire, youngest son of Hobson Gamgee and brother of Hamfast Gamgee. He lived in Overhill. (III 477)

**HALIFIRIEN** The seventh and last of the northern beacontower hills of Gondor, located in the Firien Wood on the border of Rohan. (III 20)

**HALIMATH** The ninth month of the Shire Reckoning (q. v.), corresponding roughly to our September.
Called Harvestmath in Bree. (III 478)

**HALLA** (Q.: 'tall') Tehta originally used in Quenya for *h*, written ), also used to make a following consonant voiceless. (III 500)

**HALLAS** (S.: 'tall-leaf'?) (d. TA 2605) Dúnadan, thirteenth Ruling Steward of Gondor (2567-2605). (III 395)

**HALL OF FIRE** Great hall in the house of Elrond. Although the Hall was used only on high days, a fire was kept lit there at all times. (I 303; II 430)

**HALL OF THE KINGS** The Tower Hall (q. v.). (III 304)

**HALLOWS** The area behind Minas Tirith where the Kings and Stewards of Gondor, and other great men of the realm, were buried. The Hallows were reached by a path from the sixth level of the city which went through Fen Hollen.
Also called the Tombs.
See: the House of the Kings, the House of the Stewards. (III 121-22, 153-60, 305, 313)

**HALLS OF EREBOR** The halls of the Kingdom under the Mountain (q. v.). (III 440)

**HÁMA** (d. TA 2759) Man of Rohan, younger son of King Helm. He was lost in the snow during the Long Winter while on a foraying mission from the Hornburg. (III 432)

**HÁMA** (d. TA 3019) Man of Rohan, doorward of King Théoden and captain of the King's guard. He was slain defending the gate in the Battle of the Hornburg. (II 146-47, 191, 237)

**HAMFAST GAMGEE** (TA 2926-FA 8) Hobbit of the Shire, son of Hobson Gamgee. He married Bell Goodchild; they had six children, including Samwise Gamgee. While young, Hamfast moved to Hobbiton and worked with his cousin Holman

Greenhand as a gardêner. About 2960 he became the gardêner at Bag End.

Hamfast was noted for his loquacity and his knowledge of
plants, especially potatoes.

Hamfast was known as the Gaffer and Old Gamgee at the
time of the WR. Hamfast, or Ham for short, is the translated
Hobbitish equivalent of the genuine Hobbitish forename
Ranugad (shortened to Ran), which meant "stay-at-home."
(I 44, 105; III 359, 362-63, 477, 517)

**HAMFAST GAMGEE** (b. FA 12) Hobbit of the Shire, fourth
son and seventh child of Sam Gamgee. (III 477)

**HAMFAST OF GAMWICH** (b. TA 2760) Hobbit of the Shire,
founder of the family of Gamwich, later Gamgee. (III 477)

**HAMSON GAMGEE** (b. TA 2965) Hobbit of the Shire, eldest
son of Hamfast Gamgee. He moved to Tighfield and worked
with his uncle Andwise Roper as a roper. (III 477)

**HANNA BRANDYBUCK** (fl. TA 2800) Hobbit of the Shire, wife
of Madoc Brandybuck. She was born a Goldworthy. (III 476)

**HARAD** (S.: 'south') The lands south of the River Harnen.
Except that oliphaunts lived there, nothing much is said of
the land, except for Umbar. Harad was most probably hot,
and perhaps had deserts.

Harad was also called Sutherland and Haradwaith, and was
divided into Near Harad and Far Harad. It was politically
divided into many kingdoms, inhabited by the Haradrim.

Called by the Hobbits of the Shire the Sunlands. (I 17,
325, 518; II 322, 338-39; III 456)

**HARADRIM** (S.: 'south-people') The primitive and savage
Men of Harad. In the Second Age some of the Haradrim paid
tribute to Númenor, but in the Third they were influenced by
Sauron and were a constant threat to Gondor's southern borders. The most serious attacks of the Haradrim on Gondor
took place in TA 1014-50, over Umbar, in 1944, when the
Haradrim were allied with the Wainriders, in 2885, when they
were defeated in the Battle of the Crossings of Poros, and
during the WR, when Haradrim fought in the Battle of the
Pelennor Fields and elsewhere. In addition, from the nineteenth century onwards, the Corsairs of Umbar were Haradrim.

The Haradrim were tall and dark-skinned, with black hair
and eyes. They loved bright clothing and ornaments, and some
tribes of Haradrim painted their bodies. In battle they used
all weapons, and were noted for their use of Oliphaunts.

Called in Westron Southerns and Southrons. Also called the Swarthy Men (by Hobbits) and the Swertings. (I 322; II 321, 322, 340-41; III 139-40, 148, 403-04, 409, 416)

**HARAD ROAD** Road running from Ithilien into Harad, passing over fords on the Poros and Harnen. At the time of the WR the southern part of the Road had fallen into disuse and had disappeared.

The Harad Road was probably built by Gondor in the early Third Age, when her power extended into Harad. (I 17)

**HARADWAITH** (S.: 'south---') Harad (q.v.).

Haradwaith and Sutherland were equivalent geographically, and perhaps also linguistically. (I 17; III 403)

**HARDBOTTLE** Village in the Shire, home of a family of Brace-girdles of which Lobelia Sackville-Baggins was a member. (III 372)

**HARDING** (d. TA 3019) Man of Rohan, killed in the Battle of the Pelennor Fields. (III 152)

**HARDING OF THE HILL** (b. FA 81) Hobbit of the Shire, son of Holfast Gardner. He probably lived in Bag End.

Harding's full name may have been Harding Gardner of the Hill. (III 477)

**HARFOOTS** The most common of the three branches of Hobbits. The Harfoots were the first Hobbits to cross the Misty Mountains into Eriador, doing so about TA 1050.

The harfoots were the most typical Hobbits. They were browner than the Stoors and Fallohides, and also smaller and shorter. They liked best highlands and hillsides, and kept the habit of living underground longer than the other strains. The Harfoots were friendlier with Dwarves than other Hobbits. (I 22; III 456)

**HARLINDON** (S.: 'south Lindon') That portion of Lindon south of the Gulf of Lune. Celeborn and Galadriel lived in Harlindon at the beginning of the Second Age.

See: Lindon. (I 16; III 452)

**HARLOND** (S.: 'south-haven') Harbor on the southern side of the Gulf of Lune. (I 16; III 411)

**HARLOND** Harbor and quays on the west side of Anduin three or four miles south of Minas Tirith, the port of the city. The Harlond was within the Rammas Echor. (III 23, 150)

**HARMA** (Q.: 'treasure') Original name for the tengwa ᚦ (number 11), having the value *ch*. Later, this *ch* became *h* at the beginning of words, and the name was changed to aha. (III 500)

HARNEN (S.: 'south-water') River flowing from the southern Ephel Dúath westward to the Bay of Belfalas, in the early Third Age the boundary between Gondor and the kingdoms of Harad. (I 17; III 403)

HARONDOR (S.: 'south Gondor') The land between the Poros and the Harnen, part of Gondor early in the Third Age and thereafter a land debated between Gondor and the Haradrim. Called in Westron South Gondor. (I 17; III 407)

HARROWDALE Valley in Rohan above Edoras. During the WR, the Muster of Rohan was held here. (III 66, 76 ff.)

HARRY GOATLEAF (fl. WR) Man of Bree, keeper of the western gate of Bree. He joined Bill Ferny and his ruffians as a bandit outside Bree during the WR. (I 207-08, 236; III 332, 335)

HARVESTMATH Name given Halimath (q. v.) in Bree. (III 483)

HASUFEL (tr. Roh.: 'dark skin'?) (fl. WR) Large grey horse of Rohan, lent by Éomer to Aragorn. (II 51)

HAUNTED MOUNTAIN The Dwimorberg (q. v.). (III 81)

HAUNTED PASS Cirith Gorgor (q. v.). (II 308)

HAVEN OF THE ELDAR A place in Eressëa, perhaps Tirion (q. v.). (III 390)

HAVENS OF UMBAR The sheltered bay and quays of Umbar (q. v.). Also called the Haven. (I 17; III 407)

HAY The High Hay (q. v.). (TB 9)

HAY GATE The Buckland Gate (q. v.). (III 342)

HAYSEND, HAYS-END Village in Buckland at the mouth of the Withywindle, so called because it was located at the southern end of the High Hay. (I 40, 142; TB 18, 19)

HAYWARD Family of Hobbits of the Eastfarthing. Probably an early member of the family was a hayward. (III 342)

HEADSTRONG Family of Hobbits of the Shire, perhaps well-to-do. (III 476)

HEATHERTOES Family of Men of Bree. (I 212)

HEDGE The High Hay (q. v.). (I 40, 155-57)

HEIRS OF ANÁRION The Kings of Gondor (q. v.). (III 394)

HEIRS OF ISILDUR The line of Isildur, unbroken  throughout

the Third Age. Isildur's son, Valandil, was King of Arnor, and his heirs were Kings of Arnor (to TA 861) or of Arthedain (861-1974), or Chieftains of the Dúnedain of the North (1974-3019). After the WR the heirs of Isildur, the Telcontari (q. v.), were the Kings of the Reunited Kingdom.

The Heirs of Isildur survived after the fall of Arthedain only because of the aid of Elrond, but most of them lived their full lifespan, which waned less rapidly than that of the Kings of Gondor.

The heirlooms of Isildur's heirs were the ring of Barahir, the shards of Narsil, the Elendilmir and the sceptre of Annúminas.

Also called the Northern Line. (III 394, 401, 402, 422)

**HELM** (TA 2691-2759) Man, ninth King of Rohan (2741-59) and last of the First Line. His reign was remembered chiefly for its end, for in 2758 Rohan was invaded by a huge horde of Dunlendings led by Wulf, son of Helm's enemy Freca (qq. v.). Helm, after losing a battle at the Crossings of Isen, retreated to the Hornburg, which he held during the Long Winter. Toward the end of the winter, Helm froze to death during a night sortie.

Helm was known as Hammerhand because of his great strength; he killed Freca with one blow of his fist. (III 431-33, 435)

**HELMINGAS** Name given by the Rohirrim to the men of Westfold, or perhaps of Rohan. (II 179)

**HELM'S DEEP** Gorge winding into the Ered Nimrais below the Thrihyrne. Helm's Deep was fortified and provisioned by the Rohirrim, who used it as a refuge in time of war. Helm's Deep was defended by Helm in 2758-59, and this defense gave it and everything in the area its name. During the WR it was defended by Théoden.

The Deeping Stream flowed out of Helm's Deep, and the Aglarond was found in it. The Deeping Wall was built across the entrance to the Deep.

"Helm's Deep" was the most common name used to refer to the entire system of fortifications in the area, including the Hornburg. (II 169 ff.; III 432)

**HELM'S DIKE** Trench and rampart built along the side of the Deeping Coomb nearest the Hornburg. (II 169 ff., esp. 171)

**HELM'S GATE** The entrance to Helm's Deep, across which the Deeping Wall was built. (II 169 ff.)

**HENDING** (b. TA 2859)  Hobbit of the Shire, of the working class, third son and fourth child of Holman the greenhanded. (III 477)

**HENNETH ANNÛN** (S.: 'sunset window, west window')  Hidden refuge of the Rangers of Ithilien, built behind a waterfall in North Ithilien by Túrin of Gondor in TA 2901. It was manned continuously until Faramir's retreat to Minas Tirith before the Siege of Gondor during the WR.

Called in Westron the Window of the Sunset and the Window on the West. (II 357 ff.; III 103, 416)

**HENSDAY** Hevenesdei (q. v.). (III 484)

*HERBLORE OF THE SHIRE*  A book written by Merry Brandybuck, describing among other things the history of pipe-weed. (I 28-29)

**HEREFARA** (d. TA 3019)  Man of Rohan, slain in the Battle of the Pelennor Fields. (III 152)

**HERION** (S.) (d. TA 2148)  Dúnadan, third Ruling Steward of Gondor (2116-48). (III 395)

**HERUBRAND** (d. TA 3019)  Man of Rohan, killed in the Battle of the Pelennor Fields. (III 152)

**HERUGRIM** The sword of Théoden. (II 157)

**HEVENESDEI** Early form of the name of the fifth day of the week in the Shire Reckoning, a translation of the Quenya Menelya. At the time of the WR, the form of the name was Hevensday or Hensday.

Called in *LotR* "Wednesday." (III 484)

**HEVENSDAY** See: Hevenesdei. (III 484)

**HIGH COURT** A court in the seventh level of Minas Tirith, not the Court of the Fountain. (III 25)

**HIGHDAY** See: Highdei. (III 484)

**HIGHDEI** Early form of the name of the seventh and chief day of the week in the Shire Reckoning, equivalent to the Eldarin and Westron Valanya. At the time of the WR, the form of the name was Highday.

Called in *LotR* "Friday." (III 484, 485)

**HIGH ELVES** The Eldar (q. v.). (III 452, 506)

**HIGH HAY** A twenty-mile-long hedge separating Buckland from the Old Forest. The High Hay was built by the Brandybucks as a defense against the Forest, and extended from the Great East Road in the north to the Withywindle in the south.

Also called the Hay and the Hedge. (I 40, 142, 155-56)

**HIGH KING OF ARNOR** Elendil, so called because he was King over both the Dúnedain realms of Arnor and Gondor, ruling Arnor directly and Gondor through his sons. After his death, however, the two kingdoms were separated and there were no further High Kings, although it is possible that some Kings of the Northern Line considered themselves High Kings. In the Fourth Age, Elessar and the later rulers of the Telcontar family may have been High Kings, although they ruled both kingdoms directly. (III 394)

**HIGH NAZGÛL** The Lord of the Nazgûl (q. v.), as called by the Orcs of Minas Morgul. (II 442)

**HIGH PASS** Pass over the Misty Mountains east of Rivendell. Toward the end of the Third Age the High Pass became one of the most important passes over the Mountains because it was believed safe from Orcs. However, about 2940 the Orcs opened an entrance to their tunnels on the Pass, and Thorin and Company were captured here in 2941. After that time, though, the Pass was kept open by the Beornings, and was an important trade route at the time of the WR. (I 301; H 64-67, 122)

**HIGH SEA** The Sea (q. v.). (III 384)

**HILD** (fl. TA 2726) Woman of Rohan, daughter of Gram and mother of Fréaláf. (III 433)

**HILDA BRANDYBUCK** (fl. TA 3000) Hobbit of the Shire, wife of Seredic Brandybuck. She was born a Bracegirdle. Hilda was a guest at the Farewell Party. (III 476)

**HILDIBRAND TOOK** (TA 2849-2934) Hobbit of the Shire, eighth son of Gerontius Took. (III 475)

**HILDIFONS TOOK** (b. TA 2844) Hobbit of the Shire, sixth son of Gerontius Took. He went on a journey and never returned. (III 475)

**HILDIGARD TOOK** (b. TA 2833 to 2837) Hobbit of the Shire, second son of Gerontius Took. He died young. (III 475)

**HILDIGRIM TOOK** (TA 2840-2941) Hobbit of the Shire, fourth son of Gerontius Took. He married Rosa Baggins; they had one son, Adalgrim. (III 474, 475)

**HILL** One of the westernmost hills of the Barrow-downs. Tom Bombadil's house was built on its western side. (I 168, 171; TB 11)

**HILL, THE**  Hobbiton Hill (q. v.). (III 486)

**HILL-MEN**  An evil people, living perhaps in the Ettenmoors or the western Misty Mountains near the Angle, allied with Angmar. The Hill-men seized control of Rhudaur about TA 1350 and fought with Angmar against Arthedain and Cardolan until the fall of Angmar in 1975, when they were probably annihilated or scattered. (III 397)

**HILL OF ERECH**  See: Erech. (III 73)

**HILL OF GUARD**  The easternmost spur of Mindolluin, upon which Minas Tirith was built. The massive Hill was joined to the main part of the mountain by a narrow ridge. (III 25)

**HILL OF HEARING**  Amon Lhaw (q. v.). (I 510)

**HILL OF ILMARIN**  Oiolosse (q. v.). (I 309)

**HILL OF SIGHT**  Amon Hen (q. v.). (I 510)

**HILL OF THE EYE**  Amon Hen (q. v.). (I 517)

**HILLS OF EVENDIM**  Hills north and south of Lake Evendim. Probably called in Sindarin Emyn Nenuial. (I 16; III 411)

**HILLS OF SCARY**  Hills in the Shire north of Scary. (I 40, III 372)

**HIRGON**  (S.: 'lord-stone') (d. TA 3019)  Man of Gondor, messenger of Denethor II. During the WR he brought the Red Arrow to Théoden, but was slain by Orcs while returning to Minas Tirith. (III 86, 134)

**HIRLUIN**  (S.: 'lord-blue') (d. TA 3019)  Man of Gondor, Lord of Pinnath Gelin. He was slain in the Battle of the Pelennor Fields.
He was known as Hirluin the Fair. (III 50, 148, 152)

**HÍSIMË**  (Q.: 'mist---')  Eleventh month of the Kings' and Stewards' Reckonings, and the eighth of the New Reckoning, corresponding roughly to our November.
The Sindarin form, used only by the Dúnedain, was Hithui. (III 483)

**HITHAIGLIN**  (S.: 'mist-point')  The Misty Mountains (q. v.). (I 16-17)

**HITHER SHORES**  Middle-earth, in Elvish poetical reference. (I 311)

**HITHLAIN**  (S.: 'mist-thread')  Substance used by the Elves of Lórien in their ropes, a tough, light, soft-feeling grey substance. (I 481; II 273; RHM III 438)

**HITHUI** (S.: 'misty') Hísimë (q. v.). (III 483)

**HLOTHRAM** (gen. Hobb.: 'cottager') A Hobbit forename. See: Cotman. (III 520)

**HLOTHRAN** (gen. Hobb.: *hloth* 'two-room dwelling + *ranu* 'collection of these on a hillside') Fairly common village-name in the Shire. (III 520)

**HLOTHRAN** A Shire surname, derived from the preceding. See: Cotton. (III 520)

*HOARD, THE* Poem written by Hobbits of the Shire in the Fourth Age, containing scraps of legends from the First Age. The Dwarf and the King in the poem seem to have been modelled on Mim and Túrin. (TB 8, 53-56)

**HOARWELL** The Mitheithel (q. v.). (I 268)

**HOBBITISH** The language used in the Shire at the time of the WR, a provincial dialect of Westron with some vocabulary taken from the Mannish languages of Dunland and the Vales of Anduin. The Hobbits seem to have freely used whatever Mannish language was used around them, and to have used these tongues carelessly and without great regard for form. These tendencies may be seen by comparing Rohirric *kuddukan* with Hobbitish *kuduk,* both forms meaning "hole-dweller, hobbit."

Since Hobbitish was so closely related to Westron, Professor Tolkien has translated it in *LotR* into real or likely (but invented) English forms of various periods related to the Old English forms he uses for Westron. There are, however, a few "genuine Hobbitish" words recorded on III 519-20, and various Hobbit personal names have been left untranslated. (III 509-10)

**HOBBITON** Village in the Shire, located in the Westfarthing north of the Great East Road.

See: Bagshot Row, the Mill, the Old Grange, etc. (I 40, 43; III 365 ff.)

**HOBBITON HILL** Hill in the Westfarthing, located between Hobbiton and Overhill.

Usually called the Hill. (I 40, 44; III 486; H 15)

**HOBBITON ROAD** Road running from Bywater over the Water and thence to Hobbiton and Overhill. (I 40; III 349)

**HOBBITRY-IN-ARMS** General mobilization of the Shire, held only in times of emergency and led by the Thain. As times of emergency did not frequently occur in the Shire, this mobilization was not common.

The Hobbitry-in-arms was probably the same as or similar to the Shire-muster. (I 30)

**HOBBITS**  One of the speaking races of Middle-earth, originally closely related to Men. Although created in the First Age, Hobbits were unobtrusive and lived in the Vales of Anduin largely unnoticed by other races until well into the Third Age. About TA 1050 the Hobbits, who by this time had become divided into three distinct groups, the Fallohides, the Harfoots and the Stoors (qq. v.), fled westward because of the evil in Mirkwood. The wanderings of each strain are described in their individual entries. In 1600 the Shire was founded, and soon almost all Hobbits came to live there or in Bree, although in 2463 there was a colony of Stoors in the Gladden Fields, and at the time of the WR there were wandering Hobbits.

Except for the Great Plague of 1636 and the Long Winter of 2758, the Hobbits of Eriador lived for the most part peacefully and comfortably in the Shire and Bree, thanks to the protection of Gandalf and the Rangers. Their population grew, and twice the boundaries of the Shire were extended; in 2340 the Oldbucks settled Buckland, and in FA 32 the Westmarch was added to the Shire by gift of King Elessar. Except for Gandalf and the Rangers, before the WR nobody was concerned with Hobbits; after the War, however, because of the heroic deeds of Frodo and his companions, Hobbits were included in songs and chronicles by other peoples, a courtesy which in general the Hobbits did not return.

A thorough description of Hobbits is given on I 19-36 and H 16, and there is no purpose in repeating these passages. It may be mentioned that the Stoors of the Gladden Fields in TA 2463 were matriarchal, and all Hobbits may at one time have been organized into matriarchal clans. It is also worth stressing that Hobbits, although comfort-loving, provincial and distrustful of the outside world, were in times of danger courageous, skillful and relatively undaunted by great terrors. Toward the end of the Third Age, the Hobbits alone in Middle-earth (with the Men of Bree) used surnames. They lived to about one hundred years of age; thirty-three was considered the age of adulthood.

Hobbits at the time of the WR spoke a provincial dialect

of Westron (See.: Hobbitish) They wrote mostly with a mode of the cirth, although some of the better-educated Hobbits knew the Tengwar.

Hobbit is an anglicization of *kuduk*, the name they called themselves; it is related to the translated Rohirric *holbytla* (pl. *holbytlan*), a translation of the genuine Rohirric *kuddukan*, meaning "hole-builder." They were called the Periannath in Sindarin and banakil (sing.) in genuine Westron; the translated Westron equivalent is "Halfling." They were also known as the Little Folk and the Little People. (I 19-36, 79, 89, 206; III 456-57, 509-10, 514, 515-16, 519-20; H 15-16, 77-78; TB 9)

**HOB GAMMIDGE** (b. TA 2846) Hobbit of the Shire, son of Wiseman Gamwich. He married Rowan, eldest daughter of Holman the greenhanded; they had at least one child, Hobson Gamgee.

Hob was known as Hob Gammidge the Roper, and also as Old Gammidgy. (III 477)

**HOB HAYWARD** (fl. WR) Hobbit of the Eastfarthing. Before the WR he guarded the Hay Gate, but during Saruman's domination of the Shire he was a guard at the Brandywine Gate.

At the time of the WR he seems to have been fairly old. (III 342)

**HOBSON GAMGEE** (TA 2885-2984) Hobbit of the Shire, son of Hob Gammidge. Like his father, he was a roper in Tighfield.

Hobson was also called Roper Gamgee. (III 477)

**HOGG** Perhaps a family of Hobbits of the Shire. Old Farmer Hogg appears in the poem *Perry-the-Winkle*, and may well have been an historical personage. (TB 42)

**HOLBYTLA, HOLBYTLAN** See: Hobbits. (II 207; III 510)

**HOLD OF DUNHARROW** See: Dunharrow. (III 80 ff.)

**HOLDWINE** Name given Merry Brandybuck (q. v.) in Rohan. (III 438)

**HOLFAST GARDNER** (b. FA 42) Hobbit of the Shire, son of Frodo Gardner. Holfast probably lived in Bag End. (III 477)

**HOLLIN** Eregion (q. v.). (I 369)

**HOLMAN** (b. TA 2810) Hobbit of the Shire, an excellent gardêner and founder of the family of Greenhand. Holman lived in Hobbiton.

Holman was known as Holman the greenhanded. (III 477)

**HOLMAN COTTON** (b. TA 2902) Hobbit of the Shire, son of Cotman. He lived in Bywater.

Holman was known as Long Hom. (III 477)

**HOLMAN GREENHAND** (b. TA 2892, d. c. 2961) Hobbit of the Shire, son of Halfred Greenhand. He lived at Number 3, Bagshot Row, Hobbiton, and was gardêner to Bilbo Baggins. Holman taught the trade of gardêning to Hamfast Gamgee. (I 44; III 477)

**HONEYBEES**  A race of creatures battled by the messenger in Bilbo Baggins' poem *Errantry*. Their existence in this context is probably fictitious. (TB 27)

**HONEYCAKES OF BEORN**  Tasty cakes prepared by Beorn. Like cram, they were very nourishing and could be preserved for long periods of time. (H 133)

**HORN**  (d. TA 3019)  Man of Rohan, killed in the Battle of the Pelennor Fields. (III 152)

**HORNBLOWER**  Family of Hobbits of the Shire, all or most of whom dwelt in the Southfarthing. The Hornblowers were probably of the upper class. (I 28, 52; III 474)

**HORNBURG**  Fortress in western Rohan, built by Gondor in the days of its power on the Hornrock near the Thrihyrne. It was said that no enemy could take the Hornburg if it were defended. Helm took refuge there against the Dunlendings in TA 2758-59, and during the WR Théoden fought the Battle of the Hornburg (q. v.) against the forces of Saruman.
　　The Hornburg was so named because a horn sounded in its tower echoed loudly in the winding depths of Helm's Deep. In times of peace it was the dwelling of the master of Westfold. (II 169 ff.; III 432)

**HORN-CALL OF BUCKLAND**  The alarm of Buckland, not used very often. (I 239; III 354)

**HORN OF THE MARK**  Small silver horn made by the Dwarves in ancient times, taken by the Éothéod from the hoard of Scatha. After the WR, Éowyn gave the horn to Merry as a keepsake, and he used it to hearten the Hobbits during the scouring of the Shire. Afterwards, it was blown each year on the anniversary of its first use in the Shire. (III 316, 353-54, 486)

**HORNROCK**  Rock upon which the Hornburg (q. v.) was built, a black spur jutting out from the northern cliff of Helm's Deep. (II 169 ff.)

**HOST OF THE WEST**  The army that defeated the Witch-king and destroyed Angmar in TA 1975 in the Battle of Fornost. The Army was composed of Elves of Lindon and Men of Arthedain and Gondor, and was led by Círdan and Eärnur. (III 411)

**HOST OF THE WEST**  The Army of the West (q. v.). (III 467)

**HOST OF VALINOR** The army that came to the aid of the Eldar and the Edain in the War of the Great Jewels, and which overthrew Morgoth and broke Thangorodrim in the Great Battle. The Host of Valinor contained some of the greatest Valar, including Araw, as well as many lesser Valar and Eldar. (I 319; III 138, 452)

**HOUSE OF DURIN** The royal family of Durin's Folk, descended from Durin I. (III 450)

**HOUSE OF EORL** The Kings of the Mark (q. v.). (II 158)

**HOUSE OF HADOR** The Third House of the Edain, the most renowned in the War of the Great Jewels. The House of Hador was golden-haired, and was related to the Rohirrim. Huor, Tuor and Eärendil were of this House, in addition to its founder, Hador. (II 364; III 389)

**HOUSE OF HÚRIN** The House of the Stewards (q. v.). (III 395-96, 414)

**HOUSE OF THE KINGS** Building in the Hallows (q. v.) of Minas Tirith where the Kings of Gondor were laid to rest. (III 427, 472)

**HOUSE OF THE STEWARDS** Noble Dúnadan family from which the Stewards of Gondor were chosen after TA 1621. The first Steward of the House was Húrin of Emyn Arnen, Steward to King Minardil. After Húrin all the Stewards were chosen from among his descendents, and after Pelendur (d. 1998) the Stewardship became hereditary.

The Stewards seem to have had hereditary lands in Emyn Arnen; Húrin came from there and Faramir was made Lord of Emyn Arnen after the WR.

The chief heirloom of the House was the Great Horn originally used by Vorondil; after his time it was carried by the heir of the House.

Also called the House of Húrin. (III 118, 414)

**HOUSE OF THE STEWARDS** Building in the Hallows of Minas Tirith where the Stewards of Gondor were laid to rest. During the WR, Denethor II burned himself in the House, which was destroyed by the fire. (III 122, 155-61)

**HOUSES OF HEALING** The hospital of Minas Tirith, built against the southern wall of the sixth level of the city. The House had a fair, tree-girt garden. (III 161, 165-80, 291-300)

**HRÍVË** (Q.: 'winter') The next-to-last division of the Eldarin loa (q. v.), called in Sindarin rhîw. Also used by Men as the name for the season "winter." (III 480, 485)

**HUGGINS** Surname of William, one of the trolls turned to stone during the expedition of Thorin and Company in TA 2941. (H 48)

**HUGO BOFFIN** (fl. TA 2900) Hobbit of the Shire. He married Donnamira Took. (III 475)

**HUGO BRACEGIRDLE** (fl. TA 3000) Hobbit of the Shire, a guest at the Farewell Party. He was noted for borrowing books and not returning them. (I 64)

**HUMMERHORNS** A probably-fictitious insect race fought by the messenger in Bilbo Baggins' poem *Errantry*. (TB 27)

**HUNTER'S MOON** The name given by the Hobbits of the Shire to the bright full moon of mid-November. (I 358-59)

**HUOR** (S.? tr. Ad.?) (First Age) Adan of the Third House of the Edain, father of Tuor. (III 389)

**HUORNS** (tr. Roh.? S.?) Creatures of Fangorn, probably Ents (or trees) that had become wild and dangerous in the Great Darkness. Huorns moved little, but when they desired they could travel quickly and could wrap themselves in shadow. Huorns could still speak, and were controlled by the true Ents. Although wild, they were not really evil, and hated Orcs. (II 186-87, 192-93, 200-01, 217)

**HÚRIN** (S.? tr. Ad.?) (First Age) Adan, elf-friend and hero. (I 355)

**HÚRIN** (fl. TA 1634) Dúnadan of Gondor, Steward of King Minardil and founder of the House of the Stewards.
He was known as Húrin of Emyn Arnen. (III 414)

**HÚRIN I** (d. TA 2244) Dúnadan, fifth Ruling Steward of Gondor (2204-44). (III 395)

**HÚRIN II** (d. TA 2628) Dúnadan, fourteenth Ruling Steward of Gondor (2605-28). (III 395)

**HÚRIN** (fl. WR) Dúnadan of Gondor of high rank, Warden of the Keys of Minas Tirith. Húrin fought in the Battle of the Pelennor Fields, and later was given charge of Minas Tirith when the Army of the West rode to the Morannon. (III 148, 292)

**HWESTA** (Q.: 'breeze') Name of the tengwa **ᴄ** (number 12), used in Quenya to represent voiceless *w* and in Sindarin to represent *chw.* (III 500)

**HWESTA SINDARINWA** (Q.: 'grey-Elven *hw')* Name for the tengwa ᴐᶅ (number 34), which seems to have been a modified form of hwesta. It was used only in Sindarin, in which it represented voiceless *w.* (III 500)

**HYARMEN** (Q.: 'south') Name for the tengwa ᴧ (number 33). This tengwa was commonly used to indicate the compass-point "south" even in languages in which the word for "south" did not begin with this sign. (III 500)

**HYARMENDACIL I** (Q.: 'south-victor') (d. TA 1149) Dúnadan, fifteenth King of Gondor (1015-1149) and the last Ship-king. He took the crown under the name Ciryaher, but changed his royal name to Hyarmendacil in 1050, after crushing the Haradrim and forcing them to acknowledge the overlordship of Gondor. During his reign Gondor reached the height of its power. (III 394, 403-04)

**HYARMENDACIL II** (d. TA 1621) Dúnadan, twenty-fourth King of Gondor (1540-1621). He was originally named Vinyarion, but took the name Hyarmendacil in commemmoration of a great victory he won over the Haradrim in 1551. (III 395, 457)

# I

**IARWAIN BEN-ADAR** (S.: 'oldest fatherless') Elvish name for Tom Bombadil (q. v.). (I 347)

**IAVAS** (S.) The Sindarin form of yávië (q. v.). (III 480)

**ICE BAY OF FOROCHEL** The great bay between the mainland of the Northern Waste and the Cape of Forochel. The Bay was frozen in winter.

The maps in *LotR,* however, label a southern inlet of the Bay proper as the "Ice Bay of Forochel." (I 16; III 399, 400)

**IDRIL CELEBRINDAL** (S.) (First Age) Eldarin princess, daughter of King Turgon of Gondolin. She married Tuor, and was the mother of Eärendil. (III 388-89)

**ILBERIC BRANDYBUCK** (b. TA 2991) Hobbit of the Shire, second son of Seredic Brandybuck. He was a guest at the Farewell Party. (III 476)

**ILMARIN** (Q.) In the Undying Lands, perhaps the palace of Manwe on Oiolosse, mainland Eldamar or the land including Oiolosse, Tirion and the Calacirian. (I 309, 310, 482)

**IMLAD MORGUL** (S.: 'valley of black magic') Valley in the western side of the Ephel Dúath, through which the Morgulduin flowed. Minas Morgul was located at the head of the valley. During the WR the Captains of the West set fire to the evil meadows of Imlad Morgul and broke the bridge across the Morgulduin, but even after the War the terror of the valley was too great for it to be resettled.

Also called Morgul Vale, Morgulvale, the Valley of the Wraiths and the valley of Living Death. (II 388, 397 ff.; III 197-98, 305)

**IMLADRIS** (S.: 'valley-cut') Rivendell (q. v.). (I 323)

**IMLOTH MELUI** (S.: 'deep-blossom ---') Valley in Gondor, perhaps in Lossarnach, noted for its roses. (III 173)

**IMRAHIL** (of Númenorean origin) (fl. WR) Dúnadan of Gondor, Prince of Belfalas and Lord of Dol Amroth. During the WR Imrahil fought in the Battle of the Pelennor Fields, and ruled Minas Tirith after the death of Denethor II while Faramir was ill. He was one of the Captains of the West, and fought in the battle outside the Morannon.

Imrahil was a great warrior, and was known as "the fair" because he bore the signs of his Dúnadan and Elvish ancestry. (III 23, 50, 119, 148-52, 181, 487)

**INCÁNUS** Name given to Gandalf (q. v.) in the south of Middle-earth. (II 353)

**INGOLD** (S.? tr. W.?) (fl. WR) Man of Gondor, leader of the soldiers at the northern gate of the Rammas Echor before the Siege of Gondor. (III 21, 115)

**INLAND SEA** The Sea of Rhûn (q. v.). (III 43)

**INZILADÛN, AR-** (Ad.) See: Tar-Palantir. (III 390)

**IORETH** (S.) (fl. WR) Woman of Gondor, originally from Lossarnach. At the time of the WR she was the eldest of the women who served in the Houses of Healing in Minas Tirith. Her folk wisdom was exceeded only by her loquacity. (III 166, 170-71, 302-03)

**IORLAS** (S.: '---leaf') (fl. WR) Man of Gondor, brother of Beregond. He probably lived in Minas Tirith. (III 47)

**IRENSAGA** Saw-toothed mountain of the Ered Nimrais. Irensaga formed the north wall of Dunharrow. (III 81)

**IRON CROWN** The crown of Morgoth, in which he set the Silmarilli. Beren stole one of them from the Crown, and as the others were separated and lost at the fall of Thangorodrim, the Iron Crown seems to have been destroyed at the end of the First Age. (I 260; II 408)

**IRON HILLS** Hills east of Erebor settled about TA 2590 by Grór and Dwarves of Durin's Folk after the desertion of the Ered Mithrin. The Dwarves of the Iron Hills under Náin, coming late to the field, turned the tide of the Battle of Azanulbizar in 2799. In 2941, five hundred Dwarves of the Iron Hills, led by Dáin, came to Erebor to support Thorin II, and fought valiantly in the Battle of the Five Armies. Dáin then became King of Erebor; the Iron Hills pass out of records after this, but they may not have been deserted.

The Dwarves of the Iron Hills seem to have been prosperous, but not wealthy. It is likely that the Hills had much iron, but no gold. (I 17; III 440, 443-44, 448; H 246, 256-57, 263-65)

**ISEMBARD TOOK** (TA 2847-2946) Hobbit of the Shire, seventh son of Gerontius Took. (III 475)

**ISEMBOLD TOOK** (TA 2842-2946) Hobbit of the Shire, fifth

son of Gerontius Took. (III 475)

**ISEN** (tr. Roh.: 'iron') River flowing from Nan Curunír south through the Gap of Rohan, and then west to the Sea. During the WR, the Ents temporarily diverted its waters in order to flood Isengard.

The Isen was the western boundary of Rohan, and was defended against the Dunlendings. The Isen seems not to have been bridged, but it was crossed by the Fords of Isen about thirty miles south of Isengard. (I 16; II 198-202; III 431)

**ISENGAR TOOK** (TA 2862-2960) Hobbit of the Shire, youngest son of Gerontius Took. He was said to have gone to sea in his youth. (III 475)

**ISENGARD** (tr. Roh.: 'iron-fortress') Fortress built by Gondor in the days of its power in Nan Curunír. Isengard consisted of a natural circular stone wall surrounding a broad plain, in the center of which was the tower of Orthanc (q. v.). Isengard had only one gate, which faced south.

When Calenardhon was given to the Rohirrim in TA 2510, Isengard was kept by Gondor, but it was deserted. About 2700 it was taken by the Dunlendings, but they were driven out in 2759 by Fréaláf. In that year, with the permission of Beren of Gondor, Saruman began to live in Isengard, and in 2963 he took it as his own and began to fortify it, replacing its grass and trees with stone and machinery. There he housed Orcs, Men and wolves until Isengard was attacked and demolished by the Ents during the WR. The Ents planted the Watchwood (q. v.) there, and renamed Isengard the Treegarth of Orthanc.

Called in Sindarin Angrenost. Also called the Ring of Isengard, which referred specifically to the physical arrangement of wall and plain. (I 338; II 203-04 ff.; III 317, 416, 417, 432, 433-34, 460, 462)

**ISENGRIM TOOK** (TA 2620-2722) Hobbit of the Shire, as Isengrim II the twenty-second Thain of the Shire (2653-2722). He began the excavation of the Great Smials. (III 459, 474, 482)

**ISENGRIM TOOK** (TA 2832-2930) Hobbit of the Shire, eldest son of Gerontius Took and, as Isengrim III, twenty-seventh Thain of the Shire (2920-30). He had no children. (III 475)

**ISENMOUTHE** Pass in Mordor between Gorgoroth and Udûn, at the meeting of the Ered Luin and the Ephel Dúath.

Called in Sindarin Carach Angren. (III 15, 241, 251)

ISILDUR (Q.: 'moon---') (d. TA 2) Dúnadan, elder son of Elendil. He escaped with his father from the ruin of Númenor, and became, with his brother Anárion, co-ruler of Gondor. He was also Lord of Ithilien. Isildur founded Minas Ithil, and ruled there until SA 3429, when Sauron took the city. He escaped to Arnor, leaving Anárion to defend Osgiliath and Minas Anor, and returned to Gondor with the army of the Last Alliance. In 3441 Isildur stood by his father in the final battle against Sauron; and, cutting off the Enemy's finger, claimed the One Ring. After ruling Gondor for two years (SA 3441-TA 2) and instructing Meneldil, Anárion's young son, in the art of kingship, Isildur went north to rule in Arnor, of which he had become King on his father's death in 3441. On the way, however, his party was ambushed in the Gladden Fields by a host of Orcs. Isildur tried to escape by putting on the Ring and swimming in the Anduin, but the Ring slipped off and he was slain. (I 83, 319, 320, 331-32; III 394)

ISILDUR'S BANE The One Ring (q. v.). (I 323, 324)

ISILYA (Q.: 'moon-day') The third day of the enquië, dedicated to the moon.
    Called in Sindarin Orithil, and by the Hobbits Monendei, later Monday. The last name is used for Isilya in *LotR*. (III 484)

ISLES OF THE WEST The Undying Lands (q. v.), or possibly Eressëa and other islands. (III 424)

ISTARI (S.? Q.?) The Wizards (q. v.). (III 455)

ISUMBRAS TOOK (fl. SA 2340) Hobbit of the Shire, as Isumbras I the thirteenth Thain of the Shire (2340-?) and the first of the Took line. (III 457)

ISUMBRAS TOOK (TA 2666-2759) Hobbit of the Shire, son of Isengrim Took and, as Isumbras III, twenty-third Thain of the Shire (2722-59). (III 475)

ISUMBRAS TOOK (TA 2838-2939) Hobbit of the Shire, third son of Gerontius Took and, as Isumbras IV, twenty-eighth Thain of the Shire (2930-39). (III 475)

ITHILDIN (S.: 'star-moon') Substance fashioned by the Noldor of Eregion from mithril, and used by them for gateways and such. Ithildin was visible only by starlight or moonlight, and only after it was touched by one who spoke certain words of lore. (I 397, 413)

**ITHILIEN** (S.: 'moon-land') Area of Gondor between Anduin and the Ephel Dúath, bounded on the south by the Poros, divided into North and South Ithilien. Ithilien was originally the fief of Isildur. Ithilien bore the brunt of the attacks on Gondor from the east and south, beginning with Sauron's capture of its chief city, Minas Ithil, in SA 3429. The city was freed, but its capture by the Nazgûl in TA 2002 caused many of the remaining inhabitants of Ithilien to flee, and more fled when Mordor-orcs began to ravage the land in 2901. The desertion was not complete, however, until 2954, when Mount Doom burst into flame and Sauron openly declared himself. Before this time, secret refuges like Henneth Annûn had been built, and the Rangers of Ithilien harried Sauron's forces in Ithilien until the WR.

Since Sauron had not controlled Ithilien for long, after the WR it was still a fair, pollen-perfumed land. In 3019, with the return of the King, Faramir became Prince of Ithilien. Legolas and other Elves of the Woodland Realm lived in Ithilien, and it became once more the fairest land in the Westlands.

Originally called Ithiliend. (I 322; II 325 ff.; III 14-15, 413, 414 ff., 451, 461, 462, 490)

**IVANNETH** Name used by the Dúnedain for Yavannië (q. v.). (III 483)

**IVORWEN** (S.) (fl. TA 2907-29) Dúnadan of the North, wife of Dírhael and mother of Gilraen. (III 420)

**IVY BUSH, THE** Tavern on the Bywater Road, frequented by Hobbits from Bywater and Hobbiton. (I 44)

# J

**JOLLY COTTON** Wilcome Cotton (q.v.). (III 354)

# K

**KALI** See: Kalimac. (III 517)

**KALIMAC** (gen. Mannish) Buckland personal name, originally derived from the language used by the Stoors before coming to the Shire. It was almost always shortened to Kali, which meant "jolly, gay" in Westron.
See: Meriadoc Brandybuck. (III 517)

**KARNINGUL** (gen. West.: 'cut valley') Rivendell (q. v.). (III 515)

**KELOS** See: Celos. (III 14)

**KEY OF ORTHANC** Actually, two black keys of intricate shape, used to lock the door of Orthanc. (III 240, 245)

**KEYS OF BARAD-DÛR** The keys of the Dark Tower, a symbol of Sauron's power. (II 240)

**KHAND** Realm southeast of Mordor, home of the Variags (q. v.). Because of its location, Khand was probably always strongly influenced by Sauron. (I 17; III 148, 409)

**KHAZÂD** (Kh.) The name given to the Dwarves (q. v.) by Aulë the Smith, their own name for themselves. (III 519)

**KHAZAD-DÛM** (Kh.: 'dwarf-mansion') The mansion and folk-home of Durin's Folk, carved by Durin I early in the First Age in the caves overlooking Azanulbizar. Here was located the tomb of Durin, and here dwelled the heart of his people. Expanded many times, Khazad-dûm ultimately took up much of the area beneath Barazinbar, Zirak-zigil and Bundushathûr, and in the Second Age a tunnel was built to Eregion. Khazad-dûm consisted of many large halls on a number of levels, as well as mines, etc.

At the end of the First Age, the population of Khazad-dûm was increased, as many skilled Dwarves from the Ered Luin came there after the ruin of Nogrod and Belegost. Early in the Second Age, mithril was discovered in Khazad-dûm, and the friendship between Durin's Folk and the Noldor of Eregion began. The gates of Khazad-dûm were closed during the War of Elves and Sauron, and thus the Dwarves survived through the Second Age.

In TA 1980, the Dwarves, while extending their mithril-mine, released the Balrog imprisoned beneath Barazinbar.

The next year, after two Kings of Khazad-dûm had been slain by the Balrog, the Dwarves fled. About 2480 Sauron began to keep Orcs in Khazad-dûm, and these Orcs murdured Thrór in 2790. This led to the War of the Dwarves and Orcs, which ended in 2799 with the Battle of Azanulbizar. Despite the Dwarves' victory, Dáin Ironfoot refused to re-enter Khazad-dûm because of the presence of the Balrog. In 2989, however, a large group of Dwarves of Erebor, led by Balin, established a Dwarf-kingdom in Khazad-dûm. However, they were trapped by the Watcher in the Water at the West-gate and a large army of Orcs at the East-gate, and they perished in 2994. In January, 3019, the Company of the Ring (and Gollum) passed through Khazad-dûm, and Gandalf slew the Balrog in a series of battles which ruined the Chamber of Mazarbul, Durin's Bridge, the Endless Stair and Durin's Tower (qq. v.). There is no mention of a recolonization of Khazad-dûm by the Dwarves in the Fourth Age, despite the death of the Balrog.

The Dwarvish kingdom of Khazad-dûm included Azanulbizar as well as the halls within the mountains. Except for Balin, all the Kings of Khazad-dûm were also Kings of Durin's Folk.

The Elvish name for Khazad-dûm was Moria. The Westron names were the Dwarrowdelf (gen. West. Phurunargian). and the Black Pit or the Black Chasm, translations of the Khuzdul and Sindarin respectively. Also known as the Mines of Moria. (I 316, 370, 402-31; II 134-35; III 438-39, 442, 444, 458, 459, 462, 519)

KHELED-ZÂRAM (Kh.) Lake in Azanulbizar. Here, early in the First Age, Durin I beheld the reflection of Durin's Crown. Ever after, these stars could be seen reflected in the water of Kheled-zâram at any time of the day or night, and the lake was always smooth. However, the faces of those who looked into the waters could not be seen.

Called in Westron the Mirromere. (I 370, 411, 412, 432-34)

KHUZDUL (Kh.: 'Dwarvish') The language of the Dwarves. It was a secret tongue of lore, and few who were not Dwarves ever learned it. Khuzdul seems to have been a rather harsh tongue, with an emphasis on stops, voiced spirants and aspiration, but it no doubt assumed some grace when properly spoken.

The only examples of Khuzdul given in LotR are a few place-names, the Dwarves' battle-cry and the inscription on the tomb of Balin. (III 488, 504, 512-13)

**KIBIL-NÂLA** (Kh.) Either the Silverlode or the springs that were its source. The springs were located in Azanulbizar and were icy cold. (I 370-71, 461)

**KÍLI** (TA 2864-2941) Dwarf of Durin's line, son of Dís and nephew of Thorin, a member of Thorin and Company. Kíli, with his brother Fíli, was slain in the Battle of the Five Armies while defending Thorin's body. (III 450; H 22, 26, 275)

**KINE OF ARAW** A kind of large white ox found near the Sea of Rhûn. The Kine were often hunted; the most famous hunters were Araw the Vala in the First Age, and Vorondil of Gondor in the Third. The Great Horn worn by the heirs of the Stewards was made from a horn of one of the Kine killed by Vorondil. (III 29, 395)

**KINGDOM UNDER THE MOUNTAIN** The Dwarf-realm in Erebor (q. v.), ruled by the King of Durin's Folk. (III 448)

**KING OF THE DEAD** (fl. SA 3429-TA 3019) Man, chief of the Men of the Mountains at the time of the founding of Gondor. On behalf of his people, he swore allegiance to Isildur at Erech, but broke the Oath when called to fight with the army of the Last Alliance. For this, he and his people were doomed to dwell in the Ered Nimrais until they repaid their debt, which they did during the WR.

While a normal Man, he was known as the King of the Mountains. (III 64, 187)

**KING OF THE MOUNTAINS** The King of the Dead (q. v.). (III 64)

**KING OF THE NINE RIDERS** The Lord of the Nazgûl (q. v.). (II 401)

**KING'S COURT** Court in Númenor, probably in the royal palace, where Nimloth grew. (III 484)

**KINGSFOIL** Athelas (q. v.). (III 170)

**KING'S HOUSE** The royal palace of Gondor, originally in Osgiliath but moved to Minas Anor by King Tarondor in TA 1640. See: the White Tower, the Tower Hall. (III 28, 457)

**KING'S MEN** Those Númenoreans who settled in Middle-earth in the Second Age, and their descendents, who were faithful to the Kings. They were corrupted by Sauron and became known as the Black Númenoreans (q. v.).

The greatest center of the King's Men in Middle-earth was Umbar. (III 403)

**KINGS OF ARNOR** The Kings of Arnor were Dúnedain, Elendil, Isildur and the Line of Isildur (qq. v.) from SA 3320 to TA 861, TA 1349 to 1974 and from TA 3019 into the Fourth Age. From 861 to 1349, Arnor was divided into three realms, but after 1349, since the royal line had died out in two of the kingdoms, the Kings of Arthedain claimed lordship over all of Arnor. From TA 1974 to 3019, the Dúnedain of the North were scattered, and although the royal line survived it did not claim kingship.

The Kings of Arnor at first dwelled in Annuminas, but before 861 the royal court was moved to Fornost. At the beginning of the Fourth Age Annúminas was rebuilt and once more became the site of the court.

The symbols of the authority of the Kings of Arnor were the sceptre of Annúminas, the Elendilmir, and the ring of Barahir; they wore no crown. (III 394, 401)

**KINGS OF ARTHEDAIN** The Kings of Arthedain were Dúnedain of the Line of Isildur, Amlaith and his descendents from TA 861 until 1974. Amlaith was the eldest son of Eärendur of Arnor, and thus the Kings of Arthedain were the heirs of Isildur. Beginning with Argeleb I in 1349, the Kings of Arthedain claimed lordship over all of Arnor, but this claim was contested by Rhudaur. The last King of Arthedain was Arvedui; with his death in 1974 and the conquest of Arthedain by Angmar the kingdom ended. (III 394)

**KINGS OF DURIN'S FOLK** The Kings of Durin's Folk were the heirs of Durin I, whether in Khazad-dûm or in exile. From its making in the Second Age, when it was given to Durin III, until TA 2845, when Sauron recovered it from Thráin II, the Kings of Durin's Folk bore the greatest of the Seven Rings.

It was believed by the Dwarves that six times the King of Durin's Folk would so resemble Durin the Deathless as to be named Durin, and that the line would end with Durin VII.

The Kings of Durin's Folk were also known at certain times as the Kings of Khazad-dûm (First Age-TA 1981) and the Kings under the Mountain (TA 1999-2190, 2590-2770, 2941-FA ?). (III 439, 450)

**KINGS OF GONDOR** The Kings of Gondor were Dúnedain, Elendil, Isildur and Anárion, the heirs of Anárion and the Telcontari. Elendil was the first King, but he committed the rule of Gondor to his sons, Isildur and Anárion. On Elendil's death, Isildur became King of Arnor, and Meneldil, the son of Anárion, King of Gondor; the two lines were separated. In the Third Age the line of the Kings was broken five times, until in 2050 King Eärnur, who was unmarried, disappeared, and the kingdom was ruled by the Stewards. The line of the Kings was restored by Elessar Telcontar, the heir of Isildur, after the WR.

The Kings wore a crown, the Silver Crown, and bore a sceptre. Their banner was black, with a blossoming white tree under seven stars.

The titles of the Kings are not given in *LotR*, but they were probably similar to those of the Ruling Stewards. The Kings, or their heirs, when capable led in person the armies and fleets of Gondor.

Also known as the Line of Anárion. (III 394-95)

**KINGS OF KHAZAD-DÛM**  Those of the Kings of Durin's Folk (q. v.) who lived in Khazad-dûm. There was such a king from the time of Durin I to TA 1981, when Khazad-dûm was deserted by the Dwarves because of the Balrog. Balin, who was not King of Durin's Folk, was King of Khazad-dûm from TA 2989-94. (III 445)

**KINGS OF MEN**  The Dúnedain (q. v.). (III 428)

**KINGS OF THE MARK**  Men, the Kings of Rohan, of the House of Eorl. The King was the First Marshal of the Mark, and had his court (after its building in TA 2569) in Meduseld.

The line of the Kings was broken twice, and so the line was divided into the First, Second and Third Lines (qq. v.). (II 158; III 434-37)

**KINGS OF THE WEST**  The Telcontari (q. v.). (III 469)

**KINGS' RECKONING**  The calendar system used in Númenor and in the Westron area of Middle-earth until about TA 2100, a synthesis of the systems of the Eldar and the Edain. The enquië (q. v.) had seven days, and the astar (q. v.) thirty. The loa (q. v.) contained twelve astari and a number of extra days, forming a total of 365 days, or 366 in leap years. The calendar for one loa was as follows:

| | |
|---|---|
| yestarë: first day* | Cermië: 31 days |
| Narvinyë: 30 days | Úrimë: 30 days |
| Nénimë: 30 days | Yavannië: 30 days |
| Súlimë: 30 days | Narquelië: 30 days |
| Víressë: 30 days | Hísimë: 30 days |
| Lótessë: 30 days | Ringarë: 30 days |
| Nárië: 31 days | mettarë: last day |
| loëndë: Midsummer's Day** | |

\* Our December 23

\*\* Replaced every fourth year except the last of a century by 2 enderi

Further adjustments were made as a result of the Deficit (q. v.).

About TA 2100 the Kings' Reckoning was replaced by the Stewards' Reckoning everywhere in the Westron area except the Shire. (See: the Shire Reckoning) The Quenya names given above were the names most commonly used, but the Dúnedain used Sindarin names and the Hobbits used Mannish ones. (III 480-81)

**KINGS UNDER THE MOUNTAIN** Dwarves, those Kings of Durin's Folk who ruled in Erebor. There was such a King during the years TA 1999-2190, 2590-2770 and 2941-FA ?. (III 439; H 190)

**KING'S WRITERS** The royal scribes of Gondor. (I 38)

**KIN-STRIFE** The great civil war of Gondor, lasting from TA 1432 to 1448. The war resulted from the belief of some of the Dúnedain that Eldacar was unfit to rule because he was not of pure Dúnadan blood, and stemmed ultimately from the discontent of various members of the royal family over the favor shown to the Northmen by Eldacar's father Valacar. Before Valacar's death in 1432 there was rebellion in southern Gondor, and on Eldacar's accession there was widespread warfare. The rebels, the most powerful of whom was Castamir, the Captain of Ships, besieged Eldacar in Osgiliath. In 1437, the king was forced to flee to his mother's kin in Rhovanion, but Osgiliath was burned and its palantír lost. Eldacar's son Ornendil was captured and put to death by Castamir, who was made king. The new king was cruel and thought only of the navy, and was soon disliked in the inland areas of Gondor. After ten years of exile, in 1447 Eldacar returned to Gondor with an army of Northmen. He received much support from the folk of Calenardhon, Ithilien and Anórien, and slew Castamir in the Battle of the Crossings of Erui. The remaining rebels were besieged in Pelargir, and in 1448 they took the entire fleet of Gondor and sailed to Umbar. There, they rapidly degenerated into Corsairs, and troubled Gondor's coasts for many generations. (III 405-07)

**KIRIL** See: Ciril. (III 14)

**KIRITH UNGOL** See: Cirith Ungol. (III 15)

**KÛD-DÛKAN** (gen. Roh.: 'hole-dweller') Rohirric name for the Hobbits (q. v.). (III 520)

**KUDUK** (gen. Hob.: 'hobbit') Name by which the Hobbits of the Shire and Bree called themselves at the time of the WR, derived from the Mannish *kûd-dûkan*. (III 519-20)

# L

**LAER** (S.) The Sindarin form of lairë (q. v.). (III 480)

**LAGDUF** (d. TA 3019) Orc of the Tower of Cirith Ungol, killed in the fight over Frodo's mithril-mail between Lagduf's company and Orcs of Minas Morgul. (III 217, 222)

**LAIRË** (Q.) The second season of the Calendar of Imladris, equivalent to summer. Lairë contained 72 days.
Called in Sindarin laer. (III 480, 485)

**LAKE NÚRNEN** Nûrnen (q. v.). (III 246)

**LAKE-TOWN** Esgaroth (q. v.). (H 172)

**LAMBE** (Q.: 'tongue') Name for the tengwa ᴎ (number 27), which seems to have had the value *l* in almost all systems. (III 500)

**LAMEDON** (S.) Area in Gondor around the headwaters of the Ciril. The chief town of Lamedon seems to have been Calembel. Lamedon was probably a fief. (III 14, 50, 75)

**LAMPWRIGHTS' STREET** Rath Celerdain (q. v.). (III 46)

**LAND OF SHADOW** Mordor (q. v.). (I 526)

**LAND OF THE STAR** Númenor (q. v.). (III 407)

**LANDROVAL** (S.) (fl. WR) Eagle of the Misty Mountains, brother of Gwaihir. He was one of the Eagles that rescued Frodo and Sam from the slopes of Orodruin. (III 278, 280-82)

**LANGSTRAND** Anfalas (q. v.). (I 16)

**LARGO BAGGINS** (TA 2820-2912) Hobbit of the Shire, third son and fourth child of Balbo Baggins. Largo married Tanta Hornblower; they had one child, Fosco. (III 474)

**LASSELANTA** (Q.: 'leaf-fall') Another name for quellë (q. v.). (III 480)

**LASSEMISTA** (Q.: 'leaf---') Rowan-tree of Fangorn, cut down by Orcs of Isengard. (II 110)

**LAST ALLIANCE OF ELVES AND MEN** Alliance made between Elendil and Gil-galad in SA 3430 to defeat Sauron. In 3434 the army of the Last Alliance marched south, won the Battle of Dagorlad and besieged the Barad-dûr. In 3441, in a battle on the slopes of Orodruin, Sauron was overthrown, but both Gil-galad and Elendil were slain. (I 319; III 454-55)

**LAST BRIDGE**   The Bridge of Mitheithel (q. v.). (I 268, 269)

**LAST DESERT**   A probably-imaginary place mentioned by Bilbo. According to him it was very far in the east, and contained wild Were-worms. (H 31)

**LAST HOMELY HOUSE EAST OF THE SEA**   The house of Elrond in Rivendell, so called because it was the easternmost true house of the Eldar in Middle-earth.
   Called for short the Last Homely House. Also called the house of Elrond. (I 296-97 ff.; H 60)

**LAST MOUNTAIN**   Methedras (q. v.). (II 92)

**LAST RIDING OF THE KEEPERS OF THE RINGS**   Procession from Rivendell to the Grey Havens in September, TA 3021. The company was composed of Galadriel, Elrond, Bilbo, and many Elves, including Gildor. Frodo and Sam joined the Last Riding in the Green Hills, and Gandalf at the Havens. All the riders, except Sam, then sailed over Sea. (III 381-84, 470)

*LAST SHIP, THE*   A Shire-poem of the Fourth Age, ultimately derived from Gondor. (TB 8, 61-64)

**LAST SHORE**   The shore of Eldamar, in Legolas' song about the Sea.
   See: the Undying Lands. (III 289)

**LAURA BAGGINS**   (fl. TA 29th Cent.)   Hobbit of the Shire, wife of Mungo Baggins. She was born a Grubb. (III 474)

**LAURELIN**   (Q.: 'gold---')   The golden tree of the Two Trees of the Valar (q. v.). There was no likeness of Laurelin in Middle-earth.
   Called the Golden Tree and the Tree of Gold. (III 388)

**LAURELINDÓRINAN**   (Q.: 'land of the valley of singing gold') Original name of Lórien (q. v.). (II 88)

*LAY OF NIMRODEL*   One of many Silvan Elvish and Mannish songs about Nimrodel and Amroth, and of Lórien in its early days. (I 440-42; III 119)

**LEAF**   Pipe-weed (q. v.). (I 24)

**LEAFLOCK**   Finglas (q. v.). (II 98)

**LEBENNIN**   (S.)   Area of Gondor, roughly those lands watered by the Gilrain, Serni, Celos, Sirith and Erui. The inhabitants of Lebennin were of mixed Dúnadan and lesser blood. (III (III 14-15, 23)

**LEBETHRON** (S.) Tree of Gondor, growing probably in the Ered Nimrais, much liked by the woodwrights of Gondor. Its wood, or at least the wood of one variety of lebethron, was black. The staffs Faramir gave to Frodo and Sam were made of lebethron, as was the casket in which the Silver Crown was kept. (II 384-85; III 302)

**LEFNUI** (S.) River in western Gondor, flowing from its source in the western Ered Nimrais south and west into the Sea. (I 16)

**LEGOLAS** (S.: 'green-leaf') (fl. TA) Sindarin Elf of the Woodland Realm, son of Thranduil. In TA 3019 Legolas went to Rivendell as a messenger, and took part in the Council of Elrond. He then became one of the Companions of the Ring, representing the Elves. In Lórien Legolas became very friendly with Gimli, a friendship which was maintained for the rest of their lives. After the breaking of the Fellowship, Legolas went with Aragorn and Gimli in search of Merry and Pippin, and fought in the Battle of the Hornburg. He was one of the Grey Company, and fought in the Battle of the Pelennor Fields. While in southern Gondor Legolas for the first time saw the Sea, and the Eldarin yearning for Eldamar was awakened in him.

　　After the WR Legolas led a number of Elves of the Woodland Realm to Ithilien, where they beautified the war-ravaged land. In FA 120, after the death of Elessar, Legolas finally sailed over Sea, taking Gimli with him. (I 315, 361, 366, 381-82, 462, 464-65, 481, 501; II 136; III 183, 185, 451)

**LEMBAS** (S.: *len* 'way' + *bas* 'bread') The waybread of the Galadrim, formed into thin cakes, each of which was enough for a day's journey. Lembas remained fresh for many days if kept unbroken in its mallorn-leaf wrapping. Unlike cram, lembas was tasty. (I 478, 502; II 35, 117, 289-90; III 233)

**LÉOD** (TA 2459-2501) Man, Lord of Éothéod, father of Eorl. Léod was a great horse-tamer, but was killed when he tried to master Felaróf. (III 429, 430)

**LÉOFA** Brytta (q. v.). (III 435)

**LHÛN** (S.) River in western Middle-earth, flowing south from the northern Ered Luin into the Gulf of Lune, and forming the boundary between Eriador and the Elvish and Dwarvish lands to the west. The Lhûn drained all the land between the Ered Luin and the Hills of Evendim.

Called in Westron the Lune. (I 16; III 396, 515)

**LIDLESS EYE** The Eye (q. v.). (III 117)

**LIGHT-ELVES** Perhaps one of the Three Kindreds of the Eldar (q. v.). (H 164)

**LIGHTFOOT** (fl. TA 3000) Meara of Rohan, sire of Snowmane. (III 146)

**LILY COTTON** (fl. WR) Hobbit of the Shire, wife of Tolman Cotton and mother of five children. She was born a Brown. (III 355, 477)

**LILY GOODBODY** (TA 2822-2912) Hobbit of the Shire, youngest child of Balbo Baggins. She married Togo Goodbody. (III 474)

**LIMLIGHT** River flowing from its source in Fangorn Forest into Anduin. At the time of the WR it marked the northern boundary of Rohan. (I 17, 493)

**LINDA PROUDFOOT** (TA 2862-2963) Hobbit of the Shire, fourth child and second daughter of Mungo Baggins. She married Bodo Proudfoot, and bore him at least one child. (III 474)

**LINDIR** (S.: 'song---') (fl. WR) Elf of Rivendell. (I 311)

**LINDON** (S.: 'song---') Elvish lands of the Second, Third and Fourth Ages, located west of the Ered Luin. Lindon, divided into Forlindon and Harlindon by the Gulf of Lune, was the remnant of Beleriand. Many of the High Elves remaining in Middle-earth after the Elder Days lived in Lindon, where they were ruled by Gil-galad and, after his fall, probably by Círdan. The Grey Havens were in Lindon.

In SA 1700 Gil-galad, fearing attack from Sauron during the War of the Elves and Sauron, appealed to Númenor for aid, and Tar-Minastir sent a fleet to Lindon, which enabled Gil-galad to drive Sauron out of Eriador. At the end of the Second Age, Gil-galad led the forces of Lindon in the army of the Last Alliance. During the Third Age Círdan aided the Dúnedain of Arnor as best he could in the wars against Angmar, especially in the Battle of Fornost. (III 383-84, 396, 452, 453, 454)

**LINE OF ANÁRION** The line of the Kings of Gondor (q.v.). (III 404)

**LINE OF ISILDUR** The royal family of the North-kingdom, whose heirs were the Kings of Arnor, Arthedain and the Reunited Kingdom, as well as Chieftains of the Dúnedain of the North. Junior branches of the family were the Kings of Cardolan and Rhudaur. (III 396)

**LINHIR** (S.) Town in Lebennin, Gondor, above the mouth of the Gilrain. During the WR, a battle was fought here between the men of Lamedon and the Corsairs; the battle ended when both sides fled at the approach of the Dead Men of Dunharrow. (III 184-85)

**LINNOD** (S.: 'song') Elvish literary form, a dualistically balanced type of aphorism with some playing on words. The line was composed of two parts, each of which was composed of a dactyl and two trochees.

It is possible that "linnod" referred only to the meter of the line, and not to the use to which it was put. (III 426)

**LITHE** The name used in Bree for Forelithe (q. v.). (III 483)

**LITHE, THE** or **THE LITHEDAYS** The name used in the Shire to refer to the three days between Forelithe and Afterlithe, which were 1 Lithe, Midyear's Day and 2 Lithe. In leap years, there were four Lithedays, including Overlithe.

Called in Bree the Summerdays. (III 478, 481-82)

**LITHLAD** (S.: 'ash-plain') One of the great plains of Mordor, located either in the southwest or the east. (II 308)

**LITTLE DELVING** Village in the northwest part of the West-farthing of the Shire. (I 40)

**LOA** (Q.: 'growth') The nature-year of the Eldar in Middle-earth, divided into six seasons. The method of division varied, but the only one recorded in *LotR* is that of the Calendar of Imladris (q. v.).

*Loa* was probably also the name used for the year of the various Dúnadan calendar systems. (III 480)

**LOBELIA SACKVILLE-BAGGINS** (b. before TA 2920, d. TA 3020) Hobbit of the Shire, wife of Otho Sackville-Baggins and mother of Lotho. She was born in Hardbottle, and was a Bracegirdle. Known for her shrewish temper and grasping ways, Lobelia tried for most of her life to gain possession of Bag End from Bilbo and Frodo by one means or another, until finally, in TA 3018 Frodo sold it to her when he left the Shire. During Saruman's control of the Shire, Lobelia was imprisoned in the Lockholes for arguing with some of the Chief's Men. On her release, she was popular for the first time in her life, but being crushed by her son's death returned to her family in Hardbottle, and gave Bag End back to Frodo. When she died, she left her money to Frodo to be used to aid Hobbits made homeless by her son and Saruman. (I 52, 64,

66-67, 101, 103-04; III 361-62, 372, 474)

**LOCKHOLES** Storage-tunnels in Michel Delving. They were used during Saruman's control of the Shire as a prison for dissident hobbits. (III 348, 356; TB 42)

**LOËNDË** (Q.: 'year-middle-day') Midsummer's Day, the middle day of the Kings' and Stewards' Reckonings. In the New Reckoning, Loëndë was the second of the three enderi; but, since the loa began in the spring, it came between Yavannië and Narquelië. (III 481)

**LONE-LANDS** Name given to the lands between Bree (or perhaps the Forsaken Inn) and Rivendell. (H 43)

**LONELY MOUNTAIN** Erebor (q.v.). (I 366)

**LONELY TROLL** A troll, a chief character in the poem *Perry-the-Winkle*. He was well-behaved but friendless, and was an excellent baker. He was probably fictitious. (TB 41-44)

**LONGBEARDS** Durin's Folk (q.v.). (III 438; H 62)

**LONGBOTTOM** Village in the Southfarthing, home of a family of Hornblowers. About TA 2670, Tobold Hornblower grew pipeweed for the first time in the Shire in Longbottom. (I 28)

**LONGBOTTOM LEAF** A variety of pipe-weed (q.v.). (I 28; II 213)

**LONG CLEEVE** Village in the Shire, home of the North-tooks. Long Cleeve was probably in the Northfarthing. (III 471, 475)

**LONGHOLES** Surname used by Hobbits of Bree, and perhaps also of the Shire. (I 212)

**LONG LAKE** An oval-shaped lake east of Mirkwood near Erebor, fed by the Forest River and the River Running. The latter flowed out of the Long Lake over a waterfall at its southern end.

Esgaroth was built on the Long Lake. (H 184-85, 194)

**LONG LIST OF THE ENTS** A lore-song of the Ents in which was listed every variety of living creature. Since the Ents would probably not have made the descriptions quite so brief, the Long List may originally have been Elvish. (II 84-85, 244)

**LONGO BAGGINS** (TA 2860-2950) Hobbit of the Shire, second son and third child of Mungo Baggins. He married Camellia Sackville, and was the father of Otho Sackville-Baggins. (III 474)

**LONG WINTER** The winter of TA 2758-59, during which Eriador and Rohan were snowbound for as much as five months. In Rohan, Helm was besieged in Helm's Deep by the Dunlendings, and both sides suffered greatly. In the Shire, great losses were averted through the aid of Gandalf, but famine was elsewhere widespread.

In the Shire this winter and its aftermath were referred to as the Days of Dearth. (I 24; III 432-33, 460)

**LÓNI** (d. TA 2994) Dwarf of Erebor. He went to Khazad-dûm with Balin in 2989, and was slain by Orcs while defending Durin's Bridge and the Second Hall. (I 419)

**LORD OF THE EAGLES** Gwaihir (q.v.). (H 107)

**LORD OF THE GLITTERING CAVES** Title of Gimli and the succeeding lords of Aglarond in the Fourth Age. (III 451)

**LORD OF THE NAZGÛL** (SA c. 1600-TA 3019) The chief Nazgûl (q.v.), the mightiest of Sauron's servants. He was originally a king and sorceror, but was enslaved by Sauron when he received the greatest of the Nine Rings. His fortunes rose and fell with Sauron's through the Second Age. With the other Nazgûl, he arose again about TA 1300. Disguising himself, he formed the evil realm of Angmar and became its Witch-king, seeking to destroy the already-weakened Dúnedain of Arnor. As the Witch-king of Angmar, he directed the wars against the North-kingdom until 1975, when, after finally crushing Arthedain, his forces were routed by armies led by Círdan, Glorfindel and Eärnur of Gondor in the Battle of Fornost. After the battle, the Lord of the Nazgûl disappeared from the North, but soon after, in 2000, he and other Nazgûl attacked Minas Ithil and took it after a two-year siege. The Nazgûl-lord renamed the city Minas Morgul and became its lord. In 2043 and 2050 he challenged Eärnur, now King of Gondor, to single combat because the latter, due to the terror of his horse, had not faced him during the Battle of Fornost. In 2050 Eärnur accepted the challenge and was slain, probably treacherously.

During the WR the Nazgûl-lord led the search for Frodo during the latter's journey to Rivendell, and seriously wounded him at Weathertop. He led the army that attacked Minas Tirith in the Siege of Gondor, and broke the gates of the city. He was prevented from entering the city by the arrival of the Rohirrim. Although he killed King Théoden in the Battle of the Pelennor Fields, he was in turn slain by Éowyn and Merry Brandybuck, fulfilling Glorfindel's prophecy at the Battle of Fornost that he was not to fall by the hand of man.

The Lord of the Nazgûl was taller than the other Nazgûl and wore a crown; his fear and power were also greater than theirs. All blades that touched him perished, and only blades with special spells could harm him.

He was called the Lord of the Nine Riders, the King of the Nine Riders, the Wraith-lord, the Wraith-king, the Morgul-lord, the Morgul-king, the King of Minas Morgul, the Lord of Morgul, the Black Captain (as head of the army of Minas Morgul during the WR), the Black Rider, the Black Shadow, the Dwimmerlaik (by Éowyn) and the High Nazgûl (by Orcs of Minas Morgul). His real name is not given. (I 263, 337; II 400-01; III 124-26, 139-43, 146, 397, 412, 413, 437)

LORD OF THE NINE RIDERS The Lord of the Nazgûl (q. v.). (II 400)

LORD OF THE RING, LORD OF THE RINGS Sauron (q. v.). (I frontispiece, 298)

LORD OF THE WESTERN LANDS A title of the Kings of the Reunited Kingdom, who were kings of Arnor and Gondor and overlords of such realms as Erebor and Dale. (III 284)

LORDS OF ANDÚNIË Dúnedain, nobles of Númenor and the leaders of the Faithful. The Lords of Andúnië were the heirs of Silmariën, eldest child of Tar-Elendil. The last Lord of Andúnië was Amandil, father of Elendil the Tall.

The heirlooms of the Lords of Andúnië were the ring of Barahir and the palantíri. The symbol of their authority was a silver sceptre, which later became known as the sceptre of Annúminas. (III 391, 393, 401)

LORDS OF THE WEST The Valar (q. v.). (III 451)

LÓRIEN (S., from Silvan) Elven realm west of Anduin, at the meeting of Celebrant and Anduin, ruled by Celeborn and Galadriel (qq. v.). The mellyrn woods of Lórien were protected from Sauron by the power of Galadriel, and here alone in Middle-earth was the true beauty and timelessness of Eldamar preserved.

Lórien was made and founded in the Second Age by Galadriel. Although most of its people were Silvan Elves, Sindarin was spoken in Lórien. In the Third Age, Lórien aided Elrond at need, especially in 1409.* In 1981, as a result of the appearance of the Balrog in Khazad-dûm, many of the Elves of Lórien fled south, among them Amroth and Nimrodel. During the Quest of Mount Doom the Companions of the Ring rested in Lórien for a month; this was the first time a Dwarf had entered Lórien for many years. In the WR,

* For the rest of the Second and Third Ages, Lórien remained isolated from the outside world.

Lórien was assaulted three times from Dol Guldur, but the attackers were defeated, and after the downfall of Sauron the forces of Lórien, led by Celeborn, took Dol Guldur, and Galadriel destroyed its pits. With the passing of Galadriel over Sea at the end of the Third Age and Celeborn's removal to East Lórien, Lórien was largely deserted.

The capital and chief city of Lórien was Caras Galadon. The Elves of Lórien were known as the Galadrim.

The original name of Lórien was Laurelindórinan, which was later changed to Lothlórien. Also called the Golden Wood and the Hidden Land in Westron, and Dwimordene by the Rohirrim.

See also: Cerin Amroth, Egladil, the Naith, the Tongue. (I 434 ff.; II 88; III 428, 468-69, 506)

**LOSSARNACH** (S.: 'snow' + *arnach)* Area of Gondor, comprising probably the mountain-valleys just southwest of Minas Tirith.

Also called Arnach. *Arnach* was a name of pre-Númenorean origin. (III 23, 152, 508)

**LOSSOTH** (S.: 'snow-people') Men dwelling on the Cape of Forochel. They were primitive and poor, and seem to have lived in the cold regions of the North since the First Age. In TA 1974 they sheltered Arvedui and his men after the fall of Arthedain.

Called in Westron the Snowmen. (III 398-99; R 62)

**LOST ISLE** Eressëa (q. v.). (III 289)

**LÓTESSË** (Q.: 'blossom-month') The fifth month of the Kings' and Stewards' Reckonings, and the second of the New Reckoning, corresponding roughly to our May.

The Sindarin name, used only by the Dúnedain, was Lothron. Called Thrimidge in the Shire. (III 483)

**LOTHÍRIEL** (S.: 'blossom---female') (fl. WR) Woman of Gondor, daughter of Imrahil. In TA 3020 she married King Éomer of Rohan. (III 438)

**LOTHLÓRIEN** (S.: 'blossom-dream-land') Lórien (q. v.).

The Westron equivalent was Dreamflower. (I 434)

**LOTHO SACKVILLE-BAGGINS** (TA 2964-3019) Hobbit of the Shire, son of Otho and Lobelia Sackville-Baggins, probably unmarried. In September, 3018, Lotho and his mother moved into Bag End after buying it from Frodo. Shortly afterward, using money obtained from Isengard and elsewhere from the sale of pipe-weed grown on his lands in the Southfarthing, he began buying up property and supporting outside Men, known as ruffians or the Chief's Men. Lotho then imprisoned Will Whitfoot, the Mayor; and, naming himself Chief Shirriff, took over the Shire, industrializing and regimenting its life. In September, 3019, with the arrival of Saruman, his power collapsed. Sometime in September or October he was slain, perhaps by Gríma.

Lotho was frequently called, at his own insistence, the Chief, which was short for Chief Shirriff. The Hobbits of the Shire called him Pimple or Little Pimple; he seems to have had a number of facial blemishes. (I 103; III 343, 360-61, 370, 474)

**LOTHRON** (S.: 'blossom---') Sindarin form of Lótessë, used only by the Dúnedain. (III 483)

**LOUDWATER** Bruinen (q. v.). (I 268)

**LOWER HALLS** The lower lever of Erebor (q.v.), where Smaug collected his hoard. The hidden door led to the Lower Halls. (H 32, 205-06, 224-29)

**LOWLAND OF THE YALE** See: the Yale. (I 114)

**LUGBÚRZ** (B. S.: 'tower-dark') The Barad-dûr (q. v.). (II 61)

**LUGDUSH** (Orkish: 'tower---') (d. TA 3019) Uruk-hai of Isengard, a member of Uglúk's band. He was slain by Éomer's éored near Fangorn. (II 64)

**LUNE** See: Lhûn. (III 396)

**LUNE, GULF OF** See: the Gulf of Lune. (II 259)

**LÚTHIEN** (S.) (First Age) Sindarin princess, daughter of King Thingol of Doriath and Melian the Vala, wife of Beren and mother of Dior. She was the most beautiful Elven-lady of all time. Beren, while fleeing from Morgoth's armies after the death of his father, came to Doriath and saw Lúthien. He fell in love with her and named her Tinúviel (Q.: 'nightingale'). She returned his love, and together they performed many great adventures, and even stole one of the Silmarilli from Morgoth's Iron Crown. However, eventually, since she had married a mortal, Lúthien died. (I 258-61; III 388)

**LÚVA** (Q.: 'bow') One of the components of the primary letters of the Tengwar. The lúva could be open, as in tinco, or closed, as in parma, and could also be doubled and reversed. (III 495-96)

# M

**MABLUNG** (S.?) (fl. WR) Man of Gondor, a Ranger of Ithilien. He led the scouts of the Army of the West. (II 338; III 198)

**MADOC BRANDYBUCK** (TA 2775-2877) Hobbit of the Shire, son of Gormadoc Brandybuck, Master of Buckland (2836-77). Madoc married Hanna Goldworthy. He was known as "Proudneck." (III 476)

**MAGGOT** Family of Hobbits of the Shire, living in the Marish. At the time of the WR, Farmer Maggot, his wife and their three daughters and two or more sons lived on a prosperous farm famous for its mushrooms. Farmer Maggot was an important Hobbit in the area, and he and Tom Bombadil exchanged visits.

Farmer Maggot was called Muddy-feet in jest by Tom Bombadil. (I 132-40, 147, 184; TB 20-21)

**MAGGOT'S LANE** Road in the Marish going from Rushey to the Maggot farmhouse. (TB 21)

**MALBETH** (S.: 'gold---') (fl. TA 20th Cent.) Dúnadan of Arthedain, seer and royal counsellor. Malbeth foretold the events of Arvedui's life, and gave him his name. He also prophesied concerning the Paths of the Dead and the role of Isildur's Heir in the final battle with Sauron.

He was generally called Malbeth the Seer. (III 63-64, 410)

**MALLOR** (S.: 'gold---') (d. TA 1110) Dúnadan, third King of Arthedain (1029-1110). (III 394)

**MALLORN** (S.: 'gold-tree,' plural *mellyrn*) The tree of Lórien, having grey or silver bark and golden blossoms. Its leaves turned to gold in the autumn and did not fall until the beginning of the spring. The trunk of the mallorn divided near the top into a crown, and here the Galadrim built their telain.

The second Party Tree was a mallorn; there also seem to have been mellyrn in Eldamar. (I 434, 443, 444, 448; II 117; III 375)

**MALLOS** (S.: 'gold-snow') Yellow flower growing in Lebennin. (III 185)

**MALTA** (Q.: 'gold') Name for the tengwa 𝍌 (number 18), which usually had the value *m*. (III 500)

**MALVA BRANDYBUCK** (fl. TA 2800) Hobbit of the Shire, wife of Gormadoc Brandybuck. She was born a Headstrong. (III 476)

**MALVEGIL** (S.: 'gold---') (d. TA 1349) Dúnadan, sixth King of Arthedain (1272-1349). (III 394)

**MAN IN THE MOON** A character of folklore, known both in the Shire and Gondor. (TB 8, 31-38)

*MAN IN THE MOON CAME DOWN TOO SOON, THE* A Shire-poem written in the Red Book of Westmarch in the Fourth Age, ultimately derived from Gondor. (TB 8, 34-38)

*MAN IN THE MOON STAYED UP TOO LATE, THE* A poem written by Bilbo Baggins and recorded in the Red Book of Westmarch. (TB 7, 31-33)

**MANNISH** General term referring to the languages of Men, especially the Men of the Vales of Anduin and others related to the Edain. Mannish tongues, which were related to Adûniac, were the basis for the original language of the Hobbits, and of the outer names of the Dwarves of Erebor. Rohirric was a Mannish tongue.

In *LotR*, Mannish forms have been translated into their Germanic, Old English, or Norse equivalents. (III 506, 509)

**MANWE** (Q.? Val.?) The greatest of the Valar, the husband of Elbereth. He lived with her in a palace on the summit of Oiolosse. Manwe commanded Elbereth to cast Valinor in shadow after the flight of the revolting Noldor.

He was also called the Elder King and the Lord of the West. (I 310, III 392; R 60, 61, 66)

**MARCHO** (fl. TA 1601) Fallohide Hobbit of Bree. In 1601, with his brother Blanco, he settled the Shire. (I 23)

**MARDIL** (Q.: '---friend') (d. TA 2080) Dúnadan, first Ruling Steward of Gondor (2050-80). He was Steward to King Eärnil and King Eärnur from 2029 to 2050, and in 2043 dissuaded Eärnur from accepting the challenge of the Lord of the Nazgûl. In 2050, however, he was unable to restrain the King, and on Eärnur's disappearance was made ruler "until the return of the King" to prevent a civil war among the members of the royal family. A wise ruler, among his accomplishments was the institution of the Stewards' Reckoning.

Mardil was called Mardil Voronwë (Q.: 'steadfast') because of his faithfulness. (III 395, 413, 481)

**MARIGOLD COTTON** (b. TA 2983) Hobbit of the Shire, youngest child of Hamfast Gamgee. She married Tolman Cotton. (III 477)

**MARISH** Fertile, boggy area in the Eastfarthing between Stock and Rushey, home of the Oldbucks before the founding of Buckland. The people of the Marish, who were largely of Stoor blood, acknowledged the authority of the Master of Buckland. (I 26, 40, 128 ff., 142, 146)

**MARK, THE** Rohan (q. v.). (II 43)

**MARMADAS BRANDYBUCK** (b. TA 2943) Hobbit of the Shire, son of Gorbulas Brandybuck. He was a guest at the Farewell Party. (III 476)

**MARMADOC BRANDYBUCK** (TA 2817-2910) Hobbit of the Shire, son of Madoc Brandybuck, Master of Buckland (2877-2910). He married Adaldrida Bolger; they had four children. Marmadoc was known as "Masterful." (III 476)

**MARROC BRANDYBUCK** (b. c. TA 2780) Hobbit of the Shire, youngest son of Gormadoc Brandybuck. (III 476)

**MASTER OF BUCKLAND** The head of the Brandybuck family. The authority of the Master was acknowledged in the Marish as well as in Buckland, but his rule was largely nominal. In FA 12 the Master of Buckland, who at that time was Meriadoc Brandybuck, was made a Counsellor of the North-kingdom.

The Masters of Buckland had attributive titles added to their names, probably by the chroniclers.

Also called the Master of the Hall, since the Master of Buckland lived in Brandy Hall. (I 142; III 471, 476)

**MASTER OF ESGAROTH** The ruler of Esgaroth, seemingly elected by the merchants of the town. The office was not hereditary. At the time of the expedition of Thorin and Company (TA 2941), the Master was greedy and selfish, and was not much good in an emergency. After the fall of Smaug, he absconded with the money given him by Bard for the repair of Esgaroth, and died in the Waste. The Master who followed him was wiser, and in his day, thanks to the refounding of Dale and Erebor, Esgaroth was very prosperous. (H 180-90, 193, 236, 238-40, 286)

**MASTER OF THE HALL** The Master of Buckland (q. v.). (I 142)

**MAT HEATHERTOES** (d. TA 3019) Man of Bree, killed in a fight between Bree-landers and Bill Ferny and his friends. (III 335, 517)

**MATHOM-HOUSE** The museum in Michel Delving, a repository of arms and other mathoms. Bilbo lent his mithril-mail to the Mathom-house, but reclaimed it before leaving the Shire in TA 3001. (I 25; H 285)

**MATTA** Genuine Hobbitish personal name, usually shortened to Mat. (III 517)

**MAUHÚR** (B. S.) (fl. WR)  Orc of Isengard, probably an Uruk. During the WR he led a band of Orcs which unsuccessfully tried to break the ring of Rohirrim surrounding Uglúk's Orc-band. (II 72, 75-76)

**MAY GAMGEE** (b. TA 2928)  Hobbit of the Shire, third child and first daughter of Hobson Gamgee. (III 477)

**MAY GAMGEE** (b. TA 2976)  Hobbit of the Shire, fourth child and second daughter of Hamfast Gamgee. (III 477)

**MAYOR OF MICHEL DELVING**  The only real official in the Shire at the time of the WR, elected every seven years at the Free Fair. The Mayor was, as First Shirriff and Postmaster, in charge of the Watch and the Messenger Service. However, his most important duty was to preside at banquets. In FA 14 the Mayor, who at that time was Sam Gamgee, was made a Counsellor of the North-kingdom.

The Mayor seems to have been chosen from among popular and responsible members of the working class.

The only Mayors mentioned in *LotR* are Will Whitfoot (TA 3013 or earlier-FA 7) and Sam Gamgee (FA 7-56). Frodo Baggins was Deputy Mayor in 3019-20.

Also called the Mayor of the Shire. (I 31; III 372-73, 471)

**MEARAS** (tr. Roh.)  Horses of Rohan, Felaróf and his descendants. Except for Shadowfax, the mearas would allow none but the King of the Mark or his sons to ride them. It was believed that Araw brought the first meara to Middle-earth from Valinor, such was their beauty and strength.

The mearas were the greatest horses of Rohan, and thus of the world, being extremely strong, swift and intelligent. They were white or grey, and lived about eighty years. (II 46, 137; III 431)

**MEDE**  Name given Afterlithe (q. v.) in Bree. (III 483)

**MEDUSELD**  The palace of the Kings of the Mark, in Edoras, built by King Brego in TA 2569. Its roof was made of gold.

Also called the Golden Hall. (II 50, 141, 145 ff.; III 84, 314, 432, 459)

**MEE**  A young Elven-princess in the Hobbit nonsense-poem *Princess Mee*. Any resemblance to historical personages is probably coincidental. (TB 28-30)

**MELCHAR** (Val.? Q.?)  The real name of Morgoth (q. v.). (RB 11/15/67)

**MELIAN** (Val.? Q.?) (fl. First Age) Vala, wife of King Thingol and mother of Lúthien. She was probably a lesser Vala. (III 388)

**MELILOT BRANDYBUCK** (b. TA 2985) Hobbit of the Shire, younger daughter of Marmadas Brandybuck. She was a guest at the Farewell Party. (I 54; III 476)

**MELLYRN** See: mallorn. (I 443)

**MEN** One of the speaking races of Middle-earth. Although rather obscure in the First Age (except for the Edain), in the Second and Third Ages their power grew, and in the Fourth Age, the Dominion of Men, they eclipsed all other races.

Men were too diverse physically and culturally to be described in one entry. The Dúnedain of Gondor divided Men into three groups: the Men of the West, or the Dúnedain, the Men of the Twilight, peoples such as the Rohirrim, and the Men of Darkness, or the Wild, men of lesser stature and nature, unrelated to the Edain. Men were called the Big People or the Big Folk by Hobbits.

See: Beornings, Dúnedain, Dunlendings, Easterlings, Edain, Haradrim, Northmen, Númenoreans, Rohirrim, Variags, Beornings and the various entries under "Men of ...." (II 364; III 506-09)

**MENEGILDA BRANDYBUCK** (fl. TA 30th Cent.) Hobbit of the Shire, wife of Rorimac Brandybuck and mother of Saradoc and Merimac. She was born a Goold. (III 476)

**MENELDIL** (Q.: 'heaven-lover') (d. TA 158) Dúnadan, son of Anárion and third King of Gondor (2-158). (I 331; III 394)

**MENELDOR** (S.: 'heaven---') (fl. WR) Eagle of the Misty Mountains, one of the Eagles that rescued Frodo and Sam from the slopes of Orodruin. (III 280-82)

**MENELDUR, TAR-** (Q.: 'heaven---') (b. c. SA 550) Dúnadan, fifth King of Númenor. (III 390, 410)

**MENELMACAR** (Q.: 'heaven-swordsman') Menelvagor (q. v.). (III 488)

**MENELTARMA** (Q.: 'king of the heavens') Mountain in western Númenor from which the far-sighted could see the Haven of the Eldar in Tirion. (III 390)

**MENELVAGOR** (S.: 'heaven-swordsman') The constellation Orion.

The Quenya form of the name was Menelmacar. Also called Telumehtar. (I 120; III 488)

**MENELYA** (Q.: 'heaven's day') Quenya name for the fifth day of the Eldarin and Dúnadan enquië, named for the heavens.

The Sindarin form was Ormenel, and the Hobbitish Hevenesdei, later Hevensday or Hensday. Called in *LotR* Wednesday. (III 484)

**MEN OF BREE** Men, related to the Dunlendings and other Men of the Ered Nimrais. In the Second Age some of these Men moved northward, and in the Third they became subject to Arnor, learned Westron and forgot their origin.

The Men of Bree were cheerful, provincial, short and brownhaired. They got on extremely well with people of all races, and were the only Men anywhere to live with Hobbits. (I 205; III 509, 516)

**MEN OF DALE** Men, at the time of the WR living in Dale, closely related to the Men of the Long Lake. The Men of Dale were related to the Edain, and in the Third Age still spoke a language akin to Adûnaic. After the destruction of Dale by Smaug in TA 2770, many of the Men of Dale lived in Esgaroth, but after the dragon's death in 2941 they returned to their home. After this time they were known as the Bardings, because they were ruled by King Bard and his descendents.

The Men of Dale were very friendly with the thrushes of Dale, and could speak with them. They wrote with a mode of the cirth. (I 301; III 493, 508; H 218, 237)

**MEN OF DARKNESS** In the lore of Gondor, those Men, such as the Easterlings and the Haradrim, not related to the Dúnedain.

Also called the Wild. (II 364)

**MEN OF ÉOTHÉOD** The Éothéod (q. v.). (III 428)

**MEN OF THE LONG LAKE** Men, closely related to the Men of Dale and more distantly to the Edain, dwelling in and near Esgaroth at the time of the WR. Like the Men of Dale they could speak with thrushes.

Also known as the Lake-men. (III 508; H 218, 239)

**MEN OF THE MOUNTAINS** See: the Dead Men of Dunharrow. (III 64)

**MEN OF THE NORTH-WEST** The Edain (q. v.). This term implies that Middle-earth extended beyond Rhûn and Harad. (III 480)

**MEN OF THE RIDDERMARK** The Rohirrim (q. v.). (III 508)

**MEN OF THE TWILIGHT** In the lore of Gondor, those of the Edain and their close kin who did not go to Númenor, and their descendents. The Men of the Twilight included the Rohirrim and the Northmen, and probably also the Beornings, the Men of Dale and of the Long Lake, the Woodmen and the other Men of the Vales of Anduin.

Also known as the Middle Peoples. (II 364)

**MEN OF THE VALES OF ANDUIN**  Various kindreds of Men living between Mirkwood and the Misty Mountains, many of them related to the Edain. Although at the time of the WR only the Beornings and the Woodmen are mentioned as living there, the Rohirrim, the Men of Dale and of the Long Lake, the Northmen and perhaps even the Edain originally dwelled there.

The Men of the Vales of Anduin spoke various languages related to Adûnaic. They were for the most part good, and aided Gondor and fought Orcs to the best of their ability, but being located between Mirkwood and the Mountains were frequently hard put to it to survive. (III 404, 483, 508)

**MENTHA BRANDYBUCK**  (b. TA 2983)  Hobbit of the Shire, elder daughter of Marmeadas Brandybuck. She was a guest at the Farewell Party. (III 476)

**MERE OF DEAD FACES**  Dark pool in the Dead Marshes containing the graves of Men and Elves killed in the Battle of Dagorlad. The faces of the dead men and lit candles showed beneath the surface of the water, but could not be reached. (II 296-97)

**MERESDEI**  Early form of the name of the sixth day of the Hobbit week, a translation of the Quenya Eärenya. By the time of the WR, the name was Mersday.

Meresdei, the day before Highdei, corresponds to our Saturday, but in *LotR* is called Thursday. (III 484, 485)

**MERETHROND**  (S.: 'feast-hall')  The Great Hall of Feasts in Minas Tirith. (III 312)

**MERIADOC BRANDYBUCK**  (TA 2982-FA c. 65)  Hobbit of the Shire, son of Saradoc Brandybuck, adventurer and Master of Buckland (FA 12-64). In his youth he was a close friend of Frodo Baggins, and therefore accompanied him to Rivendell in 3018. There he became one of the Companions of the Ring, and travelled with the Company until Parth Galen, where he and Peregrin Took were captured by Orcs. While taking the Hobbits to Isengard the Orc-band was attacked by the Rohirrim, and Merry and Pippin escaped into Fangorn. There they were befriended by Fangorn the Ent, and were instrumental in launching the Ents' attack on Isengard. Merry later took service with King Théoden of Rohan, and as his esquire returned with him to Edoras. Although ordered to remain in Rohan when the Rohirrim rode to Gondor, Merry rode to Minas Tirith with Éowyn, and together they slew the Lord of the Nazgûl during the Battle of the Pelennor Fields. Merry nearly died from the contact with the Lord of the Nazgûl, but was healed by Aragorn.

After the WR, Merry was made a knight of Rohan and was rewarded for his valor. He then returned to the Shire, and was one of the leaders of the Hobbit forces in the Battle of Bywater. On his father's death, Merry became Master of Buckland, and in FA 14 he was made a Counsellor of the Northkingdom. Throughout his life he maintained contact with the friends he had made during the war, and in 64 he and Pippin resigned their offices and rode to Rohan and Gondor. They died a few years later in the latter realm, and were buried in the House of the Kings.

Merry wrote *Herblore of the Shire, The Reckoning of Years, Old Words and Names in the Shire,* and other scholarly works.

Because he drank ent-draughts while in Fangorn, Merry was, with Pippin, the largest Hobbit in history, being probably at least four and a half feet tall.

Meriadoc was always called Merry. He was also known as Master Holbytla and Holdwine of the Shire in Rohan, and Master Perian in Gondor. As Master of Buckland, he was known as Meriadoc the Magnificent. Merry's real name, in genuine Hobbitish, was Kalimac, which was usually abbreviated to Kali, which meant "jolly, gay" in genuine Westron. (I 28, 71; III 58-59, 89-90, 141-47, 177-78, 316, 363-64, 377, 471, 472, 476, 517)

**MERIMAC BRANDYBUCK** (TA 2942-FA 10) Hobbit of the Shire, second son of Rorimac Brandybuck. He was a guest at the Farewell Party. (III 476)

**MERIMAS BRANDYBUCK** (b. TA 2981) Hobbit of the Shire, son of Marmadas Brandybuck. He was a guest at the Farewell Party. (III 476)

**MERING STREAM** Stream flowing from the Ered Nimrais through the Firien Wood and into the Mouths of Entwash. The Mering Stream marked the boundary between Gondor and Rohan. (III 14)

**MERLOCK MOUNTAINS** Probably, the mountains where the

Merlocks lived. The Merlock Mountains were probably fictitious, since they are only mentioned in a traditional Shire
poem, but they were possibly based on what little the Hobbits knew about the Misty Mountains. (TB 45, 46)

**MERRY BRANDYBUCK**   See: Meriadoc Brandybuck. (III 517)

**MERRY GAMGEE**   (b. FA 7)  Hobbit of the Shire, fourth child
and second son of Sam Gamgee. (III 382, 477)

**MERSDAY**   See: Meresdei. (III 484)

**MESSENGER SERVICE**   The mail system of the Shire, run by
the Mayor in his capacity of Postmaster. The Messenger
Service probably included the Quick Post. (I 31)

**MESSRS. GRUBB, GRUBB, AND BURROWES**   A Shire firm,
either of lawyers or of auctioneers. (H 284)

**METHEDRAS**   (S.: 'last-peak')  The southernmost peak of the
Misty Mountains east of Nan Curunír. Its eastern slopes were
part of Fangorn Forest.
    Called in Westron the Last Mountain. (II 38, 91, 92)

**METTARË**   (Q.: 'last-day')  The last day of the loa in the
Eldarin and Dúnadan calendars. In the former, mettarë was
not part of any season, and in the latter, it was not part of
any month. In the Stewards' Reckoning, and perhaps in the
other Dúnadan systems as well, mettarë was a holiday. (III
480, 481, 486)

**MEWLIPS**   In the Shire-poem of the same name, a probably-
fictional evil race perhaps modelled on Orcs. (TB 45-46)

*MEWLIPS, THE*   A poem written by a Hobbit of the Shire. Although perhaps totally fictitious, there may be echoes in the
poem of the Misty ("Merlock") Mountains, Mirkwood ("spider-
shadows" and "wood of hanging trees and the gallows-weed")
and the marsh at the eastern end of the Old Forest Road. The
Mewlips themselves could be patterned on vague rumors of
Orcs. (TB 45-46)

**MICHEL DELVING**   Town in the Westfarthing, located on the
White Downs, chief township and more or less the capital of
the Shire. Michel Delving contained the dwelling of the Mayor,
the Lockholes and the Mathom-house.
    Also called Delving. (I 25; III 356; TB 41)

**MIDDLE DAYS**   The Second and Third Ages, the years between
the Eldar Days, the First Age of the Elves, and the Younger
Days, the Fourth Age of Men. (I 339)

**MIDDLE-EARTH** Those lands east of the Sea, extending at least as far south and east as Harad and Rhûn. In Volume II, Number 2, page 1 of the *Tolkien Journal,* Henry Resnick quotes Professor Tolkien as saying that "Middle-earth is Europe." However, this seems to mean only that Europe and the setting of the events of *LotR* are related. Certainly it would seem that Middle-earth should include all those lands not part of Over-heaven or the Underworld, and this belief is strengthened by the use of the term "Men of the North-west" for the Edain on III 480.

Native races of Middle-earth included Dwarves, Orcs, Men, Trolls and Hobbits, and perhaps also the Elves.

Called in Sindarin Ennor and in Quenya Endóre. Also called the Great Lands, the Wide World and, by Galadriel, the Hither Shore. (III 303; H 164)

**MIDDLE PEOPLES** The Men of the Twilight (q. v.). (II 364)

**MIDGEWATER MARSHES** Marshes north of the Great East Road between Bree and Weathertop, infested with midges and other insects. (I 245, 246-47)

**MIDYEAR'S DAY** The middle day of the year in the Shire Reckoning, corresponding roughly with the day of the summer solstice.

Cf.: the enderi, Loëndë. (III 478)

**MILL** The mill of Hobbiton, located on the Water, run toward the end of the Third Age by the Sandymans. During Lotho's control of the Shire, the Mill was torn down and replaced by a brick building that polluted both air and stream. This in turn was torn down after the death of Saruman. (III 360, 361, 365-66)

**MILO BROCKHOUSE** A misprint for Milo Burrows. (RHM III 420)

**MILO BURROWS** (b. TA 2947) Hobbit of the Shire, son of Rufus Burrows and Peony Baggins. He was a guest at the Farewell Party. (I 64; III 474, 476)

**MIM** (First Age) Dwarf. Mim possessed a great treasure but was slain by a dragon who coveted it. (TB 8, 53-54)

**MIMOSA BAGGINS** (fl. TA 29th Cent.) Hobbit of the Shire, wife of Ponto Baggins. She was born a Bunce. (III 474)

**MINALCAR** (Q.: 'tower-glorious') Rómendacil II (q. v.). (III 395, 404)

**MINARDIL** (Q.: 'tower-lover') (d. TA 1634) Dúnadan, twenty-fifth King of Gondor (1621-34). He was slain in a battle at

Pelargir with the Corsairs of Umbar. (III 395, 407)

**MINAS ANOR** (S.: 'tower of the sun') The fortress-city of Anárion, built in Anórien on the eastern slopes of Mindolluin in SA 3320. As Osgiliath and Minas Ithil decreased in importance in the first part of the Third Age, Minas Anor became the chief city of Gondor. In 420 the city was rebuilt, and in 1640 the King's House was moved there from Osgiliath. In 1900 the White Tower (q. v.) was built. Soon after the fall of Minas Ithil in 2002, Minas Anor was renamed Minas Tirith, and it was under this name that it was known ever after.

A palantír was kept in Minas Anor.

Also called the Tower of the Rising Sun. (I 321; II 259; III 403, 408, 413, 456-58)

**MINAS ITHIL** (S.: 'tower of the moon') Fortress-city of Isildur, built high on a western spur of the Ephel Dúath in SA 3320. Taken by Sauron in SA 3429, it was re-inhabited at the beginning of the Third Age, but never regained its equality with Minas Anor, for the heirs of Isildur did not dwell there. In TA 2000 Minas Ithil was besieged by the Nazgûl and fell after two years. The city was then called in Gondor Minas Morgul (q. v.). After the WR it was again called Minas Ithil, but was not inhabited because of the dread remaining there.

A palantír was kept there, but it was captured by the Nazgûl and taken to the Barad-dûr.

Minas Ithil was lit at night by moonlight welling through its marble halls.

Also called the Tower of the Rising Moon and the Tower of the Moon. (I 321; II 259, 396; III 305, 412, 454)

**MINAS MORGUL** (S.: 'tower of black-magic') Name given Minas Ithil in TA 2002 after its capture by the Nazgûl, who made it their home. Terror and war were directed against Gondor from Minas Morgul until Ithilien was deserted. During the WR, the army that attacked Osgiliath and undertook the Siege of Gondor came from Minas Morgul.

In fashion Minas Morgul seems to have been much like Minas Ithil, except for the replacement of beauty by terror. The topmost course of the tower revolved slowly, and the walls of Morgul shone with a pale, frightening light.

Minas Morgul seems to have been guarded by the Silent Watchers (q. v.), who also detected enemies on the Stairs.

Also called the Tower of Sorcery and the Dead City. (I 321; II 396 ff.; III 305, 412-13)

**MINASTAN** (Q.: 'tower-*adan*') (fl. TA 17th Cent.) Dúnadan of Gondor, second son of King Minardil and father of King Tarondor. He probably died in the Great Plague of 1636, or earlier. (III 395)

**MINASTIR, TAR** (Q.: 'tower-watch') (fl. SA 1700) Dúnadan, eleventh King of Númenor. In 1700 he sent a great fleet to aid Gil-galad in the War of the Elves and Sauron, and with this aid Sauron was defeated. (III 390, 391, 454)

**MINAS TIRITH** (S.: 'tower of guard') The name given to Minas Anor after the fall of Minas Ithil in TA 2002. Minas Tirith was built in seven levels on the Hill of Guard (q. v.) in such a manner that the gate of each of the levels faced a different direction from the one beneath it, with the Great Gate facing eastward. Behind the Great Gate a cliff rose seven hundred feet to the wall of the seventh level, the Citadel (q. v.). So strong was the city that no enemy was able to enter it until the WR.

As the chief city of Gondor, Minas Tirith was the focal point of the struggle to contain Sauron in the Third Age. However, as Gondor slowly declined over the centuries, Minas Tirith became underpopulated. The city was not attacked until TA 3019, when the forces of Mordor, led by the Lord of the Nazgûl, undertook the Siege of Gondor and broke the Great Gate. However, the enemy was prevented from entering beyond the courtyard of the Great Gate by the arrival of the Rohirrim and the subsequent victory of the West in the Battle of the Pelennor Fields. After the WR the Great Gate was rebuilt by the Dwarves of Aglarond, the White Tree was replanted and Minas Tirith remained the capital and chief city of Gondor.

Called in Westron the Tower of Guard and the Guarded City, and in translated Rohirric Mundburg. Ghân-buri-Ghân called it Stone-city and Stone-houses, referring to its position as the chief city of Gondor and to its construction.

See: the White Tower, the Houses of Healing, the Hallows, Merethrond, etc. (I 321; III 25 ff., 116, 413)

**MINDOLLUIN** (S.: 'tower-hill-blue'?) The easternmost mountain of the Ered Nimrais, located just west of Minas Tirith, which was built on the Hill of Guard, an eastern spur of the mountain. The Hallows were located on an eastern flank of Mindolluin. (II 371; III 25-26, 307-08)

**MINES OF MORIA** Khazad-dûm (q. v.). (I 386)

**MINHIRIATH** (S.) Area of Arnor (later Cardolan) between the Gwathlo and the Bruinen. Minhiriath was the most severely affected by the Great Plague of TA 1636 of all Eriador, and was more or less deserted after that time. In 2912 great floods devastated the remnant of its people. (I 16; III 398, 461)

**MIN-RIMMON** (S.) The fifth of the northern beacon-towers of Gondor, built on Rimmon. (III 14, 20)

**MINTO BURROWS** (b. TA 2996) Hobbit of the Shire, youngest son of Milo Burrows. (III 474)

**MINUIAL** (S.) See: tindómë. (III 485)

**MINYATUR, TAR-** (Q.: 'tower---') Elros (q. v.). (III 390)

**MIRABELLA BRANDYBUCK** (TA 2860-2960) Hobbit of the Shire, youngest daughter of Gerontius Took. She married Gorbadoc Brandybuck and had seven children by him. (III 475, 476)

**MÍRIEL** (Q.: 'jewel-woman') (fl. SA 3255) Dúnadan of Númenor, daughter and heir of Tar-Palantir. She should have been the twenty-fourth ruler of Númenor, but her cousin usurped the sceptre from her and became Ar-Pharazon. (III 390)

**MIRKWOOD** Name given Greenwood the Great (q. v.) when the shadow of Dol Guldur fell on it about TA 1050. With the growth of the power of Sauron in Dol Guldur, black squirrels, Orcs, and great spiders spread through the forest, but the Woodman and the Elves of the Woodland Realm of northern Mirkwood remained in Mirkwood. In the course of the Third Age the Old Forest Road fell into disuse.

In TA 2941 Thorin and Company passed through Mirkwood on an old elf-path and encountered an enchanted stream, queer eyes and insects at night, the great spiders and a feeling of oppression and darkness.

After the WR, Mirkwood was cleansed and renamed Eryn Lasgalen (q. v.).

Called in Sindarin Taur e-Ndaedelos. Also called the Wood and the Great Wood.

See also: the Forest River, the Enchanted River, the Mountains of Mirkwood and the Narrows. (I 17, 81; III 456, 515; H 12-13, 136, 140 ff.)

**MIRROMERE** Kheled-zâram (q. v.). (I 370)

**MIRROR OF GALADRIEL** Basin in Caras Galadon, which when filled with water gave glimpses of scenes far away in time or space. (I 468-72)

**MIRUVOR** or **MIRUVÓRE** (Q., from Val.: 'jewel---') The clear, fragrant cordial of the Eldar, believed to have been made from the undying flowers of the gardens of Yavanna. Elrond gave a flask of miruvor to Gandalf at the beginning of the Quest of Mount Doom, and this saved the Hobbits' lives on Caradhras. (I 379, 385; R 61)

**MISTY MOUNTAINS** Great mountain chain of Middle-earth, running nine hundred miles from the Northern Waste to the Gap of Rohan. Throughout the Third Age the Misty Mountains were infested with Orcs.

Individual peaks of the Misty Mountains included Gundabad, Zirak-zigil, Barazinbar, Bundushathûr and Methedras, while the High Pass and the Redhorn Pass were two of the important passes over the Mountains.

In addition to its habitation by Orcs, the great Dwarf-palace of Khazad-dûm was delved beneath the Misty Mountains. Carn Dûm may also originally have been a dwelling-place of the Dwarves.

Called in Sindarin the Hithaiglin. (I 16-17, 252; II 124; H 65-66)

**MITHE** The outflow of the Shirebourn into the Baranduin. A landing-stage was built here from which a road led to Deephallow. (TB 9, 17)

**MITHEITHEL** (S.: 'grey---') River flowing southwest from the Ettenmoors, crossed by the Great East Road on the Bridge of Mitheithel. At Tharbad the Mitheithel was joined by the Glanduin, and was then called the Gwathlo. Its principal tributary was the Bruinen.

Called in Westron the Hoarwell. (I 16, 268, 269)

**MITHE STEPS** The landing-stage at the Mithe. (TB 20)

**MITHLOND** (S.: 'grey-haven') The Grey Havens (q.v.). (II 259)

**MITHRANDIR** (S.: 'grey pilgrim') Gandalf (q.v.). (I 465)

**MITHRIL** (S.: 'silver-flame') Metal, found only in Khazad-dûm. Mithril was loved by the Dwarves above all things, and was also treasured greatly by the Elves, the Dúnedain and Sauron. Mithril could be beaten and polished without being weakened, and it was both light and hard. Its silver color did not tarnish.

The Noldor of Eregion made ithildin from mithril. Bilbo's mail, Nenya and the helms of the Guards of the Citadel were made of mithril.

The mithril-vein of Khazad-dûm was what made Durin's

Folk wealthy, and what drew them to their ancestral home despite all danger. This vein also caused the Noldor, under Celebrimbor, to settle Eregion in the Second Age. However, the vein led north, under Barazinbar, and by TA 1980 the Dwarves had delved so deeply that they released the Balrog imprisoned there. Such was his terror that even the Orcs refused to mine there, and so no more mithril was produced after TA 1980. By the end of the Third Age, therefore, mithril had become priceless.

Also called silver-steel, Moria-silver and true silver. ( I 413-14, 418; III 439; H 228)

**MITHRIL-MAIL** A corselet and helmet of mithril made in Erebor for a young elf-prince and incorporated into Smaug's hoard. During the expedition of Thorin and Company, Thorin gave it to Bilbo Baggins, who in turn later gave it to Frodo. Frodo wore the corselet during the Quest of Mount Doom, and it saved his life in Khazad-dûm. The mithril corselet was captured with Frodo in Cirith Ungol, and when two Orc-bands quarreled over its possession Frodo was able to escape. Gandalf reclaimed the corselet from the Mouth of Sauron, and Frodo wore it on his return to the Shire, where it foiled Saruman's attempt on his life. (I 363, 413-14; II 203, 205; H 228, 285)

**MODE OF BELERIAND** A system of the Tengwar in which vowels were represented by full letters. Diphthongs were made by using the vowel-sign plus the tengwa for *w* or *y*, or by placing the "following *y*" tehta or a modified *u*-curl ( ƍ ) over the vowel. The West-gate inscription exemplifies a normal adaptation of the mode of Beleriand. (I 399; III 498-99)

**MODE OF EREBOR** A variation of the Angerthas Moria. It was fundamentally the same, but had perhaps a dozen differences, some of which represented a return to the Angerthas Daeron. This mode was developed by the Dwarves of Erebor, and was used in the Book of Mazarbul. (III 504)

**MODE OF FËANOR** The most common system of the Tengwar (q. v.). (III 491, 493)

**MONDAY** See: Monendei. (III 484)

**MONENDEI** Early form of the name of the third day of the Hobbit week. The name was a translation of the Quenya Isilya. By the time of the WR the name had changed to Monday. Called Monday in *LotR*. (III 484)

**MONEY**   Contrary to the claims of some, there are references
to money in *LotR,* chiefly in connection with Bree. There, a
pony was worth about four silver pennies, the loss of thirty
silver pennies was a hard blow to the well-off Barliman Butterbur, and a gold piece was a truly extravagant reward for
good news. Nár was given "a few coins of little worth" by
Azog as an insult. Bilbo's gold and silver from Erebor were
probably minted. In all probability there were many different
kinds of currency, and these currencies were no doubt mutual-
ly exchangeable, as in medieval Europe. (I 242, 345; III 442)

**MOON-LETTERS**   Runes that could only be seen when they
were exposed to a moon of the same phase and on the same
day of the year as when they were written. Moon-letters were
invented by the Dwarves, and were written with silver pens.
(H 62)

**MORANNON**   (S.: 'black-gate')   The rampart across Cirith Gorgor, the exit from Mordor best suited to large armies. The
Morannon had one iron gate, with three vast doors. It was
ruined when the One Ring was unmade during the WR.
   Called in Westron the Black Gate. (II 308; III 200-06, 279)

**MORDOR**   (S.: 'black-land')   Realm east of the lower Anduin,
bounded and protected on the north by the Ered Lithui and on
the south and west by the Ephel Dúath. First settled by Sauron about SA 1000, Mordor was ever after a stronghold of evil.
From Mordor Sauron directed the War of the Elves and Sauron,
and remained there until he submitted to Ar-Pharazôn in 3262.
After the fall of Númenor, Sauron returned to Mordor, and in
3429 attacked Gondor. Mordor was invaded by the army of the
Last Alliance in 3434, and with Sauron's defeat in 3441 Mordor was cleansed of his servants. In the Third Age Gondor
built fortresses such as Durthang, the Towers of the Teeth
and the Tower of Cirith Ungol to prevent any evil thing from
re-entering Mordor, but after the Great Plague of 1636 these
fortresses were abandoned, and the Nazgûl entered Mordor and
began the slow preparation of the land for the return of Sauron, who was then dwelling in disguise in Dol Guldur. In 2942
Sauron returned to his home, and in 2951 openly declared himself and began the rebuilding of the Barad-dûr. During the WR
the armies gathered in Mordor were unleashed against Gondor,
but with the unmaking of the One Ring many of Sauron's works
were destroyed and Mordor was devastated by earthquakes.
   Points of interest in Mordor included Gorgoroth, Lithlad
and Núrn, three of its chief plains, the Sea of Núrnen, Udûn,
Orodruin, Cirith Gorgor, the Isenmouthe, Cirith Ungol, the

Nameless Pass, the Morgai, etc.

Called in Westron the Black Land, the Land of Shadow or the Dark Country. Also called the Nameless Land. (I 17; III 15, 213 ff., 404, 408, 412, 417, 453-68)

**MORGAI** (S.: 'black---') Mountain-ridge east of, and lower than, the Ephel Dúath, the inner fence of western Mordor. Although dreary, the Morgai was not altogether desolate, since hardy shrubs and thorn bushes grew there. (III 214, 243-45)

**MORGOTH** (S.: 'black-power'?) (First Age) A Vala of high rank and great power, living originally in Valinor. Sometime in the First Age Morgoth became evil and, coveting the Silmarilli and their light, poisoned the Two Trees and stole the three Silmarilli. With a number of lesser Valar, Morgoth fled to Middle-earth and founded the realm of Angband and built the great fortress of Thangorodrim. He set the Silmarilli in his Iron Crown. Fëanor and a great number of Noldor followed him to Middle-earth; and, aided by the Sindar and the Edain, fought against Morgoth in the War of the Great Jewels, which lasted for a number of generations of the Edain. Finally, Morgoth had the victory, but Eärendil, with the aid of the Silmaril that Beren had stolen from the Iron Crown, sailed to Valinor and gained the support of the Valar. In the Great Battle at the end of the First Age, Morgoth was overthrown and Thangorodrim broken.

Among Morgoth's accomplishments was the breeding of Orcs and Trolls.

Also known as the Great Enemy, the Enemy, Morgoth the Enemy and the Dark Power of the North. His real name was Melchar. (I 260; III 388, 389, 452, 507, 511; RB 11/15/67)

**MORGULDUIN** (S.: 'black-magic-river') Stream flowing into Anduin from Imlad Morgul. Morgulduin glowed with a pale, evil light and smelled noisome. (II 388, 397 ff.)

**MORGUL-KNIFE** An enchanted knife with which the Lord of the Nazgûl stabbed Frodo on Weathertop. A fragment of the knife-blade remained in the wound, and slowly worked its way toward Frodo's heart, but it was extricated by Elrond. The knife-blade vaporized when it was exposed to the sun. (I 263, 265-66, 281, 292)

**MORGUL PASS** Pass leading from Minas Morgul over the Ephel Dúath into Mordor.

Also called the Nameless Pass. (II 405; III 215)

**MORGUL-RATS** The Orcs of Minas Morgul, so called by an

Orc of the Tower of Cirith Ungol. (III 222)

**MORGUL VALE**   Imlad Morgul (q. v.). (I 332)

**MORIA**   (S.: 'black pit')   Khazad-dûm (q. v.). (I 316; H 65)

**MORIA-SILVER**   Mithril (q. v.). (I 413)

**MORO BURROWS**   (b. TA 2991)   Hobbit of the Shire, second son of Milo Burrows. He was a guest at the Farewell Party. (III 474)

**MORROWDIM**   Tindómë (q. v.). (III 485)

**MORTHOND**   (S.: 'black-root')   River in Gondor, flowing from its source in the Paths of the Dead past Erech and south to the Sea, which it entered near Dol Amroth.
Called in Westron the Blackroot. (III 49, 72-3; TB 8)

**MORTHOND VALE**   The Blackroot Vale (q. v.). (III 73)

**MORWEN**   (S.: 'black---') (b. TA 2922)   Dúnadan of Gondor, born in Lossarnach. In 2943 she married King Thengel of Rohan, and bore him five children, including Théoden and Théodwyn.
Morwen was called Steelsheen by the Rohirrim. (III 436, 437)

**MOSCO BURROWS**   (b. TA 2987)   Hobbit of the Shire, eldest son of Milo Burrows. He was a guest at the Farewell Party. (III 474)

**MOUNDS OF MUNDBURG**   The burial-mounds of those slain in the Battle of the Pelennor Fields, as called by the Rohirrim. (III 152)

**MOUNTAIN, THE**   Erebor (q. v.). (I 51)

**MOUNTAIN, THE**   Oiolosse (q. v.). (I 309, 310)

**MOUNTAIN OF FIRE**   Orodruin (q. v.). (I 318)

**MOUNTAIN OF SHADOW**   Probably a misprint for the Mountains of Shadow (q. v.). (I 321)

**MOUNTAINS OF LUNE**   The Ered Luin (q. v.). (II 90)

**MOUNTAINS OF MIRKWOOD**   The mountains of northern Mirkwood, the source of the Enchanted River. After the WR the Mountains became the southern boundary of the Woodland Realm. (I 17; III 468; H 13)

**MOUNTAINS OF MORIA**   Bundushathûr, Zirak-zigil and Barazinbar, the three mountains under which Khazad-dûm was delved. (I 432)

**MOUNTAINS OF SHADOW**   The Ephel Dúath (q. v.). (I 17, 330)

**MOUNTAINS OF TERROR**   Mountains in Beleriand near Doriath. The great spiders dwelled in the Mountains of Terror, and probably other perils as well. (I 260; II 422)

**MOUNTAINS OF THE MOON** The home of the Man in the Moon, in a Hobbit poem originally derived from Gondor. Although the Mountains were probably imaginary, it is possible that some sort of jesting reference to the Ered Luin, which were in the Shire called the Mountains of Lune, was being made. (TB 38)

**MOUNTAINS OF VALINOR** The Pelóri (q. v.). (R 61)

**MOUNTAIN WALL** Probably the Pelóri (q. v.). (I 310)

**MOUNT DOOM** Orodruin (q. v.). (III 393)

**MOUNT EVERWHITE** Oiolosse (q. v.). (I 489)

**MOUNT FANG** Orthanc (q. v.). (II 204)

**MOUNT GRAM** One of the Misty Mountains, home of the Orcs that attacked the Shire in TA 2747 and were defeated in the Battle of Greenfields. (H 30)

**MOUTH OF SAURON** (SA ?-TA 3019) Black Númenorean. In the Third Age (and perhaps in the Second as well) he served Sauron, and rose in his service because of his cunning and evil. He became a great sorcerer, which is probably how he preserved his life for thousands of years. By the time of the WR he had become the Lieutenant of the Tower of Barad-dûr, and had forgotten his real name. He was doubtless killed when Sauron fell, or in the battle with the Army of the West which followed. (III 202-06)

**MOUTHS OF ANDUIN** Ethir Anduin (q. v.). (III 14)

**MOUTHS OF ENTWASH** Marshy area in Gondor on the border with Rohan, where the Entwash flowed into Anduin.

For more information, see Entwash Vale, of which the Mouth of Entwash was a part. (III 14-15, 94)

**MUGWORT** Family of Hobbits of Bree. (I 212)

**MÛMAKIL** (S.?) Oliphaunts (q. v.). (II 341)

**MUNDBURG** Name by which Minas Tirith was called by the Rohirrim. (II 143)

**MUNGO BAGGINS** (TA 2807-2900) Hobbit of the Shire, eldest son of Balbo Baggins. He married Laura Grubb; they had five children. (III 474)

**MUZGASH** (Orkish?) (d. TA 3019) Orc of Cirith Ungol, killed in the battle between his company and one from Minas Morgul over Frodo's mithril-mail. (III 217, 222)

**MYRTLE BURROWS** (b. TA 2993) Hobbit of the Shire, third child and only daughter of Milo Burrows. She was a guest at the Farewell Party. (III 474)

# N

**NAHALD** (gen. Mannish: 'secret') See: Déagol. (III 518)

**NÁIN I** (TA 1832-1981) Dwarf, King of Durin's Folk and King of Khazad-dûm (1980-81). He was slain by the Balrog. (III 439, 450)

**NÁIN II** (TA 2338-2585) Dwarf, King of Durin's Folk (2488-2585) in the Ered Mithrin. (III 450)

**NÁIN** (TA 2665-2799) Dwarf of the House of Durin, son of Grór and father of Dáin Ironfoot. Náin was slain by Azog in the Battle of Azanulbizar. (III 443, 450)

**NAITH** That part of Lórien between Celebrant and Anduin. The Naith included Egladil but was of greater extent.
    Called in Westron the Gore. (I 450)

**NÁLI** (d. TA 2994) Dwarf of Erebor. Náli went to Khazad-dûm with Balin in 2989, and was slain by Orcs while defending Durin's Bridge and the Second Hall. (I 419)

**NAMELESS LAND** Mordor (q. v.). (II 384)

**NAMELESS PASS** Morgul Pass (q. v.). (II 405)

**NAN CURUNÍR** (S.: 'valley of Saruman') Great valley in the southern Misty Mountains, opening into the Gap of Rohan. Isengard was located in Nan Curunír. Nan Curunír was at one time a fertile and fruitfully-tilled valley watered by the Isen, but at the time of the WR only a few acres near Isengard were cultivated by the slaves of Saruman; the rest of the valley had become a bramble-infested waste.
    Called in Westron the Wizard's Vale. (II 115, 202ff.)

**NANDUHIRION** (S.: 'valley---') Azanulbizar (q. v.). (I 370)

**NAN-TASARION** (S.: 'valley-willow') Tasarian (q. v.). (II 90)

**NÁR** (fl. TA 28th Cent.) Dwarf, companion of Thór in his wanderings. Nár was used by the Orcs of Khazad-dûm as a messenger to tell the Dwarves of the murder of Thrór. (III 441-42)

**NARBELETH** (S.: 'sun-waning') Another name for firith (q.v.). (III 480)

**NARBELETH** The Sindarin form of Narquelië, used only by the Dúnedain. (III 483)

**NARCHOST** (S.: 'fire-tooth') One of the Towers of the Teeth

(q. v.). (III 215)

**NARDOL** (S.: 'fire-hill') The third of the northern beacon-tower hills of Gondor, located west of Druadan Forest. (III 20)

**NARGOTHROND** (S.: 'fire-stone-hall'?) Elven kingdom in Beleriand, ruled by Finrod Felagund (q. v.). Nargothrond fell to Morgoth sometime in the First Age. (I 412; III 453, 506)

**NÁRIË** (Q.) The sixth month of the Kings' and Stewards' Reckonings and the third of the New Reckoning, corresponding roughly to our June.
The Sindarin form, used only by the Dúnedain, was Nórui. (III 483)

**NARQUELIË** (Q.: 'sun-waning') The tenth month of the Kings' and Stewards' Reckonings and the seventh of the New Reckoning, corresponding roughly to our October.
The Sindarin form, used only by the Dúnedain, was Narbeleth. (III 483, 486)

**NARMACIL I** (Q.: 'sun---') (d. TA 1294) Dúnadan, seventeenth King of Gondor (1226-94). Narmacil was both lazy and childless, and in 1240 he entrusted the rule of Gondor to his nephew Minalcar. (III 395, 404)

**NARMACIL II** (d. TA 1856) Dúnadan, twenty-ninth King of Gondor (1850-56). He was slain fighting the Wainriders. (III 395, 408)

**NARROW ICE** Some place to which Eärendil sailed in his wanderings before meeting Elwing. The Narrow Ice may have been imaginary and merely poetic. (I 308)

**NARROWS** Area in southern Mirkwood where the western and eastern borders of the wood drew together to form a narrow waist. In the Fourth Age the Narrows formed the northern boundary of East Lórien. (III 468)

**NARSIL** (Q.: 'sun---') The mighty sword of Elendil, forged by Telchar in the First Age. Narsil broke when Elendil fell in SA 3441 while fighting Sauron, and the shards were one of the heirlooms of the Line of Isildur through the Third Age. Elrond presented the shards to Aragorn when he came of age, and on the eve of the WR the sword was reforged and named Andúril (q. v.).
Called the Sword of Elendil and the Sword or Blade that was Broken. The Elvish name carried a connotation of ''red and white flame.'' (I 231, 233, 319, 320, 323-25; II 147; III 401, 421; RHM III 438)

**NARVI** (fl. SA 750) Dwarf of Khazad-dûm, maker of the West-gate. (I 398)

**NARVINYË** (Q.) The first month of the Kings' and Stewards' Reckonings and the tenth of the New Reckoning, correspond-ing roughly to our January.

The Sindarin form, used only by the Dúnedain, was Narwain. (III 483)

**NARWAIN** (S.) The Sindarin form of Narvinyë (q. v.), used only by the Dúnedain. (III 483)

**NARYA** (S.? Q.?: 'sun—') The third of the Three Rings of the Elves (q. v.), originally worn by Círdan, but given by him to Gandalf when the latter came to Middle-earth. Narya was the Ring of Fire, and had a red stone. It had the power to strength-en hearts.

Called Narya the Great. (III 383-84, 456)

**NAUGRIM** (S.: 'fire-people') The Dwarves (q. v.), as called by the Elves in the First Age. (III 518)

**NAZGÛL** (B. S.: 'those of the Ring or Rings') Nine beings, slaves of the Nine Rings and the chief servants of Sauron. Originally Men, perhaps Black Númenoreans, the Nazgûl were each given one of the Nine Rings by Sauron in the Second Age; and, being desirous of power, were easily corrupted. About SA 2250 they first appeared as the Nazgûl, beings ut-terly dependent on Sauron; or, more accurately, on his power acting through the One Ring. When Sauron fell at the end of the Second Age, the Nazgûl were overthrown or went into hiding. They reappeared about TA 1300, at which time their chief, the Lord of the Nazgûl (q. v.), became the Witch-king of Angmar. The other eight stayed in the East until about 1640, when they secretly entered Mordor and began to prepare that realm for Sauron, who was in Dol Guldur. In 2000, joined by their Lord, the Nazgûl besieged Minas Ithil, and captured the city and its palantír in 2002. From this time, the Nazgûl were closely associated with Minas Morgul, as Minas Ithil was then called. In 2951, ten years after its desertion by Sauron, three Nazgûl went to Dol Guldur, and stayed there until the WR.

In 3018 Sauron sent the Nazgûl, who at this time were known as the Black Riders because they rode swift black horses, to the Shire to search for Frodo and the Ring. Although the Lord of the Nazgûl wounded Frodo on Weathertop, he escaped from them, and their steeds were later destroyed in the Ford of Bruinen. A few months later, in 3019, they reappeared, mounted on flying beasts. The Nazgûl were active in the Siege of Gondor and the Battle of the Pelennor Fields, in which their Lord was slain, but the remaining Nazgûl were destroyed, with their Rings, when the One Ring was unmade in Orodruin.

The Nazgûl were the principal tools through which Sauron worked; they wielded a great power and terror, and were used as messengers and scouts, and to lead Sauron's armies and cow his enemies. Their power together at night was nearly as great as Gandalf's. They could be wounded only by weapons with special spells on them, and any blade which touched them melted. The Nazgûl were strongest at night and in deserted places, and were afraid of fire and the name of Elbereth. Because of their evil power, people who were near them for long developed the Black Breath (q. v.). As with others corrupted by the Rings, they were invisible to normal eyes, and could be seen only by their black clothing. The Nazgûl had a keen sense of smell, but may have been blind by normal standards. They could emit extremely loud, piercing, frightening cries. The Nazgûl used the Black Speech.

None of the names of the Nazgûl are given in *LotR,* although Gothmog was possibly the name of the second highest Nazgûl.

The Nazgûl were called in Westron the Ringwraiths. They were also called the Black Riders, the Fell Riders, the Nine Riders, and the Black Wings when appropriate, and the Nine, the Nine Servants of the Lord of the Rings and, by Orcs of the Tower of Cirith Ungol, the Shriekers. (I 82, 111-13, 135, 236, 263, 284-86, 337, 345-46, 357, 501; II 256; III 98-100, 276, 409, 412-13, 414, 454, 457, 462, 511)

**NEAR HARAD** That portion of Harad (q. v.) west of Khand, so called because it was near Gondor. (III 409)

**NECROMANCER** Sauron (q. v.). (H 37; I 328)

**NEEDLEHOLE** Village in the Westfarthing, located on the Water north of Rushock Bog. (I 40)

**NEEKERBREEKERS** Sam Gamgee's name for a kind of noisy insect found in the Midgewater Marshes. (I 247)

**NELDORETH** (S.) Forest in Beleriand in the First Age, containing the kingdom of Doriath. Its trees included hemlocks and beeches.

Also called Taur-na-neldor. (I 260; II 90)

**NEN HITHOEL** (S.: 'misty lake') A long, pale lake on Anduin. The northern entrance to Nen Hithoel was the Argonath, and at its southern end stood Tol Brandir and Emyn Lhaw and Hen, and beyond them the falls of Rauros. (I 17, 509)

NÉNIMË  (Q.: 'water---') The second month of the Kings' and Stewards' Reckonings and the eleventh of the New Reckoning, corresponding roughly to our February.

The Sindarin form, used only by the Dúnedain, was Nínui. (III 483)

NENUIAL  (S.: 'lake of twilight') Lake in Arnor north of the Shire. On its shores was built Annúminas.

Called in Westron Lake Evendim. (I 16, 320; III 411)

NENYA  (Q.: 'water--') The second of the Three Rings of the Elves (q. v.), worn by Galadriel. Nenya was made of mithril and had a white stone with a soft, flickering light.

Also called the Ring of Adamant. (I 472-73; III 381, 456)

NEW AGE  The Fourth Age, so called by Gandalf at the end of the Third. (III 318)

NEWBURY  Village in Buckland north of Crickhollow. (I 40)

NEW RECKONING  The calendar adopted by the Reunited Kingdom under King Elessar in TA 3021. The New Reckoning was basically the same as the Kings' Reckoning, but began in the spring, like the Eldarin loa, and contained various holidays commemorating the WR and its heroes. All of the months had thirty days.

The calendar for one year was;

> yestarë—first day; old Súlimë 25, the day of the downfall of Sauron.

Víressë
Lótessë
Nárië
Cermië
Úrimë
Yavannië
enderi—three days, the second called Loëndë.
Narquelië
Hísimë
Ringarë
Narvinyë
Nénimë
Súlimë
mettarë—last day.

The leap year was provided for by doubling Yavannië 30,

Frodo's birthday, which was called Cormarë. The week and the millenial adjustments seem to have been the same as those of the Kings' Reckoning. (III 486)

**NEW ROW** Name given the street in Hobbiton that had been Bagshot Row (q. v.), after it was completely rebuilt following its ruin by the Chief's Men in TA 3018-19.

New Row was jokingly called Sharkey's End in Bywater, since Saruman had been killed here. (III 373-74)

**NGOLDO** (Q.) Older form of noldo (q. v.). (III 500)

**NGWALME** (Q.) Older form of nwalme (q. v.). (III 500)

**NIBS COTTON** Carl Cotton (q. v.). (III 354-55)

**NICK COTTON** Bowman Cotton (q. v.). (III 354)

**NIGHT OF NAUGHT** The Shadows (q. v.). (I 308)

**NIMBRETHIL** (S.: 'white-birch') Forest or land where Eärendil obtained the wood for his ship. (I 308)

**NIMLOTH** (S.: 'white-blossom') The White Tree that grew in the King's Court in Númenor, a descendent of Galathilion. A sapling of Nimloth was carried to Middle-earth by Isildur when Númenor fell and Nimloth was destroyed. (III 308, 393, 484)

**NIMRODEL** (S.: 'white—') Shallow stream flowing from the Misty Mountains into the Silverlode, which it met at the boundary of Lórien. Its water was refreshing and cold.

*Nimrodel* was of Silvan origin adapted to Sindarin. (I 16-17, 439; III 506)

**NIMRODEL** (fl. TA 1980) Elf of Lórien, the lover of Amroth. She lived near the river Nimrodel. Nimrodel was one of the Elves who fled from Lórien when the Balrog arose in Khazad-dûm, but on her way to Dol Amroth she was lost in the Ered Nimrais. (I 440-42; III 181)

**NINDALF** (S.) Marshes east of Anduin and south of the Emyn Muil, caused by the merging of Anduin and the Entwash and the division of Anduin into many channels.

Called in Westron the Wetwang. (I 17, 483-84)

**NINE COMPANIONS** The Companions of the Ring (q. v.). (III 182)

**NINE RIDERS** The Nazgûl (q. v.). (I 360)

**NINE RINGS** The Rings of Power (q. v.) given to Men. The bearers of the Nine, the Nazgûl, were easily corrupted by

Sauron and showed themselves in their new form about SA 2250. The Nine Rings preserved them, but they became invisible and totally dependent on Sauron and the One Ring. The Nine Rings were destroyed in Orodruin when the One was destroyed during the WR, although the greatest of the Nine, worn by the Lord of the Nazgûl, may have been preserved, although it was powerless.

As with the other lesser Rings of Power, the Nine were each set with a gem. (I 82, 330; III 276)

**NINE WALKERS** The Companions of the Ring (q. v.). (I 360)

**NÍNUI** (S.) The Sindarin form of Nénime (q. v.), used only by the Dúnedain. (III 483)

**NIPHREDIL** (S.) Pale winter flower of Lórien. (I 454; III 428)

**NOAKES** Family of working-class Hobbits of the Shire. At the time of the WR Old Noakes lived in Bywater and frequented the Ivy Bush. (I 45)

**NOB** (fl. WR) Hobbit of Bree, servant at the Prancing Pony. (I 210, 211, 241; III 333)

**NOBOTTLE** Village in the Westfarthing. (I 40)

**NOGROD** (S.: 'dwarf-mountain') Dwarfish city of the First Age, located in the Ered Luin. Nogrod was ruined at the breaking of Thangorodrim. (III 439)

**NOLDO** (Q.: 'one of the Noldor') Later form of the name for the tengwa **ccʃ** (number 19). The original name, ngoldo, was given because the letter usually had the value **ŋɔ** , but this sound later changed to *n*. (III 500)

**NOLDOR** (Q.) One of the Three Kindreds of the Eldar (q. v.). All, or almost all, of the Exiles were Noldor, since Fëanor was a Noldorin prince. In the Second and Third Ages most of the Noldor who remained in Middle-earth dwelled in Lindon, Eregion or Rivendell.

The Noldor were the craftsmen of the Eldar, and were also more interested in such things as devising alphabets than other kindreds of the Eldar. Noldorin inventions and products included the Silmarilli, the Palantíri, ithildin and the Tengwar. The Noldor were also less unfriendly to Dwarves than other Elves, no doubt because of their more common interests.

The Noldor were possibly the Deep-elves and Gnomes of H 164. (III 452, 453, 493; R 60)

**NOMAN-LANDS** The Brown Lands (q. v.). (I 484)

**NORI** (fl. TA 2941)  Dwarf of the House of Durin, one of the members of Thorin and Company. (III 450; H 22, 26, 44)

**NORLAND**  A northern land of Middle-earth in the First Age. See: Forodwaith. (I 310)

**NORTH DOWNS**  High hills in Arnor about one hundred and fifty miles northeast of the Shire. Fornost was located on the North Downs. (I 16, 320; III 411)

**NORTHERN ARMY OF GONDOR**  One of the two armies of Gondor in the days of its greatest power. The Northern Army engaged in battles north and east of Minas Tirith, mostly against Easterlings.
Cf.: the Southern Army of Gondor. (III 409, 429)

**NORTHERN FENCES**  The northern border of Lórien (q. v.). (I 480)

**NORTHERN LINE**  The Line of Isildur (q. v.). (III 402)

**NORTHERN MIRKWOOD**  The Woodland Realm (q. v.). (I 315)

**NORTHERN WASTE**  The lands north of the Misty Mountains and the Ered Mithrin.
See: Forodwaith. (I 17)

**NORTHFARTHING**  One of the four Farthings of the Shire, where the barley for the Shire's beer was grown. Only in the Northfarthing was snow common in the Shire. The Northfarthing was also the site of hunting. (I 40, 377; II 325; III 375)

**NORTH ITHILIEN**  That portion of Ithilien north of the Morgulduin. (III 15)

**NORTH KINGDOM** or **NORTH-KINGDOM**  The northern Dúnadan realm, either Arnor or Arthedain. (I 23)

**NORTH MARCH**  The area around Rauros, the northern border of Gondor at the time of the WR. (III 350)

**NORTHMEN**  Men related to the Rohirrim and the Edain. The Northmen originally came from northern Rhovanion, but because of their distant relation to the Dúnedain and Gondor's need for a defense against the Easterlings, they were given much land east and south of Mirkwood about TA 1000. Rómendacil II ensured their doubtful loyalty by crushing the Easterlings in TA 1248 and by taking many Northmen into the army of Gondor. The Northmen remained loyal to Gondor thereafter as long as Gondor had any power in the East, and Northmen formed a considerable part of the army that restored Eldacar in 1447.

In 1856 the Northmen were enslaved by the Easterlings,
but in 1899 they revolted and, thanks to an attack by King
Calimehtar of Gondor at the same time, freed themselves.
After this, however, Gondor could not aid the Northmen, and
they fought off the Easterlings for the next thousand years
with varying success. During this time various tribes of
Northmen allied themselves with Gondor, and Northmen warriors comprised part of the army of Eärnur at the Battle of
Fornost in 1975.

In the Twenty-seventh and Twenty-eighth Centuries the
Northmen between Celduin and Carnen were allied with the
Dwarves of Erebor, and using Dwarvish weapons drove their
enemies back into Rhûn. By the time of the WR, however,
they were again weak, and the Easterlings reached the gates
of Erebor in 3019. In the Fourth Age those Northmen who
survived this invasion were probably allied with the Reunited
Kingdom. (III 404 ff., 408-09, 411, 440)

**NORTH MOORS** Moors in the Northfarthing. In TA 3001 Halfast of Overhill saw an Ent there. (I 73)

**NORTH ROAD** Road running from below Tharbad to Fornost,
crossing the Great East Road at Bree. After the fall of the
North-kingdom and the desolation of Eriador the North Road
became known as the Greenway because of its disuse.

Also called the Old South Road south of Tharbad. (I 210,
359)

**NORTH STAIR** Portage-way leading from the southern end of
Nen Hithoel to the foot of Rauros, made by Gondor early in
the Third Age. (I 504)

**NORTH-TOOKS** A branch of the Took family, living in Long
Cleeve. The North-tooks were descended from Bandobras
Took. (III 475)

**NORTH-WAY** This, of course, is another name for the West
Road. It all depended where one was standing when it was
named. (III 306)

**NÓRUI** (S.) Sindarin form of Nárië (q. v.), used only by the
Dúnedain. (III 483)

**NUMBER 3 BAGSHOT ROW** Hole in Bagshot Row where the
Gamgees lived at the time of the WR. It was ruined by the
Chief's Men during Lotho's control of the Shire, but was later
rebuilt and lined with brick. (I 44; III 373)

**NUMEN** (Q.: 'west') Name for the tengwa ⲣⳛ (number 17),

which usually had the value *n*. This tengwa was commonly used to indicate the compass-direction "west" even in languages in which the word for "west" did not begin with this letter. (III 500)

**NÚMENOR**   (Q.: 'west-land')   Rich and powerful kingdom of the Dúnedain, founded in SA 32 on the great island of Elenna. This island, westernmost of mortal lands, was granted to the Edain by the Valar as a reward for their part in the War of the Great Jewels. The Kings of Númenor were Elros Tar-Minyatur (q. v.) and his descendents; after SA 1075 the crown passed to the eldest child of the King, whether male or female.

Enriched by gifts from the Eldar, the Númenoreans became powerful and wise, but they were forbidden to set foot on the Undying Lands or to become immortal. About 600 ships of Númenor first returned to Middle-earth, and six hundred years later the Númenoreans began to make permanent havens in Middle-earth, of which Umbar was the greatest. In 1700 Tar-Minastir sent a great fleet to the aid of Gil-galad, and with this aid Sauron, who had overrun all of Eriador in the War of the Elves and Sauron, was defeated. A hundred years later the Men of Númenor began to establish dominions on the coasts of Middle-earth, exacting tribute where previously they had freely given aid, for Númenor was becoming enamored of power. At the same time, as great and proud mariners, the Númenoreans began to object to the fact that the western seas were closed to them. About this time the fear of death became widespread, for the lifespan of the Dúnedain was slowly dwindling.

In 2251 Tar-Atanamir became King, and he openly spoke against the Eldar and the Ban of the Valar (q. v.). All the people of Númenor followed him, except for the Faithful (q. v.). Succeeding generations abandoned the use of the Elven tongues, persecuted the Faithful and lost the joy of life through the fear of death. The Kings in 2899 began to take their royal names in Adûnaic, and the dwindling of their life-spans increased. In 3175 Tar-Palantir tried to return to the old ways, but his reign was marked by civil war, and on his death in 3255 his nephew usurped the crown and became Ar-Pharazôn.

Resolving to gain the kingship of the world, Ar-Pharazôn humbled Sauron in 3262 and took him to Númenor as a prisoner. Sauron quickly corrupted Númenor and persuaded Ar-Pharazôn to take Valinor and immortality by force. When he tried to do so in 3319, the Valar laid aside their Guardianship and called upon Eru, and Númenor was destroyed. Elendil, son of the Lord of Andúnië, escaped from the ruin with his sons and a small following of the Faithful, and came to Middle-earth. Sauron also escaped, but his body was destroyed.

Called in Westron Westernesse. Also known as the Land of the Star, a Westron translation of Elenna. The full Quenya form of the name was Númenóre. (I 489; III 297, 390-93, 407, 453-54, 507)

**NÚMENOREAN** Adûnaic (q. v.). (III 488)

**NÚMENOREANS** The Men of Númenor.
See: the Dúnedain, Númenor. (III 383-93, 507)

**NURN** (S.?) Area in southwestern Mordor around Nûrnen. At the time of the WR the slave-tilled fields of Nurn provided food for the armies of Mordor. After the War the slaves were freed and King Elessar gave the fields to them for their own. (I 17; III 246, 305)

**NÛRNEN** (S.: 'Nurn water') Bitter inland sea in southern Mordor. Into Nûrnen flowed rivers draining all of Mordor except for Gorgoroth and Udûn; it had no outlet.
Also called Lake Núrnen and the Sea of Nurnen. (I 17; II 308; III 246)

**NWALME** (Q.: 'torment') Later form of the name of the tengwa ᴆ (number 20), originally called ngwalme. The change was due to a phonological change in Quenya as it was spoken in Middle-earth. (III 500)

O

**OATBARTON**   Village in the Northfarthing.
Spelled in error "Catbarion" on I 40. (RHM I 26)

**OATH OF EORL**   Oath sworn by Eorl the Young to Cirion, the
Steward of Gondor, in TA 2510. The Oath stated that Eorl
and his descendents would aid the Stewards of Gondor at
need, in return for the gift of Calenardhon. The token of this
call for aid seems to have been the Red Arrow (q. v.). Rohan
fulfilled the Oath a number of times in the Third Age, especially in the time of King Folcwine and Steward Turin II
(2885), and during the WR. After the WR Éomer of Rohan renewed the Oath with the Kings of Gondor. (III 415, 416, 438)

**ODO PROUDFOOT**   (TA 2904-3005)  Hobbit of the Shire, son
of Bodo Proudfoot and Linda Baggins. He was a guest at
the Farewell Party. (I 53-54, 56; III 474)

**ODOVACAR BOLGER**   (fl. TA 30th Cent.)  Hobbit of the Shire,
father of Fredegar Bolger. He was a guest at the Farewell
Party.
The name "Odovacar" may possibly have been influenced
by the Quenya *vacar*. (III 475)

**OHTAR**   (S.) (fl. TA 1st Cent.)  Dúnadan of Arnor, the esquire
of Isildur. He was one of the three survivors of the Battle of
Gladden Fields, and brought the shards of Narsil to Arnor.
(I 320)

**ÓIN**   (TA 2238-2488)  Dwarf, King of Durin's Folk (2385-2488)
in the Ered Mithrin. (III 450)

**ÓIN**   (TA 2774-2994)  Dwarf of the House of Durin, elder son
of Gróin. He was a member of Thorin and Company, and lived
in Erebor after its recovery. In 2989 Óin went with Balin to
Khazad-dûm, and in 2994 he was taken by the Watcher in the
Water. (I 302, 418, 419; III 450; H 22, 26)

**OIOLOSSE**   (Q.: 'ever-snow-white')  The highest peak of the
Pelóri, and thus the highest mountain of the world. Upon its
summit were the halls of Manwe and Varda, and here Varda
stood when enveloping Valinor in darkness, and when hearing
the prayers of those in Middle-earth.
The Sindarin form was Uilos, and another Quenya name was
Taniquetil. Called in Westron Mount Everwhite. Also called

the Mountain and the Hill of Ilmarin. (I 309, 310, 489; R 60, 61)

**OLDBUCK** A Hobbit family, originally living in the Marish, where they were quite influential. It seems that the family was descended from Bucca of the Marish, the first Thain of the Shire. His heirs were also Thains until TA 2340, when Gorhendad Oldbuck moved to Buckland and changed the family name to Brandybuck (q. v.).

The genuine Hobbitish form of the name was Zaragamba. (III 459, 476, 520)

**OLD FARMER HOGG** See: Hogg. (TB 42)

**OLD FORD** Ford across Anduin, for ponies or horses, on the Old Forest Road. (H 13, 134)

**OLD FOREST** Forest between Buckland and the Barrow-downs, remnant of the great forest that once covered most of Eriador. The trees of the Old Forest, especially Old Man Willow (q.v.) and others by the Withywindle (q. v.), were malevolent and mobile. In appearance the trees were much like those of Fangorn Forest, and may have been as old. Tom Bombadil, who lived just outside the eastern end of the Forest, had great power over all the inhabitants of the Old Forest.

In TA 1409 some of the Dúnedain of Cardolan took refuge in the Old Forest when their land was overrun by Angmar. At some time later in the Third Age, the trees of the Forest attacked Buckland and tried to get over the Hay, but they were driven off when the Hobbits set a fire in the area later known as the Bonfire Glade. (I 16, 40, 156-71, 347; II 89)

**OLD FOREST ROAD** Road leading east from the High Pass and, crossing Anduin at the Old Ford, going through Mirkwood south of the Mountains. By TA 2941 the eastern end of the Road had become marshy and impassible, and the Road had been deserted because of the fear of Orcs. (I 17; H 12-13, 134)

**OLD GRANGE** Granary on the west side of the Hobbiton Road north of the Water. The Old Grange was torn down by the Chief's Men during Lotho's control of the Shire. (III 366)

**OLD GUESTHOUSE** Large building in Minas Tirith, in Rath Celerdain. During the Siege of Gondor the few boys remaining in the city stayed here. (III 46, 47)

**OLD MAN WILLOW** See: Willow, Old Man.

**OLD SOUTH ROAD** A name for that part of the North Road south of Tharbad. (I 16)

**OLD SWAN** Swan, one of the denizens of the Withywindle in a Shire poem about Tom Bombadil. (TB 19, 23)

**OLD TOBY** A variety of pipe-weed (q. v.). (I 28)

**OLD TOOK** Gerontius Took (q. v.). (II 80)

**OLD WINYARDS** A strong red Hobbit wine, made in the South-farthing. (I 65, 103)

*OLD WORDS AND NAMES IN THE SHIRE* A book by Merry Brandybuck discussing the relationship between Rohirric and Hobbitish. (I 39)

*OLIPHAUNT* A Shire-poem traditional at the time of the WR. (II 322; TB 47)

**OLIPHAUNTS** Elephants, used by the Haradrim as beasts of war. They carried war-towers, and also frightened horses; being virtually invulnerable, they formed centers of Haradrim defense in battle. They could be killed only by being shot in the eye, although they did have a tendency to go mad. Oliphaunts were considerably larger than modern elephants, but otherwise were very much the same.

The Rangers of Ithilien called Oliphaunts *mûmakil* (sing. *mûmak)*, which may have been their name in Westron, Sindarin or the language of the Haradrim. "Oliphaunt" was the name given them by the Hobbits. (II 322, 341-42; III 141, 147-48; TB 7, 47)

**OLOG-HAI** (B. S.: 'troll-people') A race of trolls of southern Mirkwood and northern Mordor, bred by Sauron toward the end of the Third Age. Unlike other trolls, the Olog-hai were cunning, and could endure the sun when controlled by Sauron. The Olog-hai probably perished when Sauron was overthrown.

The Olog-hai used the Black Speech; they knew no other language. (III 512)

**OLO PROUDFOOT** (TA 2946-FA 15) Hobbit of the Shire, son of Odo Proudfoot. He was a guest at the Farewell Party. (III 474)

**OLÓRIN** (Val.? Q.? S.?) Gandalf's real name, given to him in the West in his youth. (II 353)

**ONDOHER** (Q.: '---lord') (d. TA 1944) Dúnadan, thirty-first King of Gondor (1936-1944). During his reign, Gondor was attacked from the east and south by the Wainriders and Haradrim allied with them, and Ondoher and both his sons were slain in the battle with the invaders on Dagorlad. (III 395, 409)

**ONE, THE**   Eru (q. v.). (III 392)

**ONE, THE**   The One Ring (q. v.). (I 321)

**ONE RING**   The greatest of the Rings of Power (q. v.). After the forging of the other Rings, Sauron secretly forged the One Ring by himself in Orodruin, intending thereby to control the other Rings and their bearers. However, Celebrimbor perceived his designs, and kept the Three Rings free from Sauron's domination. Sauron did, however, control the Nine Rings through the One Ring. He let much of his power pass into the Ring, and many of his works, including the Barad-dûr, were linked to its power. The Ring was completely evil.

At the first downfall of Sauron in SA 3441, Isildur took the Ring, but it slipped off his finger during the Battle of the Gladden Fields and was lost in Anduin. About TA 2463 Déagol the Stoor found the Ring, and Gollum immediately murdered him to get it. Gollum then hid in the Misty Mountains with the Ring until 2941, when he lost it and Bilbo Baggins found it. Bilbo gave the Ring to Frodo in 3001. In the meantime, Gandalf, suspecting that the ring was indeed the One Ring, did research in Gondor, confirmed his suspicions and decided that something had to be done. Frodo, despite the efforts of Sauron to recover the Ring and of the Ring to corrupt him, eventually destroyed the One Ring in Orodruin in 3019, thus permanently (we hope) crippling Sauron and preventing him from ever taking shape again.

In appearance the Ring was a plain gold band. The Ring-inscription (q. v.) was finely engraved on it, but could only be read when the Ring was heated. The Ring could only be melted in the Fire of Doom in which it was forged.

Because of its great evil power, the Ring had curious properties. It possessed a certain measure of self-determination; Gandalf, who had wisdom in such matters, claimed that Bilbo found the Ring because it wanted to be found in order to be re-united with Sauron. The Ring also used and devoured its bearers unless, like Sauron, they were of very high rank. Their lives were extended, but they became enslaved to it and were physically changed (see: Gollum) as their bodies and souls were consumed by the Ring's hunger. The Ring also incited greed on the part of others to possess it, and jealous hate and fear on the part of its bearer. Bilbo and Frodo became distrustful of each other and of Gandalf while under the influence of the Ring, Boromir tried to kill Frodo to obtain it, and Gollum killed his friend and cousin Déagol for the Ring. Only the very wise, such as Gandalf, Galadriel and Aragorn, or the very simple, such as Sam and Tom Bombadil, could resist the lure of the Ring. Those of little power who wore the Ring became invisible, but their sight and hearing were increased, and this sensory acuteness remained to an extent even when they did not wear the Ring. The awareness of Sauron and of the other Rings of Power was especially heightened. The Ring was a constant weight and torment to Frodo's mind and body because he bore it at a time when Sauron's power was very great, and because he bore it in Mordor.

Called also the Great Ring, the One, the Ring, the Ring of Rings, the Ring of Doom, the Ring of Power, the Ruling Ring, the Master-ring, the Burden (in connection with Frodo) and Preciouss (by Gollum). (I vii, 55, 80-88, 94, 184-85, 188-89, 263, 276, 319-21, 330, 331-32, 352, 406, 472-74; II 300-01; III 189-90, 216, 276, 453; H 77, 87, 89)

**ONODRIM**  (S.: 'ent-people')  The Ents (q. v.). (II 55; III 510)

**ORAEARON**  (S.: 'day-sea')  Eärenya (q. v.). (III 484)

**ORALD**  Mannish name for Tom Bombadil (q. v.).

The name is actually translated Mannish; it meant "very old" in Old English. (I 347)

**ORANOR**  (S.: 'day-sun')  Anarya (q. v.). (III 484)

**ORBELAIN**  (S.: 'day-Valar')  Valanya (q. v.). (III 484)

**ORCH**  (S.)  See: Orcs. (III 511)

**ORCRIST**  (S.: 'goblin cleaver')  The sword of Thorin Oakenshield, the mate of Glamdring (q. v.). Although taken from Thorin in the halls of Taranduil, Orcrist was later placed on his tomb, and warned the Dwarves of Erebor of the approach of any enemy.

Called Biter by the Orcs. (I 366; H 53, 61, 72, 189, 275)

**ORCS**  Evil race of Middle-earth, first bred by Morgoth in the First Age from some unknown stock, and used by him as soldiers and servants in the War of the Great Jewels. After the overthrow of Morgoth, tribes of Orcs survived in the Misty Mountains and elsewhere, and in the Second and Third Ages they were Sauron's chief servants, although they were also used by Saruman and seem to have acted independently on occasion.

In the Third Age, Orcs began to multiply in the Misty Mountains about 1300, and by the time of the WR they were found there and in Mordor, Minas Morgul, Mirkwood and other areas controlled by Sauron. Orcs took part in all the vast enterprises of Sauron, from the realm of Angmar in the north to the assaults on Gondor in the south. They occupied Khazad-dûm after it was deserted by the Dwarves, and destroyed Balin's colony there in 2994, waylaid travellers in the passes of the Misty Mountains, raided in eastern Eriador and even attacked the Shire in 2747, invaded Rohan in 2800 and constantly troubled the Elves of Lórien and Mirkwood. After 2950 Saruman used Orcs in his attacks on Rohan. Although all the many conflicts between the Free Peoples and the Orcs cannot be mentioned here, two especially should be noted: the War of the Dwarves and Orcs, which destroyed a large part of the Orcs of the Misty Mountains in TA 2793-99, and the Battle of the Five Armies, which did the same thing in 2941.

Orcs were bred in mockery of Elves, and like Elves they were fierce warriors and did not die naturally. However, in all else they were different. Although Orcs varied from tribe to tribe, they tended to be short, squat and bow-legged, with long arms, dark faces, squinty eyes and long fangs. Most Orcs, except for the Uruk-hai, were weakened in the sun, and all Orcs preferred the dark. They were skilled in tunneling, in making weapons and in other practical skills; their medicines were harsh but extremely effective. Orcs wore foul, coarse clothing and heavy shoes. They hated all things of beauty, and loved to kill and destroy. Orcs used many weapons, including bows, spears, stabbing swords and long knives, but they seem to have preferred scimitar-like swords. Orcs liked blood and raw flesh and ate, among other things, Men, ponies and their own kind.

There were many different tribes of Orcs, and although there was cooperation within the tribe, between tribes Orcs hated each other as much as they did everything else. However, there was some organization among tribes, and the Orcs of the Misty Mountains had a capital, Gundabad. Cooperation was, not surprisingly, greater in wartime, when large numbers of Orcs, often under the control of Sauron, were able to work together to fight the Free Peoples. Nothing is said about Orkish tribal structures or female Orcs; Orcs were said to be spawned. Physical variation between tribes was not very great, although some tribes of Orcs (such as the tracking Orcs of III 246-49) may have been specially bred for certain functions. The Uruk-hai (q. v.), however, were a different strain and were quite different physically, being larger and more warlike. Orc tribes mentioned in *LotR* are those of Minas Morgul, the Tower of Cirith Ungol, the Barad-dûr, Isengard and various tribes of the Misty Mountains and Mirkwood. Some of these places may have had more than one tribe of Orcs, and in most of them there were probably Uruk-hai commanding lesser Orcs.

The Orkish tribes invented exceedingly crude languages for intra-tribal communication, and most of these languages included a few words of the Black Speech. For communication between tribes, Orcs used a debased form of Westron. (See: Orkish) Those Orcs who could write used a form of the Cirth.

The names for the Orcs were similar in most languages: *orch* in Sindarin (pl. *yrch)*, *uruk* in the Black Speech, *orc* in translated (and perhaps genuine) Rohirric *(orc* in Old English means 'demon') and *gorgûn* in the language of the Woses. The Hobbits, however, called them goblins. (I 83, 387, 422-23; II 20, 30, 60-75, 96, 113; III 133, 232, 246-49, 493, 511, 514; H 65, 68-72, 88, 95)

ORE   (Q.: 'heart' or 'inner mind')   Name for the tengwa ?? (number 21, which had the value of weak (untrilled) *r* in most systems. (III 500)

ORGALADH   (S.: 'day-tree')   Aldëa (q. v.). (III 484)

ORGALADHAD   (S.: 'day-trees')   Aldúya (q. v.). (III 484)

ORGILION   (S.: 'day-stars')   Elenya (q. v.). (III 484)

ORGULAS BRANDYBUCK   (b. TA 2868)   Hobbit of the Shire, youngest child of Marmadoc Brandybuck and father of Gorbulas Brandybuck. (III 476)

ORI   (d. TA 2994)   Dwarf of the House of Durin, a member of Thorin and Company. In 2989 Ori left Erebor and went to Khazad-dûm with Balin, where he died in the last defense of the Dwarves in the Chamber of Mazarbul. (I 302, 418; III 450; H 22, 26)

ORITHIL   (S.: 'day-moon')   Isilya (q. v.). (III 484)

ORKISH   The languages, such as they were, of the Orcs. They were mostly composed of snatches of other languages put together coarsely. For communication between tribes, a debased form of Westron was used, and Westron was the base of some of the tribal tongues. A few common inter-tribe words were derived from the Black Speech, and a few tribes had made a debased Black Speech their tribal tongue in the Third Age. The Orkish tongues were rich in curses, but weak in grammar, grammar being the one thing Orkish was not cursed with. (III 511)

ORMENEL (S.: 'day-heaven') Menelya (q. v.). (III 484)

ORNENDIL (Q.: '---water-lover') (d. TA 1437) Dúnadan of Gondor, son of King Eldacar. He was captured and slain by Castamir during the Kin-strife. (III 406, 457)

OROD-NA-THÔN (S.: 'mountain---pine') Dorthonion (q. v.). (II 90)

ORODROTH (S.: 'mountain--') (d. TA 2685) Dúnadan, sixteenth Ruling Steward of Gondor (2655-85). (III 395)

ORODRUIN (S.: 'the fire mountain') Volcanic mountain in Mordor, on the plain of Gorgoroth. In its fires about SA 1600 Sauron forged the One Ring, and always at his rising Orodruin erupted. Orodruin burst into flame in SA 3429, and erupted intermittently from TA 2954 until the end of the WR. When Gollum fell into the Fire of Doom with the One Ring in 3019, there was a major eruption.

Orodruin was only about 4500 feet high, but stood alone on a great plain, and so appeared higher. It had a great base about 3000 feet high, and on top of that there rose a tall cone ending in a wide crater. The Sammath Naur (q. v.) were located in this cone, and entering these chambers one came to the Crack of Doom, a great fissure in the mountain, in the depths of which burned the Fire of Doom (q. v.).

Also called Mount Doom (Sindarin: Amon Amarth), which was a name given the mountain by the people of Gondor when it erupted at the end of the Second Age. Called in Westron the Fire-mountain, the Fiery Mountain or the Mountain of Fire. (I 94; III 214, 269-72, 393, 453, 462)

OROFARNË (Q.) Rowan tree of Fangorn, cut down by Orcs of Isengard toward the end of the Third Age. (II 110)

OROMË (Q.) Araw (q. v.). (III 138, 395, 431)

OROPHIN (S.? Silvan?) (fl. WR) Silvan Elf of Lórien, brother of Haldir. He was a guard on the northern border of Lórien. (I 445, 448)

ORTHANC (S.: 'mount fang') The tower of Isengard, built from four pillars of black rock by the Dúnedain of Gondor. The top of Orthanc, a flat floor inscribed with astronomical figures, stood 500 feet above the plain of Isengard.

Orthanc was deserted by the Dúnedain sometime in the Second Age, and stood deserted until 2759, when Saruman came to dwell there. During the WR Orthanc defied the Ents, who could break other stone with ease, and so the tower passed unharmed through the War, and was again controlled by Gondor in the Fourth Age.

In translated Rohirric *Orthanc* meant "the cunning mind." (I 338, 341-43; II 204, 232 ff.; III 319)

**OSGILIATH** (S.: 'citadel of the stars') City and first capital of Gondor, built on both sides of Anduin between Minas Anor and Minas Ithil. Osgiliath was burnt during the Kin-strife and its greatest building, the Dome of Stars, was ruined. Many of its inhabitants died during the Great Plague of TA 1636, and most of its inhabitants who survived by fleeing refused to return. In 2475 Osgiliath was taken by Uruks of Mordor; and, although soon liberated by Boromir, the city was completely deserted, and became an outpost guarded against attack from the East. During the WR, Osgiliath was attacked in June, 3018; its last bridge was broken and the eastern half of the city was taken by Sauron's forces. Later, in March, 3019, the western half of the city was defended by the Rangers of Ithilien, but was easily captured. There is no record of its rebuilding in the Fourth Age.

The chief palantír was kept in Osgiliath until its loss during the Kin-strife. (I 321, 322; III 15, 41, 406, 408, 414, 457, 459, 465)

**OSSIRIAND** (S.: '--stream-land') Land in Beleriand in the First Age. Ossiriand had elm-woods and seven rivers. (II 90)

**OSTOHER** (Q.: 'fortress-lord') (d. TA 492) Dúnadan, seventh King of Gondor (411-92). Ostoher rebuilt Minas Anor and began the custom of dwelling there in summer. (III 394, 403)

**OTHO SACKVILLE-BAGGINS** (TA 2910-3012) Hobbit of the Shire, son of Longo Baggins and Camellia Sackville, and founder of the family of Sackville-Baggins. Otho married Lobelia Bracegirdle; their only child was Lotho. He was a guest at the Farewell Party.

Like the rest of his family, Otho was offensive and greedy. (I 52, 66; III 474)

**OUTLANDS** The areas of Gondor excluding Minas Tirith and

Anórien, and perhaps also Ithilien. Politically, the Outlands were the fiefs of Gondor. (III 48, 49)

**OUTSIDE**  In Tom Bombadil's world-view, everything not a part of Middle-earth; specifically, the Undying Lands. (I 182)

**OUTSIDERS**  Hobbits who did not live in the Shire, so called by the Hobbits of the Shire. (I 206)

**OVERBOURN MARSHES**  Marshes in the Shire south of the lower Shirebourn. (I 40)

**OVER-HEAVEN**  The Undying Lands (q. v.). (II 260)

**OVERHILL**  Village in the Westfarthing north of Hobbiton Hill. (I 40)

**OVERLITHE**  The leap-day in the Shire Reckoning, coming after Midyear's Day every fourth year except the last of a century. Overlithe was a special holiday. (III 478, 482)

## p

**PALADIN TOOK** (TA 2933-FA 14) Hobbit of the Shire, son of Adalgrim and father of Peregrin Took. Paladin was, as Paladin II, the thirty-first Thain of the Shire. When Lotho took over the Shire during the WR, Paladin refused to give up control of the Tookland or let the Chief's Men enter it, and organized an armed defense of the area. (III 356-57, 475)

**PALANTIR, TAR-** (Q.: 'farsighted') (d. SA 3255) Dúnadan, twenty-third King of Númenor (before 3175-3255). He took the sceptre as Ar-Inziladûn, but in 3175 he repented of the ways of his forebears and changed his royal name to Tar-Palantir. This pro-Eldarin policy caused civil war in Númenor, and when Palantir died the sceptre was usurped by the leader of the rebels, his nephew Ar-Pharazôn. (III 390, 392, 454)

**PALANTÍRI** (Q.: 'far-seer'; sing. *palantír*) Seven crystal globes wrought by the Noldor in Eldamar and given to the Lords of Andúnië by the Eldar. The palantíri showed scenes far away in space and time, and the views could be controlled by a person of strong will; two palantíri could be used for communication.

At the fall of Númenor, Elendil brought the palantíri to Middle-earth, and placed them throughout his realm. The chief palantír he placed in the Dome of Stars in Osgiliath; this stone alone could view all the others at one time. The others were placed in Minas Ithil, Minas Anor, Orthanc, Annúminas, the Tower Hills and the Tower of Amon Sûl. After the fall of Elendil the Eldar took back into their care the palantír of the Tower Hills, which only looked to the Undying Lands, and from time to time the Eldar made pilgrimages to the Tower Hills to look at Eldamar and Valinor. This palantír was put aboard the white ship of the Last Riding of the Keepers of the Rings in TA 3021. The palantír of Amon Sûl was long coveted by Rhudaur and Cardolan, for it was the chief stone of the North-kingdom and the other two were possessed by Arthedain and the Eldar. In TA 1409 the Tower of Amon Sûl was destroyed by Angmar, but Arthedain recovered the palantír and carried it to Fornost. The palantíri of Amon Sûl and Annúminas were kept at Fornost until the fall of Arthedain, when they were lost in the shipwreck that killed Arvedui.

In Gondor, the palantír of Osgiliath was lost when the city was burned during the Kin-strife. The palantír of Minas Ithil was captured by the Nazgûl when they took the city in TA 2002, and Sauron gained control of it. This made the other palantíri dangerous to use, especially the stone of Minas Anor, to which the Ithil-stone was most closely aligned. The Ithil-stone was probably destroyed when Sauron fell in the WR. The Kings and Stewards of Gondor did not use the palantír of Minas Anor after the fall of Minas Ithil until the time of the WR, when Denethor II, grown grim after the death of his wife, felt that he needed the knowledge that the palantír could give him in order to defeat Sauron. However, Sauron so manipulated Denethor's visions and assaulted his mind that the Steward went mad during the Battle of the Pelennor Fields, and burned himself with the palantír in his hands. After this time, the only picture that could be seen in the palantír, except by one of very strong will, was of two burning hands. The seventh palantír, that of Orthanc, was unused for most of the Third Age. In 2759, Saruman came to Orthanc in order to find the stone, but in using it was ensnared by Sauron. During the WR, Gríma threw the Orthanc-stone out of the tower, and it was recovered by Aragorn, who as its rightful user wrested it to his own will. With the palantír of Orthanc Aragorn discovered many things, including the fleet of the Corsairs that was approaching Gondor, and with this knowledge he planned the course of action that resulted in the victory of the West in the Battle of the Pelennor Fields. After the WR, Aragorn used this palantír to show him the state of his kingdom.

Also called the Seeing-stones. The palantír of the Tower Hills was called the Stone of Elendil. (II 241-42, 250-53, 254, 258-60; III 62-63, 159, 161-62, 321, 393, 397, 400, 406, 412, 418-19; R 65)

**PANSY BOLGER** (b. TA 2812) Hobbit of the Shire, second child of Balbo Baggins. She married Fastolph Bolger. (III 474)

**PARADISE** A land with dragon-flies, in Bilbo's poem *Errantry*. Any resemblance to places real, East or West, is probably coincidental. (TB 27)

**PARMA** (Q.: 'book') Name for the tengwa ꝑ (number 2), which had the value p in most systems. (III 500)

**PARMATÉMA** (Q.: 'p-series') The second series of the Tengwar. In the Third Age the parmatéma was usually applied to the labials and bilabials. Number 22, in the sixth grade, was generally not rigidly incorporated into the series, although its commonest value, w, was a bilabial. (III 496-97, 500)

**PARTH GALEN** (S.) Fair lawn running from Nen Hithoel to the slopes of Amon Hen. (I 511)

**PARTY FIELD** Field behind Bagshot Row in Hobbiton, site of Bilbo's Farewell Party in TA 3001. The Party Tree (q. v.) grew in the middle of the Field. (III 375)

**PARTY TREE** Tree in the Party Field, under which Bilbo made his speech at the Farewell Party. The Party Tree was cut down by the Chief's Men during the WR, but after the War Sam Gamgee planted the seed given him by Galadriel on the spot where it had grown. The new Party Tree was the only mallorn in Eriador. (I 53; III 366)

**PASS OF CIRITH UNGOL** Cirith Ungol (q. v.). (III 412)

**PATHS OF THE DEAD** Road under the Ered Nimrais leading from the Dead Door above Dunharrow to the source of the Morthond near Erech. The Paths of the Dead were closed to all save the Dead, who lived there, and the heir of Isildur. (II 136; III 63-64, 69-72)

**PEARL TOOK** (b. TA 2975) Hobbit of the Shire, eldest child of Paladin Took. She was a guest at the Farewell Party. (III 475)

**PEEPING JACK** Hobbit of Michel Delving, in the poem *Perry-the-Winkle*. He may have been an historical character. (TB 43)

**PELARGIR** (S.) City, the chief port of Gondor, built on Anduin at the mouth of the Sirith. Pelargir was built in SA 2350 as the greatest haven of the Faithful in Middle-earth, and Elendil landed here after the downfall of Númenor. Pelargir was rebuilt by Eärnil I of Gondor about TA 920, and was used by the Ship-kings as the base for Gondor's many assaults in the Umbar area. During the Kin-strife Pelargir was seized by the rebels after the Battle of the Crossings of Erui and held for one year against Eldacar's siege. During the WR Pelargir was taken by the Corsairs, but they were in turn defeated by the Dead. (III 14, 186-87, 403, 406, 454)

**PELENNOR** (S.: 'fenced land') The area of Gondor surrounding Minas Tirith, a fair and fertile land. The Pelennor was enclosed by the Rammas Echor (q. v.). During the WR, the Battle of the Pelennor Fields was fought here.

Also called the Pelennor Fields and the Fields of Pelennor. (III 23, 151; RHM III 435)

**PELENDUR** (Q.) (d. TA 1998) Dúnadan of the House of Húrin, Steward of Gondor from before 1944 until his death. Pelendur ruled Gondor for one year, after King Ondoher's death in 1944, and was instrumental in rejecting Arvedui's claim to the crown. (III 395, 409-10)

**PELÓRI** (Q.: 'fence---') The great mountain chain of Valinor, the highest in the world. The highest peak of the Pelóri was Oiolosse (q. v.). The Pelóri ran north and south, and the chief (and perhaps the only) pass through the great range was Calacirya.

Probably equivalent to the Mountain Wall. Also called the Mountains of Valinor. (R 62)

**PEONY BURROWS** (b. TA 2950) Hobbit of the Shire, youngest child of Posco Baggins. She married Milo Burrows, and bore him four children. She was a guest at the Farewell Party. (III 474, 476)

**PEOPLE OF THE GREAT JOURNEY** The Eldar (q.v.). (III 519)

**PEOPLE OF THE STARS** The Eldar (q. v.). (III 519)

**PEREDHIL** (S.: 'half-elven') Elros and Elrond, the two children of Eärendil and Elwing. They were called the Peredhil because of their extremely mixed Adan and Eldarin blood. At the end of the First Age, the Peredhil were given the choice of which race they wished to belong to. Elros chose to remain with the Edain, and he was given by the Valar a life-span many times that of lesser Men. Elrond became an Elven-lord of great power and wisdom. Elrond's children were also given the choice of which kindred they wished to belong to; the choice was to be made when Elrond left Middle-earth. All three of his children chose mortality. (III 389)

**PEREGRIN TOOK** (TA 2990-FA c. 65) Hobbit of the Shire, the thirty-second Thain of the Shire (14-64) and a Counsellor of the North-kingdom (14-64). In his youth Pippin was a close friend of Frodo Baggins, and accompanied him to Rivendell in 3018. There he became one of the Companions of the Ring. At Parth Galen he and Merry were befriended by Fangorn the

Ent, with whom they went to Isengard. There Pippin recovered the palantír which Gríma threw out of Orthanc, and being extremely curious by nature looked in it and was questioned by Sauron. Gandalf later took him to Gondor, where he entered into the service of Denethor II and was made a Guard of the Citadel. During the Siege of Gondor Pippin warned Beregond and Gandalf of Denethor's madness, and thus helped to save Faramir's life. Later, Pippin marched with the Army of the West to the Morannon and in the final battle slew a great troll.

After the WR Pippin was rewarded by King Elessar and was made a knight of Gondor and a King's messenger. He then returned to the Shire and helped mobilize the Hobbits against the Chief's Men. Throughout his life Pippin maintained contact with the outside world, and in FA 64 he and Merry resigned their offices and rode to Rohan and Gondor. They died in Gondor a few years later and were buried in Minas Tirith with great honor.

Peregrin was universally known as Pippin. In Gondor during the WR he was erroneously called Ernil i Pheriannath, or Prince of the Halflings. (I 38, 71; II 241-42, 249-54; III 29-31, 195, 207-08, 289, 321, 363, 471-72, 475, 514)

**PERIANNATH** (S.: 'halflings') Hobbits (q. v.). (III 510)

**PERRY-THE-WINKLE** Young Hobbit of Michel Delving, in the poem of the same name.

Also called the Winkle. The character of Perry-the-Winkle may have been based on a real Hobbit. (TB 42-44)

*PERRY-THE-WINKLE* Humorous poem written by Sam Gamgee and recorded in the Red Book of Westmarch. Although the Lonely Troll, one of the main characters, is probably fictitious, the Hobbits mentioned in the poem may have been modelled on real people. (TB 7, 41-44)

**PERVINCA TOOK** (b. TA 2985) Hobbit of the Shire, third daughter of Paladin Took. She was a guest at the Farewell Party. (III 475)

**PHARAZÔN, AR-** (Ad.: 'golden') (d. SA 3319) Dúnadan, twenty-fourth and last King of Númenor (3255-3319). The nephew of Tar-Palantir, he led the rebellious Númenoreans during his uncle's reign, and on his death usurped the sceptre from his cousin, Tar-Míriel. A great and proud king, Ar-Pharazôn desired to become master of the world, and so in 3261 sailed to Umbar to conquer Sauron. The latter submitted to the great army of Ar-Pharazôn and was taken to Númenor as a prisoner. There he quickly corrupted Ar-Pharazôn and the court, and persuaded the King to attack Valinor and obtain immortality by force. For nine years, beginning in 3310, the King built the Great Armament, and in 3319 he landed on the forbidden shore of Aman the Blessed. Ar-Pharazôn, his fleet and all of Númenor were immediately destroyed by Eru, on whom the Valar called for aid.

Ar-Pharazôn was known as "the Golden." (III 390, 392, 454)

**PHIAL OF GALADRIEL**    Jar of crystal, containing the light of Eärendil caught in the water of the fountain that filled the Mirror of Galadriel. The Phial was given by Galadriel to Frodo as a parting gift when he left Lórien during the Quest. The Phial had the virtue of shining in dark places and of bringing strength and courage, and its light was in turn increased by the hope and bravery of its bearer. With the Phial Frodo was able to overcome the desire for the Ring, and Sam used the Phial to cow and blind Shelob. It also aided the breaking of the spell of the gate of the Tower of Cirith Ungol. After the WR, Frodo bore the Phial with him to the West. (I 487-88; II 401, 408, 417-20, 430; III 218, 234-35, 384)

**PHURUNARGIAN**    (gen. West.: 'dwarf-delving')    Khazad-dûm (q. v.). (III 519)

**PICKTHORN**    Family of Men of Bree. (III 335)

**PILLARS OF THE KING**    The Argonath (q. v.). (I 508)

**PIMPERNEL TOOK**    (b. TA 2979)    Hobbit of the Shire, second daughter of Paladin Took. She was a guest at the Farewell Party. (III 475)

**PINCUP**    Village in the Southfarthing, in the Green Hill Country. (I 40)

**PINNATH GELIN**    (S.: 'ridges green')    Hills in southwestern Gondor, north of Anfalas.

Called in Westron the Green Hills. (I 17; III 50, 152)

**PIPE-WEED**    The tobacco of Middle-earth. Originally brought to Middle-earth from Númenor, pipe-weed grew abundantly in Gondor but only with great care in the North, in places like Longbottom and Bree. In Gondor pipe-weed was esteemed for the fragrance of its flowers, but Hobbits, probably in Bree, were the first to smoke it. Dwarves, Rangers, Gandalf and other wanderers picked up the habit at the Prancing Pony, and about TA 2670 Tobold Hornblower grew pipe-weed for

the first time in the Shire. Of the Companions of the Ring,
Gandalf, Aragorn, Merry, Pippin and Gimli were avid smokers,
but Legolas, perhaps in common with all Elves, disapproved
of the habit.

Famous strains of pipe-weed from the Southfarthing included
Longbottom Leaf, Old Toby and Southern Star. Southlinch was
a strain grown in Bree.

Called also in the Shire leaf. Called in Gondor (in Sindarin)
galenas or sweet galenas, and in Westron westmansweed.
(I 28-29; II 213-14; III 178, 334, 459)

**PIPPIN**   Peregrin Took (q. v.). (I 71)

**PIPPIN GAMGEE**   (b. FA 9)  Hobbit of the Shire, fifth child of
Sam Gamgee. His real name may have been Peregrin. (III 382,
477)

**PLACE OF THE FOUNTAIN**   The Court of the Fountain (q.
v.). (III 25, 27)

**POLO BAGGINS**   (b. c. TA 2860)  Hobbit of the Shire, son of
Ponto Baggins. (III 474)

**PONTO BAGGINS**   (TA 2816-2911)  Hobbit of the Shire, third
child of Balbo Baggins. He married Mimosa Bunce; they had
two children. (III 474)

**PONTO BAGGINS**   (b. TA 2946)  Hobbit of the Shire, first child
of Posco Baggins. He was a guest at the Farewell Party.
(III 474)

**POOL OF BYWATER**   Wide pool in Bywater, part of the Water.
Another stream, flowing from the north, joined the Water in
the Pool.

Also called the Bywater Pool and the Pool. (I 40; III 265,
349)

**POOL SIDE**   The portion of the Hobbiton Road next to the Pool
of Bywater. A row of ugly brick houses was built there during
Lotho's control of the Shire. (III 349)

**POPPY BOLGER**   (b. TA 2944)  Hobbit of the Shire, daughter
of Falco Chubb-Baggins. She married Filibert Bolger and was
a guest at the Farewell Party. (III 474)

**POROS**   (S.)  River flowing from the southern Ephel Dúath into
Anduin just above its delta. The Poros formed the southern
boundary of Ithilien. It was crossed by the Harad Road at the
Crossings of Poros (q.v.), the site of an important battle with
the Haradrim in TA 2885. (III 14-15, 409)

**PORTO BAGGINS**   (b. TA 2948)  Hobbit of the Shire, second son
of Posco Baggins. He was a guest at the Farewell Party.

(III 474)

**POSCO BAGGINS** (b. TA 2902, d. before 3001) Hobbit of the Shire, son of Polo Baggins. He married Lily Brownlock; they had three children. (III 474)

**POSTMASTER** An office and title of the Mayor of Michel Delving in his capacity of head of the Messenger Service. (I 31)

**POTT** A Hobbit surname, in Sam Gamgee's poem *Perry-the-Winkle.* Old Pott was Mayor of Michel Delving in the poem. (TB 42)

**PRANCING PONY, THE** The inn at Bree, owned and operated for many generations by the Butterbur family. At the time of the WR the proprietor was Barliman Butterbur. The Prancing Pony was the home and center of the art of smoking pipeweed, and in prosperous times was one of the great centers of news in Eriador.

Called for short the Pony. (I 29, 209-41; III 332-39)

**PRIMARY LETTERS** The first twenty-four letters of the Tengwar, divided into series (témar) and grades (tyeller) and given values according to consistent articulatory linguistic principles. (III 495-96)

**PRIMROSE GAMGEE** (b. FA 15) Hobbit of the Shire, ninth child of Samwise Gamgee. (III 477)

**PRIMULA BAGGINS** (TA 2920-80) Hobbit of the Shire, youngest child of Gorbadoc Brandybuck. She married Drogo Baggins and bore him one child, Frodo. She and her husband were drowned in a boating accident on the Brandywine. (I 45; III 474, 476)

*PRINCESS MEE* A nonsense poem written by an unknown Hobbit in a margin of the Red Book of Westmarch. (TB 7, 28-30)

**PRISCA BOLGER** (b. TA 2906, d. before 3001) Hobbit of the Shire, second child of Polo Baggins. She married Wilibald Bolger. (III 474)

**PROUDFOOT** Family of Hobbits of the Shire, perhaps of the upper class. (I 52, 53; III 474)

**PUDDIFOOT** Family of Hobbits, at least one branch of which lived in Stock at the time of the WR. (I 133)

**PÚKEL-MEN** Name given by the Rohirrim to the grotesque statues on the road leading from Edoras to Dunharrow, carved early in the Second Age by a forgotten race. The Púkel-men resembled the Woses, and perhaps they were carved by a related people. (III 80, 81, 129)

# Q

QUARRY   Village in the Eastfarthing, near Scary. (I 40)

QUELLË   (q.: 'fading')   The fourth season of the Eldarin loa (q. v.), very roughly equivalent to our October and November. The Sindarin form of the name was firith. Other names for this season were lasse-lanta and narbeleth.

Quellë or lasse-lanta was the name given by Men to the end of yávië and the beginning of hrívë. (III 480, 485)

QUENDI   (Q.: 'the speakers')   The Elves (q. v.). (III 519)

QUENYA   (Q.: 'the language')   The first recorded language of the Eldar. Quenya was first written in Eldamar, and shows signs of being related to Valinorean, but because of its relation to Sindarin Quenya must first have been spoken in Middle-earth during or before the Great Journey. Being a language of an undying race, Quenya changed slowly or not at all. In Middle-earth, it had become by the Third Age for the Eldar a language of ceremony. The Dúnedain and the Ents greatly loved and honored Quenya.

Quenya was a soft, flowing, rhythmic, beautiful, inflected language. Examples of Quenya include the names of the Tengwar and the divisions of the calendar, Galadriel's poem, the names of various Elves and Dúnedain and some Entish.

Also called the Ancient Tongue, High-elven and Eldarin. (III 119, 487-501 passim., 506, 507, 510)

QUESSE   (Q.: 'feather')   Name for the tengwa ꡑ (number 4), originally having the value *kw*. (III 500)

QUESSETÉMA   (Q.: '*kw*-series')   A labialized series of the Tengwar, applied in Quenya to Series IV. The first four values of the quessetéma had the values *kw, gw, khw* or *hw* and *ghw* or *w*. The actual Quenya values of the first four tyeller of this series, however, were *kw, ngw, gw* and *nw*. (III 496-97, 500)

**QUEST OF MOUNT DOOM**   Frodo Baggin's mission to destroy the One Ring in the Sammath Naur of Orodruin. Frodo resolved to undertake the Quest at the Council of Elrond, November 25, TA 3018, and he achieved it on March 25, 3019. (I 367)

**QUICKBEAM** Bregalad (q. v.). (II 109)

**QUICK POST** Some sort of fast-delivery mail and message system in the Shire, probably a part of the Messenger service. During his control of the Shire, Lotho Sackville-Baggins used the Quick Post system for his own purposes. (III 348)

# R

**RADAGAST** (tr. Mannish) (fl. TA 1000-3018) One of the Istari. Radagast dwelled at Rhosgobel, and was a master of herb- and beast-lore. He was especially friendly with birds. Aside from unwittingly causing Gandalf to be captured by Saruman, and equally unwittingly arranging for his escape, Radagast does not seem to have done very much during the WR.

Radagast was, in the order of the Istari, Radagast the Brown. (I 336-37, 342, 359; H 121)

**RADBUG** (d. TA 3019) Orc of the Tower of Cirith Ungol. Shagrat squeezed his eyes out when he refused to obey an order after the fight between the Orcs of the Tower of Cirith Ungol and Gorbag's company from Minas Morgul. (III 222)

**RAMMAS ECHOR** (S.) The wall built around the Pelennor by Steward Ecthelion II after the desertion of Ithilien in TA 2954. The Rammas was repaired at the time of the WR but was easily breached by the army of the Lord of the Nazgûl on March 13, 3019.

See also: the Causeway Forts. (III 23, 136)

**RANGERS OF THE NORTH** Those of the Dúnedain of the North who guarded Eriador from Orcs, wild animals and other evil things after the fall of Arthedain. The Rangers gave special protection to the Shire, especially during the period just before the WR. It seems that most of the male Dúnedain were Rangers, and that they were led by the Chieftain of the Dúnedain, who was the heir of Isildur.

The Rangers were grim in life, appearance and dress. They wore grey or dark green cloaks, with no ornament save for a cloak-clasp shaped like a six-pointed star. The Rangers rode rough-haired, sturdy horses and carried spears, bows and swords.

The Hobbits of the Shire called them the Watchers or the Watchers at Sarn Ford; they were generally considered rather disreputable in the Shire and Bree. (I 205, 214, 291, 325-26; III 59-60, 61-62, 463, 464; TB 21)

**RANGERS OF ITHILIEN** Soldiers of Gondor, Dúnedain descended from the inhabitants of Ithilien. After Ithilien was overrun by Orcs in 2901 the Rangers crossed the Anduin from time to time to harry Sauron's forces in Ithilien. They used various secret retreats, of which the most important was Henneth Annûn. At the time of the WR, Faramir was the Captain of the Rangers.

After the WR, the Rangers may have formed the bulk of the White Company.

The Rangers wore brown and green camoflage uniforms, with green gloves and masks. They carried spears or great bows as well as swords. (II 335, 338; III 198, 416)

**RANUGAD** (gen. Hobb.: 'stay-at-home') Hamfast (q. v.). (III 517)

**RATH CELERDAIN** (S.: 'street of the lampwrights') Broad street in the first level of Minas Tirith, leading to the Great Gate. The Old Guesthouse was located on Rath Celerdain. Called in Westron the Lampwrights' Street. (III 46, 47)

**RATH DÍNEN** (S.: 'silent street') The main street of the Hallows (q. v.) of Minas Tirith. (III 121-22, 427, 472)

**RAUROS** (S.) Waterfalls on Anduin south of Nen Hithoel, where Anduin fell from the height of the Emyn Muil. Rauros was bypassed by the North Stair, a portage-way built by the Kings of Gondor. (I 483, 518)

**RAVENHILL** Hill south of Erebor at the end of the great southern spur of that mountain. The Dwarves of Erebor built a guardhouse on Ravenhill, and gave the hill its name because ravens, wise and famous Dwarf-friends, lived in a nest on top of the guardhouse.

During the expedition of Thorin and Company, the Dwarves stayed here one night, during which they met Roäc and learned of the death of Smaug. During the Battle of the Five Armies the Elves of Mirkwood, and also Gandalf and Bilbo, made their stand on Ravenhill. (H 195, 231-33, 244, 269-70)

**RAVENS** Birds of Middle-earth. The ravens of Erebor were friendly with the Dwarves, and spoke Westron. They were very large, and lived to a great age; Roäc was 153 years old in TA 2941. (H 243-44)

**RÉ** (Q.: 'day') The solar day of the Eldar, measured from sunset to sunset. The ré may also have been the day of the Dúnedain calendars. (III 479)

**RECKONING OF RIVENDELL** The Calendar of Imladris (q. v.), so called by the Hobbits of the Shire. (III 480)

**RECKONING OF YEARS, THE**  A book by Merry Brandybuck discussing the relationship between the calendars of the Shire, Bree, Rivendell, Gondor and Rohan. (I 38)

**RED ARROW**  A black-feathered arrow barbed with steel; its tip was painted red. The Red Arrow was sent from Gondor to Rohan when the former needed aid, and may have been associated with the Oath of Eorl. (III 86)

**RED BOOK OF WESTMARCH**  Large book with red leather covers, written by Bilbo, Frodo and Sam, and containing additions and notes by other hands. The Red Book contained the story of Bilbo's adventures with Thorin in TA 2941, and an account of the WR and the events of the end of the Third Age as seen by Hobbits. Attached to the Red Book were the three volumes of Bilbo's *Translations from the Elvish* and a volume of genealogies and other Shire matters compiled by one of Sam's descendents. The Red Book was given by Sam to his daughter Elanor, and was kept by the Fairbairns in Westmarch, whence its name. Although the original of the Red Book was lost, many copies of it were made. The first, and most important, was the Thain's Book (q. v.). An exact copy of this copy was made by Findegil in FA 172, and was kept at the Great Smials. This copy was the only extant one to contain all of Bilbo's *Translations,* and also contained annotations and corrections made by the scholars of Gondor, as well as various marginalia written by many generations of Hobbits. This copy seems to be the one used by Professor Tolkien. Also known as the Red Book and (in Gondor) the Red Book of the Periannath. (I 19, 37; III 365, 379-80; TB 7)

**REDHORN**  Barazinbar (q. v.). (I 370)

**REDHORN GATE**  One of the most important passes over the Misty Mountains, located on the southern side of Barazinbar, and connecting Eregion and Azanulbizar. The eastern approach to the Redhorn Gate was known as the Dimrill Stair. Also called the Redhorn Pass. (I 370, 376 ff.; III 401)

**REDHORN PASS**  The Redhorn Gate (q. v.). (III 401)

**REDWATER**  Carnen (q. v.). (III 440)

**REGINARD TOOK**  (b. TA 2969) Hobbit of the Shire, eldest son of Adelard Took. He was a guest at the Farewell Party. (III 475)

**REMMIRATH**  (S.: 'net-jewel-collective plural') The Pleiades.

Called in Westron the Netted Stars. (I 120; III 490)

**RETHE** The third month of the Shire Reckoning and the calendar of Bree, corresponding roughly to our March. (III 478, 483)

**REUNITED KINGDOM** The realm ruled by Elessar and the Telcontari who succeeded him, so called because it included all the lands of both Gondor and Arnor claimed by Elendil and divided after his death. The capitals of the Reunited Kingdom were Annúminas and Minas Tirith. At the beginning of the Fourth Age the Reunited Kingdom included all those lands which were part of Arnor and Gondor at their greatest extent, except for Rohan. In addition, the King of the Reunited Kingdom was overlord of Dale and Erebor, and probably received tribute from much of Harad and Rhûn. (I 37)

**RHÎW** (S.: 'winter') The Sindarin form of hrívë (q. v.). (III 480)

**RHOSGOBEL** (S.) The dwelling-place of Radagast, near the southern border of Mirkwood. Rhosgobel was probably located in the Vales of Anduin. (I 336, 359; H 121)

**RHOVANION** (S.) General name given to the area including Mirkwood, the Brown Lands and the Vales of Anduin, and possibly all the lands east of Rivendell.

Called in Westron Wilderland. Rhovanion was probably equivalent to the Wild. (I 17; III 405, 406; H 14)

**RHUDAUR** (S.) Kingdom in Eriador, founded in TA 861 by one of the sons of King Eärendur of Arnor. Rhudaur included all the lands between the Weather Hills, the Ettenmoors and the Misty Mountains, and also included the Angle. The Dúnedain were few in Rhudaur, and by 1350 the kingdom was controlled by Hill-men and was in league with Angmar. With the defeat of the Witch-king of Angmar in 1975 Rhudaur fell and all its people were scattered or destroyed. (I 269 ff.; III 396, 397)

**RHÛN** (S.: 'east') Name given by the Dúnedain of Gondor to the area east of the Sea of Rhûn (q. v.). In the First Age Araw came here to hunt, and at the height of its power Gondor ruled the western part of Rhûn. After the fifth century of the Third Age, however, the Easterlings (q. v.), Men of various races living in the many countries of Rhûn, made war on Gondor, often at the incitement of Sauron.

Called in Westron the East or the Eastlands. (I 17, 325, 518; III 29, 403, 404 ff.)

**RHYMES OF LORE** Poems designed to aid the retention of

various ancient facts. Men, Elves, Hobbits and probably other races had Rhymes of Lore. The Long List of the Ents may be an example of one. (II 258, 259)

**RIDDERMARK OF ROHAN** Rohan (q. v.). (I 343)

**RIDERS OF ROHAN** The knights of Rohan. Those riders who were grouped in éoreds served one particular lord, as for example Théoden's knights, who were called the Riders of the King's House. However, in addition to the knights of the noble households there also seem to have been many Riders who were soldiers at need only; these men were probably bound by feudal ties to various lords of Rohan.

The Riders were excellent horsemen, and rode together with great skill. They were armed with sword, shield and lance.

The cavalry of this people was known as the Riders even in Éothéod, and from them derived the Rohirrim's name for their new land, the Riddermark.

Also called the Riders of the Mark. (II 40-41; III 79-80, 139-40, 314, 429-30)

**RIDDLE-GAME** A game of set and sacred rules, in which two people asked each other riddles, and the first one unable to answer a riddle lost the pre-determined stakes. The Riddle-game seems to have been played throughout Middle-earth, and was included in the guardianship of the Valar. (I 33. 89; H 80-87, esp. 86)

**RIMMON** Mountain in the northern Ered Nimrais upon which was built the beacon-tower of Min-Rimmon.

The name *Rimmon* was of forgotten origin, and originated in the Second Age before the settlement of Gondor. (III 14, 130, 508)

**RING** The One Ring (q. v.). (I 32, etc.)

**RINGARË** (Q.) The twelfth month of the Kings' and Stewards' Reckonings, and the ninth of the New Reckoning, corresponding Roughly to our December.

The Sindarin form of the name, used only by the Dúnedain, was Girithron. (III 483)

**RING-INSCRIPTION** The inscription on the One Ring, written by Sauron in a special Tengwar mode in the Black Speech. The inscription read:

Ash nazg durbatulûk, ash nazg gimbatul,
Ash nazg thrakatulûk agh burzum ishi krimpatul.

and meant:

One Ring to rule them all, One Ring to find them,
One Ring to bring them all and in the darkness bind them.

The Ring-inscription, which was visible only when the Ring
was heated, was designed to ensnare the other Rings of
Power. (I 80-81, 333)

RINGLÓ  (S.)  River in Lamedon, Gondor, the largest tributary of the Morthond, which it joined just above its mouth.
The Kiril flowed into the Ringló. (III 14, 184)

RINGLÓ VALE  The valley of the Ringló, in Lamedon. (III 49)

RING OF BARAHIR  An Elven-ring, one of the heirlooms of
the House of Isildur. Originally given to Barahir by Finrod,
Beren recovered it after his father's death. At the end of
the First Age the ring went to Númenor, and somehow passed
into the hands of the Faithful. In Middle-earth it was one of
the heirlooms of the North-kingdom, and after the fall of
Arthedain was kept safe in Rivendell. (III 400, 401, 421)

RING OF ISENGARD  See: Isengard. (II 203)

RINGS OF POWER  The greatest rings of Middle-earth, forged
by the Noldorin smiths of Eregion and by Sauron between SA
1500 and 1590. There were Nine Rings for Men, Seven Rings
for Dwarves and Three Rings for the Elves (qq. v.). Ten years
after the forging of these Rings, Sauron treacherously forged
the One Ring (q. v.) to rule the others, but his designs were
perceived by Celebrimbor. Although the Elves managed to
escape from this trap, and the Dwarves proved untameable
through the Rings, the Nine Rings ensnared the Nazgûl (q.
v.). After the unmaking of the One Ring during the WR, however, all the Rings of Power lost their power.

Any mortal possessing one of the Rings would not die, but
would continue living in great weariness; the Dwarves, however, were unaffected.

All the Rings except for the One consisted of a metal band
set with a gem.

Also called the Great Rings and the Rings. (I 76, 321,
330, 333, 352, 472-73; III 445-46, 453)

RINGWRAITHS  The Nazgûl (q. v.). (I 82)

RIVENDELL  Elven-refuge in a steep and hidden valley in the
Angle, founded in SA 1697 by Elrond, who was fleeing from
the destruction of Eregion with the remnant of the Noldor of

that land. From Rivendell Elrond succoured the Dúnedain at need in the Third Age, and fought against Angmar. Valandil, the son of Isildur, was raised here, as were, later, all the Chieftains of the Dúnedain. Rivendell survived the War of the Elves and Sauron and the wars against Angmar because of the great Elven-power there; besides Elrond, Glorfindel, Gildor and a number of other great Elven-lords lived there.

After the WR, Elrond and many of the Elves of Rivendell went over Sea, but Elladan and Elrohir remained there, and they were joined by Celeborn. There is no record of when Rivendell was finally deserted.

Called in Sindarin Imladris and in genuine Westron Karningul. (I 17, 39, 289-368; III 397, 401, 421, 454, 468; H 57-63)

**RIVER RUNNING** River flowing from the Front Gate of Erebor to the Sea of Rhûn, about 600 miles long. The River Running passed through the Long Lake, which it left by a waterfall. Its principal tributaries were the Forest River and the Carnen.

The River Running was an important trade route.

Called in Sindarin the Celduin. Also called the Running River. (I 17; III 405; H 185, 194-95, 230)

**RIVER-WOMAN** Denizen of the Old Forest, living in a deep pool of the Withywindle. She was the mother of Goldberry. (TB 11, 15)

**ROÄC** (b. TA 2788) Chief of the great ravens of Erebor, son of Carc, friendly to the Dwarves. In 2941 Roäc acted as counsellor and messenger to Thorin, telling him of the death of Smaug and sending ravens to bring Dwarves of Durin's Folk to Erebor. (H 244-46)

**ROBIN GAMGEE** (b. FA 20) Hobbit of the Shire, twelfth child of Samwise Gamgee. (III 477)

**ROBIN SMALLBURROW** (fl. WR) Hobbit of the Shire, living in Hobbiton. Robin became a Shirriff before the WR because it was an easy job, but with the expansion of the Shirriffs under Lotho Sackville-Baggins he became, unwillingly, part of the First Eastfarthing Troop.

Also called Cock-robin. (III 346-49)

**RODYN** (S.) See: Valanya. (III 484)

**ROHAN** (S.: 'horse-land') Kingdom of the Rohirrim, bounded by the Ered Nimrais, the Isen, the Misty Mountains, Fangorn, the Limlight, Anduin, the Mouths of Entwash and the Mering Stream. Once a province of Gondor, Calenardhon, the land was given to the Men of Éothéod by Cirion of Gondor in TA 2510 in return for their aid in the Battle of the Fields of Celebrant and their swearing of the Oath of Eorl. Rohan, as the country was then called in Gondor, was ruled by King Eorl and his descendents.

The Rohirrim farmed and raised horses on the green plains of their country, and built or took over fortresses and refuges in the Ered Nimrais, the most important of which were Dunharrow and Helm's Deep. The first kings built the capital of Edoras below Dunharrow, but most of the Rohirrim dwelled in small villages or on farms. Their greatest concern was for their horses, which were the best in the world.

In 2758 Rohan was overrun by Dunlendings led by Wulf, but the invaders were defeated the next spring by Fréaláf. In 2799, Orcs fleeing from the Battle of Nanduhirion troubled Rohan, and they were not entirely driven out of the Ered Nimrais until 2864. About 2960 Saruman began to trouble Rohan, and his harrassments increased until the WR, when Rohan was invaded by an enormous army of Orcs and Dunlendings. Although the Rohirrim were defeated in the two Battles of the Fords of Isen, the invaders were crushed, with the aid of Gandalf and the Huorns, in the Battle of the Hornburg.

Throughout its history, Rohan was closely allied with Gondor, and Rohan performed its greatest service to the Dúnadan realm during the WR, when the Riders of Rohan played a crucial role in the Battle of the Pelennor Fields.

Rohan was the name given the land in Gondor; the Rohirrim called their land the Riddermark, the Mark of the Riders or the Mark.

See also: entries for individual kings of Rohan, Eastfold, Westfold, etc. (I 343; II 30 ff.; III 428-38, 459-72)

**ROHERYN** (S.: 'horse of the woods') (fl. WR) The horse of Aragorn, shaggy, proud and strong. During the WR Halbarad brought Roheryn to Aragorn in Rohan, and he rode him for the remainder of the War. (III 59)

**ROHIRRIC** The language of the Rohirrim, related to the languages of the Men of the Vales of Anduin. Rohirric was probably descended from Adûnaic or a related language, and was thus distantly related to Westron, than which it was more archaic. Rohirric was closely related to the former language of the northern Hobbits, and even by the time of the WR many words in Rohirric and Hobbitish were clearly related.

The Rohirrim continued to speak their ancestral tongue into the Fourth Age, even though their neighbors spoke Westron. (III 508, 510, 517)

**ROHIRRIM** (S.: 'horse-lord people') Men, the inhabitants of Rohan, descended from the Éothéod. Because of the Oath of Eorl and their natural nobility, the Rohirrim were friendly to Gondor and deadly foes of her enemies.

The Rohirrim were tall and blond, with fair faces; they lived to be about eighty, and retained their strength even in old age. The Rohirrim loved their horses above all else; they raised the noblest horses and were the best horsemen in all of Middle-earth. The Rohirrim were culturally conservative, keeping even into the Fourth Age their ancient customs and language. They wrote with a primitive mode of the Cirth.

The Rohirrim called themselves the Eorlingas (tr. Roh.: 'sons of Eorl'); Rohirrim was the name given them in Gondor. Also called the Sons of Eorl, the Horse-lords, the Horse-men (by Ghân-buri-Ghân), the Riders (by synecdoche) and the North-men (in opposition to the Haradrim). (I 343; II 39-41, 363-64; III 415, 428-30, 493, 508)

**RÓMEN** (Q.: 'east') Name for the tengwa 𝖞 (number 25), which was usually used for full *r*. This tengwa was commonly used to indicate the compass-direction "east" even in languages in which the word for "east" did not begin with this letter. (III 500)

**RÓMENDACIL I** (Q.: 'east-victor') (d. TA 541) Dúnadan, eighth King of Gondor (492-541). He took his royal name to commemorate his victories over the Easterlings, but he was later slain in battle with them.

His birth-name was Tarostar. (III 394, 403)

**RÓMENDACIL II** (d. TA 1366) Dúnadan, nineteenth King of Gondor (1304-66), originally called Minalcar. The nephew of King Narmacil, he was a man of great vigor and talent, and so Narmacil, and later his own father Calmacil, made him Regent (1240-1304). In 1248 he won a great victory over the Easterlings, and extended Gondor's power to the Sea of Rhûn. After this victory he took the name Rómendacil, with which he was later crowned. Among his other accomplishments, Rómendacil fortified the Anduin frontier and built the Argonath.

Realizing that Gondor was weak in manpower, Rómendacil showed great favor to the Northmen, and in 1250 sent his son Valacar to the court of Vidugavia. This action, although in itself wise, later led to the Kin-strife. (III 395, 404-05)

ROPER  Family of Hobbits of the Shire, descended from Andwise Roper, the eldest son of Hobson "Roper" Gamgee. For at least two generations the Ropers kept a rope-walk in Tighfield. (III 477)

ROPER GAMGEE  Hobson Gamgee (q. v.). (III 477)

RORIMAC BRANDYBUCK  (TA 2902-3008) Hobbit of the Shire, Master of Buckland (2963-3008). He married Menegilda Goold, and had by her two children. He was a guest at the Farewell Party.

Rorimac was known as "Goldfather"; and, in later life, as Old Rory. (I 56; III 476)

ROSA TOOK  (b. TA 2856) Hobbit of the Shire, daughter of Ponto Baggins. She married Hildigrim Took and bore him one child, Adalgrim. (III 474, 475)

ROSAMUNDA BOLGER  (b. TA 2938, d. after 3001) Hobbit of the Shire, daughter of Sigismund Took. She married Odovacar Bolger and bore him one child, Fredegar. She was a guest at the Farewell Party. (III 475)

ROSE  (b. TA 2862) Hobbit of the Shire, youngest child of Holman the greenhanded. She married Cotman and bore him one child, Holman Cotton. (III 477)

ROSE GAMGEE  (TA 2984-FA 62) Hobbit of the Shire, second son of Tolman Cotton. In 3020 she married Samwise Gamgee, and bore him thirteen children.

Also known as Rosie. (III 354-55, 376-77, 472, 477)

ROSE GAMGEE  (b. FA 5) Hobbit of the Shire, third child of Sam Gamgee. (III 382, 477)

ROWAN  (b. TA 2849) Hobbit of the Shire, eldest child of Holman the greenhanded. She married Hob Gammidge and bore him one child, Hobson Gamgee. (III 477)

ROWLIE APPLEDORE  (d. TA 3019) Man of Bree, killed in the fight between people of the Bree-land and Bill Ferny and his friends. (III 335)

RUBY BAGGINS  (fl. TA 2900) Hobbit of the Shire, wife of Fosco Baggins. She was born a Bolger. (III 474)

RUBY GAMGEE  (b. FA 18) Hobbit of the Shire, eleventh child of Samwise Gamgee. (III 477)

RUDIGAR BOLGER  (fl. TA 2900) Hobbit of the Shire. He married Belba Baggins. (III 474)

**RUFUS BURROWS** (fl. TA 3000) Hobbit of the Shire, a guest at the Farewell Party. He married Asphodel Brandybuck. (III 476)

**RULES, THE** The laws of the Shire, originally set down by the Kings of Arthedain. They were kept voluntarily because of their heritage and their justness. During Lotho's and Saruman's control of the Shire in TA 3018-19, the Rules were greatly increased and became a system of oppression. (I 30; III 344 ff.)

**RULING STEWARDS OF GONDOR** Those of the Stewards of Gondor (q. v.) who held their office when there was no King. Pelendur ruled in TA 1944-45 during the interregnum following the death of King Ondoher, and all the Stewards from Mardil to Denethor (TA 2050-3019) were Ruling Stewards.

Although the Stewards held their office awaiting the return of the King, few believed in such a return, and the Ruling Stewards did not look with favor on the idea of giving the crown to any heir of Isildur. Still, none of the Ruling Stewards sat on the throne of Gondor or wore the crown; they bore a white rod of office and used a plain white banner. In all other ways, however, their power and position were the same as that of the Kings in whose place they ruled.

Titles of the Ruling Stewards included the Lord and Steward of Minas Tirith, Lord of the City and Lord of the White Tower. The heir of the Steward was usually the Captain and High Warden of the White Tower. (III 395-96; III 414)

**RUMBLE** Family of Hobbits of the Shire of the working class, at least one branch of which lived in Hobbiton. At the beginning of the Fourth Age, Widow Rumble looked after Hamfast Gamgee after Sam was married. (III 376)

**RÚMIL** (S.) (First Age) Elda of Valinor. He devised the oldest Eldarin writing system. (III 493)

**RÚMIL** (fl. WR) Silvan Elf of Lórien, brother of Haldir. He was a guard on the northern border of Lórien. (I 445)

**RUSHEY** Hobbit village in the Marish, on the Causeway. Spelled "Rushy" on the Shire-map. (I 40, 142; TB 9, 21)

**RUSHLIGHT** Family of Men of Bree. (I 212)

**RUSHOCK BOG** Bog in the Westfarthing on the Water, south of Needlehole. (I 40)

**RUSHY** Rushey (q. v.). (I 40)

# S

**SACKVILLE** Family of Hobbits of the Shire, probably of the upper class. (III 474)

**SACKVILLE-BAGGINS** Family of Hobbits of the Shire, founded by Otho, the son of Longo Baggins and Camellia Sackville. The entire family seems to have been extremely obnoxious, but died out after two generations. (I 43, 46; III 474; H 284-85)

**SADOC BRANDYBUCK** (b. TA 2779) Hobbit of the Shire, second son of Gormadoc Brandybuck. (III 476)

**SAKALTHÔR, AR-** (Ad.) (fl. SA 31st Cent.) Dúnadan, twenty-first King of Númenor. (III 390)

**SALVIA BOLGER** (b. TA 2826) Hobbit of the Shire, third child of Sadoc Brandybuck. She married Gundabald Bolger. (III 476)

**SAM** (gen. Hobb.) Shortened version of an actual Hobbit forename, probably Samba. (III 517)

**SAM** or **SAM GAMGEE** See: Samwise Gamgee.

**SAMMATH NAUR** (S.: 'chambers of fire') Chambers high in the core of Orodruin (q. v.), containing the Crack of Doom. The Sammath Naur was reached by Sauron's Road.
 Called in Westron the Chambers of Fire. (III 265, 273-76)

**SAMWISE GAMGEE** (TA 2980-   ) Hobbit of the Shire, youngest son of Hamfast Gamgee. Like his father, Sam was a gardener, and took care of Bag End when Hamfast grew old. In this way he came to know Bilbo Baggins, who told him stories of his adventures and taught him to read; from this Sam probably derived his love of Elves and lore. Because of his curiosity about such things Sam was selected (after being caught eavesdropping) by Gandalf to accompany Frodo, as his servant, to Rivendell in 3018. There, under similar circumstances, he became one of the Companions of the Ring. When the Company was split at Parth Galen, Sam alone accompanied Frodo. On the journey to Mordor Sam many times proved his loyalty and devotion to Frodo. After Frodo was paralyzed by Shelob, Sam, thinking him dead, took the One Ring and vowed to continue the Quest, thus preventing the Ring from falling into the hands of the Orcs. Although tempted, he rejected the lure of the Ring because of his great practicality and honesty. With the aid of the Phial of Galadriel, Sam blinded Shelob and rescued Frodo from the Tower of Cirith Ungol, and went with him to Orodruin.

After the WR, Sam returned to the Shire and married Rose Cotton. They had thirteen children, including Elanor the Fair and Frodo Gardner, and lived in Bag End, which was given to Sam by Frodo when the latter went over Sea in 3021. Because of the fame he had acquired as a result of his adventures, his friendship with the Thain and the Master of Buckland, his connection with the Cottons and, as the heir of Frodo, his financial independence, Sam was elected Mayor of the Shire seven times (FA 7-56). In FA 82, after the death of his wife, Sam sailed over Sea, which he was permitted to do because he had been a Ringbearer.

Sam was somewhat of an author. He contributed to the Red Book of Westmarch and also wrote numerous individual poems.

Sam's name in genuine Hobbitish was Banazîr, usually shortened to Ban. (I 44, 47, 73-74, 250, 355, 525-26; III 216, 382-85, 471-72, 477, 517; TB 7)

**SANCHO PROUDFOOT** (b. TA 2990) Hobbit of the Shire, son of Olo Proudfoot. He was a guest at the Farewell Party, and was discovered after the Party searching for Bilbo's treasure in Bag End. (I 67; III 474)

**SANDHEAVER** Family of Hobbits of Bree. There may also have been Sandheavers in the Shire. (I 212)

**SANDYMAN** Family of working-class Hobbits of the Shire, one branch of which owned and operated the Hobbiton mill before the WR. (I 46)

**SANGAHYANDO** (fl. TA 1634) Dúnadan, great-grandson of Castamir the Usurper. With his brother Angamaitë he led the Corsairs of Umbar on a raid on Pelargir in which King Minardil of Gondor was slain. (III 407)

**SARADAS BRANDYBUCK** (TA 2908-3007) Hobbit of the Shire, third child of Gorbadoc Brandybuck. He was a guest at the Farewell Party. (III 476)

**SARADOC BRANDYBUCK** (TA 2940-FA 12) Hobbit of the Shire, son of Rorimac Brandybuck and Master of Buckland (TA 3008-FA 12). He married Esmeralda Took; they had one child, Meriadoc. Saradoc was a guest at the Farewell Party. As Master of Buckland he was known as "Scattergold." (III 475, 476)

**SARN FORD** Ford on the Brandywine south of the Shire. Sarn Ford was guarded by the Rangers as part of their protection of the Shire, since the road leading to the Shire from the south crossed the Brandywine here. (I 16, 234; III 464)

**SARN GEBIR** (S.) Unnavigable rapids on the Anduin above the Argonath. A portage-way was built on the western bank of the river to bypass the rapids.

Also called the Rapids. (I 499-500, 505-06)

**SARUMAN** (d. TA 3019) One of the Istari, as Saruman the White the greatest of the Order. Saruman had great power over men's minds and great skill in his hands, and was especially learned in the lore of the Elven-rings and the devices of Sauron. In TA 2463 he was made head of the White Council. Saruman had travelled much in the East, but in 2759, with the consent of Steward Beren of Gondor, he settled in Isengard. At first, Saruman was a true friend to Rohan, but it slowly became apparent that he wished to become a power, and eventually it was learned that he coveted the One Ring. It is for this reason that he settled in Isengard, for he thought to use its palantír. Also for this reason he persuaded the White Council not to drive the Necromancer out of Dol Guldur, since he hoped that the Ring, seeking its master, would reveal itself if Sauron was not disturbed. His duplicity toward the White Council, which trusted him as its Ring-expert, delayed many actions and lulled many justified fears. In 2953 Saruman took Isengard for his own and fortified it. There he gathered Orcs and Dunlendings, and began harrassing Rohan and Fangorn; he also began spying on Gandalf and keeping agents in Bree and the Shire. About 3000 he used his palantír and was trapped by Sauron; after this time, although he thought himself free he was actually controlled by Sauron. His pride grew even more rapidly than his power at this time, and by the time of the WR he called himself Saruman the Many-Coloured. About 3010, through his agent Gríma, he caused Théoden of Rohan to decline into old age, but the King was revived by Gandalf in 3019. During the WR Saruman brought on his own destruction by capturing Merry and Pippin; they escaped into Fangorn Forest where their presence aroused the Ents, who attacked Isengard and imprisoned Saruman in Orthanc. Gandalf then cast him out of the order of the wizards. He was later released by Fangorn, and with Gríma went to the Shire, where he had financed Lotho Sackville-Baggins' rise to power. Frodo cast Saruman out of the Shire after he returned from Gondor, and he was slain by Gríma.

Saruman, or Saruman the Wise, was the name given him by Men in the north of Middle-earth; he was called Curunír by the Elves. His emblem, which was also used attributively to refer to him, was the White Hand. He was called Sharkey by the Orcs of Isengard and his Men in the Shire. (I 78, 328-44; II 48, 55-56, 95-96, 219, 234-41; III 318-19, 322-25, 361, 367-71, 416, 417, 433-34, 455, 460-63)

**SATURDAY** See: Sterrendei. (III 478)

**SAURON**  (S.: 'enemy'?)  Evil being, probably a Vala, a servant of Morgoth in the First Age. During the War of the Great Jewels he imprisoned Beren. Somehow Sauron survived the fall of Morgoth, and about SA 500 began to stir again in Middle-earth. His power slowly returned, and by 1000 he had settled in Mordor and begun the building of the Barad-dûr. About 1200 Sauron seduced the Noldor of Eregion, and in the sixteenth century they forged the Rings of Power with him, with which he hoped to ensnare the Free Peoples. Sauron placed much of his power in the One Ring, with which he completed the Barad-dûr. Celebrimbor of Eregion discovered Sauron's treachery with the Rings, and this led to the War of the Elves and Sauron (1693-1700), in which Sauron destroyed Eregion and overran Eriador, but was defeated by Gil-galad and a fleet sent to Middle-earth by Tar-Minastir of Númenor. After this, Sauron extended his power eastward for fifteen hundred years. In 3262 Ar-Pharazôn of Númenor landed at Umbar with a vast army to contest the rule of Middle-earth with Sauron. Sauron was deserted by his armies and was forced to submit to Ar-Pharazôn, who took him back to Númenor. In less than fifty years Sauron corrupted the court and persuaded Ar-Pharazôn to take the Undying Lands, and immortality, by force. This led to the destruction of Númenor. Sauron escaped the wreck, but his body perished, and he was thereafter unable to assume a fair-seeming body. He returned to Mordor, and in 3429 he attacked Gondor. In 3434, however, he was defeated in the Battle of Dagorlad by the army of the Last Alliance and was besieged in the Barad-dûr. In 3441, in a final battle on the slopes of Orodruin, Sauron was overthrown by Gil-galad and Elendil, but killed both his foes. Isildur cut off his finger and took the Ring.

In the Third Age, without the One Ring which formed the base of his power, Sauron was extremely cautious. His policy was twofold: to weaken the Dúnedain kingdoms without provoking massive retaliation, and to recover the Ring. The latter policy was clouded by Sauron's uncertainty about the fate of the Ring, which should have been destroyed by Isildur. After Sauron rose again about TA 1000, he hid his identity and was known as the Necromancer. Since Mordor was guarded by Gondor, he dwelled in Dol Guldur. About 1300 he began to attack the Free Peoples, especially the Dúnedain. He sent the Lord of the Nazgûl to the North, where he founded Angmar. In the South, Sauron stirred up the Haradrim and the

Easterlings against Gondor.

After the Great Plague of 1636, which may have been sent by Sauron, Gondor's watch on Mordor was relaxed, and the Nazgûl re-entered that realm and prepared it for Sauron. In 2002 the Nazgûl took Minas Ithil, thus obtaining a palantír for Sauron, which he later used to ensnare Saruman and trick Denethor II. In 2063, Gandalf went to Dol Guldur to learn the identity of the Necromancer, but Sauron fled to the East. He returned to Dol Guldur in 2460 with increased strength and renewed his plots until 2941, when he was driven out of Dol Guldur by the White Council. Sauron willingly retreated to Mordor, where he openly proclaimed himself, rebuilt the Barad-dûr and prepared to defeat the West by overwhelming Gondor and the smaller realms of the North with his vast armies of Orcs, trolls, Haradrim, Easterlings and creatures more foul.

Even though Sauron did not have the Ring, its very existence gave him enough strength to crush the West. Gandalf and Elrond, realizing this, saw that the only way to defeat Sauron was to destroy the Ring. Frodo Baggins volunteered to undertake the Quest of Mount Doom; and, escaping Sauron's servants searching for him and the Ring, destroyed the Ring in the Fire of Doom. The Nazgûl were destroyed and Sauron so weakened that he was unable ever to take shape again.

It is almost impossible to describe all the plots of Sauron, the master of deceit and treachery, and so only an outline of his policies is presented here. Among Sauron's other accomplishments stand the invention of the Black Speech and the breeding of the Olog-hai and, perhaps, the Uruk-hai.

After the ruin of his body in the destruction of Númenor, Sauron had the form of a Man; his skin was black and burning hot. In the Third Age he most frequently appeared as a fearsome, ever-searching Eye.

Sauron's real name is not given; he was called Sauron in Sindarin and the Enemy in Westron. He was also called the Power, the Dark Lord, the Lord of Mordor, the Dark Lord of Mordor, the Power of the Black Land, the Black Master, the Black One, the Lord of Barad-dûr, the Lord of the Dark Tower and the Shadow. He was also called, attributively, the Great Eye, the Red Eye, the Eye of Barad-dûr, the Lidless Eye and the Evil Eye. Also called the Unnamed, the Nameless One, the Nameless Eye and He or Him. Also the Lord of the Rings, the Lord of the Ring and the Ring-maker. Also, by Gollum, the Black Hand. (I 81, 82, 83, 260, 318, 328-29, 377, 471-72, 519; II 300-01; III 190-91, 275, 278-79, 391-93, 408, 415, 416, 417, 453-55, 456 ff., 511, 512, 515; H 37)

**SAURON'S ROAD**  Road leading from the Barad-dûr to the Sammath Naur. Leaving the Dark Tower by a great iron bridge, Sauron's Road went across Gorgoroth and then rose up to Orodruin on a causeway. It then wound counterclockwise up the mountain, and entered an eastern opening of the Sammath Naur. The Road was frequently obstructed by eruptions of Orodruin, but was always repaired. (III 269-74)

**SCARY**  Village in the Eastfarthing, the site of quarries. (I 40)

**SCATHA**  (d. c. TA 2000)  Great dragon of the Ered Mithrin, possessor of a large dwarf-hoard. He was slain by Fram of Éothéod. (III 316, 430)

**SCEPTRE OF ANNÚMINAS**  Silver rod, once the sceptre of the Lords of Andúnië. It was brought to Middle-earth by Elendil, and was the chief mark of royalty of Arnor. After the end of the North-kingdom the sceptre was kept at Rivendell. Elrond gave it to Elessar at his wedding, and it then became once more the mark of royalty of Arnor. (III 310, 401, 421)

**SEA**  The body of water of indefinite size west of Middle-earth. Its western reaches were accessible to all (assuming the proper weather) until the end of the Second Age, when the Undying Lands were "removed from the circles of the world." After this time the physical and metaphysical nature of the Sea were changed; the Undying Lands, which now were not on the surface of the world, were still reached by sailing west over Sea.

Also called the High Sea, the Great Sea and the Sundering Sea (q. v.). (I 452; III 384)

**SEA-BELL, THE**  Hobbit poem of the Fourth Age reflecting the Shire distrust of the Sea and of things outside the Shire.

The poem was subtitled *Frodos Dreme,* and was no doubt associated in the Shire with Frodo's unquiet dreams after the WR. (TB 9, 57-60)

**SEA-ELVES**  One of the Three Kindreds of the Eldar (q. v.). (H 164)

**SEA OF NURNEN**  Núrnen (q. v.). (I 17)

**SEA OF RHÛN**  Great inland sea northeast of Mordor. According to the maps, the Sea of Rhûn was fed only by the Celduin-Carnen, and had no outlet.

Also called the Inland Sea. (I 17; III 395, 404, 405, 438)

**SEAT OF SEEING** The throne on Amon Hen (q. v.), built by the Kings of Gondor. One who sat in the Seat of Seeing could see all the lands for hundreds of miles around.

Also called the Seat of Amon Hen. (I 518)

**SEA-WARD TOWER** The tower of Dol Amroth (q. v.), looking toward the Sea.

Called in Sindarin Tirith Aear. (TB 8, 37)

**SECOND AGE** The age of Middle-earth comprising the time between the overthrow of Morgoth and the first overthrow of Sauron. For much of the Age, Sauron controlled large parts of Middle-earth; Men were killed or enslaved, and the Elves and Dwarves hid. The seeds of later evil were sown with the forging of the Rings of Power, and the Dúnedain realms of Gondor and Arnor were founded after the destruction of Númenor. (III 393, 452-55)

**SECOND BATTLE OF THE FORDS OF ISEN** See: the Battles of the Fords of Isen. (III 466)

**SECOND HALL** Hall in the First Deep of Khazad-dûm, containing Durin's Bridge. (I 426 ff.)

**SECOND LINE** The second series of Kings of Rohan, beginning with Fréaláf, Helm's nephew, in TA 2759, and ending with the death of King Théoden and his only son Théodred during the WR. The Second Line contained eight Kings. (III 435-36)

**SECRET FIRE** Whatever it was that Gandalf was a servant of. (I 429)

**SEREDIC BRANDYBUCK** (b. TA 2948) Hobbit of the Shire, son of Saradas Brandybuck. Seredic married Hilda Bracegirdle, and was a guest at the Farewell Party. (III 476)

**SERNI** or **SERNUI** (S.) River in Lebennin, Gondor, flowing into the Gilrain above Linhir. (III 15; TB 8)

**SEVEN FATHERS OF THE DWARVES** The first seven Dwarves, founders of the seven houses of the Dwarves. (III 438)

**SEVEN RINGS** The Rings of Power (q.v.) of the Dwarves. They were probably given to the Kings of each of the seven houses of the Dwarves. Despite Sauron's plans, the Seven

could not dominate the Dwarves either by making them evil
or by lengthening their lives. They did, however, cause their
bearers to lust after gold and other precious materials. This
failure caused Sauron to hate the Dwarves more than he did
already, and he tried to recover the Seven.

Sauron was successful in recovering three of the Rings,
and dragons consumed the other four. The only Ring about
which much is said is the Ring of Durin's Folk. It was said
to have been given to Durin III by the Elves and not by
Sauron, and was probably the greatest of the Seven. It was
long kept hidden, but the Dwarves believed that Sauron at
last discovered its location, and for this reason especially
persecuted the Kings of Durin's Folk. The ring was taken
from Thráin in Dol Guldur about TA 2845.

The Seven had metal bands and were set with single gems.
(I 82, 330, 351; III 445-47)

SEVEN RIVERS  The major rivers of southern Gondor, the Lefnui, Morthond-Ciril-Ringló, Gilrain-Serni and Anduin. (TB 8,
64)

SEVEN RIVERS OF OSSIR  The rivers (guess how many) of
Ossiriand. (II 90)

SEVEN STARS  The six-pointed stars that served as the emblem of Elendil and his heirs. They represented the single
stars on the banners of each of the ships of the Faithful that
bore a palantír. (III 150; RHM III 439-40)

SEVENTH LEVEL  One of the levels of Khazad-dûm, the sixth
above the Great Gates. The Seventh Level contained many
halls, including the Chamber of Mazarbul. (I 420)

SHADOW  Sauron, and also the extent of his influence and cor-
ruption. (I 82, 229, 451; II 266; III 43, 171, 408)

SHADOW  According to Gandalf, where the Balrog should return
to. (I 429)

SHADOW-BRIDE  A Hobbit poem recorded on a margin of the
Red Book of Westmarch. The poem seems to have some sig-
nificance, and may refer to a tale not told in LotR. (TB 7, 52)

SHADOWFAX  (fl. WR)  Meara, the greatest horse of Rohan at
the time of the WR. In 3018 King Théoden gave Gandalf any
horse of his choosing, and the wizard chose Shadowfax. The
horse bore him faithfully without bridle or saddle throughout
the WR.

Shadowfax was extremely strong and swift; he could run

twelve hours at a stretch, and could outrun the steeds of the Nazgûl. Shadowfax got his name because his coat was silver-grey. (I 343, 344; II 46, 137-38; III 125, 518)

**SHADOW-LAND**  A land in Bilbo's poem *Errantry*, a dreary place near the Derrilyn. Although possibly an imaginary place, "Shadow-land" is an acceptable Westron translation of Mordor. If this was intentional, then the Derrilyn could be Anduin. (TB 24)

**SHADOWMERE**  Lake in Eldamar in which were reflected the lamps of Tirion. (I 309)

**SHADOWS**  The eternal twilight of Valinor, summoned by Varda at the decree of Manwe after the destruction of the Two Trees and the revolt of the Noldor. The Shadows seem to have been impenetrable to any who sought to pass them without the permission of the Valar or without great power, and they extended out into the Sea.

However, Frodo's ship reached a land with a "swift sunrise," and so the Shadows may have been lifted sometime after the end of the First Age, perhaps when the Undying Lands were removed from the circles of the world after the destruction of Númenor.

The Night of Naught, the Twilight and Evernight refer to the same darkness. (I 308-11; III 389; R 60)

**SHADOWY MOUNTAINS**  The Ephel Dúath (q. v.), as called by Gollum. (II 316)

**SHAGRAT**  (fl. WR)  Uruk, Captain of the Tower of Cirith Ungol. He was one of the few survivors of the battle between his band and Gorbag's over Frodo's mithril-mail, and kept the mail for Sauron despite the fact that he lost an arm in the battle. (II 437, 439-46; III 222-25)

**SHARKEY**  (fr. Orkish *sharkū* 'old man')  Name given Saruman by the Men and Orcs of Isengard, and the name by which he was known in the Shire. (III 367-68)

**SHARKEY'S END**  See: New Row. (III 374)

**SHARP-EARS**  (fl. WR)  One of the ponies provided by Merry for the journey from Buckland to Imladris in 3018. He was driven off in Bree, but was later recovered and spent the rest of his life working for Barliman Butterbur.

Sharp-ears was named by Tom Bombadil. (I 198, 199)

**SHATHÛR**  Bundushathûr (q. v.). (I 370)

**SHEE**  The reflection of Princess Mee, in the Shire poem. (TB

29-30)

**SHELOB** (S.) (First Age-Fourth Age) Great spider, akin to those of the Mountains of Terror. Somehow Shelob escaped the ruin of Beleriand, and she and her offspring dwelled in the Ephel Dúath and in Mirkwood. Shelob herself had a vast den in Cirith Ungol, and for two ages of Middle-earth she lived on Men, Elves and Orcs, and served as a sure guard to prevent anyone from entering Mordor by that route. About TA 3000 she trapped Gollum, but released him on the condition that he bring her food. In 3019, during the Quest of Mount Doom, Gollum guided Frodo and Sam to Shelob's Lair. Shelob paralyzed Frodo, but was herself blinded and stabbed by Sam, who used the Phial of Galadriel and Sting. Shelob may have eventually died of her wounds, or of starvation caused by her inability to hunt while blind.

Shelob was called Her Ladyship by the Orcs of the Tower of Cirith Ungol. She was also known as Shelob the Great. (II 418 ff., esp. 422-24, 425)

**SHELOB'S LAIR** The dwelling-place of Shelob, a foul and many-tunnelled lair under the Ephel Dúath near Cirith Ungol. It was necessary to pass through the Lair in order to get over the Ephel Dúath by that route. Shelob built tunnels from her Lair that intersected every Orc-path built to avoid her. (II 414)

**SHIP-KINGS** Tarannon Falastur, Eärnil I, Ciryandil and Hyarmendacil I, the Kings of Gondor from TA 830 to 1149 under whom Gondor reached the height of its power. They were so named because the most important element of their policy was the expansion southward and westward of the borders of Gondor through the efforts of her fleets. (III 394, 403-04)

**SHIRE, THE** Area in Eriador between the Baranduin and the Far Downs, originally a fertile and well-tilled part of Arnor. In the course of the waning of the North-kingdom the area was deserted, and in TA 1601 it was ceded by King Argeleb II of Arthedain to the Hobbits, led by Marcho and Blanco. By 1630 most of the Hobbits in Middle-earth lived in the Shire, which they divided into four Farthings and a number of folklands. The Hobbits lived comfortably in their new land; the only adversities they faced in the Third Age were the Great Plague of 1636, the Battle of Greenfields (2747), the Long Winter and the Days of Dearth (2758-60), the Fell Winter of 2911 and the domination of the Shire by Lotho Sackville-

Baggins, Saruman and evil Men during the WR. Indeed, the Hobbits of the Shire managed to ignore the outside world for so long they almost forgot it existed, even though the Great East Road went through the middle of the Shire. In part, this safety was due to the ceaseless protection of the Rangers.

Because of over-population, the Oldbucks of the Marish crossed the Brandywine in 2340 and settled Buckland. In FA 32 King Elessar formally added Buckland to the Shire, and also gave the Hobbits the Westmarch, extending from the Far Downs to the Tower Hills. Earlier, in 17, he had issued a decree making the Shire a Free Land under his protection, and forbade any Men to enter the Shire.

Before the death of Arvedui, the Shire had acknowledged the rule of the King, but was so divorced from outside affairs that this rule was only nominal. After the end of the North-kingdom the Hobbits chose a Thain to rule until the return of the King; the Thain's duties were mostly ceremonial. The only official with active duties was the Mayor of Michel Delving, who had charge of the Watch and the Messenger Service.

The social structure of the Shire seems to have been rather simple. There were a few members of the landed gentry, who were well enough off not to have to work, but most Hobbits were farmers, tradesmen or laborers. There were some poor, but their plight was not extreme. The Shire was primarily agricultural.

Also called the Four Farthings. The genuine Hobbitish name was Sûza. (I 17, 23-25, 29-31, 40, 43 ff.; III 457-71)

**SHIREBOURN** River in the Shire, flowing from its source in the Green Hills south and then east to the Brandywine, which it entered south of Deephallow. The Mithe was at its outflow. The lower Shirebourn formed part of the boundary between the East- and Southfarthings. (I 40; TB 9)

**SHIRE-MOOT** A gathering of Hobbits of the Shire held in times of emergency to take counsel, presided over by the Thain. (I 31)

**SHIRE-MUSTER** See: Hobbitry-in-arms. (I 31)

**SHIRE-RECKONING or SHIRE RECKONING** The calendar system of the Shire and (under a different name) of Bree, an adaptation of the Kings' Reckoning. The year 1 was equal to TA 1601 in the Shire and 1300 in Bree. The week had seven days, which were Sterrendei, Sunnendei, Monendei, Trewesdei, Hevenesdei, Meresdei and the chief day, Highdei. (In *LotR* the names are given by their modern equivalents, with Sunnendei equal to Sunday.) The year had twelve months and a number of extra days, with leap years being formed by the addition of Overlithe. The yearly calendar for the Shire is shown on III 478; there was some difference in the names used in Bree and the Eastfarthing.

The only major difference between the Shire-reckoning and the Kings' Reckoning was the Shire-reform (q. v.). (III 478, 479, 481, 483-85, 486)

**SHIRE-REFORM**    Calendar reform invented and adopted in the Shire about TA 2700, and adopted in Bree somewhat later. The Shire-reform removed the week-day names from Midyear's Day and Overlithe, thus giving the year exactly 52 weeks and providing each day of the year with an unchanging week-day name. (III 482)

**SHIRRIFFS**    the Watch (q. v.). (I 31)

**SICKLE**    The Big Dipper, as called by the Hobbits. Also called the Wain. (I 237; H 185)

**SIEGE OF GONDOR**    The siege of Minas Tirith during the WR, lasting from the night of March 13, TA 3019 until the dawn of March 15. The Siege began when the army of the Lord of the Nazgûl broke through the Rammas Echor and swept across the Pelennor, driving the forces of Gondor into Minas Tirith. On March 14, catapults set the first level of the city on fire, and the Nazgûl demoralized the defenders. The next day, before dawn, the Great Gate was broken by the Lord of the Nazgûl, but before he could enter the city the Rohirrim arrived at the Pelennor, and in the Battle of the Pelennor Fields which followed the Siege was lifted. (III 115-26)

**SIEGE OF THE BARAD-DÛR**    The final phase of the war between Sauron and the Last Alliance, in which Sauron, after his defeat in the Battle of Dagorlad in SA 3434, was besieged in the Barad-dûr for seven years. In 3440 Anárion was slain by a stone-cast from the Dark Tower, but in the following year Sauron was forced to fight, and he was slain in a final battle on the slopes of Orodruin. (I 319; III 401, 455)

**SIGISMOND TOOK**    (TA 2890-2991)    Hobbit of the Shire, son of Hildibrand Took. (III 475)

**SILENT WATCHERS**    The Two Watchers (q. v.). (II 316, 441)

**SILIMA** (Q.) A crystalline substance which shone from within. Fëanor invented silima, and he alone could make it. The Silmarilli were made of silima. (R 65)

**SILMARIËN** (Q.) (b. SA 548) Dúnadan of Númenor, eldest child of Tar-Elendil. Her son Valandil was the first Lord of Andúnië. (III 391, 453)

**SILMARILLI** (Q.: 'jewels of silima'; sing. *silmaril)* The three great jewels made by Fëanor of silima, filled with the light of the Two Trees. The Silmarilli were Fëanor's greatest pride and one of the treasures of Eldamar, and were among the greatest works of craft of all time.

Morgoth stole the Silmarilli when he poisoned the Two Trees and fled to Middle-earth, and he later set them in his Iron Crown. This theft caused the revolt of the Noldor and the War of the Great Jewels. Beren and Lúthien recovered one of the Silmarilli, and Eärendil used it as a token to gain entrance to the West, where he obtained the aid that defeated Morgoth. He and the Silmaril were placed in the heavens as the star Eärendil. The other two Silmarilli were lost forever when Beleriand was ruined, one under the earth and the other in the depths of the Sea.

Also called the Great Jewels and the Three Jewels. The Westronized plural of *silmaril* is *silmarils*. (I 260, 309, 310; III 281, 388, 389; R 65; RP 1/12/66)

*SILMARILLION, THE* (Q.: 'of the Silmarilli') Book of lore telling much about the First Age, especially concerned with events related to the Silmarilli. *The Silmarillion* is extant, and was probably part of Bilbo's *Translations from the Elvish.* (III 389)

**SILME** (Q.: 'starlight') Name for the tengwa **ᘯ** (number 29), which was almost universally used for *s.* (III 500)

**SILME NUQUERNA** (Q.: 'reversed *s')* Name for the tengwa **ᘰ** (number 30), usually a variant of silme used with diacritics. (III 500)

**SILVAN ELVES** Those tribes of Elves who were not of the Eldar, than whom they were far more numerous. Although less noble and wise in spirit and body than the Eldar, they were still good. The Silvan Elves dwelled in forests or mountains, and in the Third Age most of them were part of various kingdoms such as Lórien and the Woodland Realm which were ruled by Eldar.

The Silvan Elves spoke their own languages which were different than, although possibly related to, Eldarin.

Also called the Wood-elves and, in opposition to the Eldar, the East-elves. (III 452, 468, 505-06; H 57-60, 150-53, 164-65)

**SILVER CROWN**    The chief mark of royalty of Gondor. Originally a plain Númenorean war-helm, said to be Isildur's, in the time of Atanatar Alcarin it was replaced by a jewelled helm. The new helm was silver and had wings like those of a sea-bird wrought of pearl and silver. The Crown had seven gems in it to represent Elendil, and also a single gem to represent Anárion.

Also called the White Crown. (II 355; III 303, 401)

**SILVERLODE**    Celebrant (q. v.). (I 370)

**SILVERTINE**    Zirak-zigil (q. v.). (I 370)

**SIMBELMYNË**    (tr. Roh.: 'evermind')    Small white flower that grew on the burial mounds of the Kings of Rohan. Simbelmynë bloomed in all seasons.

Also called Evermind. (II 142; III 433)

**SINDAR**    (Q.: 'sinda-plural')    Those of the Eldar who, after coming to Beleriand, did not go over Sea at the beginning of the First Age. There they were ruled by King Thingol of Doriath, and aided the Noldor in the War of the Great Jewels.

At the end of the First Age many Sindar went over Sea, and throughout succeeding ages there was a steady migration of Sindar to the West. Those of the Sindar who remained in Middle-earth dwelled in Lindon or in Elven-realms such as the Woodland Realm.

The Sindar were happy in Middle-earth, but once the desire for the Sea was aroused in them they could not be content until they sailed to Eldamar.

The Sindar originally spoke Quenya, but living in Middle-earth their language changed, and by the end of the First Age had evolved into Sindarin (q. v.). The Sindar invented the Cirth, but also used the Tengwar.

Also called the Grey-elves. (II 136, 185, 289; III 452, 493, 506, 519)

**SINDARIN**    (Q.: 'grey-elven')    The language of the Sindar, evolved from Quenya as a result of the changeableness of Middle-earth. Although less noble than Quenya, Sindarin was still very beautiful and gentle. It was adopted by the Exiles, and was also spoken by the Elves of Lórien and (as a second

language) by the Dúnedain. Sindarin words were prominent
in Westron and Entish.

Examples of Sindarin include many place-names and personal names, and also the various songs to Elebereth. (III
487-504, 506, 507, 508)

**SIRANNON**  (S.: 'gate-stream')  Stream flowing from its source
near the West-gate of Khazad-dûm. The Sirannon was dammed
by the Watcher in the Water. The ancient road from Eregion
to Khazad-dûm ran along the Sirannon.

Called in Westron the Gate-stream.

See also: the Stair Falls. (I 392-403)

**SIRIONDIL**  (Q.: 'stream-lover') (d. TA 830)  Dúnadan, eleventh
King of Gondor (748-830). (III 394)

**SIRIONDIL**  (fl. TA 19th Cent.)  Dúnadan of Gondor, father of
King Eärnil II. (III 410)

**SIRITH**  (S.: 'stream---')  River in Lebennin, Gondor, flowing
from its sources in the Ered Nimrais south to Pelargir, where
it flowed into Anduin. Its principal tributary was the Celos.
(III 15)

**SKINBARK**  Fladrif (q. v.). (II 98)

**SLAG-HILLS**  The mounds of wasted metal, stone and earth
left by Orcs in the Desolation of the Morannon, especially
those two hills near the Morannon on which the Army of the
West was grouped in the battle fought on March 25, TA 3019.
(III 200, 201, 206, 467)

**SLINKER**  Sam's name for the nobler, politer "Sméagol" aspect
of Gollum (q. v.). (II 311)

**SMALLBURROW**  Family of working-class Hobbits of the Shire.
At the time of the WR, at least one branch of the family lived
in Hobbiton. (III 281)

**SMAUG**  (d. TA 2941)  Dragon of the Ered Mithrin, the greatest
dragon of his time. In 2770, hearing of the wealth of Erebor,
Smaug destroyed Dale and drove the Dwarves away from the
Kingdom under the Mountain. For nearly two hundred years
he gloried in his treasure, until in 2941, disturbed and angered by Thorin and Company, he attacked Esgaroth and was
slain by Bard the Bowman.

In addition to the various honorifics bestowed on him by
the frightened Bilbo, Smaug was known as Smaug the Golden.
(III 440; H 35-36, 206, 207-38, 248)

**SMÉAGOL**   See: Gollum. (I 84-85; III 518)

**SMIALS**   The large tunnels inhabited by well-to-do Hobbits of the Shire. Smials had rounded walls and many branches. Bag End was a smial. Some smials, like the Great Smials or Brandy Hall, were very large, and had room for a hundred or more Hobbits. (I 26, 27)

**SMIALS, THE**   The Great Smials (q. v.). (II 80)

**SNAGA**   (B. S.: 'slave')   Name given lesser Orcs, especially by the Uruk-hai. (III 511)

**SNAGA**   (d. TA 3019)   Orc of Isengard, one of Uglúk's band. He was slain by Éomer's éored.
      The name may have been just an epithet. (II 67)

**SNAGA**   (d. TA 3019)   Orc of the Tower of Cirith Ungol, one of the few survivors of the battle between his company and Gorbag's. He was Frodo's guard, and died when he broke his neck trying to escape from Sam.
      The name may have been just an epithet. (III 222-23, 226-27)

**SNOWBOURN**   River in Rohan, flowing from Dunharrow to Edoras, and then east until it joined the Entwash. (III 76, 78, 91, 93)

**SNOWMANE**   (d. TA 3019)   Meara, the mount of King Théoden. He was slain by the Lord of the Nazgûl in the Battle of the Pelennor Fields, and in his fall killed Théoden. (II 168-69; III 140, 146)

**SNOWMANE'S HOWE**   The grave of Snowmane, in the Pelennor. Long green grass grew on the Howe, and a carven stone was set over it. (III 146)

**SOLMATH**   The second month of the Shire Reckoning, corresponding roughly to our February. It was pronounced, and often written, "Somath." (III 478, 483)

**SOMATH**   Solmath (q. v.). (III 483)

**SOUTH DOWNS**   Dreary, partly-wooded downs south of the Great East Road between Bree and the Mitheithel. (I 16, 252, 255, 267-68)

**SOUTHERN ARMY OF GONDOR**   One of the two armies of Gondor in the days of its might. The Southern Army fought in Harad, but at least once, in TA 1944, reinforced the Northern Army. (III 409)

**SOUTHERN STAR** A variety of pipe-weed (q. v.) grown in the Southfarthing. (I 28)

**SOUTHFARTHING** One of the four farthings of the Shire, the warmest and the furthest south. Pipe-weed was grown here. The Southfarthing was the first area of the Shire to fall under the control of Lotho Sackville-Baggins, and Saruman kept agents here as early as TA 2953. (I 28, 40; III 360, 462)

**SOUTH ITHILIEN** That portion of Ithilien south of the Morgulduin. (III 15)

**SOUTH LANE** Road in the Shire leading south from Bywater. At the time of the WR, the Cottons lived on South Lane. (III 353)

**SOUTHLINCH** A variety of pipe-weed (q. v.) grown in Bree. (III 334)

**SOUTH ROAD** One of the main roads of Gondor, running from Minas Tirith to Pelargir, crossing the Erui at the Crossings of Erui. (III 48)

**SPRINGLE-RING** (tr. Hobb.: 'war horse-ring') A rather vigorous Hobbit dance. The dancers probably imitated horses or horsemen. (I 54; TB 21)

**STADDLE** Village of Men and Hobbits in the Bree-land, on the southeastern side of Bree Hill. (I 205, 245)

**STAIR FALLS** Waterfalls in the Sirannon (q. v.) near the Westgate, next to a flight of steps in the road from Eregion to Khazad-dûm. (I 393)

**STAIR OF THE HOLD** Steep switchback road in Rohan, leading from Edoras to Dunharrow, built by a forgotten race. As each section overlooked the ones below, it was impossible for any enemy to take the Stair (and Dunharrow) save by siege or by aerial attack.

The Púkel-men (q. v.) were carved at each turn of the Stair. (III 80, 85)

**STAIRS** The two flights of steps, the Straight Stair and the Winding Stair (qq. v.), leading from Imlad Morgul to Cirith Ungol. (II 442)

**STANDELF** Village in southern Buckland. (I 40)

**STANDING SILENCE** Moment of silence observed in Gondor before meals. The diners stood and looked toward the West, toward Númenor, Eldamar and Valinor. (II 361; III 287)

**STARKHORN** Mountain in the Ered Nimrais overlooking the

southern end of Dunharrow. (III 76, 81)

**STAR OF ELENDIL**  A diamond, one of the heirlooms of the North-kingdom. It represented Eärendil, which had served as a guide to the Edain when they sailed to Númenor. The Star was worn on the brow of the Kings of the North-kingdom until Elessar gave it to Sam Gamgee in FA 16.

Also called the Star of the Dúnedain, the Star of the North and the Elendilmir. (III 150, 401, 471; RHM III 439)

**STAR OF THE DÚNEDAIN**  The Star of Elendil (q. v.). (III 471)

**STAR OF THE HOUSE OF FËANOR**  The emblem of Fëanor and his heirs, an eight-rayed star made of silver. (I 397; RHM III 439)

**STAR OF THE NORTH**  The Star of Elendil (q. v.). (III 302)

**STEELSHEEN**  Morwen (q. v.). (III 437)

**STERDAY**  See: Sterrendei. (III 484)

**STERRENDEI**  Early form of the name of the first day of the Hobbit week, a translation of Elenya. By the time of the WR, the form of the name was Sterday.

Called in *LotR* Saturday. (III 484)

**STEWARD'S DOOR**  Fen Hollen (q. v.). (III 160)

**STEWARDS OF THE HOUSE OF ANÁRION**  The chief officials of Gondor, head of the King's Council. Every King had a Steward, but after the time of King Minardil all the Stewards were chosen from the House of Húrin (q. v.), and after Steward Pelendur (d. TA 1998) the office was made hereditary. When the line of the Kings failed, the Stewards became the rulers of Gondor. (See: the Ruling Stewards) When the kingdom was restored by Elessar at the end of the Third Age, Faramir, the heir of the last Ruling Steward, was made Steward to the King. (III 158, 395-96, 409, 414 ff.)

**STEWARDS' RECKONING**  A revision of the Kings' Reckoning made by Steward Mardil about TA 2100 and eventually adopted throughout the Westron area, except in the Shire and Bree. All the months had thirty days, and the five days outside the months were holidays. The calendar was the same as that of the Kings' Reckoning except that tuilérë came after Súlimë 30, Nárië and Cermië had thirty days each, and yáviérë came after Yavannië 30.

The Stewards' Reckoning was replaced by the New Reckoning at the beginning of the Fourth Age. (III 481)

**STING**   A well-forged long knife made in Beleriand in the First Age, named by Bilbo Baggins. Sting shone with a blue light when Orcs were near. Bilbo found Sting in a troll-cave during the expedition of Thorin and Company, and he and Frodo used it as a sword throughout their adventures. Frodo gave Sting to Sam in the Tower of Cirith Ungol, after Sam had seriously wounded Shelob with it. (I 363, 421-22; II 428-29; III 250, 287; H 53, 77, 154)

**STINKER**   Sam's name for the nastier, more vicious "Gollum-ish" aspect of Gollum (q. v.). (II 311)

**STOCK**   Village in the northern Marish, south of the Brandy-wine Bridge. (I 40, 142; TB 9)

**STOCKBROOK**   Stream in the Eastfarthing, flowing from its source in the Woody End through Stock and then into the Brandywine. (I 40)

**STOCK ROAD**   Road in the Shire, leaving the Great East Road west of Bywater and running through the Green Hills and the Woody End to Stock. Frodo and Sam met the Last Riding of the Keepers of the Rings in Woody End on the Stock Road. (I 40; III 380)

**STONE-GIANTS**   Creatures of great size and strength living in the high passes of the northern Misty Mountains.
   The stone-giants are mentioned only in *The Hobbit,* and may be no more serious than Golfimbul. (H 65, 99-100)

**STONE-HOUSES**   The Woses' name for Minas Tirith (q. v.). (III 129)

**STONE OF ELENDIL**   The Palantír (q. v.) of the Tower Hills. (R 65)

**STONE OF ERECH**   Black stone brought to Middle-earth from Númenor by Isildur and set on the hill of Erech at the time of the founding of Gondor. The King of the Mountains swore allegiance to Isildur on the Stone, and during the WR was brought to the Stone by Aragorn to fulfill his oath.
   The Stone was round and black, and was perhaps six feet in diameter. (III 64, 74-75)

*STONE TROLL, THE*   A humorous poem composed by Sam Gamgee in TA 3018.
   See: Tom. (I 276-78; TB 7, 39-40)

**STONE-TROLLS**   A kind of troll (q. v.) found in Eriador. Bert, Tom and William Huggins were probably Stone-trolls, since they spoke Westron, which Stone-trolls alone of their kind did. (III 512)

**STONEWAIN VALLEY**   Valley running through Druadan Forest. The Men of Gondor had built a great road through the Stonewain Valley which, although overgrown at the time of the WR, was used by the Rohirrim on their ride to Minas Tirith before the Battle of the Pelennor Fields. (III 15, 131-32)

**STONINGLAND**   Gondor (q. v.), as called in Rohan. (III 152)

**STOORS**   The southernmost of the three strains of Hobbits. The Stoors stayed in the Vales of Anduin longest of any of the three groups, but about TA 1300 they went over the Redhorn Pass and settled in Dunland or the Angle. The Stoors of the Angle fled to Dunland or Rhovanion about a hundred years later because of the threat of Angmar. The Stoor settlement in Rhovanion was in the Gladden Fields, and survived until well after 2460. The Stoors of Dunland emigrated to the Shire about 1630, and settled mostly in the East- and Southfarthings. At the time of the WR, Stoors were common in the Marish and Buckland.

Stoors were broader and heavier than other Hobbits, and were the only Hobbits to grow beards. Some Stoors wore boots in muddy weather. The Stoors were friendlier with Men than the other strains, and they preferred flat lands and riversides. Stoors were almost the only Hobbits to know anything of boating, swimming and fishing.

The Stoors of Dunland learned there a language related to Dunlending, and even at the end of the Third Age they retained many strange words and names. (I 22, 84; III 398, 457, 509)

**STRAIGHT STAIR**   The first stair in the ascent to Cirith Ungol from Imlad Morgul. The Straight was a long, steep flight of aged steps, many broken or cracked, and had a wall on both sides. (II 403-04)

**STRIDER**   See: Aragorn, Telcontar. (I 222; III 380)

**STYBBA**   (fl. WR)   Pony of Rohan, given to Merry by Théoden. Merry rode him from the Hornburg to Dunharrow before the Muster of Rohan. (III 60)

**SÚLE**   See: thúle. (III 500)

**SÚLIMË**   (Q.: 'wind---')   The third month of the Kings' and

Stewards' Reckonings, and the twelfth of the New Reckoning, corresponding roughly to our March.

The Sindarin name, used only by the Dúnedain, was Gwaeron, and the Shire equivalent was Rethe. (III 483)

**SUMMERDAYS**   The Lithe (q. v.). (III 481-82)

**SUNDAY**   See: Sunnendei. (III 484)

**SUNDERING SEAS**   The Sea, which separated Middle-earth from the Undying Lands. (I 260, 261, 482; II 260)

**SUNLENDING**   Rohirric name for Anórien (q. v.). (III 92)

**SUNLESS YEAR**   Probably, the time when the Undying Lands were darkened by the Shadows. (I 117)

**SUNNENDEI**   Early form of the name of the second day of the Hobbit week. The form at the time of the WR, and that used in *LotR,* was Sunday. The name was a translation of the Quenya Anarya. (III 484)

**SÚRION, TAR-**   (Q.: 'wind---') (fl. c. SA 1400) Dúnadan, ninth King of Númenor. (III 390)

**SUTHERLAND**   Haradwaith (q. v.). (I 17)

**SÛZA**   (gen. Hobb.: 'shire') The Shire (q. v.). (III 515)

**SWANFLEET**   Glanduin (q. v.). (III 325)

**SWEET GALENAS**   Pipe-weed (q. v.). (I 29)

**SWISH-TAIL**   (fl. WR)   One of the ponies provided by Merry for Frodo's journey from Buckland to Rivendell in TA 3018. He was driven off in Bree, but was later recovered and claimed by Barliman Butterbur.

He was named by Tom Bombadil. (I 198, 199, 242)

**SWORD OF ELENDIL**   Narsil (q. v.). (I 319)

**SWORD THAT WAS BROKEN**   Narsil or Andúril (qq.v.). (I 231-32, 323, 324)

## τ

**TALAN** (S.) The open platform built in the mellyrn of Lórien as living-places for the Elves. The talan was reached by a ladder through a hole in its center. A light screen could be fixed to any side of the platform to keep out the wind.

Called in Westron "flet." The Sindarin plural was probably *telain*. (I 444, 446)

**TALE OF ARAGORN AND ARWEN, THE** Chronicle of Gondor, said to have been written by Barahir in the second century of the Fourth Age. Parts of the *Tale* were added to the Gondor copy of the Thain's Book (q. v.). The excerpts given in Appendix A of *LotR* show evidence of having been edited by a Hobbit. (I 38; III 420-28)

**TALE OF YEARS, THE** A chronology of the Second, Third and early Fourth Ages, compiled by the Tooks in the early years of the Fourth Age, and kept at the Great Smials. Material gathered by Merry Brandybuck in Rivendell was incorporated into the *Tale*, which was thus quite accurate. Appendix B of *LotR* is a shortened version of this book.

The subtitle of the *Tale* was "Chronology of the Westlands." (I 39; III 452-472)

**TANIQUETIL** (Q.: 'high white peak') Another, and in time less common, name for Oiolosse (q. v.). (R 61)

**TANTA BAGGINS** (fl. TA 29th Cent.) Hobbit of the Shire, wife of Largo Baggins. She was born a Hornblower. (III 474)

**TAR-** (Q.: 'royal, king') Royal prefix attached to the names of those Kings and Ruling Queens of Númenor who took their names in Quenya. The rulers are entered in this Glossary under the main part of their names. (III 390)

**TARANNON** (Q.: 'royal-gate') See: Falastur. (III 403)

**TARCIL** (Q.: 'royal---') (d. TA 515) Dúnadan, sixth King of Arnor (435-515). (III 394)

**TARCIRYAN** (Q.: 'lord-ship---') (fl. TA 900) Dúnadan of Gondor, brother of King Falastur and father of Eärnil I. (III 394)

**TARGON** (Q.: 'royal-stone'?) (fl. WR) Man of Gondor, a cook for the Third Company of the Guards of the Citadel. (III 39)

**TÁRION** (Q.: 'powers') See: Valanya. (III 484)

**TARLANG'S NECK** Tall, thin outcropping of rock in Lamedon, on the road between Erech and Calembel about sixty miles north of Calembel. (III 75)

**TARMENEL** (Q.: 'king-heavens') Whence came the wind of power that blew Eärendil to the West, possibly Meneltarma. (I 309)

**TARONDOR** (Q.: 'lord---') (d. TA 602) Dúnadan, seventh King of Arnor (515-602). (III 394)

**TARONDOR** (d. TA 1798) Dúnadan, twenty-seventh King of Gondor (1656-1798). He ruled after the Great Plague, and throughout his reign, the longest of any King of Gondor, he was occupied with recovering Gondor's strength. He planted a sapling of the White Tree and permanently moved the King's residence to Minas Anor. (III 395, 408)

**TAROSTAR** (Q.: 'royal-fortress') Rómendacil I (q. v.). (III 394, 403)

**TASARINAN** (S.: 'willow-valley') Willow-meads in Beleriand. Also called Nan-tasarion. (II 90; III 321)

**TAUREMORNA** (Q.: 'forest-black') Epithet applied by Fangorn the Ent to Fangorn Forest (q. v.). (II 91)

**TAUREMORNALÓMË** (Q.: 'forest-black-shadowed') Epithet applied by Fangorn the Ent to Fangorn Forest (q. v.). (II 91)

**TAUR E-NDAEDELOS** (S.: 'forest of the great fear') Mirkwood (q. v.). (III 515)

**TAUR-NA-NELDOR** (S.) Neldoreth (q. v.). (II 90)

**TED SANDYMAN** (fl. WR) Hobbit of the Shire, from Hobbiton. He was associated with Lotho Sackville-Baggins during the latter's control of the Shire. (I 73; III 361, 366-67)

**TEETH OF MORDOR** See: the Towers of the Teeth. (II 308)

**TEHTAR** (Q.: 'signs'; sing. *tehta)* The additional signs of the Tengwar, principally used to represent vowels, vowel length (see: andaith), diphthongs, various consonantal abbreviations such as following s and preceding nasal, and abbreviations for short, very common words. (III 495, 498)

**TELCHAR** (S.) (First or Second Age?) Most probably a Noldorin smith. He forged Narsil. (II 147)

**TELCO** (Q.: 'stem') One of the basic components of a tengwa. The tyeller of the Tengwar were differentiated by differences in the telco and by the doubling of the lúva in even-numbered tyeller. In Grades 1 and 2 the telco was normal, while it was raised in 3 and 4 and reduced in 5 and 6. An extended stem, which extended both above and below the line, was also available, and was used in the original Fëanorian system. (III 495-96)

**TELCONTAR**  (Q.)  The name of the house of Elessar, the Kings of the Reunited Kingdom.

The name Telcontar was the Quenya form of Strider, the name given Aragorn the Ranger, founder of the house, by the Men of Bree. (III 469)

**TELEMMAITË, TAR-**  (Q.) (fl. SA 26th Cent.)  Dúnadan, fifteenth King of Númenor. (III 390)

**TELEMNAR**  (Q.) (d. TA 1636)  Dúnadan, twenty-sixth King of Gondor. He and both his sons died in the Great Plague. (III 395, 407-08)

**TELPERIËN, TAR-**  (Q.) (fl. SA 1600)  Dúnadan, tenth Ruler of Númenor, and the second Ruling Queen. (III 390)

**TELPERION**  (Q.)  The white tree of the Two Trees of the Valar (q. v.). Telperion was the elder of the two, and was called Eldest of Trees. Galathilion (q. v.) was a sapling of Telperion.

Telperion was poisoned by Morgoth in the First Age. (I 260; III 308-09)

**TELUMEHTAR**  (Q.)  Menelvagor (q. v.). (III 488)

**TELUMEHTAR UMBARDACIL**  (Q.: 'Orion Umbar-victor') (d. TA 1850)  Dúnadan, twenty-eighth King of Gondor (1798-1850). In 1810, troubled by Corsair raids, Telumehtar took Umbar. After this victory, Telumehtar added the title "Umbardacil" to his name. (III 395, 408)

**TÉMAR**  (Q.: 'series'; sing. *téma*)  The verical groupings of the Tengwar, representing points of articulation. The four témar were differentiated by variations in the lúvar. (III 495)

**TENGWAR**  (Q.: 'letters')  The writing system first developed by Rúmil in Eldamar, and later reworked by Fëanor. The Tengwar later spread to Númenor and large portions of the Elvish and Westron areas of Middle-earth. The Tengwar were a phonetic writing system written with brush or pen, in which the consonantal letters (tengwar) were arranged into grades (tyeller) representing modes of articulation and series (témar) representing points of articulation. Individual values could be assigned on the basis of the needs of the language in question.

Some of the adaptations of the Fëanorian system, such as the mode of Beleriand, were alphabetic and had full vocalic signs, while in other modes diacritic marks were used to represent vowels. Vowels, abbreviations and other values required by the system were represented by additional signs (tehtar).

The Tengwar, which were generally thirty-six in number, although two more grades were theoretically available, each had a universal Quenya "full name," which was a Quenya word beginning with the sound of the tengwa as used in an early Quenya mode. The Tengwar were also given unique names based on their values in different languages. (III 493-500)

**THAIN**   The ruler of the Shire after the end of the North-kingdom, who ruled until the return of the King. The Thain was master of the Shire-moot and captain of the Hobbitry-in-arms. Since these met only in emergencies, which rarely occurred in the Shire, and since the laws were voluntarily kept, the Thainship was a nominal position.

Bucca of the Marish, the first Thain, was chosen by the chieftains of the Shire in TA 1979, and the Thainship remained in the Oldbuck family until 2340, when, with the removal of the Oldbucks to Buckland, Isumbras Took became Isumbras I, the thirteenth Thain. The Thainship then became hereditary in the Took family into the Fourth Age. In FA 14, on the accession of Peregrin I, the Thain was made a Counsellor of the North-kingdom. (I 24, 30)

**THAIN'S BOOK**   A copy of the original Red Book of Westmarch, made at the request of King Elessar and brought to Gondor by Peregrin Took in FA 64. The Thain's Book was heavily annotated and expanded in Gondor, and a century later a copy of it was made in Gondor and kept at the Great Smials. This copy is the most important surviving version of the Red Book. (I 38)

**THANGORODRIM**   (S.: 'fang-mountain--') The fortress of Morgoth, broken by the Host of Valinor at the end of the First Age. (I 319; III 388, 452)

**THARBAD** (S.)   City in southern Eriador at the meeting of the Glanduin and Mitheithel. The Old South Road crossed the Mitheithel at a ford here. In TA 2912 Tharbad was ruined by great floods and deserted. (I 359; III 461)

**THARKÛN** (? Kh.)   Dwarvish name for Gandalf (q. v.). (II 353)

**THELLAMIE**   A country, in Bilbo's poem *Errantry*. The name is an imitation of Elvish, and Thellamie was probably imaginary. (TB 8, 25)

**THENGEL** (TA 2905-80)   Man, sixteenth King of Rohan (2953-80). From about 2925 to 2953 he lived in Gondor because he did not get on well with his father, King Fengel. During his reign Saruman first troubled Rohan.

Thengel married Morwen of Lossarnach in 2943, and she bore him five children, including Théoden and Théodwyn. (III 436)

**THÉODEN** (TA 2948-3019)   Man, seventeenth King of Rohan (2980-3019). Under Saruman's spells, which he worked through Théoden's evil counsellor Gríma, Théoden decayed toward the end of his reign, but in 3019 he was healed by Gandalf. Théoden led the Rohirrim against Saruman in the Battle of the Hornburg and against Mordor in the Battle of the Pelennor Fields. In the latter battle he defeated an army of Haradrim, but was slain by the Lord of the Nazgûl.

He was known as Théoden the Renowned, and, because of his decline and recovery, as Théoden Ednew (tr. Roh.: 'renewed fortune'). (II 148 ff.; III 137-45, 314, 436, 437)

**THÉODRED** (TA 2978-3019)   Man of Rohan, only child of King Théoden. He was the Second Marshal of the Mark, and was slain in the First Battle of the Fords of Isen during the WR. (II 149; III 437)

**THÉODWYN** (TA 2963-3002)   Woman of Rohan, youngest child of King Thengel. In 2889 she married Éomund of Eastfold and bore him two children, Éomer and Éowyn. Théodwyn died soon after her husband was slain. (III 436, 437)

**THINGOL** (S.: 'grey---') (First Age)   Sindarin Elf, King of Doriath and lord of the Sindar of Beleriand. He married Melian, and they had one child, Lúthien. Thingol seems to have died some time after Beren and Lúthien.

Thingol was also called Thingol Greycloak. (I 260, 261; III 388, 506)

**THIRD AGE**   The age of Middle-earth beginning with the first downfall of Sauron and the death of Gil-galad and ending with the War of the Rings, the second and final downfall of Sauron and the Last Riding of the Keepers of the Rings, in which the greatest of the Eldar departed over Sea. In this Age the Elves and Dwarves remained in Middle-earth but did little new, while Men increased in power and numbers. The Dúnedain kingdoms of Arnor and Gondor prospered at first, but waned as the evils of the Second Age, especially the Nazgûl and Sauron, rose again. In the end, however, the desperate gamble of the Wise to preserve the Free Peoples succeeded and great evil was banished, but at the same time much good and beauty was lost to Middle-earth. (III 387, 452)

**THIRD HOUSE OF THE EDAIN**   The House of Hador (q. v.). (III 389)

**THIRD LINE**   The third group of the Kings of Rohan. The first King of the Third Line was Éomer, who acceded in TA 3019 after the deaths of Théoden and his only son Théodred in the WR. (III 437-38)

**THISTLE BROOK**   Brook flowing into the Shirebourn near Willowbottom. Its source was in the Green Hill Country. (I 40)

**THISTLEWOOL**   Family of Men of Bree.
    In the RHM index, the name is given as "Thistlewood," which seems more likely to be the proper spelling. (I 212; RHM III 428)

**THORIN I**   (TA 2035-2289)   Dwarf, King of Durin's Folk (2190-2289). He led a large number of Durin's Folk from Erebor to the Ered Mithrin. (III 440, 450)

**THORIN II**   (TA 2746-2941)   Dwarf, King of Durin's Folk in exile (2845-2941). In his youth Thorin fought bravely in the Battle of Azanulbizar, and after that battle went with his father Thráin II and their folk to the Ered Luin. In 2845, after the disappearance of Thráin, Thorin became the King of Durin's Folk. For a hundred years he slowly increased the numbers and wealth of his people in the Ered Luin, until in 2941, long troubled by thoughts of the wrongs done his house, he met Gandalf and decided to reclaim Erebor from Smaug. This expedition of Thorin and Company met with success, but Thorin was killed soon after in the Battle of the Five Armies.

He was known as Thorin Oakenshield, because in the Battle of Azanulbizar he used an oak-branch as a shield and club. (III 440, 443, 445, 447-48, 450; H 23, 25-26, 29, 49-50, 268-69, 272-73)

**THORIN III** (TA 2866-FA ?) Dwarf, King of Durin's Folk in Erebor (3019-?). After the downfall of Sauron, Thorin and Bard II of Dale routed the army of Easterlings besieging Erebor.

He was known as Thorin Stonehelm. (III 450, 469)

**THORIN AND COMPANY** Business concern and expedition, organized by Thorin II, which in TA 2941 planned to recover the hoard of Smaug in Erebor. The members of the expedition were Thorin, Balin, Dwalin, Fíli, Kíli, Dori, Ori, Nori, Óin, Glóin, Bifur, Bofur, Bombur and Bilbo Baggins, their burglar. Gandalf accompanied them part of the way in an advisory capacity.

Although Smaug was destroyed and Erebor restored, the expedition had far more important results. Bilbo stole the One Ring, Gandalf found Glamdring and killed the Great Goblin of the Misty Mountains and the Battle of the Five Armies was fought.

Since the entire *Hobbit* is concerned with Thorin and Company, a more complete description of the expedition seems out of place here. (III 447-48; H 41)

**THORONDIR** (S.: 'eagle---') (d. TA 2882) Dúnadan, twenty-second Ruling Steward of Gondor (2872-82). (III 395)

**THORONDOR** (S.: 'eagle---') (First Age?) Eagle of the Encircling Mountains, from whom were descended the Eagles of the Misty Mountains. (III 278)

**THORONGIL** (S.: 'eagle of the star') The name by which Aragorn (q. v.) was known in Gondor when he served Ecthelion II. The name was given him because he was swift and keen-sighted and wore the star of the Rangers of the North on his cloak. (III 417-18)

**THRÁIN I** (TA 1934-2190) Dwarf, King of Durin's Folk (1981-2190). He led his people from Khazad-dûm to Erebor, where he founded the Kingdom under the Mountain in 1999 and discovered the Arkenstone.

Called Thráin the Old by Thorin II. (III 439-40, 450; H 9, 34)

**THRÁIN II** (TA 2644-2850) Dwarf, King of Durin's Folk in exile (2790-2850). He led the Dwarves in the War of the Dwarves and Orcs, and lost an eye in the Battle of Azanulbizar. In 2841 Thráin, restless with the greed for gold, left the Ered Luin with a few companions and resolved to go to Erebor. His journey was troubled by evil things, and in 2845 he was captured by Sauron and imprisoned in Dol Guldur. He was tormented for five years, and his Ring of Power was taken from him, but before he died he gave the key of Erebor to Gandalf. (I 351; III 440, 441, 442-45, 446-47; H 37)

**THRANDUIL** (First Age-   ) Sindarin Elf, King of the Woodland Realm, father of Legolas. At the beginning of the Second Age, Thranduil lived in Lindon, but before SA 1000 he established a kingdom in Greenwood the Great. This kingdom survived, despite attacks by the great spiders and the Orcs and a war with the Dwarves, for more than two ages of Middle-earth. In TA 2941 Thranduil led the Elven forces in the Battle of the Five Armies, and during the WR repulsed an attack from Dol Guldur. After the fall of Sauron in the WR Thranduil fixed the southern boundary of his realm as the Mountains of Mirkwood, and the Woodland Realm flourished well into the Fourth Age.

Thranduil had a great love for jewels and riches, and it may have been that this love led him to excesses, especially with the Dwarves.

Thranduil is the Elvenking of *The Hobbit*. (I 315; III 452, 467, 468; H 152, 165-66, 167-69)

**THREE-FARTHING STONE** Stone on the Great East Road marking the place where the East-, West- and Southfarthings met. The Three-Farthing Stone more or less marked the center of the Shire. (I 40; III 349)

**THREE HOUSES OF MEN** The Three Houses of the Elf-friends (q. v.). (II 364)

**THREE HOUSES OF THE ELF-FRIENDS** The three branches of the Edain (q. v.).

Also called the Ancient Houses and the Three Houses of Men. (II 127, 364; III 506)

**THREE HUNTERS** The name given by Aragorn to himself, Legolas and Gimli, when during the WR they followed the Orc-band that had captured Merry and Pippin across Rohan. (II

26 ff.)

**THREE KINDREDS** The three tribes of the Eldar (q. v.). (III 519)

**THREE RINGS** The Elven Rings of Power (q. v.). They were forged without Sauron's assistance, and thus his taint was not directly on them. However, they and their works could be controlled by the One, and their wielders would be revealed to Sauron if he had the One Ring. Unlike the other Rings, the Three gave power to build, understand and heal, not to control or conquer.

The Three were somehow successfully hidden through the Second Age, and were used in secret in the Third. However, when the One was destroyed they became powerless, and the things wrought with them failed. The Rings were taken to the West with the Last Riding of their keepers at the end of the Third Age.

The Three Rings, each of which was a band set with a single gem, were Vilya, Nenya and Narya (qq. v.). (I 318, 321, 330, 351-52, 472-73; III 308, 381-82, 456)

**THRIHYRNE** The three tall peaks of the Ered Nimrais behind the Hornburg. Helm's Deep wound into the Thrihyrne, and the Hornrock was an outlying northern spur of the mountains. (II 167, 169)

**THRIMICH** See: Thrimidge. (III 483)

**THRIMIDGE** The fifth month of the Shire Reckoning, corresponding roughly to our May. At the time of the WR the name was also spelled "Thrimich." An earlier form of the name was Thrimilch. (III 478, 483)

**THRIMILCH** Thrimidge (q. v.). (III 483)

**THRÓR** (TA 2542-2790) Dwarf, King of Durin's Folk (2589-2790). In 2590 he led his people back to Erebor from the Ered Mithrin because of the danger of dragons. In 2770 he and his people were driven from Erebor by Smaug, and they wandered off to the south. In 2790 Thrór left his people and went wandering, and was slain and his body defiled by Azog of Moria. (III 440-41, 450; H 32, 34)

**THRUSHES** Birds of Middle-earth. The thrushes of Erebor and Dale could understand Westron. They were friendly with the Men of Dale, who could understand their language and used them as messengers. These thrushes were very long-lived, and perhaps attained the same age as the ravens of Erebor. (H 217-18, 237, 243)

**THÚLE** (Q.: 'spirit') Name for the tengwa **b** (number 9), which had the value *th* in most systems. An alternate name was súle, since in Quenya *th* was usually pronounced *s*. (III 500)

**TIGHFIELD** Village in the Shire, where the Gamwiches, Gammidges and Ropers lived. (II 276; III 477)

**TIM** Tom's "nuncle" in Sam Gamgee's poem *The Stone Troll*, a corpse whose shinbone was being gnawed on by the Troll. Tim was most probably imaginary and fictitious. (I 276; TB 39)

**TINCO** (Q.: 'metal') Name for the tengwa **ρ** (number 1), which had the value *t* in most systems. (III 500)

**TINCOTÉMA** (Q.: '*t*-series') Dental and alveolar series of the Tengwar, generally applied in the Third Age to Series I. (III 496-97, 500)

**TINDÓMË** (Q.) The period of the day near dawn when the stars faded.
Called minuial in Sindarin and morrowdim by the Hobbits. (III 485)

**TINDROCK** Tol Brandir (q. v.). (I 483)

**TIRION** (Q.: 'great watch-tower') Eldarin city and tower in Valinor or Eressea. Its fashion, when Eärendil beheld it, was a white, lamp-lit tower in a sheer valley; at its foot was the Shadowmere.
Also called the Haven of the Eldar and Tirion the Fair. (I 309, 482; II 260; III 390; R 65)

**TIRITH AEAR** (S.: 'watch sea') The Sea-ward Tower (q. v.). (TB 8)

**TÎW** (S.: 'letters') The Tengwar (q. v.). (III 493)

**TOBOLD HORNBLOWER** (fl. TA 2670) Hobbit of the Shire, a resident of Longbottom. He was the first to grow pipe-weed in the Shire.
Tobold was known as Old Toby. (I 28; III 459)

**TODE** Marsh in *The Mewlips*, on the other side of the Merlock Mountains. Although possibly fictitious, Tode may have been patterned on the marsh at the eastern end of the Old Forest Road. (TB 46)

**TOGO GOODBODY** (fl. TA 29th Cent.) Hobbit of the Shire. He married Lily Baggins. (III 474)

**TOL BRANDIR** (S.) Sheer-sided mountain-island jutting out of the waters at the southern end of Nen Hithoel. It was said that no man or beast had ever set foot on it.
Called in Westron the Tindrock. (I 483, 509-10)

**TOLFALAS** (S.: '---coast') Island on the Bay of Belfalas near the Ethir Anduin. (I 16-17)

**TOLMA** (gen. Hobb.) A Hobbit forename usually shortened to Tom. (III 517)

**TOLMAN COTTON** (TA 2941-FA 20) Hobbit of the Shire, a farmer of Bywater. At the time of the WR he was influential in his neighborhood.
Tolman was known as Tom or Farmer Cotton. (III 353, 354 ff., 477)

**TOLMAN COTTON** (b. TA 2980) Hobbit of the Shire, eldest son of Tolman Cotton. In FA 22 he acted as Deputy Mayor for a year while Sam travelled to Gondor.
At the time of the WR, Tolman was known as Young Tom to distinguish him from his father. (III 471, 477)

**TOLMAN GAMGEE** (b. FA 22) Hobbit of the Shire, youngest son of Samwise Gamgee.
Tolman was known as Tom. (III 477)

**TOM** (d. TA 2941) Troll of the Trollshaws, one of the three encountered by Thorin and Company. He was turned to stone through Gandalf's trick. (H 46-52)

**TOM** The protagonist of *The Stone Troll*. It is likely that Tom was to some extent modelled on Tom Bombadil, since Sam Gamgee composed the poem soon after meeting Bombadil. (I 276-78; III 517; TB 39-40)

**TOMBA** Genuine Hobbit forename, usually abbreviated as Tom. (III 517)

**TOM BOMBADIL** A being, lord and master of the Old Forest. His race is unknown, although it is possible that he was a Vala. Tom's power within the Old Forest was absolute, and even the Ring could not affect him, but he did not go beyond the boundaries of the Forest, save for occasional visits to the Barrow-downs and the Shire.
Tom called himself Eldest, and claimed to have been alive

since early in the First Age. He looked like a Man, but was short and red-faced. He wore a pointed hat with a blue feather and large yellow boots. Tom was merry and blithe, good-hearted but unconcerned with the problems of the outside world.

"Tom Bombadil" was the name given him by the Hobbits of Buckland. He was called Iarwain Ben-adar and the First by the Elves, Forn by the Dwarves and Orald (tr. Mannish: 'very old') by northern Men. (I 167-86, 196-204, 347-48; TB 9, 11-23)

**TOMBS** the Hallows (q. v.). (III 152)

**TOM COTTON** Tolman Cotton (q. v.). (III 353, 354)

**TOM PICKTHORN** (d. TA 3019) Man of the Bree-land, killed in the fight between the Bree-landers and Bill Ferny and his friends. (III 335, 517)

**TONGUE** The lawn at the southernmost tip of Lórien between Celebrant and Anduin. Celeborn and Galadriel's farewell feast for the Company of the Ring was held there. (I 480, 482)

**TOOK** Influential Hobbitish family, living in the Tookland in the Westfarthing. The Tooks, because of their Fallohide blood, were (for Hobbits) rather adventurous, and tended to be leaders. The Thainship was hereditary in the Took family from the time of Isumbras I (TA 2340), and Tooks were from time to time known to go off on adventures or even to become sailors.

From the time of Isengrim II (fl. 2683), the Tooks closely related to the Thain lived in the Great Smials.

Took is an anglicization of the actual Hobbitish name Tûk, of forgotten origin. (I 22; III 475, 516; H 16)

**TOOK, THE** The head of the Took family. (III 471)

**TOOKBANK** Village in the Westfarthing, in the western Green Hills. (I 40)

**TOOKLAND** Folkland of the Tooks, in the South- and West-farthings in and around the Green Hills. Most of the Tooks still lived there at the time of the WR. (I 30; III 357)

**TORECH UNGOL** (S.: '--- spider') Shelob's Lair (q. v.). (II 414 ff.)

**TOROG** (S.: 'troll') See: Trolls. (III 511)

**TOWER HALL** The great audience-hall of the White Tower of

Minas Tirith, an awesome room with tall pillars, stone statues of the Kings of Gondor; and, behind the throne, a carven and gem-set image of a White Tree in flower.

Also called the Hall of the Kings. (III 28, 95, 304)

**TOWER HILLS** Hills marking the western boundary of the Shire after FA 32. A palantír was kept here until the end of the Third Age in the tallest of the White Towers (q. v.) built on the Hills.

Called in Sindarin Emyn Beraid. (I 26-27; II 259, 471)

**TOWER OF AMON SÛL** The watch-tower on Weathertop, built by Elendil in the Second. Age. The chief palantír of the North-kingdom was kept in the Tower, and for this reason in the Third Age the Tower, which was on the border of the three realms, was fought for by Arthedain, Cardolan and Rhudaur. In 1409 the combined forces of Rhudaur and Angmar took the Tower and burned it, killing King Arveleg I of Arthedain. At the time of the WR, all that remained of the Tower was an uneven ring of stones. (I 250; III 397)

**TOWER OF CIRITH UNGOL** Tower on Cirith Ungol, originally built by Gondor to prevent any evil beings from entering Mordor early in the Third Age. The Tower was later deserted by Gondor and manned by Orcs.

The Tower was built in three tiers against a mountainside, and at the time of the WR the main gate was guarded by the Two Watchers. When Frodo and Sam escaped from the Tower, the Watchers were so shaken up by the Phial of Galadriel that the gateway crumbled.

See also: the Undergate. (II 405-06; 446-47; III 214-15, 217-35, 248)

**TOWER OF ECTHELION** the White Tower (q. v.). (III 24)

**TOWER OF THE STONE OF OSGILIATH** The Dome of Stars (q. v.). (III 406)

**TOWERS OF THE TEETH** Two towers, Narchost and Carchost, built on either side of Cirith Gorgor by Gondor as a guard on Mordor. Deserted about TA 1636 and later re-occupied by Sauron, the Towers became strong Orc-holds, but they were ruined at the unmaking of the One Ring during the WR.

Also called the Teeth of Mordor. (II 308; III 200, 215, 279)

**TOWN HOLE** Building in Michel Delving where the Mayor

resided. (I 214)

**TRAHALD** (gen. Mannish: 'burrowing') See: Gollum. (III 518)

*TRANSLATIONS FROM THE ELVISH* Book of lore by Bilbo Baggins, written between TA 3003 and 3018 at Rivendell, in which he incorporated all the Elvish lore and history of the First Age he could cull from living or written records. The *Translations*, which were written in Westron, formed three volumes of the Red Book of Westmarch. (I 37, 38)

**TRAVELLERS** Name given to Frodo, Sam, Merry and Pippin by the Hobbits of the Shire after their return from their adventures during the WR. (III 374)

**TREEBEARD** Fangorn (q. v.). (II 84)

**TREEGARTH OF ORTHANC** Name given to Isengard by Fangorn after his landscaping program there during the WR. See also: the Watchwood. (III 317)

**TREE OF THE HIGH ELVES** The emblem of the Eldar, representing Galathilion. (I 397)

**TREWESDEI** The oldest recorded form of the name of the fourth day of the Hobbit week, a translation of the Quenya Aldëa. The form of the name at the time of the WR was Trewsday.
Called Tuesday in *LotR*. (III 484)

**TREWSDAY** Trewesdei (q. v.). (III 484)

**TROLL** A fictitious troll in Sam Gamgee's poem *The Stone Troll*. (I 276-78; TB 39-40)

**TROLLS** Evil race of Middle-earth. Trolls were originally bred by Morgoth in the First Age from some unknown stock in mockery and imitation of Ents. They were used by Morgoth and Sauron, although their usefulness was limited by their stupidity. Trolls probably became extinct in the Fourth Age.

Trolls were very large (perhaps as large as Ents), strong, ugly and stupid. They hoarded treasure, killed for pleasure and ate raw flesh of all kinds. Although they could never be really intelligent, Sauron increased their wits with wickedness, and toward the end of the Third Age some trolls became quite dangerous. The one interesting characteristic of trolls was that they turned to stone when exposed to the sunlight.

There seem to have been at least four strains of trolls: the Stone-trolls (q. v.) of the Trollshaws and other parts of

Eriador, the cave-trolls of Moria, the hill-trolls of Gorgoroth and Eriador and the Olog-hai. The Stone-trolls spoke a debased Westron and seem to have been the most human; Bert, Tom and William Huggins were Stone-trolls. The cave-trolls and hill-trolls spoke a debased version of Orkish, when they spoke at all, and were scaled; the cave-trolls were greenish. The Olog-hai were bred by Sauron toward the end of the Third Age, and dwelled in southern Mirkwood and the mountains of Mordor. They were more agile and cunning than other trolls, and could endure the sun as long as Sauron controlled them. The Olog-hai used the Black Speech.

The Sindarin word for "troll" was *torog,* to which the Black Speech *olog* may have been related in some way. (I 274-78, 421-22; II 83, 113; III 207-08, 420, 511-12, 514; H 49-53)

**TROLLSHAWS** Woods in the Angle north of the Great East Road. Rhudaur had built castles there; and, although long deserted at the time of the WR, they and the entire area had an unpleasant feeling. The Trollshaws were infested with trolls. (I 17, 270-79; H 43-53)

**TRUE-SILVER** Mithril (q. v.). (I 413)

**TUCKBOROUGH** Town in the Westfarthing in the Green Hills, site of the Great Smials. (I 40; II 80)

**TUILË** (Q.: 'spring') The first season of the loa of the Calendar of Imladris, corresponding roughly to our spring. Tuilë was also one of the seasons in the Dúnedain calendars.

The Sindarin form of the name was ethuil. (III 480, 485)

**TUILÉRË** (Q.: 'spring-day') Holiday of the Stewards' Reckoning occurring between Súlimë 30 and Víressë 1. Tuilérë fell near the vernal equinox. (III 481)

**TÛK** (gen. Hobb.) See: Took. (III 516)

**TUMLADEN** (S.) Valley in Gondor south of Minas Tirith, near or in Lossarnach. (III 41)

**TUNNELLY** Surname used by Hobbits of Bree, and perhaps also of the Shire. (I 212)

**TUOR** (tr. Ad.) (First Age) Adan of the House of Hador, husband of Idril Celebrindal and father of Eärendil. (III 388, 389)

**TURAMBAR** (Q.: 'lord-world') (d. TA 667) Dúnadan, ninth King of Gondor (541-667). He won a great victory over the

Easterlings, and increased Gondor's eastern territory. (III 394, 403)

**TURGON** (S.: 'lord-stone'?) (First Age) Elda, King of Gondolin. He was the father of Idril. Turgon probably died when Gondolin fell to Morgoth.

Turgon's sword was the famous blade Glamdring, which was made for him. (III 388-89; H 61)

**TURGON** (d. TA 2753) Dúnadan, twenty-fourth Ruling Steward of Gondor (2914-53). (III 395, 416-17)

**TÚRIN** (S.? tr. Ad.?) (First Age) Adan, elf-friend and hero. Túrin seems to have killed a dragon in his youth and later to have become a king. He was perhaps slain in old age by an invading army. (I 355; TB 8, 54-56)

**TÚRIN I** (d. TA 2278) Dúnadan, sixth Ruling Steward of Gondor (2244-78). (III 395)

**TÚRIN II** (d. TA 2914) Dúnadan, twenty-third Ruling Steward of Gondor (2882-2914). He built refuges such as Henneth Annûn for the Rangers of Ithilien, and refortified Cair Andros against the threat of Mordor. He also won a great victory, with the aid of Rohan, over the Haradrim in the Battle of the Crossings of Poros (2885). (III 395, 416)

**TURTLE-FISH** A probably-mythical race of fish of the Sea, whose last member was Fastitocalon (q. v.). (TB 49)

**TWENTY-FIRST HALL OF THE NORTH-END** The Chamber of Mazarbul (q. v.). (I 419, 420)

**TWILIGHT** Figurative name for the Undying Lands, deriving from their darkened state after the rebellions of Morgoth and the Noldor. (III 425)

**TWILIGHT** A period early in the First Age of Middle-earth, perhaps the domination of Morgoth. (III 511, 512)

**TWOFOOT** Family of Hobbits of the Shire, at least one branch of which lived in Hobbiton. At the time of the Farewell Party (TA 3001), Daddy Twofoot lived in Bagshot Row. (I 45)

**TWO TREES OF THE VALAR** Telperion and Laurelin (qq. v.), which grew on a mound near Valimar. The light of the Trees shone throughout Valinor. Telperion, the White Tree, was older than Laurelin, the Golden, and was known as Eldest of Trees. Both Trees were poisoned by Morgoth, and their light was preserved only in the Silmarilli. There were no saplings of Laurelin, but Galathilion sprang from Telperion. However, Galathilion and its saplings did not shine.

Also called the Trees of Silver and Gold and the White Tree and Golden. (II 260, 319; III 388, 389; R 62)

**TWO WATCHERS**  Evil sentient statues guarding the gate of the Tower of Cirith Ungol at the time of the WR. Each had three joined bodies and three heads, facing outward, inward and across the gateway. They barred entry or exit to any enemy unless he had a stronger will than they, and gave an alarm if one did pass. During the Quest of Mount Doom, Sam Gamgee gained entry and exit by using the Phial of Galadriel.

The Two Watchers seem also to have given the Orcs of the Tower warning of intruders anywhere in the neighborhood.

Also called the Watchers and the Silent Watchers. (II 316, 441; III 218, 234-35)

**TYELLER**  (Q.: 'grades'; sing. *tyelle)*  The horizontal divisions of the Tengwar, usually six in number, although theoretically eight tyeller were available. The tyeller in general represented different modes of articulation, and were differentiated by the shape of the telco and the number of lúvar. (III 495)

**TYELPETÉMA**  (Q.: *'ty*-series')  Name for the voiceless alveopalatal series of the Tengwar used in writing Quenya, *ty, dy, thy, dhy,* etc. The tyelpetéma was usually represented by the tincotéma plus the tehta for following *y,* which was two underposed dots. (III 496-97, 500)

**TYRN GORTHAD**  the Barrow-downs (q. v.). (III 398)

# u

**UDÛN**  (S.: 'un-west, hell')  The Underworld (q. v.).  (I 429, RHM III 436)

**UDÛN**  The circular plain in Mordor between Isenmouthe and Cirith Gorgor.  (III 251)

**UFTHAK**  (d. TA ?)  Orc of the Tower of Cirith Ungol. At some time, he was captured and bound by Shelob. He was seen by his fellow-Orcs, but was not released because they feared to anger Shelob.  (II 445)

**UGLÚK**  (d. TA 3019)  Uruk-hai of Isengard, captain of the band that captured Merry and Pippin. He was slain by Éomer of Rohan.  (II 60-62 ff., 78)

**UIAL**  (S.)  The name for the twilight periods of morning and evening, which were very important to the Eldar.
See: tindómë, undómë.  (III 485)

**UILOS**  (S.)  The Sindarin form of Oiolosse (q. v.).  (R 62)

**UMBAR**  (Q.: 'fate')  Name for the tengwa ϼ (number 6), used for *mb* in Quenya and *b* in most other languages.  (III 500)

**UMBAR**  Coastal area in Harad, consisting of a cape, firth, havens and fortress, and also the surrounding land. The harbor was first developed by the Númenoreans in the Second Age, and by SA 2280 it was a great fortress and the chief Númenorean harbor in Middle-earth. In 3261 Ar-Pharazôn landed here to contest the power of Sauron. After the fall of Númenor (and perhaps before that time), the Dúnedain of Umbar fell under the influence of Sauron, and became known as Black Númenoreans (q. v.). In the Third Age, Gondor and the Corsairs of Umbar (q. v.) were frequently at war, and Umbar changed hands many times. King Eärnil I took Umbar in 933, and despite a lengthly siege (933-1050) it was held by Gondor until 1448, when the defeated rebels of the Kin-strife escaped from Pelargir and established themselves at Umbar. In 1810 Telumehtar recaptured the havens, but they were soon after lost to the Haradrim. In 2980, a small fleet of Gondor, led by Thorongil, attacked Umbar in a surprise raid and burned many of the ships of the Corsairs. During the WR a large Corsair fleet attacked Pelargir but was defeated by Aragorn and the Dead, and in the Fourth Age Umbar once more was controlled by Gondor, under King Elessar.

The name *Umbar* was of pre-Númenorean origin. The city of Umbar was also known as the City of the Corsairs at the time of the WR. (I 16; II 339; III 42, 186, 392, 403, 406-07, 408, 417, 454, 456, 457, 508)

**UMBARDACIL**   (Q.: 'Umbar-victor')   King Telumehtar (q. v.). (III 408)

**UNDERGATE**   The lower gate of the Tower of Cirith Ungol, entered by a tunnel going through Shelob's Lair. (II 438)

**UNDERHARROW**   Hamlet in Rohan, located in Harrowdale. (III 91)

**UNDER-HILL**   Neighborhood in Hobbiton comprising those holes which, like Bag End, were built in Hobbiton Hill. (H 28)

**UNDERHILL**   A family of Hobbits with branches in the Shire and in Staddle. Underhill was Frodo's incognito on his flight to Rivendell in TA 3018. (I 97, 212-13)

**UNDERTOWERS**   The home of the Fairbairns of the Tower, built on or in the Tower Hills. The original of the Red Book of Westmarch was kept at Undertowers. (I 37; III 471)

**UNDER-WAY**   Orc-path in Shelob's Lair, probably the tunnel between the Undergate and the stone door blocking Shelob from approaching the Tower of Cirith Ungol. (II 440)

**UNDERWORLD**   Hell, in opposition to Middle-earth and Over-heaven.
Called in Sindarin Udûn. (III 124)

**UNDÓMË**   (Q.: 'twilight')   The period of the day near evening when the stars first began to shine.
Called aduial in Sindarin and evendim by the Hobbits. (III 485)

**UNDÓMIEL**   (Q.: 'evenstar')   Name given Arwen because she was the most beautiful Elven-lady of the fading years of the Eldar in Middle-earth. (I 300)

**UNDYING LANDS**   General name given the lands west of the Sea. Here lived for all time the Valar and, most probably,

Eru. Until the end of the Second Age the Undying Lands were connected to Middle-earth by the Sea, but at the ruin of Númenor the Undying Lands were removed from the circles of the world, and the route to them was hidden. "Over-heaven" may refer to the West in this state.

Two lands in the Undying Lands are mentioned, Eressëa and Valinor. Eressëa was an island west of Elenna, and Valinor was probably to the west of Eressëa. The Pelóri Mountains ran north and south through Valinor, and that part of Valinor east of the Mountains, as well as Eressëa, comprised Eldamar. West of the Mountains, which were crossed by the great pass of Calacirya, were Valimar and the mound on which had grown the Two Trees. Oiolosse was the tallest of the Pelóri. The chief city of Eldamar was Tirion.

The Undying Lands were also called the Far West, the West; and, figuratively, Evereven and the Twilight. They were also called Arda by the Valar, and perhaps were identical to the Isles of the West, the Uttermost West, Aman the Blessed, World's End and the Blessed Realm. (III 390, 392; R 60-62 passim.)

**UNGOLIANT** (S.: 'spider---') (First Age) Great spider of Beleriand, parent of Shelob. (II 423)

**UNGWE** (Q.: 'spider's web') Name for the tengwa ⱬ (number 8). (III 500)

**UNQUE** (Q.: 'hollow') Name for the tengwa ⱬ (number 16). (III 500)

**UPBOURN** Hamlet in Rohan, located between Dunharrow and Edoras. (III 91)

**ÚR** (Q.: 'heat') Name for the tengwa ○ (number 36). (III 500)

**ÚRIMË** (Q.: 'heat---') The eighth month of the Kings' and Stewards' Reckonings, and the fifth of the New Reckoning, corresponding roughly to our August.

The Sindarin form, used only by the Dúnedain, was Úrui. (III 483)

**ÚRUI** (S.: 'heat---') Úrimë (q. v.). (III 483)

**URUK, URUKS** See: the Uruk-hai. (III 511)

**URUK-HAI** (B. S.: 'Orc-race') Strain of Orcs bred by Sauron in the Third Age in Mordor. The Uruk-hai first appeared about

TA 2475, when they overran Ithilien and took Osgiliath. By the time of the WR, uruks were used by Sauron and Saruman as soldiers on all fronts; Gorbag, Shagrat, Uglúk and perhaps Azog and Bolg were uruks.

The Uruk-hai were used as soldiers more than other strains because, unlike other Orcs, they were almost as tall as Men and had straight, strong legs. Uruks were black and slanty-eyed. They regarded themselves as superior to other Orcs.

Saruman's spies in Bree and the Chief's Men may have been Uruk-hai, and almost certainly had some uruk blood in them.

*Uruk-hai* was the generic name for the breed; the singular was *uruk* and the plural *uruks*. They were also called the Great Orcs. (I 421; II 20, 61, 441, III 255, 414, 511)

**UTTERMOST WEST**  Valinor, perhaps especially that part west of the Pelóri. (I 321; III 389)

# $\mathcal{V}$

**VALA** (Q.: 'angelic power') Name for the tengwa **ᚈ** (number 22). (III 500)

**VALACAR** (Q.: 'vala---') (d. TA 1432) Dúnadan, twentieth King of Gondor (1366-1432). In his youth (1250), Valacar was sent by his father Rómendacil II to the court of Vidugavia to improve relations between Gondor and the Northmen and to enable Valacar to learn the ways of these important allies. Valacar, however, went far beyond this, for he came to love the Northmen, and he married Vidumavi, Vidugavia's daughter. Their child, Eldacar, was thus only half Dúnadan; this favoritism toward the Northmen led to the Kin-strife. (III 395, 405)

**VALANDIL** (Q.: 'vala-lover') (b. SA 6th Cent.) Dúnadan of Númenor, son of Silmariën and first Lord of Andúnië. (III 391)

**VALANDIL** (SA 3430?-TA 249) Dúnadan, third King of Arnor (TA 10-249). Valandil was born in Imladris, and became King when his father Isildur and his three elder brothers were slain in the Battle of the Gladden Fields. He received the sceptre of Annúminas in TA 10 on reaching his majority. (III 394, 456)

**VALANDUR** (Q.: 'vala---') (d. TA 652) Dúnadan, eighth King of Arnor (602-52). He died a violent death. (III 394)

**VALANYA** (Q.: 'day of the Valar') The sixth day of the Eldarin week and the seventh in Dúnedain calendars, named for the Valar. It was the chief day of the week.

The Sindarin form was Orbelain. Alternate names were the Quenya Tárion and the Sindarin Rodyn. The Hobbitish name was Highdei. (III 484)

**VALAR** (Q.: 'vala+plural') Angelic powers, second in might and authority only to their lord, Eru. The Valar aided Eru in making of the the world, although they did not have any part in the making of Elves or Men. They prepared Arda for the Erusēn and for themselves, and dwelled there ever after as the guardians of Middle-earth. In this guardianship four events stand out. The first is the rebellion of Morgoth, a great

Vala, and the decision of the Valar to give up that which they most cherished, the light of the two Trees, in order to preserve their peace; from this revolt resulted the rebellion of the Noldor and their exile from Valinor for having returned to Middle-earth. This in turn led to the mission of Eärendil at the end of the First Age, and the decision of the Valar to overthrow Morgoth, place the Silmaril of Eärendil in the heavens as a star, reward the Edain with Elenna and forgive all the Exiles save Galadriel. It was the gift of Elenna to the Edain which led to the greatest crisis of the Valar, for in SA 3319 Ar-Pharazôn of Númenor, corrupted by Sauron, assaulted Valinor; the Valar laid down their guardianship for the moment and Eru destroyed Númenor. Sauron, however, survived into the Third Age, and so about TA 1000 the Valar sent the Wizards to Middle-earth, and with their aid the Free Peoples of Middle-earth eventually worked out their destiny and overthrew Sauron. Thus at the end of the Third Age the last major personalities (Sauron, Galadriel, Elrond, the Wizards) brought to Middle-earth by the actions of the Valar were through their wisdom removed from Middle-earth. In all this, the policy of the Valar was to act directly as little as possible, but to bolster goodness and courage on the part of the Free Peoples with strength to enable them to meet their foes on equal terms.

The Valar seem to have had numerous functions in Middle-Earth, although by the Third Age their power and authority were remote and often ignored. For example, the Valar interpreted and enforced the rules of the Riddle-game.

The Valar seem to have been beings of pure spirit, but they presented themselves to physical eyes in majestic, luminous bodies called by the Eldar *fanar,* which physically resembled those of Elves and Men. The Valar dwelled in Valinor, and only Oromë came frequently to Middle-earth. The Valar seem to have had a number of kings and queens, the chief of whom were Manwe and Elbereth. The Valar in general, but especially Elbereth, were venerated and worshipped by the Eldar and the Dúnedain.

The chief Valar seem to have had specialized natures and functions somewhat similar to those of the Greek gods, and probably also ruled over lesser Valar. However, of all the Valar only Aulë, Elbereth, Manwe, Melian, Morgoth and Oromë

are named, so not much can be said about this. Oromë was
the huntsman of the Valar and Aulë was their smith; Manwe
would seem to correspond to Zeus, but Elbereth was far
greater than Hera.

The Valar were also known as the Authorities, the Guardians of the World, the Lords of the West and the Powers. The
Sindarin form of their name was Belain, of which the singular
was *balan.* (I 33; II 341; III 138, 388, 389, 390, 395; R 66;
RP 9/12/65)

**VALES OF ANDUIN** The lands between Mirkwood and the Misty
Mountains, home of the Hobbits and the Men of the Vales of
Anduin. Although a fair and fertile land, by the time of the WR
the Vales of Anduin were nearly deserted because of the dread
of Dol Guldur; only the Beornings and the Stoors of the Gladden Fields are mentioned as living there. (I 21; III 404, 429)

**VALIMAR** (Q.: 'dwelling of the Valar') Properly, the city of the
Valar, the mound upon which the Two Trees stood. However,
in time Valimar came to refer to Valinor as a whole. (I 489;
R 62)

**VALINOR** (Q.: 'land of the Valar') Part of the Undying Lands,
where the Valar dwelt. Valinor was divided from north to
south by the Pelóri, and that part of Valinor east of the Mountains comprised mainland Eldamar.

The Valar settled in Valinor after their demiurgic labors in
the creation of the world, and prepared the eastern portion of
their realm for the Eldar, who arrived there early in the First
Age. However, the rebellion of Morgoth caused grief and dissension, for Fëanor and many of the Eldar followed him to
Middle-earth to recover the Silmarils. At the command of the
Elder King, Elbereth summoned up Shadows, and Valinor was
darkened. Most of the Eldar who survived the War of the Great
Jewels returned to Valinor at the end of the First Age.

Also called the Blessed Realm and Valimar. Arda was the
name given to the region by the Valar when they first came
there. (I 309, 489; III 311, 388, 452; R 60)

**VALINOREAN** The language of the Valar. The only example
of Valinorean given in *LotR, asëa aranion,* looks very much
like Quenya, but it is nonetheless possible that Valinorean
was a separate language. Some of the names of the Valar and
places in Valinor, may be Valinorean.

Elements of Valinorean should appear in Quenya and the
Black Speech. It is possible that "Valinorean" means merely

"the speech of Valinor," in which case it would probably be a reference to Quenya. (III 172)

**VANIMELDË, TAR-** (Q.) (fl. SA 2600)   Dúnadan, sixteenth Ruler of Númenor and the third Ruling Queen. (III 390)

**VARDA** (Q.: 'exalted')   Elbereth (q. v.). (I 489)

**VARDAMIR** (Q.: 'exalted jewel, jewel of Elbereth') (fl. SA 5th Cent.)   Dúnadan, fifth King of Númenor (442-?). (III 390)

**VARIAGS**   A race, probably of Men, dwelling in Khand. In the WR they were allied with Sauron. (III 148)

**VIDUGAVIA** (? gen. Northmen) (fl. TA 13th Cent.)   Northman, self-styled King of Rhovanion. He was the most powerful Northern prince of his time; his realm lay between Mirkwood and the Celeduin. Vidugavia was friendly with Rómendacil II of Gondor, and aided him in his great victory over the Easterlings in 1248. (III 405)

**VIDUMAVI** (? gen. Northmen) (fl. TA 13th Cent.)   Northman, daughter of Vidugavia. She married Valacar of Gondor. (III 405)

**VILYA** (Q.: 'air, sky')   Later and more usual name for the tengwa ᴜ (number 24). The earlier form was wilya, but this changed because of a change in the pronunciation of Quenya in Middle-earth. (III 500)

**VILYA**   The mightiest of the Three Rings of the Elves (q. v.). Vilya was originally worn by Gil-galad, but it was given by him to Elrond. Vilya was made of gold, and had a great blue stone. (III 381, 456)

**VINITHARYA** (? gen. Northmen)   The name given Eldacar (q. v.) in his youth. (III 405)

**VINYARION** (Q.)   Hyarmendacil II (q. v.). (III 395)

**VÍRESSË** (Q.)   The fourth month of the Kings' and Stewards' Reckonings and the first of the New Reckoning, corresponding roughly to our April.

The Sindarin name, used only by the Dúnedain, was Gwirith. (III 483, 486)

**VORONDIL** (Q.: '---lover') (d. TA 2029)   Dúnadan, Steward from 1998 to 2029 of Eärnil II of Gondor. Vorondil was a great hunter, which is why he was known as Vorondil the Hunter, and he made the Great Horn from the horn of one of the Kine of Araw which he slew. (III 29, 395)

# W

**WAIN** the Sickle (q. v.). (H 185)

**WAINRIDERS** An Easterling people or confederacy. They first ventured west of the Sea of Rhûn in TA 1851. In 1856, stirred up by Sauron, they attacked Gondor, taking Rhovanion and killing King Narmacil II. In 1899, the enslaved Northmen of Rhovanion revolted against the Wainriders, and Gondor, under King Calimehtar, took advantage of this to defeat the Wainriders in a battle on Dagorlad. In fifty years, however, the Wainriders had recovered their strength and, allied with Men of Khand and Near Harad, launched a great two-pronged assault on Gondor from the east and south in 1944. Although the northern Wainrider force defeated the Northern Army of Gondor and killed King Ondoher and both his sons, the southern assault was defeated by Eärnil, who then brought his army north and crushed the main Wainrider force in the Battle of the Camp. The Wainriders were totally destroyed, and never again troubled Gondor.

The Wainriders were so called because they travelled in large wagons. Their chieftains fought in chariots, and in general they were better armed than previous Easterling invaders. (III 408-09)

**WALDA** (TA 2780-2851) Man, twelfth King of Rohan (2842-51). He was ambushed and slain by Orcs near Dunharrow. (III 435)

**WANDERING COMPANIES** Groups of Elves that had no permanent home in Middle-earth, but wandered about together. (I 117 ff., 124)

**WANDERING DAYS** The period, lasting from about TA 1000 to 1630, during which the Hobbits gradually migrated from the Vales of Anduin to Bree or the Shire, prompted by the rise of Dol Guldur and Angmar. About 1050 the Harfoots came to Eriador, and the Fallohides followed about a century later, while the Stoors went to Dunland or the Angle. When Angmar rose, the Hobbits migrated further west, many settling at Bree. Some Stoors, however, returned to the Gladden Fields. In TA 1600 the Shire was settled by a large number of Hobbits from Bree, and thirty years later the Stoors of Dunland moved there as well. (I 21; III 456, 457)

**WANDLIMB**  Fimbrethil (q. v.). (II 99)

**WARDEN OF THE HOUSES OF HEALING**  The head of the hospital of Minas Tirith. At the time of the WR, the Warden was somewhat pedantic. (III 179, 291 ff.)

**WARGS**  Evil wolves of Rhovanion, allies of the Orcs and servants of Sauron.

The Wargs of I 388-91 do not seem to have been true Wargs, in that they were west of the Misty Mountains and weren't real. (I 388-91; H 103-09, 265, 268)

**WAR OF THE DWARVES AND ORCS**  War fought from TA 2793 to 2799 between the Orcs of the Misty Mountains and the Dwarves, especially Durin's Folk. The war was caused by the murder and mutilation of Thrór in 2790 by Orcs of Moria. After mustering their forces, in 2793 the Dwarves began sacking every Orc-hold they could find in the Misty Mountains, searching for Azog, Thrór's murderer. In 2799 all the surviving Orcs gathered in Moria, and the Dwarves met them in the Battle of Azanulbizar (q. v.). Most of the Orcs were killed in this War, and this made the Misty Mountains safer for a century and a half, but many Dwarves were also slain. A large number of Orcs fled across Rohan and settled in the Ered Nimrais, but they were killed by 2864. (III 416, 442-44)

**WAR OF THE ELVES AND SAURON**  War fought from SA 1693 to 1701 between the Eldar of Eregion and Lindon and Sauron and his allies. The War began after Celebrimbor discovered Sauron's treachery in the forging of the Rings of Power, and Sauron decided to crush the now implacably hostile Elves. The Three Rings were hidden by the Eldar, but in 1697 Eregion was overrun and Celebrimbor slain. Elrond, who had been sent to Eregion by Gil-galad, fled with the remaining Noldor and founded Rivendell. In the next two years Sauron overran all of Eriador except for Rivendell. Gil-galad asked Tar-Minastir of Númenor for aid, and in 1700 the latter sent a navy to Middle-earth with whose aid Sauron was defeated. In 1701 he was driven out of Eriador and the war ended.

Aside from greatly reducing the power and numbers of the Eldar, the War ended the last close link between the Elves and the Dwarves, the friendship between Khazad-dûm and

Eregion. (III 454)

**WAR OF THE GREAT JEWELS**  The great war of the First
Age, fought between Morgoth and the Noldor, led by Fëanor.
After Morgoth stole the Silmarilli, the Noldor, against the
wishes of the Valar, came to Middle-earth to recover them.
The Noldor were aided by the Sindar and the Edain, but despite the deeds of great heroes such as Beren, Lúthien and
Finrod they were utterly defeated. However, Eärendil obtained
aid from the Valar, and in the great battle between the Host
of Valinor and Morgoth the latter was overthrown and Beleriand destroyed.

Also called the Goblin-wars. (III 388, 507; H 61, 72)

**WAR OF THE RING**  The great war fought at the end of the
Third Age between Sauron and the Free Peoples, the subject
of *LotR*. In the War Sauron was overthrown for the final time
and the One Ring destroyed. (I 23, 291; III 371, 379)

**WASTE**  Perhaps the Desolation of Smaug. (H 286)

**WATCH**  The official name for the Shirriffs, the Shire police.
There were three in each Farthing for Inside Work, which
consisted mostly of catching stray animals, and a variable
number of Bounders to keep undesirable outsiders from entering the Shire. The Watch was run by the Mayor of Michel
Delving, who was First Shirriff.

During the WR, Saruman and Lotho greatly increased the
Watch, and the Shirriffs were assigned to arrest those who
broke the Rules. The hundreds of Shirriffs were organized
into companies, of which only one, the First Eastfarthing
Troop, is named in *LotR*.

The members of the Watch wore feathers in their caps to
identify themselves. (I 31; III 346-48, 355-56)

**WATCHER IN THE WATER**  A many-tentacled creature who
guarded the West-gate of Moria at least between the years
TA 2994 and 3019, perhaps related to the nameless things
below Khazad-dûm. The Watcher was definitely evil, but it
is unclear whether he was under the control of Sauron or the
Balrog.

The Watcher lived in a lake created by his damming of the
Sirannon. (I 402-03, 419)

**WATCHERS**  the Rangers of the North (q. v.). (TB 21)

**WATCHFUL PEACE**  the period from TA 2063 to 2460, during

which Sauron remained hidden in the East and the Nazgûl were quiet in Minas Morgul. The Watchful Peace began when Sauron fled from Dol Guldur to avoid identification by Gandalf, and ended with his return to the tower with increased strength. During this period the West was relatively peaceful, although Eriador was troubled by evil creatures, especially wolves. (III 401, 414, 459)

**WATCHWOOD**   Forest of Ents and Huorns in the Ring of Isengard during the WR, so named because it guarded Saruman, who was a prisoner in Orthanc. (II 245)

**WATER**   Stream in the Shire, running through Needlehole and Bywater and emptying into the Brandywine just above the Bridge of Stonebows. Rushock Bog and the Pool of Bywater were on the Water. (I 40, 106, 365; H 16)

**WATER-VALLEY**   the valley of the Water, in the Shire. Part of the Great East Road went through the Water-valley. (I 107)

**WAYBREAD**   Lembas (q. v.). (I 478)

**WAYMEET**   Village in the Westfarthing on the Great East Road, fifteen miles west of Bywater. Waymeet was so called because the main road from Sarn Ford joined the Great East Road at Waymeet. Waymeet was one of the headquarters of the Chief's Men during the WR.
  Called Waymoot on the Shire-map. (I 40; III 356, 357)

**WAYMOOT**   Waymeet (q. v.). (I 40)

**WEATHER HILLS**   Hills north of the Great East Road between Bree and Mitheithel, at one time the boundary between Arthedain and Rhudaur. Arthedain fortified the Hills against Angmar, but they were taken in TA 1409 and later recovered.
  The chief peak of the Weather Hills was the southernmost, Weathertop. (I 16, 247, 249; III 397)

**WEATHERTOP**   The southernmost of the Westher Hills, on which was built the Tower of Amon Sûl (q. v.).
  Called in Sindarin Amon Sûl. (I 16, 233, 250-67, 346; TB 41)

**WEDMATH**   The eighth month of the Shire Reckoning, corresponding roughly to our August. (III 478, 483)

**WELLINGHALL**   A dwelling of Fangorn near the roots of Methedras and the source of the Entwash. Its walls and roof consisted of the branches and trunks of evergreen trees, and there was a little waterfall in the back of the large room. (II 91-92, 216)

**WERE-WORMS** Probably-mythical monsters of the far East of Middle-earth. (H 31)

**WEST** The Undying Lands (q. v.). (II 353)

**WEST** That part of Middle-earth including Gondor and the lands to the north and west, or the peoples of those lands. (III 195, 469)

**WEST-ELVES** the Eldar (q. v.). (III 505)

**WESTEMNET** That portion of Rohan west of the Entwash. (I 17; II 42)

**WESTERNESSE** Westron name for Númenor (q. v.). (I 23)

**WESTERN SEAS** Either the Sea (q. v.) as a whole, or that portion of it near the Undying Lands. (I 117, 412; III 381)

**WESTFARTHING** One of the four Farthings of the Shire, seemingly the most important. Michel Delving, the "capital" of the Shire, was in the Westfarthing, and the Free Fair was held here. Other places of note in the Westfarthing included Bywater and Hobbiton. (I 40)

**WESTFOLD** Area in Rohan in the vicinity of Helm's Deep. The master of Westfold dwelled in the Hornburg. (II 168, 170)

**WESTFOLD VALE** Valley in the Westfold of Rohan through which ran the Deeping Stream. (II 169)

**WEST-GATE OF MORIA** Gate in Khazad-dûm built by Narvi in the Second Age to facilitate trade between the Dwarves and the Noldor of Eregion. The gate was controlled by the spell placed on it by Celebrimbor. When Sauron overran Eregion the West-gate was closed. Sometime after TA 1981, the gate was blocked by the Watcher in the Water, who in 2994 prevented Balin's Dwarf-colony from escaping by that route. When the Company of the Ring opened the West-gate in 3019, the Watcher closed the doors and barricaded them with boulders and holly trees.

The West-gate was made of ithildin, and only opened when it was visible and when the person desiring entry spoke the word *mellon.*

Also called the Elven Door, the Doors of Durin and the Gate. (I 388, 394-403)

**WESTMANSWEED** Pipe-weed (q. v.). (III 178)

**WESTMARCH**   Area added to the Shire in FA 32 by gift of King Elessar, lying between the Far Downs and the Tower Hills. In 35 Fastred and Elanor moved to Undertowers in Westmarch, and Fastred was named Warden of Westmarch. His descendents, the Fairbairns, retained that office and had in their possession the Red Book of Westmarch. (I 30; III 471)

**WEST ROAD**   The road leading from Minas Tirith to Edoras. Also called the North-way and the Great West Road. (III 14-15, 93-94, 127-29, 193, 306)

**WESTRON**   The native language at the time of the WR of all those Men and Hobbits living in the old areas of Gondor and Arnor, and also of those inhabitants of the west bank of Anduin as far north as the Gladden Fields, with the exception of the Woses, the Dunlendings and the Rohirrim. In addition, Westron was the common tongue for all inter-lingual meetings, and as such was known to some degree by everybody west of Rhûn. Westron was also the public language of the Dwarves and the base for many Orkish tongues.

Westron was in origin a mingling of Adûnaic and the languages of the coastlands of Middle-earth, and developed in the third millenium of the Second Age with the establishment of Númenorean settlements in Middle-earth. With the coming of Elendil to Middle-earth, the language was enriched with many Sindarin words, and this was the form in which Westron spread throughout Middle-earth.

Westron also served as a cultural medium, as may be seen by the spread of the Gondor calendar systems, and the term "Westron area" has been used in this Glossary with this sense.

Hobbitish was in part a rustic form of Westron. The languages of the Men of Rhovanion and the Rohirrim were distinctly related to Westron, since all descended from the languages of the Edain and their kin.

There are very few examples of genuine Westron given in *LotR*, as most Westron names have been translated into equivalent English forms.

Westron was also called the Common Speech. (I 23; III 487, 504, 505, 506-09, 511, 512, 513-20 passim.)

**WETWANG**   Nindalf (q. v.). (I 483)

**WHISKER-LAD**   A young otter of the Withywindle, in the poem

*Bombadil Goes Boating.* (TB 18-19, 23)

**WHITE COMPANY** The guard of the Princes of Ithilien in the Fourth Age, formed by King Elessar after the WR to serve Faramir, the first Prince. Beregond was the first Captain of the White Company.

Also called the Guard of Faramir. (III 305)

**WHITE COUNCIL** Council of the Wise formed at the summons of Galadriel to plan the strategy to be used against Sauron. The White Council was composed of the Wizards, Galadriel, Elrond and perhaps others of the chief Eldar. Saruman was chosen as its head.

The first meeting of the Council was held in TA 2463, three years after the end of the Watchful Peace. The next important meeting was held in 2851, at which Saruman, who desired the One Ring, overruled Gandalf's plan to attack Dol Guldur. At the next meeting, in 2941, Saruman agreed to the attack, and the Council drove Sauron to Mordor. The last meeting of the Council was held in 2953, and was held to discuss the Rings of Power. At this meeting Saruman lied about the fate of the One, saying it had gone into the Sea, and thus quieted Gandalf's suspicions about Bilbo's ring.

The Council as an organization seems to have been a formality, since the Wise and the Council were the same people. The reference to the Council on III 414 is incorrect, since the Wise, not the yet-unformed Council, drove Sauron from Dol Guldur in 2063.

Also called the Council and the Council of the Wise. (I 77, 78, 462; II 95-96; III 414, 434, 459, 462; H 280-81)

**WHITE CROWN** the Silver Crown (q. v.). (III 304)

**WHITE DOWNS** Downs in the Westfarthing, on which Michel Delving was built. The Free Fair was held on the White Downs. (I 31; III 383)

**WHITE HAND** The emblem of Saruman. (II 20, 202, 246)

**WHITE HORSE UPON GREEN** The emblem of Rohan, showing a meara running over a grassy plain. (III 438)

**WHITE MOUNTAINS** the Ered Nimrais (q. v.). (I 16, 321)

**WHITE RIDER** Gandalf (q. v.) while riding Shadowfax, in opposition to the Black Riders, the Nazgûl. (II 133)

**WHITE SHIPS** The ships built by the Elves to sail from Middle-earth to Eldamar. They had both oars and sails. The white ships sailed from Dol Amroth until about TA 2000, and also down Anduin and from the Grey Havens.

Also called Elven-ships and grey ships. (I 74, 441, 483; III 181, 383; TB 62-64)

**WHITE-SOCKS** (fl. WR) One of the ponies provided by Merry for Frodo's flight to Rivendell. He was driven off in Bree, but was later recovered and claimed by Barliman Butterbur.

White-socks was named by Tom Bombadil. (I 198, 199, 242)

**WHITE TOWER** The tower in the Citadel of Minas Tirith, built by King Calimehtar in TA 1900. In 2698 it was rebuilt by Steward Ecthelion I. The White Tower seems to have been the site of the royal court from the time of its construction. The main room of the Tower was the Tower Hall (q. v.), and the palantír of Minas Anor was kept in a chamber under the dome of the Tower.

Also called the Tower of Ecthelion. (III 24, 25, 115, 458, 459)

**WHITE TOWERS** Three towers on the Tower Hills, built by the Elves in the First or Second Age. A palantír (q. v.) was kept in the tallest of these towers, from which one could see the Sea.

Called also the Towers. (I 26-27, 74, 349; III 383)

**WHITE TREE OF GONDOR** Any of the descendents of Nimloth growing in Gondor. Isildur brought with him from Númenor a sapling in Nimloth which he planted in Minas Anor. In TA 1636, during the Great Plague, the White Tree died, but soon after King Tarondor planted a sapling in the Court of the Fountain. This tree died in 2852 with the death of Steward Belecthor II, and as no sapling could be found the Withered Tree (q. v.) was left standing. After the WR, Aragorn found a sapling of the White Tree on the slopes of Mindolluin, and this was planted in the Citadel.

The White Tree had leaves dark on top and silver beneath, and clusters of flowers with white petals. (I 321, 331; III 26, 308, 311, 393, 408, 416, 457)

**WHITE WOLVES** Animals of Middle-earth, found in Forodwaith. In the Fell Winter of TA 2911 White Wolves came south and troubled the inhabitants of Eriador. (III 461)

**WHITFOOT** Family of Hobbits of the Shire, not of the upper class but of some prominence. (I 214)

**WHITFURROWS**  Village in the Eastfarthing on the Great East Road. (I 40)

**WHITWELL**  Village in the Shire near Tuckborough. Paladin Took owned farm lands in Whitwell. (III 47)

**WÍDFARA**  (fl. WR)  Man of Rohan, from the Wold. He fought in the Battle of the Pelennor Fields. (III 135)

**WILCOME COTTON**  (b. TA 2946)  Hobbit of the Shire, second child of Holman Cotton.
He was usually called Will. (III 477)

**WILCOME COTTON**  (b. TA 2984)  Hobbit of the Shire, third child of Tolman Cotton.
He was usually called Jolly. (III 354, 477)

**WILD**  The area east of the Ford of Bruinen, where nothing was as safe or dependable as it was in the Shire.
The Wild may be identical to Rhovanion. (I 307; H 12, 65)

**WILD**  The Men of Darkness (q. v.). (II 364)

**WILDERLAND**  Rhovanion (q. v.). (I 17, 330; H 14)

**WILD MEN**  The Woses (q. v.). (III 505)

**WILD WOOD**  The wood whence came the first Elf-children at the beginning of the world. (II 78)

**WILIBALD BOLGER**  (b. c. TA 2900, d. before 3001)  Hobbit of the Shire. He married Prisca Baggins. (III 474)

**WILLIAM HUGGINS**  (d. TA 2941)  Troll of the Trollshaws, one of the three encountered by Thorin and Company and turned to stone through Gandalf's trickery.
He was usually called Bill. (H 44-52)

**WILLIE BANKS**  (d. TA 3019)  Hobbit of the Bree-land, killed in the fight between Breelanders and Bill Ferny and his friends. (III 335)

**WILLOWBOTTOM**  Village in the Eastfarthing, near the place where Thistle Brook flowed into the Shirebourn. (I 40)

**WILLOW, OLD MAN**  (First Age-Fourth Age)  Evil-hearted willow tree in the Old Forest, standing near the Withywindle. Old Man Willow had power over much of the Forest, although he was not as powerful as Tom Bombadil. (I 164-69, 180-81; TB 12, 17)

**WILLOW-WREN**  Bird of the Old Forest, in the poem *Bombadil*

*Goes Boating.* (TB 17, 23)

**WILL WHITFOOT** (fl. WR) Hobbit of the Shire, Mayor of Michel Delving from TA 3013 or earlier to FA 7. Will was the first Hobbit put in the Lockholes by the Chief's Men. Before his imprisonment he was the fattest Hobbit in the Westfarthing.

Will was known as old Will and old Flourdumpling. (I 214; III 347, 360, 372-73, 377, 471)

**WILYA** Older form of vilya (q. v.). (III 500)

**WINDFOLA** (fl. WR) Horse of Rohan, ridden by Éowyn and Merry to the Battle of the Pelennor Fields. (III 93, 141)

**WINDING STAIR** The second stairway in the ascent from Imlad Morgul to Cirith Ungol. The Winding Stair zig-zagged up the face of the Ephel Dúath. (II 404-05)

**WINDLE-REACH** Straight portion of the lower Withywindle between Grindwall and the Withy-weir. (TB 19)

**WINDOW-CURTAIN** The waterfall behind which Henneth Annûn (q. v.) was built.

Also called the Curtain. (II 358, 370)

**WINDOW OF THE EYE** The window high in the western side of Barad-dûr whence watched the Eye of Sauron. Although Sauron could look in many directions from the Window, the Window actually looked directly at the Sammath Naur. (III 270)

**WINDOW OF THE SUNSET, WINDOW ON THE WEST** Henneth Annûn (q. v.). (II 358)

**WINGED MESSENGER** One of the Nazgûl (q. v.), whose steed was shot by Legolas over Anduin during the Quest. (I 501; II 129)

**WINTERFILTH** The tenth month of the Shire Reckoning, corresponding to our October. The name in Bree was Wintring, but Winterfilth was claimed by Shire-hobbits to be the older name. The name referred to the completing (filling) of the days remaining before winter, and dated from the time before the adoption of the Kings' Reckoning when the Hobbit year began after the harvest. (III 478, 483)

**WINTRING** See: Winterfilth. (III 483)

**WISE** The wizards and the chief Eldar, who in the Third Age acted together to face the menace of Dol Guldur. In TA 2463 the Wise formed the White Council (q. v.). (I 326, 327; III 420, 456)

**WISEMAN GAMWICH** (b. TA 2800) Hobbit of the Shire, son of Hamfast of Gamwich. He moved to Tighfield, and was probably a roper. (III 477)

**WISE-NOSE** (fl. WR) One of the ponies provided by Merry for Frodo's flight to Rivendell. Wise-nose was driven off in Bree, but was later recovered and claimed by Barliman Butterbur.

He was named by Tom Bombadil. (I 198, 199)

**WITCH-KING OF ANGMAR** The name by which the Lord of the Nazgûl (q. v.) was known in Angmar. (III 397, 398, 399, 411-12)

**WITHERED HEATH** Area in the eastern Ered Nimrais whence came dragons and other evil creatures that plagued the Dwarves of the Ered Mithrin. (I 17; H 13, 32)

**WITHERED TREE** The dead White Tree of Gondor which remained in the Court of the Fountain from TA 2852 to 3019, as no sapling could be found to replace it. In 3019, when Gandalf and Aragorn found a sapling, the Withered Tree was laid to rest in Rath Dínen. (III 26-27, 309, 416)

**WITHY-WEIR** Weir in the Withywindle above Windle-reach, made most probably by the Hobbits of Buckland. (TB 19, 23)

**WITHYWINDLE** River flowing from its source in the Barrow-downs through the Old Forest (q.v.) and into the Brandywine at the southern end of Buckland. In its valley, the Dingle, grew many willow trees, and this area was the center of the evil of the Old Forest.

Goldberry, Bombadil's wife, was the daughter of the River-woman (q.v.) of the Withywindle.

See also: the Withy-weir, Windle-reach. (I 40, 160, 163-71, 176; TB 8-9, 11-23 passim.)

**WIZARDS** Five beings, Valar "of a sort," sent to Middle-earth by the Valar about TA 1000 to unite and counsel the enemies of Sauron. They were forbidden to dominate the peoples of Middle-earth or to match Sauron's power with power. When Saruman, the greatest of the Wizards, disobeyed this injunction, he was cast from the order. At the end of the Third Age the Wizards passed from sight, for with the fall of Sauron their work was done. Gandalf passed over Sea with the Last Riding of the Keepers of the Rings, and the other surviving Wizards may also have returned to the West.

The Wizards had the shape of Old Men. They possessed great powers, which they used and controlled with their staffs. Each of the Wizards had his own color and grade within the order of Wizards. Saruman the White was the greatest and Gandalf the Grey second; of the other three Wizards only Radagast the Brown is named in *LotR*.

Called in Quenya the Istari (sing.: *istar*). (I 429; II 241; III 33-34, 308, 325-26, 455; RP oral communication, summer 1967)

**WIZARD'S VALE**   Nan Curunír (q. v.). (II 167)

**WOLD OF ROHAN**   The grassy upland plain of northeastern Rohan. (I 17; II 38 ff.)

**WOLF, THE**   (First Age)   Creature from Angband who slew Beren. (I 260)

**WOLF**   (fl. WR)   One of Farmer Maggot's guard-dogs. (I 133, 134)

**WOLF-RIDERS**   Evil beings who rode wolves of some sort. In the Battle of the Five Armies the wolf-riders were clearly Orcs mounted on Wargs, but the identity of the Wolf-riders serving Saruman in the WR is less certain. (II 48; H 265, 267)

**WOLVES**   See: Wargs, White Wolves, Wolf-riders.

**WOOD-ELVES**   The Silvan Elves (q. v.). (H 164)

**WOODHALL**   Village in the Eastfarthing on the northern eaves of the Woody End. (I 40)

**WOODLAND REALM**   The Elven-realm of Thranduil (q. v.) in northern Mirkwood, founded early in the Second Age. Its boundaries were uncertain until the end of the Third Age, when they were fixed so as to include all of Eryn Lasgalen north of the Mountains of Mirkwood.

The Elves of the Woodland Realm were untroubled, except for their constant struggle (after TA 1000) with the Orcs and great spiders of Mirkwood, and a war with the Dwarves. (II

342; H 165)

**WOODMEN OF WESTERN MIRKWOOD** Men, related to the Edain, who inhabited the western portion of central Mirkwood in the Third Age. Although troubled by Orcs, spiders and other evils out of Dol Guldur, they survived until the end of the Third Age. When Mirkwood was cleansed after the WR, the Woodmen and the Beornings were given that portion of the forest between the Mountains and the Narrows. (III 429, 468, 508; H 13)

**WOODY END** Woods in the Eastfarthing of the Shire. (I 40, 107)

**WORLD'S END** Somewhere beyond the Pelóri, seemingly the border between earth and sky. (I 310)

**WORMTONGUE** Gríma (q. v.). (II 149)

**WOSES** Primitive Men living in Druadan Forest at the time of the WR. They lived there at least since the Second Age, and although they did not dare to oppose Sauron openly they hated and feared him. In the Third Age they seem occasionally to have been hunted for sport by the Rohirrim. During the WR, the Woses, under their chieftain, Ghân-buri-Ghân, led the Rohirrim through Druadan Forest so that they could avoid the Orc-army on the West Road. In return for this service, King Elessar at the beginning of the Fourth Age gave Druadan Forest to the Woses, and forbade any outsider to enter it without their permission.

The Woses were culturally primitive, but were very woodcrafty; they used poison arrows. Their language was entirely alien to Adûnaic.

Also called the Wild Men of the Woods or of Druadan Forest. (III 128, 129, 313, 505, 508-09)

**WULF** (d. TA 2759) Man of Rohan, son of Freca. After his father's death in 2754, Wulf fled to Dunland, and in 2758 invaded Rohan with a large army of Dunlendings. He easily overran the country and took Meduseld, killing Prince Haleth. During the Long Winter, Wulf's armies besieged Helm in the Hornburg and Fréaláf, Helm's nephew, in Dunharrow. Although Helm and his second son Háma perished during the Winter, in early spring Fréaláf surprised Wulf in Meduseld and slew him. (III 431-33)

# Υ

**YALE**  Lowland area in the Eastfarthing. The Yale was west of Stock. (I 114)

**YANTA**  (Q.: 'bridge')  Name for the tengwa ⟨ (number 35), which usually represented consonantal *y* or (in the mode of Beleriand) *e*. (III 500)

**YAVANNA**  (Q.)  Site or owner of famed gardens of undying flowers, in Middle-earth or in the West. It was believed that miruvor was made from these flowers. (R 61)

**YAVANNIË**  (Q.)  The ninth month of the Kings' and Stewards' Reckonings and the sixth of the new Reckoning, corresponding roughly to our September.

The Sindarin name, used only by the Dúnedain, was Ivanneth. (III 483)

**YÁVIË**  (Q.)  The third of the seasons of the loa of the Calendar of Imladris, corresponding roughly to our August and September. The name was also used by Men for the season of autumn.

Called in Sindarin iavas. (III 480, 485)

**YÁVIÉRË**  (Q.: 'autumn-day')  In the Stewards' Reckoning, a holiday coming between Yavannië 30 and Narquelië 1, falling near the autumnal equinox. (III 481)

**YEAR-BOOK OF TUCKBOROUGH**  Yellowskin (q. v.). (III 484)

**YELLOWSKIN**  Book kept by the Tooks recording Took births, deaths, marriages and land-sales, and also various Shire events. It ·was begun about TA 2000, and contained much information cited in the Red Book of Westmarch. Yellowskin was the most ancient document in the Shire at the end of the Third Age.

Also called the Year-book of Tuckborough. (III 484) ·

**YÉN**  (Q.: 'year')  The long year of the Eldar in Middle-earth, equal to 144 solar years. (III 479)

**YESTARË**  (Q.: 'first-day')  The first day of the year in the Calendar of Imladris and the three Dúnedain calendars. In the Kings' and Stewards' Reckonings it fell at the winter solstice, but in the Rivendell and New Reckonings it came near the vernal equinox, on our March 29 and 17, respectively.

Yestarë fell outside the months. (III 480, 481, 486)

**YOUNGER DAYS** The Fourth Age, the Age of Men, as opposed to the Elder and Middle Days of the Elves, so called by Saruman. (I 339)

**YOUNG TOM COTTON** Tolman Cotton (2) (q. v.). (III 354)

**YULEDAYS** The first and last days of the year in the Shire Reckoning, with the Lithedays the chief holidays of the year. The two Yuledays did not belong to any month. (III 478, 482)

**YULEMATH** The name given Foreyule (q. v.) in Bree and the Eastfarthing. (III 483)

**YULETIDE** The six-day winter holiday period in the Shire, lasting from 29 Foreyule to 2 Afteryule. (III 482)

*Z*

**ZARAGAMBA** (gen. Hobb.) The Oldbucks (q. v.). (III 520)

**ZIMRATHÔN, AR-** (Ad.) (fl. c. SA 3000) Dúnadan, twentieth King of Númenor. (III 390)

**ZIRAK** Zirak-zigil (q. v.). (I 370)

**ZIRAK-ZIGIL** (Kh.) One of the three Mountains of Moria. In its pinnacle was built Durin's Tower, and here Gandalf threw down the Balrog.

Called in Sindarin Celebdil and in Westron Silvertine. Also called Zirak for short by the Dwarves. (I 370, 432; II 134)

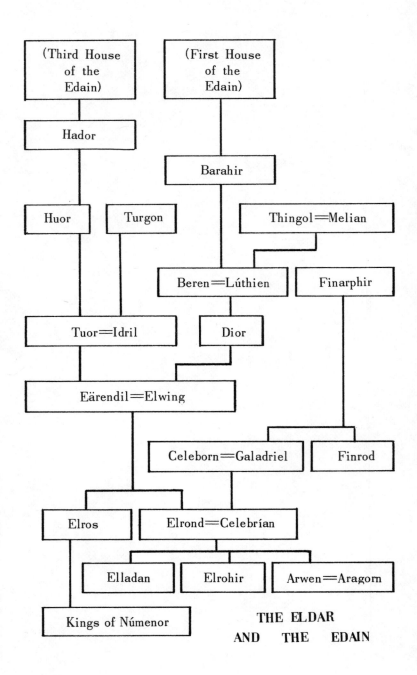

THE ELDAR
AND THE EDAIN

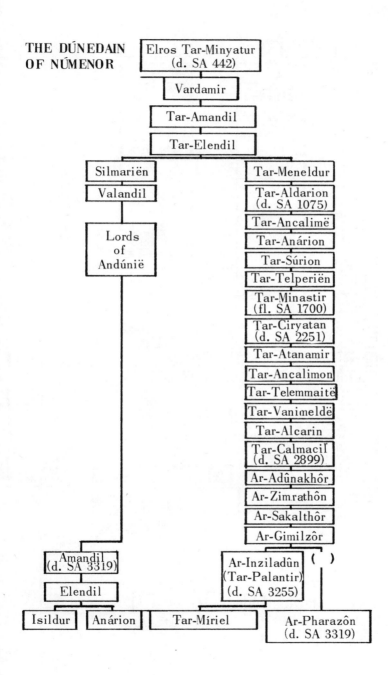

**THE DÚNEDAIN OF NÚMENOR**

Elros Tar-Minyatur (d. SA 442)

Vardamir

Tar-Amandil

Tar-Elendil

Silmariën — Tar-Meneldur

Valandil — Tar-Aldarion (d. SA 1075)

Tar-Ancalimë

Tar-Anárion

Tar-Súrion

Tar-Telperiën

Tar-Minastir (fl. SA 1700)

Tar-Ciryatan (d. SA 2251)

Tar-Atanamir

Tar-Ancalimon

Tar-Telemmaitë

Tar-Vanimeldë

Tar-Alcarin

Tar-Calmacil (d. SA 2899)

Ar-Adûnakhôr

Ar-Zimrathôn

Ar-Sakalthôr

Ar-Gimilzôr

Lords of Andúnië

Amandil (d. SA 3319)

Elendil

Ar-Inziladûn (Tar-Palantir) (d. SA 3255) — ( )

Isildur — Anárion — Tar-Míriel — Ar-Pharazôn (d. SA 3319)

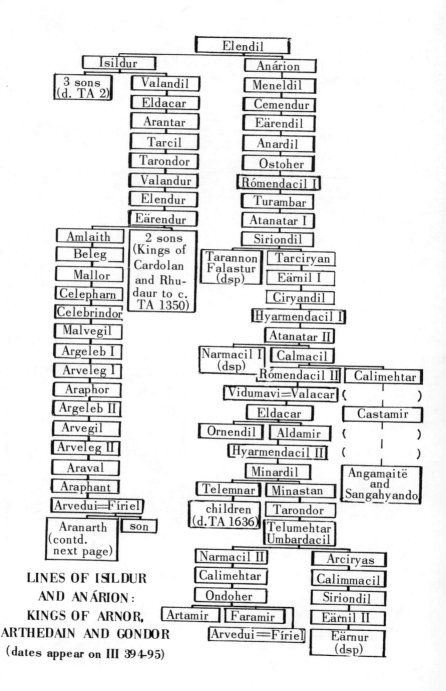

LINES OF ISILDUR
AND ANÁRION:
KINGS OF ARNOR,
ARTHEDAIN AND GONDOR
(dates appear on III 394-95)

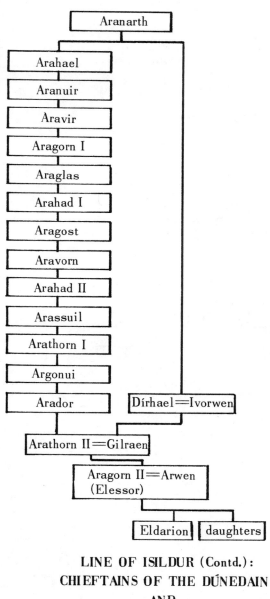

Aranarth

Arahael
Aranuir
Aravir
Aragorn I
Araglas
Arahad I
Aragost
Aravorn
Arahad II
Arassuil
Arathorn I
Argonui
Arador

Dírhael═Ivorwen

Arathorn II═Gilraen

Aragorn II═Arwen
(Elessor)

Eldarion    daughters

LINE OF ISILDUR (Contd.):
CHIEFTAINS OF THE DÚNEDAIN
AND
KINGS OF THE REUNITED KINGDOM

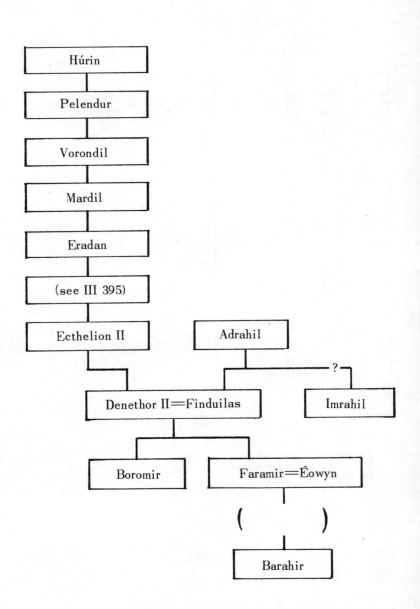

**THE HOUSE OF HÚRIN**
**(THE HOUSE OF THE STEWARDS)**

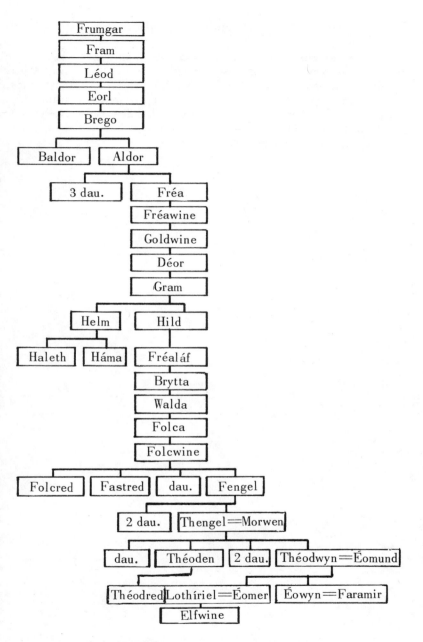

**THE ÉOTHÉOD AND THE ROHIRRIM**

## FIVE THOUSAND

copies, approximately, of A *Guide to Middle Earth* have been printed and bound by Malloy Lithographing Co., Inc., Ann Arbor, Michigan, and John Dekker & Sons, Bookbinders, Grand Rapids, Michigan, for The Mirage Press, a joint non-stock partnership, Jack L. Chalker editorial director and sales manager, William Osten typographer and production manager. Earlier editions and printings of this book were numbered.